Geoeconomic Shifts and Strategic Business Responses

Bryan Christiansen
https://orcid.org/0000-0001-7282-8497
Southern New Hampshire University, USA

John D. Branch
https://orcid.org/0000-0002-5201-125X
University of Michigan, USA

IGI Global
Scientific Publishing
Publishing Tomorrow's Research Today

Vice President of Editorial Melissa Wagner
Director of Acquisitions Mikaela Felty
Director of Book Development Jocelynn Hessler
Production Manager Mike Brehm
Cover Design Jose Rosado

Published in the United States of America by
IGI Global Scientific Publishing
701 East Chocolate Avenue
Hershey, PA, 17033, USA
Tel: 717-533-8845 | Fax: 717-533-7115
Website: https://www.igi-global.com E-mail: cust@igi-global.com

Library of Congress Cataloging-in-Publication Data

No LCCN (CIP Data Pending)
ISBN13: 9798337379074
Isbn13Softcover: 9798337379081
EISBN13: 9798337379098

British Cataloguing in Publication Data
A Cataloguing in Publication record for this book is available from the British Library.

Table of Contents

Detailed Table of Contents

This research observes the first effects of one of the most recent agreements for international cooperation – i.e., the Regional Comprehensive Economic Partnership (RCEP) – due to the facilitation it brought to international trade. A multiple linear regression on longitudinal data shows the variables depicting the first – besides contrasting – effects of new measures favouring the trade exchange among 15 partner countries in the Asia-Pacific region. Resilience emerges as a key topic in this investigation, due to the advantages of considering new and closer destination markets when planning the further development of international trade.

The war in Ukraine has triggered severe economic disruptions in the Eurozone, thus leading to high inflation. In response, the European Central Bank (ECB) adopted contractionary monetary policies grounded in Friedman's theory. While effective in curbing inflation, these measures have intensified social inequalities. This chapter analyzes the intersection of geoeconomics, inflation control, and fiscal policy, highlighting impacts on national economies and global business. It draws on key economic theories—diminishing marginal utility, the Phillips Curve, Okun's Law, and the Laffer Curve—to examine equity and competitiveness. The chapter proposes a more balanced approach: combining monetary tightening with adaptive fiscal measures and a novel "Savings Policy" led by the ECB. This integrated strategy aims to stabilize prices while promoting social justice and resilience. Ultimately, it argues for inclusive policies that safeguard the most vulnerable, ensuring fair burden-sharing and sustainable recovery.

This chapter explores the interconnected development of trade policy and international business. Trade policy has developed from the creation of the multilateral governance system to the increasing influence of sustainable development, digitalization, and security. At the same time, the ways of conducting international business have evolved from the rise of multinational companies to global value chains binding together highly specialised companies. By highlighting some of the key developments and related challenges, this chapter provides multiple perspectives to explore the possible future developments of the dynamics of trade policy and international business environment. The chapter highlights ongoing and expected changes in international business environment and their interconnections with geoeconomic developments.

This chapter considers the development of BRICS (Brazil, Russia, India, China, and South Africa) as one of the most interesting and efficient agents of reforming the global currency system in the late neoliberal era in the context of changing geoeconomics and geopolitical conditions. It examines how BRICS projects—such as the New Development Bank, the Contingent Reserve Arrangement, and currency swaps—undermine conventional reserve currencies' supremacy and shape a multipolar financial order. The study illuminates the strategic response of BRICS to trade wars, sanctions, systemic inequities, digital currency innovations, and sustainable development. The chapter ends by examining future perspectives for world financial governance as influenced by BRICS-led reforms and institutional options.

Increased international trade has led to interconnection of supply chains across continents and countries. With the disruptions existing in the global economy, the domestic economies of many countries feel the resulting impact whenever there are any major world events that intertwine with the supply chain, for example, the adoption of green supply chain practices, disruption of shipping logistics, and economic trade wars. While the developed countries have made noticeable movements in moving towards green supply chains, countries in Africa and more specifically East Africa are yet to make substantial changes. In this chapter, green supply chain management has exhibited quantifiable benefits that range from reduction in CO2 emissions, reduction in waste, cost savings arising from use of clean energy, incorporation of local sourcing, and sourcing from suppliers who would be classified as disadvantaged from an economic perspective.

The chapter examines the long-run and short-run impact of GDP on NIFTY 50 in India using data from April 2011 to July 2024. The study employs ARDL Bounds testing, Granger Causality test, and other econometric tools to explore the relationship. GDP, as the independent variable, and NIFTY 50, as the dependent variable, are transformed into natural logarithms to stabilize the data. Results reveal no long-term cointegration between GDP and NIFTY 50, as indicated by the F-statistic from the ARDL Bounds test. However, Granger causality results suggest that NIFTY 50 influences GDP in the short run, while GDP does not Granger-cause NIFTY 50. The study highlights the significance of these findings for policymakers and investors, suggesting further exploration into stock market dynamics with other macroeconomic variables.

This chapter examines the determinants of foreign direct investment inflows in 23 emerging countries over the period 2004–2023, using three tree-based machine learning models, decision tree, XGBoost, and random forest, to analyze 44 distinct indicators. The study evaluates how crises alter investor priorities by comparing stable and turbulent periods. Results show that during stable periods geopolitical risk, lagged unemployment, and digital infrastructure dominate, while trade openness and geopolitical stability gain prominence during crises, and capital openness and institutional quality become critical post COVID-19. Grounded in institutional and internationalization theories, these findings underscore the context-dependent adaptability of investor behavior. The study provides policy insights for emerging markets, advocating crisis-responsive strategies like digital infrastructure upgrades, trade openness during shocks, and institutional reforms to boost foreign investment and long-term growth.

This research focuses on the dynamics of international trade laws within the rapidly changing geopolitical and geo-economic environment for trade. It analyses the emergence of new powers, China, and the place of the U.S., given protectionism, focusing on the impact on the multilateral trading system. The chapter analyses the issues which relate to the WTO, the dispute settlement, relationship between national security and free trade, and the role of regional trade agreements. Moreover, it continues where others start: the intricacies of law in the use of trade as an instrument of foreign policy, export controls, tariffs, and sanctions. The chapter outlines recommendations for the enhancement of the organization's structure, modern issues' incorporation into the WTO, and rebuilding of multilateralism. Finally, it seeks to establish the

Preface

INTRODUCTION

In recent years, the intersection between geoeconomics and global business strategy has undergone profound transformation. Shifts in power relations, trade alignments, and economic governance have redefined the principles upon which international business operates. The rise of multipolarity, disruptions from global conflicts, and new frameworks of cooperation—such as the Regional Comprehensive Economic Partnership (RCEP)—illustrate how economic interests increasingly serve as tools of geopolitical influence. *Geoeconomic Shifts and Strategic Business Responses* emerges at this critical juncture, offering a timely examination of how states, institutions, and corporations are recalibrating their strategies in an era marked by volatility, competition, and redefined alliances.

This volume captures the growing complexity of the international business landscape by integrating diverse perspectives that span economics, finance, policy, and sustainability. It seeks not only to analyze the structural changes shaping trade, monetary systems, and investment flows but also to highlight the adaptive responses of businesses confronting these systemic shifts. By blending theoretical insight with empirical evidence, the chapters in this book shed light on how strategic agility, policy reform, and digital transformation are becoming the bedrocks of business resilience amid uncertainty.

As editors, we recognize that the emerging global order requires a multidisciplinary lens. The interplay between economics and geopolitics cannot be viewed in isolation from social, technological, and environmental dimensions. Thus, this collection draws from a wide range of academic and professional expertise across continents, providing an integrated understanding of how geoeconomic transformations are reshaping strategic business responses worldwide. It is our hope that the analyses herein will equip scholars, practitioners, and policymakers with the tools to navigate—and even anticipate—the next wave of global economic realignment.

CHAPTER OVERVIEW

Chapter 1, "Business in Conflicting Times – A Resilience-Based View on International Agreements" by Rossana Simeoli, Marco Tregua, and Pasquale Sarnacchiaro, explores the early effects of the Regional Comprehensive Economic Partnership (RCEP). Through empirical data and regression analysis, the chapter highlights the contrasting outcomes of trade facilitation among Asia-Pacific nations and underscores resilience as a central theme in developing international cooperation frameworks.

Chapter 2, "Geoeconomic Tensions and the Rethinking of Inflation Policies" by João Rodrigues dos Santos and colleagues, delves into the European Central Bank's policy responses to inflationary shocks arising from geopolitical disruptions. Using classical and contemporary economic theories, the authors argue for a balanced approach that integrates monetary tightening with adaptive fiscal and savings-based policies to promote social equity and sustainable recovery.

Chapter 3, "Trade Policy and International Business Dynamics at the Time of Increasing Geoeconomic Challenges" by Anna Karhu, provides a comprehensive look at how trade policy evolution—from multilateral governance to sustainability-driven reform—has redefined international business operations. The chapter offers valuable insight into how policy and corporate strategy must evolve together to ensure long-term competitiveness in a shifting global environment.

Chapter 4, "The BRICS Influence: Reshaping Global Monetary Systems Amid Geoeconomics Shifts" by Surjit Singha, examines the transformative potential of BRICS nations in reforming global monetary systems. By evaluating the New Development Bank, reserve arrangements, and digital currency initiatives, the author illustrates how emerging economies are challenging Western-dominated financial hierarchies and promoting a multipolar order.

Chapter 5, "Economic Disruptions and Business Risks: The Role of Regional Conflicts in Global Trade" by Rismawati Rismawati and co-authors, investigates how geopolitical conflicts—from Ukraine to the Middle East—have redefined trade risks and corporate strategy. The analysis emphasizes the increasing importance of diversification, nearshoring, and AI-driven risk management as firms strive for operational continuity amid turbulence.

Chapter 6, "Reconfiguring Global Trade – The Economic Impact of the Russia-Ukraine Conflict and Strategic Responses" by Puneett Bhatnagr, presents a mixed-method evaluation of how the Russia-Ukraine conflict reshaped trade flows and GDP trajectories. The study highlights uneven regional outcomes and provides policy recommendations for enhancing national and corporate resilience in the face of geopolitical shocks.

Chapter 7, "Adoption of Green Concepts and Technology in Supply Chains – Case Study of East Africa" by Rehema Kiarie, focuses on the environmental and economic imperatives driving green supply chain adoption. Centered on East Africa, the chapter identifies barriers, benefits, and policy pathways for developing economies seeking to align sustainability goals with economic growth and trade integration.

Chapter 8, "Analyzing the Long-Run and Short-Run Impact of GDP on NIFTY 50: Evidence from ARDL Approach" by Shefali Saini and Gurpreet Kaur, examines the dynamic relationship between India's GDP and stock market performance. Using advanced econometric techniques, the study reveals short-term causality effects and offers valuable insights for investors and policymakers navigating volatile market conditions.

Chapter 9, "Reassessing FDI Determinants in Emerging Countries: A Geoeconomic Perspective via Machine Learning Approach" by Ichrak Dridi and Mohamed Malek Belhoula, employs machine learning models to uncover the evolving determinants of foreign direct investment. Their findings illuminate how geopolitical risk, institutional quality, and digital infrastructure shape investor behavior during periods of global crisis and recovery.

Chapter 10, "Recasting International Trade Law in the Age of Geopolitical Shifts and Geo-Economic Pressures" by Sheikh Mansoor and Syed Rashid, explores the legal dimensions of international trade amid growing protectionism and geopolitical tension. The chapter offers a compelling call for modernizing multilateral trade institutions, strengthening the WTO framework, and redefining the balance between national security and free trade.

CONCLUSION

The contributions within this volume collectively underscore that geoeconomic shifts are not isolated phenomena but systemic forces influencing every aspect of international business. The world's economic architecture is undergoing a period of recalibration—one where the strategic responses of nations, institutions, and corporations must be not only reactive but anticipatory. By addressing themes ranging from trade law to green innovation, this book reflects the diverse strategies required to maintain stability and foster progress in uncertain times.

As the boundaries between economic and geopolitical spheres continue to blur, businesses must learn to interpret global events through a geoeconomic lens. The need for adaptability—both in corporate decision-making and policy design—has never been more urgent. The insights presented in this book emphasize that resilience is not merely about withstanding disruption but about building the capacity to transform and thrive amid systemic change.

We extend our gratitude to the scholars who contributed their expertise and to the institutions that support academic inquiry into the complex realities of international business. It is our belief that *Geoeconomic Shifts and Strategic Business Responses* will serve as a valuable resource for academics, policymakers, and business leaders seeking to understand and shape the evolving contours of the global economy.

Chapter 1
Business in Conflicting Times:
A Resilience-Based View on International Agreements

Rossana Simeoli
https://orcid.org/0009-0002-3591-4294
University of Naples Federico II, Italy

Marco Tregua
https://orcid.org/0000-0003-1579-7676
University of Naples Federico II, Italy

Pasquale Sarnacchiaro
University of Naples Federico II, Italy

ABSTRACT

This research observes the first effects of one of the most recent agreements for international cooperation – i.e., the Regional Comprehensive Economic Partnership (RCEP) – due to the facilitation it brought to international trade. A multiple linear regression on longitudinal data shows the variables depicting the first – besides contrasting – effects of new measures favouring the trade exchange among 15 partner countries in the Asia-Pacific region. Resilience emerges as a key topic in this investigation, due to the advantages of considering new and closer destination markets when planning the further development of international trade.

DOI: 10.4018/979-8-3373-7907-4.ch001

INTRODUCTION

Free trade agreements (FTAs) and programs for foreign direct investments (FDIs) flourished in the global economy in recent decades; however, there are some contrasting views on such efforts to widen the global scope of markets. On one hand, businesses had the opportunity to expand their trade relations, market share, and organizational structure, as well as most governing bodies tried to support such a posture with international agreements and policies to make exchanges and FDIs more viable. On the other hand, not only disruptive events (as wars and pandemics have been in the last decade), but also political perspectives jeopardized the further widening of markets' scope. Scholars recently debated on such conditions for businesses by means of the notion of resilience, described as the capability of reacting to external shocks. Indeed, resilience has been theorized in multiple ways, with reference to the factors allowing it, namely experience (Puhr & Müllner, 2022) and geographic factors (Oh et al., 2020), among others.

Therefore, this research aims at observing the topics mentioned above in the realm shaped by one of the most recent agreements for international cooperation – i.e., the Regional Comprehensive Economic Partnership (RCEP). This agreement has been recently at the edge of research attention, due to the expectations of reducing geopolitical risks (Guo et al., 2023), via offering new chances for business and lowering the dependence on few industries and countries. Besides not explicitly mentioning resilience, Guo et al. (2023) referred to reducing the dependence on certain businesses and trade agreements with countries in a challenging scenario.

Previously these scholars had also started simulating the effects on trade and income (Li & Moon, 2018), thus calling for further investigation once the agreement would have come into force. Therefore, this research is centred on whether RCEP had effects on international trade and foreign investments. In 2022, two years after the formal implementation of RCEP, the Chinese news agency Qiushi reported significant economic impacts resulting from the agreement. According to published data, China's total trade with the other 14 RCEP members reached 12.95 trillion yuan (approximately 1.786 trillion USD), accounting for 30.8% of the country's total foreign trade. Similarly, Japan experienced a marked increase in FDIs flows towards RCEP member states, totalling 55.8 trillion yen (approximately 353.2 billion USD) and representing 26.3% of Japan's total outward FDIs. These preliminary data underscore RCEP's role as a driver for deep regional economic integration, fostering trade expansion, investment growth, and economic cooperation.

Due to the aforementioned goals, this chapter is structured as follows: first, a theoretical background is set to frame studies on international business in light of international cooperation and to address the notion of resilience at both business' and context's level. The review of extant theories and recent contributions allowed a focus on the dynamics affecting international trade and foreign direct investments, even in light of facilitation brought by international agreements. Indeed, there is a focus on the impacts of international agreement on trade, paying attention to shocks that can occur in markets and resilience as a way to show how companies react to disruptive scenarios, alternatively levering on the opportunities in different markets. Additionally, there is an in-depth consideration of the Asia-Pacific context, due to RCEP being the center of the investigation; this theoretical analysis allows the authors to depict key features and changes of the area, including some recent trends. Finally, there is a review on the most relevant variables used in extant studies in investigating and describing the effects on international trade.

Then the research design is described, aimed at setting the ground for the understanding of the impacts performed by RCEP on the international trade among partner countries, thus showing whether the expected goals have already been achieved and which are the consequences when it comes to the resilience of local economies, in light of geographical closer partnerships, thus potentially reducing the costs and the dependence from single partner economies. Then findings are shown through a multiple linear regression on key countries of the region and with reference to both agricultural goods and manufactured products; consequently, implications are offered at both country and industrial level, then the chapter ends with suggestions for further research in this domain, also due to the recentness of RCEP.

THEORETICAL BACKGROUND

International businesses have been proliferating for decades and scholars paid attention to such a trend in multiple ways, mostly with reference to the goals of the internationalization process and the entry modes, as well as the impacts on societies. As it regards the goals, chasing them in the international arena led to a key contribution discerning the attention paid to different forms of advantages, all in all stimulating new trade routes as well as foreign direct investments (e.g., Dunning, 1991); parallel to this, the ways to widen the scope of a business to the international arena were investigated from a strategic perspective (e.g., Sarkar and Cavusgil, 1996). When it comes to the effects on society, several topics are relevant, ranging from the impacts on employment to the increasing competition for local companies; indeed, Hymer (1968) stressed the bright and dark side of the multinational corporations (MNCs) due to the contrastive effects on local contexts.

Lots of changes occurred in the complex international domain, making businesses more prone to internationalization – as with born global companies (Cavusgil and Knight, 2009) – as well as facing fierce competition (Wright and Dana, 2003), due to the increase in the openness of economies, the flourishing of international agreements, and the ease of trade through e-commerce. The changes brought to light by scholars shaped a wide and intricate debate juxtaposing the aforementioned bright and dark side of international business, as it is highlighted in the concurrent widening and narrowing down of market opportunities for small and medium enterprises (SMEs), also due to their constraints (Ayob and Senik, 2015). Indeed, SMEs are struggling to find their space in the international arenas, even in this case with contrasting results, since they suffer from the more fierce competition depending on companies from foreign countries, while they have the chance to benefit from internationalization, due to new global markets – including online ones – and the being international of supply chains (Sin et al., 2016). Parallel to this, the debate on MNCs continues struggling with Hymer's view, thus frames MNCs as *janus bifrons* (Forsgren, 2024), due to their contribution to economic development and their growing market power, hindering the access to international arenas to new competitors.

The access to international markets is favoured in a general fashion also by FTAs that contributed to market expansion, since the liberalization of markets and the fading away of barriers stimulated business internationalization, both in terms of trade and foreign direct investments, besides the current scenario seems to offer an opposite posture. Sin et al. (2016) showed such results also with reference to small and medium enterprise, since they considered the opportunities brought by internet technologies in favouring international sales – e.g., e-commerce – and the growing competition, making local markets harder to be dealt with due to the massive entry of relevant operators from other countries. Therefore, the two sides of a coin are also evident in international sales with reference to e-commerce, making internationalization easier and markets closer to offering saturation. In such a scenario, FTAs were meant as regulators of international flows of goods, besides the significant differences featuring some national and supranational markets (Bieron and Ahmed, 2012). FTAs – as well as other forms of cooperation – are meant to be supportive in the achievement of economic resilience at country level, thanks to the facilitation and the widening of market access (Erixon et al., 2024); additionally, Kuźnar (2024) observed resilience as a beneficial outcome of FTAs and other international agreements in East Asia, with particular reference to developing countries. However, she stressed the reduction in bureaucratic tasks – also thanks to digitalization – and a limited achievement of expected goals – e.g., trade growth – as an unexpected outcome that overlapping agreements might lead to, due to the contrasting measures proposed.

As it concerns investments abroad, the option for foreign direct investments is observed through the proliferation of subsidiaries (McDonald et al., 2011), even with contradictory considerations on the advantage brought by taxation (Richter, 2024), making investments flowing from an area to another for reasons different than manufacturing advantage(-s) or market growth, thus just chasing the most advantageous fiscal system. Similarly, international trade is directly affected by changes (e.g., lower or no barriers, leaner processes, and so on) infused into global markets by means of FTAs (Baggs and Brander, 2006), with NAFTA, European Union, ASEAN, and – more recently – RCEP representing some of the key examples. Even in this case, there are some contrasting views on the expected effects (Dent, 2010) in terms of regulation, increase in dependency from other countries, trade balance, job increase, new business relationships, and loss of opportunities for local companies. Such recent advances are aligned to the goals emerging from previous studies; indeed, Hofmann et al. (2018) identified the contribution of preferential trade agreements – namely, measures addressing barriers or incentives to specific countries, industries or processes – to the development of international businesses. The authors found such agreements having a direct effect on goods trade, as well as being shaped according to the income level of the country members; moreover, they observed a lack of information in implementing the norms brought by the agreements, as well as a limited action from national governments in properly aligning the local laws to the international posture. More recently, scholars focused on the drawbacks of international agreements, namely the limitation to market diversification, making some countries – and the local firms – depending on single markets, the undermining of local production in industries with a relevant specialization abroad, as well as the risk of sociopolitical tensions in case of a market requiring the further exploitation of natural resources (Oxford Analytica, 2024). Therefore, the debate is very vibrant in grasping the impacts of international agreements on trade, mostly in light of recent changes due to the creation of new incentives to international sales.

The Impact Of International Agreements on Trade

An Overview

The relevance of international agreements widened the scope of the debate on international business from business studies to geopolitical studies, due to the key role played by governments – also supranational entities – in furthering investments, as well as in the power that businesses might exert on governing bodies, in line with the pioneering view of Hymer (1960) as addressed also in recent studies (Forsgren & Yamin, 2023). Indeed, scholars paid attention to the contribution of international agreements to business reaction to shocks; Luo & Van Assche (2023) defined cooperative areas as the suitable context to consider investments abroad as a way to react to shocks. They framed such a chance to contrast shocks in both new investments and relocation of extant ones and described the deriving effect as geopolitical resilience. Similarly, Schotter (2021) identified resilience in MNCs by means of FTAs and regional cooperation as they favour the rise of new solutions to locate business activities in areas with lower costs.

However, resilience is not an innate feature of a business, nor of contexts, and it may depend on the portfolio activities (White III et al., 2021), but it also has to be set in order to perform activities that might contrast external shocks. Additionally, resilience has been framed also at a level wider than business, indeed supply chain resilience is a feature that contributes to both businesses and contexts. More recently, Statsenko et al. (2023) observed how FTAs can favour vertical disintegration, agreements to use intellectual property abroad, and outsourcing in a general vein, thus giving businesses the opportunity to be flexible and visible, two key features in the path towards resilience. Indeed, operations in business domains are thought to be resilient when a response might be offered in light of negative and unexpected events. This capability of reacting has been observed in companies operating at multinational level (Nielsen et al., 2023).

The analysis of the impact of FTAs has historically been dependent upon a robust methodological framework grounded in the utilisation of quantitative models. Of these, the gravity model occupies a central position. The gravity model, initially proposed by Tinbergen (1962), is a theoretical framework employed to estimate trade flows between countries. This model utilises dummy variables – such as geographical distance, cultural proximity, and the presence of shared land borders – to predict trade patterns. Additionally, it incorporates the role of joint participation in trade agreements as a determining factor. In this regard, the gravity model has become a cornerstone for assessing the *ex-post* effects of FTAs, due to its ability to isolate the impact of such agreements on import and export flows between member countries (Baier & Bergstrand, 2007).

The model has been subjected to a process of refinement over time to address the limitations that are evident from the data (such as the presence of zero trade flows). In response to this issue, Silva and Tenreyro (2006) proposed the use of the Poisson Pseudo-Maximum Likelihood (PPML) estimator, which effectively accounts for zero values. Furthermore, Helpman et al. (2008) proposed a two-stage estimation approach that differentiates between a firm's decision to engage in trade (selection stage) and the intensity of trade flows (outcome stage), thereby enhancing the robustness of the estimates. The potential impact of a trade agreement can also be assessed *ex-ante* by Computable General Equilibrium (CGE) models, which simulate the systemic effects of trade policies on a general equilibrium economy (Okabe, 2015).

In the context of FTAs, it is also essential to differentiate between direct and indirect effects. Direct effects refer to the increase in trade between member countries, primarily driven by the reduction or progressive elimination of tariff barriers. Conversely, indirect effects emerge when such agreements result in a decline in trade flows with third countries, due to a reallocation of trade preferences (Carrère, 2006).

The integration of these quantitative approaches has thus enabled the literature to provide both *ex-ante* and *ex-post* evaluations of trade agreements, contributing to a deeper understanding of their effects on trade flows, economic dynamics, and the structural resilience of the economies involved.

A focus on Asia and Oceania

The models examined in the preceding section are highly suitable for the estimation of the potential impact of international agreements in the Sino-Pacific region, most notably the RCEP. From an economic perspective, the adoption of Rules of Origin (RoO) is among the most salient features of the agreement for member states, in terms of economic returns. These provisions have been designed as key instruments for trade facilitation within the region, acting as drivers for the strengthening of regional value chains and the gradual reduction of transaction costs (Estrades et al., 2022; Dib et al., 2020). One of the first investigations on RCEP is challenging the expected effects of RCEP, through a simulation of the effects on trade for China and Korea (Li & Moon, 2018). The analysis highlights the expected increase in trade with contrasting effects on income, due to the counterbalancing impact on services; indeed, scholars stress the different consequences of liberalization on services and goods, stating that China might experience a limited benefit from an increase in trade due to the weak competitiveness in service industry. Such a limited competitiveness might jeopardize the expected increase in the income due to higher amounts of exports.

The view on the improvement in transaction costs is further supported by the study by Chung et al. (2022), who utilized a gravity model to estimate that the reduction in trade costs attributable to the new RoO framework could range from 7.8% to 25.9% in 2035. Their findings underscore the importance of RoO as a pivotal element in maximising the potential benefits of the agreement. Beyond the gravity model, the potential economic effects of RCEP have also been explored through dynamic Computable General Equilibrium (CGE) models, such as ENVISAGE. Simulations using this framework suggest a projected increase in real income by 2035 of 4.9% for Vietnam and 4.6% for Malaysia by 2035. At the sectoral level, the model forecasts substantial growth in exports from RCEP members in specific categories, including meat-based products (+16.3%) and tourism-related services (+15.7%) by 2035. With specific regard to intra-regional trade, it is expected that the agreement will stimulate regional sourcing, with projected increases in imports in sectors such as apparel (+10.7%), food and beverages (+7.53%), and textiles (+8.84%) (Estrades et al., 2022). Focusing on the textile sector, Lu (2019) argues that RCEP will incentivise members to increasingly source inputs within the region, progressively reducing reliance on non-member countries and fostering a more deeply integrated regional supply chain. More recently – and in line with Lu (2019) – Guo et al. (2023) considers the beneficial effects of RCEP on geopolitical risk, since the opportunity to increase trade with member countries would limit the dependence on some industries and partner countries, thus increasing the bargaining power of the countries affiliated with RCEP.

In conclusion, the utilisation of quantitative models – encompassing the CGE model and the gravity model – has facilitated scholars in delineating the potential sector-specific impacts of the RCEP. A particular focus has been placed on the transformative role of RoO provisions, which appear to be pivotal to the agreement's potential to foster trade integration and regional economic resilience. A study on New Zealand try to depict the relevance of international relationships for the New Zealander context to contrast a decrease in export in disruptive cases, as it was with pandemics (Fath et al., 2021).

A comparison between RCEP and CPTPP

The RCEP and the Comprehensive and Progressive Agreement for Trans-Pacific Partnership (CPTPP) represent two economic integration models in the Asia-Pacific region, delineating complementary yet diversified approaches with regard to strategic objectives, degrees of openness, and regulatory ambition. The CPTPP, which entered into force in 2018 – following the withdrawal of the United States from the Trans-Pacific Partnership (TPP) framework – constitutes a next-generation trade agreement marked by extensive liberalization and a broad regulatory scope that goes beyond the exchange of goods and services (Kong & Yamada, 2025). Indeed, the agreement incorporates advanced provisions on intellectual property rights (in accordance with the standards of the WTO's Agreement on Trade-Related Aspects of Intellectual Property Rights), public procurement, state-owned enterprises (SOEs), competition policy and digital trade, and is characterized by the exclusive use of negative lists (Jiang & Yu, 2021). Furthermore, its document comprises chapters of a binding nature on subjects including environmental protection, labour rights, data governance and fair competition. In contrast, RCEP adopts a more pragmatic and inclusive approach, aimed at fostering gradual integration among countries with heterogeneous levels of development. The agreement places a high priority on trade in goods, with a commitment to the elimination of approximately 90% of tariffs (compared to the CPTPP's more ambitious target of 99%), with particular attention to agricultural quotas and flexible implementation timelines (Gao et al., 2025). From a regulatory perspective, RCEP employs a hybrid structure that combines positive and negative lists for services liberalization, and excludes binding provisions on labour, environment, and SOEs. Moreover, RCEP focuses on developing trade facilitation measures, harmonising regulations, and strengthening regional value chains (Park et al., 2021). However, the two agreements are not mutually exclusive and share a substantial overlap in membership: Australia, Brunei, Japan, Malaysia, New Zealand, Singapore, and Vietnam are parties to both frameworks (see Figure 1). These countries benefit from the legal and economic advantages provided by each agreement, placing them in a strategic position within the regional integration process and enabling a potential convergence between differing yet complementary regulatory models (Li & Whalley, 2021). On the same topic Kuźnar (2024) offers a different view, since she observed a weaken effect from new agreements in case of overlaps with extant ones, due to either contrasting or hard to combine measures.

As "megaregional" trade agreements (as defined by Park et al., 2021), both the RCEP and the CPTPP are shaping contemporary trade and investment patterns in the Asia-Pacific, functioning as instruments of economic governance, capable of influencing the global regulatory architecture and the development trajectories of their member economies.

Figure 1. Members of RCEP and CPTPP

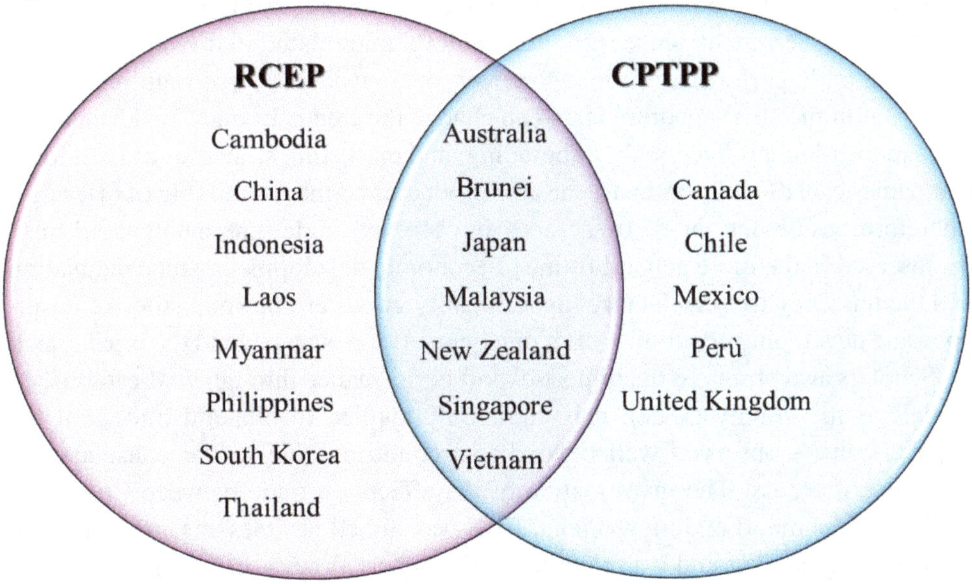

Source: Authors' elaboration

SCOPE AND DRIVERS OF RESEARCH ON INTERNATIONAL AGREEMENTS AND TRADE

The research on international agreements and their effect on worldwide trade offers a variety of interpretations and factors taken into account to describe how new norms can change the export performance, with effects on employment, taxes, investments, and a new framing of geopolitics.

In 2020 Flach & Gräf observed the effects of trade agreements on world export, stressing the effects on prices; following the highlighting of this tie, they observed the consequences on competitiveness and the preference for investments, in case of prices being changing the attractiveness of a market in terms of destination for export flows. In order to investigate this issue, the authors analysed tariffs, gross domestic products (GDPs) of country members, the competitiveness of a country, the import-export flows, and the prices at different shipping conditions – i.e., CIF (cost, insurance, and freight) and FOB (free on board). They wrapped up their research confirming international trade being a multi-variable phenomenon, with trade promotion in the realm of international agreements being just a part of the efforts of a government, since rules at local level and related to investments might affect the trade performance too. Moreover, the consideration of multiple effects occurring in the short-medium term can change the trends in trade besides tariffs, since innovation, product quality upgrading, and marketing strategies of individual companies can affect the attractiveness of products and the positioning of offerings. Therefore, besides the variety of factors to be observed, trade agreements should also be observed in the more general frame of economic development, since innovation and the tendency to manufacture higher quality goods are pre-requisites of developed and developing economies affecting competition even beyond the price effect.

Scholars also observed the import-export performance through well-established models as the gravity model; it is commonly applied to bilateral trade, but the impacts can be observed well beyond two countries, due to the consequences on competitiveness. The investigation of the effects on trade between China and Pakistan (Mahmood & Jongwanich, 2018) was aimed at assessing the impact of a bilateral agreement and was centred on the export flows – including a focus on agricultural products and manufactured ones –, the GDP of country members, the tariff gap, the population, and the opportunity to opt for other countries as an export destination in case of tariffs being unbearable. The results show two main effects, namely a wider effect of bilateral agreement than FTAs among multiple countries and the wider effects on agricultural than manufactured products, due to the ease of complying with the new norms.

The gravity model was also used by Kaushal (2022), as she also assessed the impact on inefficiencies in trade partnerships, thus she considered the promotion embedded in regional agreements to stimulate products exchange, with a focus on the Indian export performance. The model proposed to reach the research goal embedded GDP, the exchange rate, the geographical distance, and the combined effect of multiple agreements into an area. In most cases the adoption of new agreements favoured an increase in competitiveness and in trade effectiveness, with significant increases in exports. This was further stimulated by a depreciation of the national currency, making local products more appealing than before for partners from other countries. However, efficiency was not fully achieved, due to detailed measures missing in some agreements, including references to quality and rules of origin. Moreover, the increase in export performance led the country being attractive also for FDIs, still with an effect on effectiveness and not in efficiency, due to a limited exploitation of the potential full advantage; this also depended on the country not being part of several global value chains, while just contributing to some of them. Consequently, the efforts of the local governments should be aimed at attracting FDIs – as well as the interest of local investors – in industries where the country is not yet part of international markets at full, also through the implementation of trade standards addressing quality and country of origin, as a result of the growing competitiveness. Similar considerations had been advanced by Frederick et al. (2015) as they investigated the reciprocity of trade relations and goods movement in Central America in light of the setting of a new free trade zone; their investigation observed the effects of the new agreement through the data on the income of a whole industry and the ratio between export flows towards a country and total export flows.

Trade facilitations have also been investigated by the WTO, due to its role in monitoring barriers and incentives to global markets. The availability of data and the chance to aggregate multiple measures made their perspective wider than the one that might be achieved at country level. Indeed, Beverelli et al. (2023) combined variables shaping the trade facilitation system, with most of the facilitation depending on trade cost reduction. One of the first effects they observed is the evolution of commitment at country level throughout time in developing countries, besides the pace of growth of such commitment emerged as lower than the average growth in some cases. Indeed, the increase in commitment was due to the effort of trading partners instead of depending on the efforts at country level. The variables considered to assess such effects were fragmented at industry level as well as data were compared in order to make a distinction between the one-side and the bilateral goals of regional agreements. Though a gravity model was not considered at first, it then emerged as significant when considering non-tariff barriers too. The key outcomes of the perspective offered by WTO were the bilateral trade results when tariff barriers are lowered and an increase in competitiveness following a reduction in barriers; contrary to this, an increase in demand generated an increase in wages in the short term, leading competitiveness to be negatively affected. The fragmentation of data with reference to multiple industries led to highlight price elasticity as an additional variable to be observed when assessing the effects of trade facilitations, as in new agreements or in changes to extant trade barriers.

Recently, a new perspective on trade – mostly with reference to the Asia-Pacific area – has been offered by the United Nations (2024) through the ESCAP (Economic and Social Commission for Asia and the Pacific), as they considered the impact of trade facilitation on trade and reviewed the variables shaping a model for assessing the effects of new trade agreements as well as other facilitating measures. The variables listed are GDP, previous ties – at both historical and economic level between partner economies –, the existence of multiple agreements, and the port connectivity index. This latter provides insights on how the transportation system can support and be reactive in mutual trade flows and its progress mirrors the increase in traffic. Their results show a significant impact of trade facilitations including a lean bureaucracy – even through the use of new digital solutions for document and data management –, a wider cooperation at national level, and a general increase in transparency, both in data exchange and in setting the rules.

Research Design

Research Gaps And Aims

The studies on the impact of international cooperation agreements and FTAs on international business are continuously flourishing due to the changing nature of such agreements. The new perspective brought by studies on businesses' and contexts' resilience fed the debate and need further attention; moreover, new measures – including restrictive ones – are being adopted by governmental entities (White III et al., 2021), thus further research has been called for. Parallel to this, some studies suggest a view wider than that of a single industry (Statsenko et al., 2023). Additionally, geopolitics offers sparks for research due to the rise of new agreements, such as the RCEP; finally, the rise of new global issues shaping conflicting times stimulate the interest for additional research. Recent studies paid attention to FTAs and their effects, as well as to RCEP, due to its novelty and the role played by Asian countries in the global economy; as a consequence, this research addresses the calls for research emerging from extant literature on such themes. Indeed, Li & Moon (2018) simulated the effects of RCEP, therefore implicitly called for an investigation after the agreement came into force to review their considerations; Guo et al. (2024) considered the chance to reduce the geopolitical risk through the new agreement, thus a resilience-based view is adopted; Erixon et al. (2024) pondered a facilitation to market access as it should be with international agreements, yet to be verified due to the novelty of the agreement when they investigated the topic; finally, Kuźnar

(2024) foresaw a possible drawback deriving from the partial overlapping of RCEP with previous international agreements.

Therefore, this research aims at describing whether businesses and contexts gained resilience by means of RCEP, despite global conflicts and other complex issues. More in detail, the aim is to assess whether member countries have continued to operate within their traditional trade networks or have started to capitalize on the opportunities presented by the new regulatory framework established by the RCEP. This would bring countries the chance to consider more destination markets than before, thus contrasting the limitations that might emerge in relation with some countries, therefore bringing resilience. Indeed, scholars reviewed extant studies to consider trade as a countermeasure to relevant negative events and highlighted both consequences and limits it might offer, thus calling for further investigation (Nielsen et al., 2023).

Research Context

RCEP is a trade agreement aimed at establishing a "modern, comprehensive, high-quality, and mutually beneficial economic partnership framework" (ASEAN, 2020) between the ASEAN member states and their FTA partner countries; all in all the new agreement currently groups 15 countries, namely Australia, Brunei, Cambodia, China, Indonesia, Japan, Laos, Malaysia, Myanmar, New Zealand, the Philippines, Singapore, South Korea, Thailand and Vietnam. Therefore, this agreement encompasses both advanced economies, such as Australia, New Zealand, and Japan, and developing economies, with the objective of ensuring widespread economic benefits for all participating nations (ASEAN, 2020). The negotiation process, initiated in 2013 and officially concluded in 2020, resulted in the creation of the largest free trade area in the world. In fact, despite India's withdrawal from the negotiations in 2019 due to political considerations, RCEP still encompasses approximately 30% of global GDP and includes a population of over three billion, underscoring its substantial impact on the global economic landscape (Chen et al., 2024). There are two main reasons for the particular significance of the agreement. Firstly, it is notable that the agreement represents the first trade agreement to simultaneously include China, Japan and South Korea — three of the region's largest and most influential economies — which, until now, had only been linked through bilateral agreements. The East Asian trade landscape has long been characterised by a dense network of free trade agreements (FTAs), often referred to as ASEAN+1 FTAs (Salamatov et al., 2022), with major regional partners – including China (ACFTA), Japan (AJCEP), South Korea (AKFTA), India (AIFTA), and Australia and New Zealand (AANZFTA) – and resulting in a consolidation of these individual accords into a unified framework. More in detail, ASEAN+1 frames the trade with external partners, while the aforementioned agreements – i.e. RCEP and CPTPP – adopt a different focus compared to ASEAN+1, since they adopt supportive measures for the exchanges among member countries, including lower barriers and liberalization. The success of ASEAN has been measured through the containers throughput volumes (Noosuwan et al., 2024) showing that the policies adopted in the area led to achieve an increase in exports due to measures facilitating the exports.

Secondly, while these extant FTAs have contributed to the enhancement of trade relations across the region, they have also resulted in rules and procedures fragmentation. In this regard, RCEP plays a crucial role in the harmonisation of regulations and the simplification of procedures, thereby facilitating trade integration and contributing to the development of a more cohesive and resilient economy in the Asia-Pacific region.

RCEP finally came into force in 2022 for most countries (except for Indonesia and the Philippines that only made their participation effective in 2023, while Myanmar has delayed the implementation due to political reasons). Beyond the liberalization of trade in goods with lowered tariffs, the agreement establishes commitments across strategic sectors – including education, healthcare, and business services, though not directly affected by tariff barriers – and incorporates provisions on intellectual property, competition policy, public procurement, and SMEs support. One of the key novelties within RCEP is the adoption of *rules of origin*, granting preferential tariffs to products with at least 40% value-added content from member states. This provision assumes considerable strategic significance, as it fosters the integration of regional supply chains, with significant effects on economic growth and competitiveness in the area (Chen et al., 2024). This norm is expected to perform effects also through FDIs, since the chance to manufacture locally to benefit from the rules of origin might encourage investors from abroad in investing to have their productive site in one of the partner countries of RCEP.

Research Method

Due to the changes occurred throughout time in the Asia-Pacific area – with multiple agreements and the unifying framework brought by RCEP – it is suitable to perform a longitudinal study, as this form of analysing data can clearly make a distinction between the years in which export took place before the implementation of RCEP and after it. Indeed, longitudinal studies capture how variables change with reference to both single units of analysis and groups, as well as at multiple time points. Additionally, it is in line with recent studies on this topic, as in Du & Shepotylo (2024). To sum up, a longitudinal study offers the opportunity to investigate sequences of data related to events, thus focusing on dynamic processes and highlighting patterns of change, if any; conversely, a cross-sectional analysis would have given only a snapshot of the data and described temporal relationships and causality associations.

More in concrete, contexts shaped by a multitude of variables potentially affecting a key result – as it is with performance export in this research – all data have to be tracked across time, and it is necessary to do so for the same set of subjects. This applies to the research context identified for this study, since there are several variables that might affect export trade and the RCEP refers to a multitude of countries; the variables focused on are described in the next sub-section, while the countries chosen for this investigation have been already described in the previous sub-section.

Additionally, index numbers are needed in longitudinal data analysis, as they offer a standardized number describing a variable at a certain point in time. This would lead to considering some variables a percentage – or a ratio – favouring comparison over time and with reference to different units of analysis. This is needed in this study, since countries vary very much when it comes to their export trade, their surface, their GDP, and so on; moreover, data have been collected from 2017 to 2023, thus it is necessary to set a year as a central reference to describe all other data in a homogeneous manner. For this analysis the authors set the starting year as an index number.

Furthermore, a multiple linear regression is the analysis that can favour the understanding of relationships among multiple variables over time; a multiple linear regression identifies the relationships between a dependent variable (the main focus of an investigation) and multiple independent variables. These latter might be considered as either predicting the effects or explaining them. This is in line with recent studies on the effect of barriers on international trade (Mrindoko and Mollel, 2024). An additional advantage of a multiple linear regression is to incorporate data from different time points, thus offering the opportunity to predict how a dependent variable can change over time, due to the changes affecting predictors. This would also lead to discard the expected effects of confounding factors, thus allowing to highlight only data that shows to affect the change over time of the dependent variable.

To sum up, the combination of longitudinal analysis, index numbers, and multiple linear regression shapes a framework of analysis useful to analyze complex and dynamic systems, encompassing the effect of time and contexts, as it is in the premises of this study, as well as in recent studies in international trade and trade agreements.

Data Collection

Following the suggestions emerged from the extant literature, the authors have identified the variables summed up in the following table (Table 1), even in light of the availability of data in the longest possible range of time for the key countries of the area. As regards the countries, the focus is on four of the partner countries of RCEP, namely (a) China – as being the most relevant partner country of the Asia-Pacific region, due to its role in global manufacturing –, (b) Australia and (c) New Zealand – as they joined RCEP, thus framing business relationship with partner countries in a new posture, while the other partners of RCEP had already benefited from previous international agreements, as ASEAN is –, and (d) Vietnam – due to its relevance in the global value chains when performing outsourcing.

Table 1. Data collection: source and reference to literature

Data	**Source**	**Reference in previous studies**	**Typology of data**
Export flows of agricultural products towards RCEP partner countries (value)	OECD	Beverelli et al., 2023; Mahmood & Jongwanich, 2018	primary
Export flows of manufactured goods towards RCEP partner countries (value)	OECD	Beverelli et al., 2023; Mahmood & Jongwanich, 2018	primary
GDP	World Bank	Kaushal, 2022	primary
Exchange rate to US$	Bank of Italy	Kaushal, 2022	primary
Globally exported agricultural products (value)	OECD	Beverelli et al., 2023	primary
Globally exported manufactured goods (value)	OECD	Beverelli et al., 2023	primary
Number of containers shipped	UNComtrade	United Nations, 2024	primary
Consumer prices index (in %)	World Bank	Flach & Gräf, 2018	primary
Port liner shipping connectivity index for the key port	UNComtrade	United Nations, 2024	primary, it's a composite index
Ratio between Exported agricultural products towards RCEP partner countries and Globally exported agricultural products	OECD	Frederick et al., 2015	Comparison between two primary data
Ratio between Exported manufactured goods towards RCEP partner countries and Globally exported manufactured goods	OECD	Frederick et al., 2015	Comparison between two primary data
Ratio between number of containers shipped to RCEP partner countries and number of globally shipped containers	OECD	Noosuwan et al., 2024	Comparison between two primary data
Ratio between Exported agricultural products towards RCEP partner countries and GDP	OECD	Mahmood & Jongwanich, 2018	Comparison between two primary data
Ratio between Exported manufactured goods towards RCEP partner countries and GDP	OECD	Mahmood & Jongwanich, 2018	Comparison between two primary data

Research Rationale

In line with the goal of observing effects at a scale wider than single industry and in the realm of RCEP, this research uses multiple reports and statistics on both international trade and FDIs from official sources as supranational institutions (United Nations and World Trade Organization - WTO) and national governments (e.g., Australian Department of Foreign Affairs and Trade). The research design is set by authors as inference on official data and the consideration on such choice are inspired by methodological suggestions by Bryman and Bell (2011). Inference on data - as per Table 1 - would provide insights on whether RCEP contributed to the increase in trade in the Asia-Pacific region, thus in making national economies more resilient over time, through the (further) development of international trade. Moreover, the emerging trends in trade among the partner countries of this agreement would provide an idea for resilience of national economies also in light of the ongoing changes in the tariffs scenario worldwide, as well as offer insights on how to leverage on agreements like this to contrast disruptive events.

The analysis offers validity depending on the sources trustworthiness, and low subjectivity, due to the variety of sources, reducing the risk of leaning on local sources lacking independence in their data collection and representation. Reliability depends on the variables used in determining such data, leading to a limited understanding of the phenomenon investigated; anyhow, such data offer an overview on the ongoing trends from reciprocal perspectives of the RCEP member countries, thus contrasting the risk of misleading interpretations.

FINDINGS

A Premise On The Years Surrounding The Implementation of RCEP

The analysis of the economic behaviour of RCEP member countries prior to the agreement's implementation provides valuable insights into potential future outcomes, assessing the impact of RCEP not only on national economies but also on import-export dynamics and the commercial strategies of the businesses involved, including foreign investments.

A review of trade data from 2019 to 2022, as reported by WTO, reveals notable trends in the Asia-Pacific region. Chinese agricultural exports to Japan and Laos exhibited significant growth, with increases of 9% and 24.7%, respectively. As it regards Laos, evidence suggests the potential for political motivations to influence these shifts. Japan, a major regional economic player, experienced an 8.5% rise in agricultural exports to China and a 5.7% rise to South Korea, indicating a strengthening of its trade relations with key Asian partners. Non-agricultural exports also exhibited growth, with Japanese exports to China rising by 12.8%, while Chinese exports to Japan and South Korea grew by 16.3% and 7%, respectively. Updated data from New Zealand also show increased exports to China (+6.3%), Australia (+8.4%), and Japan (+7.2%), although imports from these countries experienced a modest decline, except for a 14% rise in imports from Australia.

In the realm of FDIs, China emerged as a significant strategic partner for Australia (the second top foreign investor), with Chinese investments rising by 21.2% (the highest increase in the country), reaching USD 3.6596 billion. At the same time, Australian exports to China exhibited a 14.1% increase during the 2022-2023 period.

These trends suggest a positive trajectory for regional trade and great opportunities for further economic integration within RCEP member states.

An Overview On Basic Trade Trends After The Implementation of RCEP

Multiple analyses have been run on the data recalled above in order to observe the ongoing trends in key countries and the interplay among the variables to frame the contribution of RCEP.

The first analysis depicts trends in the export performance for Australia, New Zealand, China, and Vietnam according to the fragmentation of data proposed by the OECD in sectors; the attention was paid to agricultural products and manufactured goods (Figure 2). The trends show some contrasting performance, indeed while in 2022 Australia had a huge increase in the export of agricultural products and a weak increase in the export of manufactured goods, China had a small decrease in the export of agricultural products and a huge increase in the export of manufactured goods. In 2023 both countries experienced a weak increase in the export of agricultural products and while Australia had a minor decrease in the export of manufactured goods, China had a huge decrease for the same goods. Trends are very contrasting also for New Zealand and Vietnam; indeed, in 2022 Vietnam had a strong increase in the export of agricultural products and New Zealand had a strong decrease for the same products, while both countries had a significant increase in the export of manufactured goods. In 2023, both countries experienced a decrease in the export of manufactured goods, while the trend for the export of agricultural products shows a significant increase for Vietnam and a significant decrease for New Zealand. These trends offered an overview on the changes experienced in the two years following the introduction of RCEP, thus in order to grasp some more meanings from such data it is worthy to run additional analyses.

Figure 2. The export volume index for agricultural products and manufactured goods (base year 2017 = 1) measures changes in the physical volume of agricultural products and manufactured goods over time, adjusting for price effects.

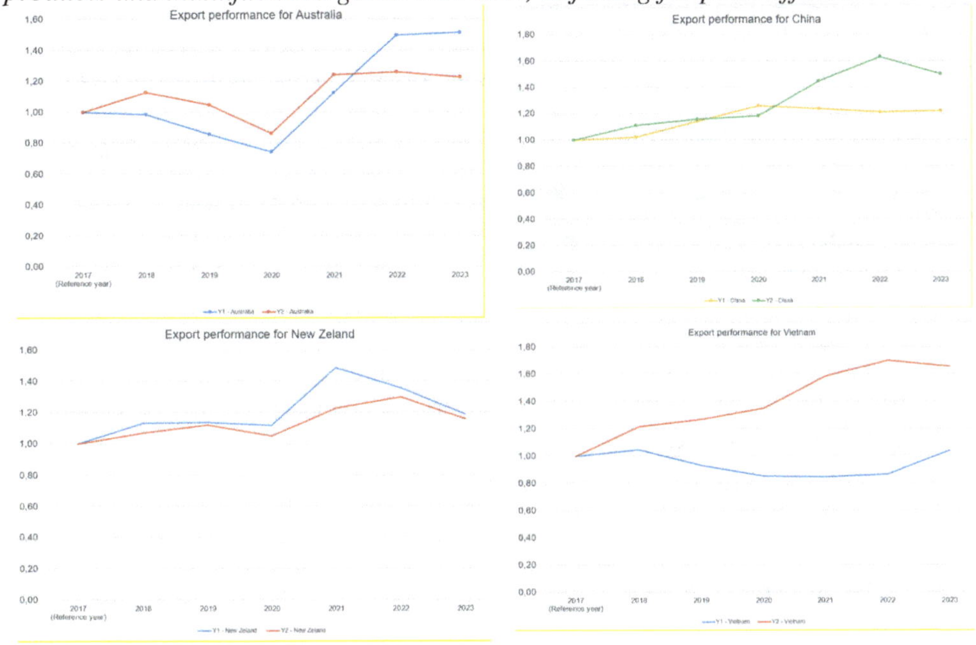

A Detailed Analysis On Trade Trends And Their Drivers

As per the previous section multiple linear regression analyses have been performed with reference to the four countries (Australia, China, New Zealand, Vietnam) and the two categories of exported items (i.e., agricultural goods and manufactured products). In order to select the best model, the Stepwise-backward procedure was used. Furthermore, for all estimated models, the basic assumptions were verified using standard residual analysis methods and variance inflation factor (VIF) for multicollinearity assessment.

The export trend for Australian agricultural products is significantly coupled with GDP, the total number of containers shipped towards the RCEP partner countries, and the index for consumer prices.

Therefore, it shows a significant tie with the general growth of the national economy, as well as an increase in shipped goods, mirroring an increase in volumes. The statistical model was found to be statistically significant (p-value <0,001), and the goodness of fit was excellent (R^2-adjusted=0,998). Multicollinearity was assessed using the VIF, and the values for the three statistically significant variables were below 5. Moreover, the significant increase in consumer prices is combined with an increase in export, thus showing a reaction of local producers. The correlations and the significance are reported below (Table 2).

Table 2. Multiple linear regression analysis on Australian agricultural goods export

Australia - Agricultural goods export

	Coefficients	Std. Error	Stat t	Sign.
Intercept	-17174274656	5627957341	-3,0516	0,0554
X1 - GDP	0,032178589	0,001514602	21,2456	0,0002
X5 - N. of containers shipped	-4086,030595	419,5835016	-9,7383	0,0023
X7 - Consumer prices index	63615001,63	15459331,41	4,1150	0,0260

As it regards the export trend for Australian manufactured goods, the only significant variable coupled to the value of export trade is GDP (Table 3), showing a general growth of the Australian economy.

The goodness of fit was good (R^2-adjusted=0,763).

Table 3. Multiple linear regression analysis on Australian manufactured products export

Australia - Manufactured products export

	Coefficients	Std. Error	Stat t	Sign.
Intercept	-2007850007	12895679070	-0,1557	0,8824
X1 - GDP	0,034498928	0,008584212	4,0189	0,0101

The analysis of export trends for China shows a significant relationship between the export of agricultural goods and the whole amount of agricultural goods exported worldwide, as well as between the export of manufactured products and the whole amount of manufactured products exported worldwide. For both models, the goodness-of-fit index R^2 was excellent, respectively 0.882 and 0.961. Therefore, tables 4 and 5 show a general growth for China exports, both locally and globally.

Table 4. Multiple linear regression analysis on Chinese agricultural goods export

China - Agricultural goods export

	Coefficients	Std. Error	Stat t	Sign.
Intercept	455194681,4	1443080613	0,3154	0,7652
X3 - Agricultural goods exported worldwide	0,442575214	0,072263072	6,1245	0,0017

Table 5. Multiple linear regression analysis on Chinese manufactured products export

China - Manufactured products export	Coefficients	Std. Error	Stat t	Sign.
Intercept	-54564222095	49389904167	-1,1048	0,3196
X4 - Manufactured products exported worldwide	0,276515592	0,017176624	16,0984	0,0000

Results for New Zealand are quite similar to the previous two countries, with a coefficient significant for GDP with reference to agricultural products, and the global export performance for both agricultural goods and manufactured products, as it is described in tables 6 and 7. Also, the R^2 index was excellent for both models (R^2-adjusted=0,987 and R=0,922).

Table 6. Multiple linear regression analysis on New Zealanders agricultural goods export

New Zealand - Agricultural goods export	Coefficients	Std. Error	Stat t	Sign.
Intercept	-2306448281	357101249,8	-6,4588	0,0030
X1 - GDP	0,008931937	0,002116431	4,2203	0,0135
X3 - Agricultural goods exported worldwide	0,761423206	0,061905638	12,2997	0,0003

Table 7. Multiple linear regression analysis on New Zealanders manufactured products export

New Zealand - Manufactured products export	Coefficients	Std. Error	Stat t	Sign.
Intercept	-3918473516	3005304874	-1,3039	0,2491
X4 - Manufactured products exported worldwide	0,688364925	0,089426671	7,6975	0,0006

Finally, the analysis for Vietnam shows a trend similar to China, thus there is a significant correlation between the export performance towards RCEP partner countries in line with the global performance, for both agricultural goods and manufactured products. Details are offered in tables 8 and 9.

Table 8. Multiple linear regression analysis on Vietnamese agricultural goods export

Vietnam - Agricultural goods export	Coefficients	Std. Error	Stat t	Sign.
Intercept	984527511,4	1365807686	0,7208	0,5033
X3 - Agricultural goods exported worldwide	0,371437048	0,165045468	2,2505	0,0742

Table 9. Multiple linear regression analysis on Vietnamese manufactured products export

Vietnam - Manufactured products export

	Coefficients	Std. Error	Stat t	Sign.
Intercept	22899728546	6469308654	3,5397	0,0166
X4 - Manufactured products exported worldwide	0,34994149	0,020377015	17,1733	0,0000

IMPLICATIONS

Overall considerations

This research shows the quite positive impacts of RCEP on the economies in South-Eastern Asia and Oceania, both on import and export flows and on foreign investments; such impacts also show that the opportunities set by the agreement have yet to be fully deployed. More in detail, the effects can be observed more frequently in agricultural goods trade and with mutual effects in some countries; indeed, in most cases reciprocal increases emerged while the trade for manufactured products shows rollercoasting trends. Moreover, such effects can occur also in developing economies, with interesting and forward-looking consequences on the political side, as it is with Myanmar that delayed the implementation of RCEP due to political reasons.

Additionally, some data used in the analysis might have limited the interpretation of data. Indeed, besides not reaching statistical significance in the multiple linear regression, some variables deserve a careful focus; the exchange rates show relevant variations over time, besides the time frame analysis is from 2017 to 2023. Some currencies experienced changes over 10% in this time frame, thus affecting both the competitiveness of a country when trading with foreign partners and the value of the export trade flows shown in the official statistics. Similarly, there have been very relevant changes in the consumer prices over time, with a great inflation in Australia, thus with potential effects on both import flows – negatively affected by the lower availability of real wage – and export flows – due to the need for local firms to find high-spending markets abroad, besides more expensive.

Finally, some effects are still hard to be fully depicted due to the long wave of pandemics; indeed, some variables used in this study show an enthusiastic trend in 2021 and 2022, due to markets restarting after the limitations due to safety reasons worldwide to limit contagium, thus making less reliable the assessment of data in 2023. This is an effect the authors observed on single variables – thus before running the multiple linear regression – for all countries investigated.

Theoretical Implications

From a theoretical perspective, this research contributes to the framing of international cooperation and FTAs as means to react to geopolitical shocks (Luo & Van Assche, 2023); indeed, RCEP entered into force in an era featured by problematic issues, as the long wave of pandemics and the rise of conflicts in various areas of the world. Besides such disruptive events, RCEP partner countries managed to encourage – and sometimes increase – their international trade and foreign investments in partner countries, mirroring the positive effect of FTAs in a general fashion (Baggs and Brander, 2006). The quick development and the promising avenues of RCEP also represent an opportunity to debate on resilience, as per the call for research launched by Nielsen et al. (2020), since an increase in trade in the Asia-Pacific area might represent a quick response to the ongoing changes worldwide and to disruptions that can affect global value chains and retailing systems.

This research addresses – and has been informed by – the calls for research from several scholars; indeed, Li & Moon (2018) had simulated the expected effects of RCEP and they properly identified the limited increase in export trends; such a limited trend might also depend on the novelty of the agreement, thus full outcomes would appear further on; indeed, this would align RCEP to ASEAN, since Noosuwan et al. (2024) only observed a significant increase in containers shipped among partners in 2024, therefore several years after the agreement came into force; similarly, Erixon et al. (2024) thought the effects would be verified in the middle-long run. Anyway, the interest generated by RCEP – besides limited in quantity – provides an answer to the chance to reduce geopolitical risks (Guo et al., 2024), since closer commercial relationships have been favoured, therefore this result might be interpreted as an increase in resilience. Another reason to interpret the limited achievement of RCEP can mirror one more call for research, since Kuźnar (2024) considered the overlapping of multiple agreements as a drawback and RCEP partially overlaps with ASEAN and CPTPP.

A closer look at the variables identified in this study offers further insights; the correlation between foreign trade and GDP confirms the posture of Hofmann et al. (2018) in stating that the effects on goods trade would emerge according to the income level of the partner countries of an agreement. This is the case for New Zealand and Australia in this investigation; for the other countries and for manufactured goods, there is a general growth of the economic performance – the entire amount of export flows – that mirrors the growth of trade towards partner countries, thus adding a different view to what previous studies had highlighted.

Time is another crucial reason in studying the effects of regional trade agreement for multiple reasons: first, the time to assess the decision to set new trade relationships abroad set a clear distinction between spotting the opportunities of such an agreement and increasing the intensity of trade flows, as Helpman et al. (2008) had stated. Indeed, the increase emerging from data related to RCEP looks still partial; second, time is a proxy of contingent issues, since some countries are still recovering from the long wave of pandemics or they are experiencing unexpected flows in foreign trade, with this effect yet to be fully investigated due to the process still being on; third, time is needed to properly design and activate new supply and retail chains to fully benefit from the incentives brought by a regional agreement. This consideration is only partially aligned to previous studies, indeed Estrades et al. (2022) consider regional value chains as a way to reduce transaction costs, but they paid limited attention to how long this process might be.

Additionally, the partially good results confirm what Kaushal (2022) observed, namely the need for promotion to be performed by governments in order to create awareness on the opportunities offered by RCEP; indeed, even if there were previous agreements to reduce barriers in this region, RCEP contributed to harmonize the barriers system as well as favouring further facilitation in some cases.

Finally, the chance of increasing trade and making the export-import trade more diversified on multiple countries create a condition that can be described through the concept of resilience; indeed, the authors consider the opportunities brought by the agreement as leading to resilience, since the partner countries – namely RCEP members – showed their willingness to change the destination of some trade flows, thus getting positive results in the region and stimulating trends by means of the opportunities brought by their international cooperation in the Asia-Pacific domain. Therefore, this research expands the view of White III et al. (2021) considering resilience as an acquired feature, deriving from cooperation. What is new in these results is the extent to which such effects emerge, since they affect different industries and countries, stressing the potentialities instead of being stuck by the constraints. This answers the call for research by Statsenko et al. (2023) addressing the need to adopt a perspective wider than an industry-based one, as well as it updates the debate in this domain by considering a new agreement, as stressed in previous studies (White III et al., 2021).

Policy Implications

The significance and extensive impact of the RCEP framework require policymakers to support it by implementing measures that ensure its effectiveness. Indeed, although the RCEP does not represent a completely new framework for the region, the expected results should have been more significant than those that emerged from this analysis. This requires further efforts from national governments to raise awareness and promote exports among partner countries through appropriate strategies. However, some efforts have already emerged in favouring the further implementation of RCEP; in doing so, the Australian government has implemented policies that facilitate digital trade and eliminate duties on electronic transmissions, demonstrating how regulatory reforms can be converted into competitive advantages for domestic firms, particularly SMEs. Moreover, beyond the liberalisation of tariffs, consideration must be given to the protection of consumer data and privacy, thereby ensuring that digital commerce flourishes on a foundation of trust. Furthermore, it is crucial to strengthen economic and technical collaboration among member nations to ensure that the economic advancement of developing countries is not compromised. Once again, Australia's strategic use of Official Development Assistance (ODA) to assist lower-income RCEP partners in adopting and implementing the agreement's provisions, serves as a pioneering example. Even the implementation of modern customs procedures fosters more integrated and resilient value chains by ensuring predictability, consistency, and transparency in the application of customs laws and regulations. Finally, RCEP measures have strengthened intellectual property protection and generated valuable opportunities for companies operating in the region. By harmonizing IP standards, the agreement fosters innovation, particularly among SMEs.

In conclusion, a comprehensive analysis of RCEP reveals its significance as a multifaceted instrument transcending the conventional boundaries of a trade agreement, but as a dynamic platform for dialogue, also establishing common benchmarks not only in the domains of digitalisation, but also in the areas of IP governance and multilateral cooperation. This first analysis mirrors some effects, still limited and suffering from limitations that would be further addressed. However, efforts are yet to be performed, especially from the most relevant countries in this area, due to their influential role in trade; this is the case for China as it ships approximately three out of every ten containers worldwide, still referring to RCEP as the future of cooperation in the Asia-Pacific region. This can also depend on the time needed to design and build supply chains in this region.

CONCLUSION

The Regional Comprehensive Economic Partnership (RCEP) represents an initiative aimed at fostering economic integration among Asia-Pacific economies by strengthening commercial ties between geographically proximate countries and reducing dependency on external economies. Nevertheless, the extant empirical evidence suggests that the agreement has yielded impacts that remain below initial expectations. This outcome should be interpreted in light of several critical exogenous factors that may have significantly influenced the implementation and early outcomes of the agreement. The COVID-19 pandemic, the ongoing geopolitical tensions in Eastern Europe and the Middle East, and the disruption to major international maritime routes have all played a substantial role in shaping the current landscape, thereby contributing to results that deviate from initial projections. Furthermore, the existence of RCEP alongside other regional and bilateral trade agreements – including ASEAN+1 and the Comprehensive and Progressive Agreement for Trans-Pacific Partnership (CPTPP) – has resulted in regulatory overlap and fragmentation, which may potentially compromise the overall effectiveness of RCEP among its member states. In this dynamic and intricate context, the role of national governments and the RCEP Joint Committee emerges as pivotal: in addition to high-level coordination, there is a clear need for targeted actions aimed at raising business awareness of the agreement's potential benefits and supporting firms in adapting to its regulatory framework. Moreover, it is also important to note, as highlighted by Kong et al. (2022), that RCEP should not be viewed merely as a conventional trade agreement; rather, it embodies significant geopolitical considerations, which may further help explain the observed asymmetries and delays in its implementation.

Nevertheless, the present study aimed to investigate whether RCEP fosters the concept of economic resilience. The agreement promotes regional integration, strengthens value chains, and reduces reliance on distant economic partners. These measures are intended to enhance member states' capacity to absorb external shocks, adapt to uncertain global scenarios, and maintain long-term economic stability. This strategic positioning of RCEP places it as a fundamental context for observing how businesses respond to disruptive environments, thereby highlighting its significance in contemporary economic and commercial dynamics.

LIMITATIONS

Given the recent implementation of RCEP, the analysis has some limitations due to the novelty of the agreement and the limited availability of data. Initially signed in 2020, the agreement did not officially enter into force for all 15 partner countries until 2023, following ratification by the last member, the Philippines, further complicating the assessment of its early effects. A major criticism that might be addressed to this investigation is the aggregate nature of the available data, which does not provide a detailed breakdown of trade and investments by industry, thus limiting the possibility of a more in-depth analysis. Nevertheless, the preliminary data do provide a first indication of the potential long-term impact of the agreement, highlighting quite a positive trend towards deeper integration of regional trade along local supply chains in some cases. Regulatory frameworks, particularly the *rules of origin*, play a key role in driving this trend by promoting deeper regional supply chain integration, facilitating intra-regional trade, and reducing barriers for businesses operating across multiple member states. A notable strength of this study lies in the availability of public data issued by the national governments published by key partner economies, such as Australia and New Zealand, which provide valuable information on international trade flows and on foreign investment trends that might be used in further analyses. However, such data is less accessible in countries with smaller economies, thus bilateral effects will be hard to be depicted. Furthermore, the integration of international sources, including Chinese sources, allows for a more comprehensive analysis that highlights economic interactions among member countries.

Analyses of the impact of the RCEP allow for assessments of the economic dynamics of single states, as well as for understanding of the broader implications for companies operating in the area. Therefore, further analyses can address these limitations; indeed, the use of more recent data as they will be available (data on 2024 have not yet be fully set, leading the authors of this research taken aside the increases in export trade some countries have already showed), the breakdown of such data at industrial level, and the chance to contrast the information achieved from different business angles would benefit the understanding of the phenomenon. Additionally, further studies might compare the trade performance with countries other than the partners in RCEP, since a substitution effect can confirm the relevance of the opportunity brought by the agreement and offer a different view. The investigation by Lu (2019) foresaw a gradual decrease in trade with countries outside the Asia-Pacific area and an increase in the exchange among the partner countries. This would also represent a further way to be resilient for the countries of this region, since it would reduce the dependency on countries that are further – thus, the supply chains might face disruptive events, as recently shown by the crisis in Yemen back in 2023 or the block to maritime transportation in Suez in 2021 –, as well as contrasting the rising tension in the commercial war with new and higher tariff barriers on the horizon. Further research is also required to assess how economic integration and development in the region will evolve over time in response to both global disruptions and policy initiatives adopted at the regional level. Consequently, as new data become available, future research could investigate the development of the agreement, as well as analyse the differential impacts of RCEP across advanced and developing economies. This would facilitate a more profound comprehension of the agreement's varying potential in diverse national contexts. Finally, a focus on additional variables and on more countries among the partners in the region can contribute to the highlighting of side effects of FTAs and international cooperation, as well as contextual issues should be brought into consideration.

REFERENCES

ASEAN. (2020). *RCEP Agreement* (full text). Available at https://asean.org/wp-content/uploads/2024/10/Regional-Comprehensive-Economic-Partnership-RCEP-Agreement-Full-Text.pdf&sa=D&source=docs&ust=1739948329527261&usg=AOvVaw1UEpjIv-z9prOG8nRVTmrH

Ayob, A. H., & Senik, Z. C. (2015). The role of competitive strategies on export market selection by SMEs in an emerging economy. *International Journal of Business and Globalisation, 14*(2), 208–225. DOI: 10.1504/IJBG.2015.067436

Baggs, J., & Brander, J. A. (2006). Trade liberalization, profitability, and financial leverage. *Journal of International Business Studies, 37*(2), 196–211. DOI: 10.1057/palgrave.jibs.8400183

Baier, S. L., & Bergstrand, J. H. (2007). Do free trade agreements actually increase members' international trade? *Journal of International Economics, 71*(1), 72–95. DOI: 10.1016/j.jinteco.2006.02.005

Beverelli, C., Gourevich, I., Heiland, I., Keck, A., Larch, M., & Yotov, Y. (2023). *Trade and welfare effects of the WTO Trade Facilitation Agreement* (No. ERSD-2023-04). WTO Staff Working Paper.

Bieron, B., & Ahmed, U. (2012). Regulating e-commerce through international policy: Understanding the international trade law issues of e-commerce. *Journal of World Trade, 46*(3).

Bryman, A., & Bell, E. (2011). *Business research methods* (3rd ed.). Oxford University Press.

Carrere, C. (2006). Revisiting the effects of regional trade agreements on trade flows with proper specification of the gravity model. *European Economic Review, 50*(2), 223–247. DOI: 10.1016/j.euroecorev.2004.06.001

Cavusgil, S. T., & Knight, G. (2009). *Born global firms: A new international enterprise*. Business Expert Press. DOI: 10.4128/9781606490136

Chen, X., Yuan, L., & Song, C. (2023). Investigating merchandise trade structure in the RCEP region from the perspective of regional integration. *Journal of Geographical Sciences, 33*(6), 1185–1204. DOI: 10.1007/s11442-023-2125-7

Chung, C., Park, I., & Park, S. (2022). Estimating the Impact of Cumulative Rules of Origin on Trade Costs: An Application to Mega-regional Free Trade Agreements in the Asia-Pacific Region. *Asian Economic Papers, 21*(1), 92–109. DOI: 10.1162/asep_a_00846

Dent, C. M. (2010). Freer trade, more regulation? Commercial regulatory provisions in Asia-Pacific free trade agreements. *Competition & Change, 14*(1), 48–79. DOI: 10.1179/102452910X12587274068114

Dib, G., Huang, F., & Poulou, A. (2020). *RCEP: Common rule of origin could boost regional trade by around USD90BN annually*. Allianz Research.

Du, J., & Shepotylo, O. (2024). Brexit and the services trade—A longitudinal analysis. *Journal of Service Research*. DOI: 10.1177/10946705241271384

Dunning, J. H. (1991). The eclectic paradigm of international production. *The nature of the transnational firm, 121*, 173-190.

Erixon, F., Guinea, O., Lamprecht, P., du Roy, O., Sisto, E., & Zilli, R. (2024). *Trading up: An EU trade policy for better market access and resilient sourcing* (No. 08/2024). ECIPE Policy Brief.

Estrades, C., Maliszewska, M., Osorio-Rodarte, I., & Pereira, M. S. (2023). Estimating the economic impacts of the regional comprehensive economic partnership. *Asia and the Global Economy, 3*(2), 100060. DOI: 10.1016/j.aglobe.2023.100060

Fath, B., Fiedler, A., Sinkovics, N., Sinkovics, R. R., & Sullivan-Taylor, B. (2021). International relationships and resilience of New Zealand SME exporters during COVID-19. *Critical Perspectives on International Business, 17*(2), 359–379. DOI: 10.1108/cpoib-05-2020-0061

Flach, L., & Gräf, F. (2020). The impact of trade agreements on world export prices. *Review of International Economics, 28*(1), 168–208. DOI: 10.1111/roie.12446

Forsgren, M. (2024). *Theories of the Multinational Firm. A Multidimensional Creature in the Global Economy* (4th ed.). Edward Elgar Publishing.

Forsgren, M., & Yamin, M. (2023). The source of MNE superiority from within or from outside?–A response to "the importance of being transnational". *Critical Perspectives on International Business, 19*(4), 523–525. DOI: 10.1108/cpoib-03-2023-0019

Frederick, S., Bair, J., & Gereffi, G. (2015). Regional trade agreements and export competitiveness: The uncertain path of Nicaragua's apparel exports under CAFTA. *Cambridge Journal of Regions, Economy and Society*, *8*(3), 403–420. DOI: 10.1093/cjres/rsv015

Gao, J., Zhao, Y., & Jia, R. (2025). RCEP regional value chain construction and global value chain position enhancement: A measurement analysis based on regional value chains. *Economia e Politica Industriale*, *52*(1), 27–58. DOI: 10.1007/s40812-024-00320-5

Guo, Y., Zheng, H., Zeng, Y., Fan, W., Albahooth, B., & Bhuiyan, R. A. (2023). Natural resources extraction of RCEP trade bloc: Examining geopolitical risk and economic situation. *Resources Policy*, *86*, 104227. DOI: 10.1016/j.resourpol.2023.104227

Helpman, E., Melitz, M., & Rubinstein, Y. (2008). Estimating trade flows: Trading partners and trading volumes. *The Quarterly Journal of Economics*, *123*(2), 441–487. DOI: 10.1162/qjec.2008.123.2.441

Hofmann, C., Osnago, A., & Ruta, M. (2019). The content of preferential trade agreements. *World Trade Review*, *18*(3), 365–398. DOI: 10.1017/S1474745618000071

Hymer, S. H. (1960). *The international operations of national firms, a study of direct foreign investment*. Doctoral dissertation, Massachusetts Institute of Technology.

Hymer, S. H. (1968). The large multinational corporation: An analysis of some motives for the international integration of business. *Revista de Economia (Curitiba)*, *19*(6), 949–973.

Jiang, H., & Yu, M. (2021). Understanding RCEP and CPTPP: From the perspective China's dual circulation economic strategy. *China Economic Journal*, *14*(2), 144–161. DOI: 10.1080/17538963.2021.1933055

Kaushal, L. A. (2022). Impact of regional trade agreements on export efficiency–A case study of India. *Cogent Economics & Finance*, *10*(1), 2008090. DOI: 10.1080/23322039.2021.2008090

Kong, Q., Yamada, M., Yang, C., & Nie, H. (2025). Competition or complementarity? Assessing the interaction effects of RCEP and CPTPP on agricultural and non-agricultural trade flows. *International Economics and Economic Policy*, *22*(1), 7. DOI: 10.1007/s10368-024-00628-6

Kuźnar, A. (2024). Shaping the economic resilience in East Asia through international trade. In *Regional Cooperation and Resilience in East Asia* (pp. 52–73). Routledge. DOI: 10.4324/9781003458357-4

Li, C., & Whalley, J. (2021). Effects of the comprehensive and progressive agreement for trans-pacific partnership. *World Economy*, *44*(5), 1312–1337. DOI: 10.1111/twec.13026

Li, Q., & Moon, H. C. (2018). The trade and income effects of RCEP: Implications for China and Korea. *Journal of Korea Trade*, *22*(3), 306–318. DOI: 10.1108/JKT-03-2018-0020

Lu, S. (2019). Regional Comprehensive Economic Partnership (RCEP): Impact on the integration of textile and apparel supply chain in the Asia-Pacific region. *Fashion Supply Chain Management in Asia: Concepts, Models, and Cases*, 21-41.

Mahmood, F., & Jongwanich, J. (2018). Export-enhancing effects of free trade agreements in South Asia: Evidence from Pakistan. *Journal of South Asian Development*, *13*(1), 24–53. DOI: 10.1177/0973174118764925

McDonald, F., Josef Tüselmann, H., Voronkova, S., & Golesorkhi, S. (2011). The strategic development of subsidiaries in regional trade blocs. *Multinational Business Review*, *19*(3), 256–271. DOI: 10.1108/15253831111172685

Mrindoko, A. E., & Mollel, A. B. (2024). Impacts of Non-Tariff Barriers to International Trade on the Growth of Small Business in Tanzania. *International Journal of Management, Accounting & Economics, 11*(6).

Nielsen, B. B., Wechtler, H., & Zheng, L. G. (2023). Disasters and international business: Insights and recommendations from a systematic review. *Journal of World Business*, *58*(4), 101458. DOI: 10.1016/j.jwb.2023.101458

Noosuwan, C., Autsadee, Y., Saengsupavanich, C., & Açık, A. (2024). Measuring economic convergence: Evidence from container throughputs of ASEAN-5 countries. *World Review of Intermodal Transportation Research*, *12*(1), 44–63. DOI: 10.1504/WRITR.2024.140467

Oh, C. H., Shin, J., & Oetzel, J. (2021). How does experience change firms' foreign investment decisions to non-market events? *Journal of International Management*, *27*(1), 100802. DOI: 10.1016/j.intman.2020.100802

Okabe, M. (2015). Impact of free trade agreements on trade in East Asia. *ERIA Discussion Paper Series, 1*, 48.

Oxford Analytica (2024). China trade deal has pros and cons for Ecuador. *Emerald Expert Briefings*, (oxan-db).

Park, C. Y., Petri, P. A., & Plummer, M. G. (2021). The economics of conflict and cooperation in the Asia-pacific: RCEP, CPTPP and the US-China trade war. *East Asian Economic Review, 25*(3), 233–272. DOI: 10.11644/KIEP.EAER.2021.25.3.397

Puhr, H., & Müllner, J. (2022). Foreign to all but fluent in many: The effect of multinationality on shock resilience. *Journal of World Business, 57*(6), 101370. DOI: 10.1016/j.jwb.2022.101370

Richter, W. F. (2024). Residual profit splitting: A theory-based approach to tax multinationals. *International Tax and Public Finance*, 1–21.

Salamatov, V., Tangaeva, A. V., & Kolomin, V. O. (2022). RCEP in the System of Mega-Regional Trade Agreements. *Mirovaia Ekonomika i Mezhdunarodnye Otnosheniia, 66*(2), 23–32. DOI: 10.20542/0131-2227-2022-66-2-23-32

Sarkar, M., & Cavusgil, S. T. (1996). Trends in international business thought and literature: A review of international market entry mode research: Integration and synthesis. *The International Executive, 38*(6), 825–847. DOI: 10.1002/tie.5060380608

Schotter, A. (2021). Resilient or not: boundary-spanning in innovation focused MNEs during global crises. *Critical Perspectives on International Business, 17*(2), 342-358.

Silva, J. S., & Tenreyro, S. (2006). The log of gravity. *The Review of Economics and Statistics, 88*(4), 641–658. DOI: 10.1162/rest.88.4.641

Sin, K. Y., Osman, A., Salahuddin, S. N., Abdullah, S., Lim, Y. J., & Sim, C. L. (2016). Relative advantage and competitive pressure towards implementation of e-commerce: Overview of small and medium enterprises (SMEs). *Procedia Economics and Finance, 35*, 434–443. DOI: 10.1016/S2212-5671(16)00054-X

Statsenko, L., Jayasinghe, R. S., & Soosay, C. (2023). Supply network resilience capabilities: A social–ecological perspective. *Supply Chain Management, 29*(1), 1–26. DOI: 10.1108/SCM-11-2022-0438

Tinbergen, J. (1962). Shaping the world economy; suggestions for an international economic policy. Academic Press.

United Nations. (2024). Asia–Pacific Trade Facilitation Report 2024 - Promoting sustainability and resilience in global value chains. ESCAP - The Economic and Social Commission for Asia and the Pacific; available online at https://repository.unescap.org/server/api/core/bitstreams/cb7a1b8a-77c2-4f60-a656-1fd49a983e49/content

White, G. O.III, Rajwani, T., & Lawton, T. C. (2021). Open for business in a closed world? Managing MNE nonmarket strategy in times of populism and geopolitical uncertainty. *Multinational Business Review*, *29*(4), 441–450. DOI: 10.1108/MBR-06-2021-0077

Wright, R. W., & Dana, L. P. (2003). Changing paradigms of international entrepreneurship strategy. *Journal of International Entrepreneurship*, *1*(1), 135–152. DOI: 10.1023/A:1023384808859

Zhao, S., & Hu, J. (2023). Gao zhiliang shishi "Quyu Quanmian Jingji Huoban Guanxi Xieding" (RCEP) (High-quality implementation of the "Regional Comprehensive Economic Partnership" (RCEP). *Qiushi*. Available at: https://www.qstheory.cn/dukan/hqwg/2023-07/11/c_1129742844.htm

Chapter 2
Geoeconomic Tensions and the Rethinking of Inflation Policies

João Rodrigues dos Santos
https://orcid.org/0000-0002-6835-680X
CETRAD, Universidade Europeia, Portugal

Andreia de Bem Machado
https://orcid.org/0000-0002-4404-0341
Universidade Federal de Santa Catarina, Brazil

António Sacavém
https://orcid.org/0000-0001-5395-5175
Universidade Europeia, Portugal

Carla Gomes da Costa
Universidade Europeia, Portugal

Maria José Sousa
https://orcid.org/0000-0001-8633-4199
ISCTE, Instituto Universitário de Lisboa, Portugal

ABSTRACT

The war in Ukraine has triggered severe economic disruptions in the Eurozone, thus leading to high inflation. In response, the European Central Bank (ECB) adopted contractionary monetary policies grounded in Friedman's theory. While effective in curbing inflation, these measures have intensified social inequalities. This chapter analyzes the intersection of geoeconomics, inflation control, and fiscal policy, highlighting impacts on national economies and global business. It draws on key

DOI: 10.4018/979-8-3373-7907-4.ch002

economic theories—diminishing marginal utility, the Phillips Curve, Okun's Law, and the Laffer Curve—to examine equity and competitiveness. The chapter proposes a more balanced approach: combining monetary tightening with adaptive fiscal measures and a novel "Savings Policy" led by the ECB. This integrated strategy aims to stabilize prices while promoting social justice and resilience. Ultimately, it argues for inclusive policies that safeguard the most vulnerable, ensuring fair burden-sharing and sustainable recovery.

1. INTRODUCTION

In recent years, the world has witnessed growing geo-economic instability, driven by political crises and international conflicts, which have had profound implications for the global economy. These crises not only generate geopolitical tensions, but also directly impact inflation and the economic stability of various nations, often exacerbating social and economic inequalities (Borghi, 2024). The case of the inflationary crisis that hit Europe in 2022, driven by Russia's invasion of Ukraine, exemplifies how political and economic issues are intertwined and how countries, particularly in the eurozone, face complex challenges when trying to manage inflation without sacrificing social justice and economic resilience. In this context, it is imperative to rethink traditional monetary policies and adapt them to contemporary challenges, such as increasing globalization and new geopolitical dynamics (Kammer, 2022). Even so, Erb & Harvey (2013) cannot fail to point out that, referring to Milton Friedman's (1963), they observe that inflation will always be a monetary phenomenon. This chapter thus aims to explore geo-economic tensions and how they require a reimagining of monetary and fiscal policies in order to mitigate the impacts of inflation and promote greater social justice, as well as increasing economic and business resilience.

1.1. The Impact of Geopolitical Crises on Inflation and Economic Stability

Inflation has historically been one of the main economic challenges faced by countries around the world. Although the causes of inflation can be varied, it is crucial to understand how geopolitical crises contribute to inflationary surprises. Rising international tensions, such as the recent war in Ukraine, can have devastating effects on the global economy, as they alter supply chains, create resource shortages and increase the prices of essential products such as energy and food. Recent studies indicate that geopolitical risks are transmitted to inflation through oil price shocks, affecting different countries in different ways (Yang et al., 2023). In a globalized world, where economies are highly interdependent, these disturbances can have repercussions beyond the borders of the countries directly involved in the conflict.

Rising energy prices, for example, have been one of the main drivers of recent inflationary pressures. According to Balteanu & Viani's analysis (2023), European countries that relied heavily on energy imports from a few suppliers, such as Russia, saw a sharp rise in inflation after the invasion of Ukraine. This is because the war has caused a supply shock in the global energy market, with oil and gas prices skyrocketing, resulting in higher costs for consumers and companies. The pressure on energy prices, as well as exacerbating inflation, also interferes with economic growth strategies, making recovery more difficult, especially for the most vulnerable countries.

This phenomenon is not exclusive to Europe. The rise in raw material prices, exacerbated by geopolitical instability, has a direct impact on the economies of countries all over the world. The increase in interest rates by central banks, often in response to inflation, can have a paradoxical effect, further slowing economic growth and creating a vicious cycle of stagnation and inequality. This scenario poses a huge challenge for traditional monetary policies, which often do not take into account the complexity of the new global crises, and more innovative and flexible approaches are needed (Stiglitz, 2020).

1.2. A Critical Examination of Inflation Surges and Their Social Consequences

When inflation reaches high levels, its social consequences can be devastating. The loss of purchasing power is one of the most immediate and visible, especially affecting the most vulnerable socio-economic groups. The prices of essential goods such as food, fuel and housing rise rapidly, making life more expensive for those already facing financial difficulties. In addition, the increase in production costs leads to a decrease in the supply of goods and services, further exacerbating scarcity and inequality. As Blanchard (2017) points out, high inflation can act as a regressive tax, disproportionately penalizing the poorest and compromising social stability.

Phillips' theory on the inverse relationship between inflation and unemployment illustrates how high levels of inflation can generate unemployment in some circumstances. The trade-off between inflation and unemployment was studied in depth by New Zealand economist William Phillips. This has “always” been a central theme for economic science. As early as 1978, Santomero & Seater highlighted the importance of the relationship established by Philips: “Twenty years have passed since Professor A. W. Philips first brought the attention of economics professionals to the relationship between inflation and unemployment” (p. 499).

Indeed, uncontrolled inflation can lead to a decrease in investment by companies, which, seeing their operating costs rise, reduce their activities or even cut jobs. This phenomenon has been amplified by the Covid-19 pandemic, which, together with rising global prices, has generated an economic slowdown in many regions, leading to a sharp drop in job creation and an increase in the unemployment rate.

Against the backdrop of the negative impacts caused by the Covid-19 pandemic in various sectors of the global economy, some of the most severe consequences are the rise in inflation and unemployment - effects which, incidentally, still persist and have been exacerbated by the military crisis in Ukraine. In this same context, Ozili and Arun (2020) point out that, faced with the consequences of the pandemic, many Fintech companies have faced a significant drop in consumer interest, resulting in losses of revenue and profit. This downturn has directly impacted venture capital investments aimed at both startups and established businesses in the sector.

Okun's Law, according to Martin (1993), points out that a marginal contribution of a 1 percentage point reduction in unemployment will result in a 2/3% increase in Gross Domestic Product.

Santos et. al (2024) point out the following:

> *Admittedly, there are many factors that can influence the relationship between the variables "growth", "inflation" and "unemployment" in an economy, but the trends defined and proven by William Phillips and Arthur Melvin Okun are absolutely logical.*

Next, the impact of inflation is particularly acute in societies where the social safety net is insufficient or where income redistribution policies are ineffective. The lower middle class and low-income workers are the most affected, since they have no means of protecting their purchasing power. The austerity policies adopted by some governments in response to economic crises tend to exacerbate this situation by cutting essential public services and social transfers, which intensifies inequality (Stiglitz, 2012).

The 2022 crisis and its effects on European society are a clear example of how geopolitical tensions and external shocks can directly affect social justice. Rising inflation, combined with reduced purchasing power and a precarious labor market, generated a cycle of impoverishment that compromised social cohesion. In this context, the need to rethink monetary and fiscal policies is urgent. Traditional inflation control policies, centered on interest rate increases and fiscal austerity, have proven to be ineffective and even harmful when global economic dynamics are so volatile and interconnected (Stiglitz, 2012; Piketty, 2020).

1.3. The Need to Reassess Traditional Monetary Policies in the Context of Modern Challenges

Traditional monetary policies, based mainly on Milton Friedman's monetarist theory, emphasize controlling the money supply in order to contain inflation. In an essay entitled Milton Friedman on Inflation, Edward Nelson, an economist at the US Federal Reserve, highlights Friedman's view of the central role of monetary policy in controlling total spending in the economy. Quoting Friedman himself, Nelson points out that monetary policy is a legitimate and effective instrument when its focus is on maintaining price stability or seeking an inflation rate considered ideal. Furthermore, Nelson notes that this principle still guides the monetary policy guidelines adopted by the world's main economies (Nelson, 2007).

However, in the current context, where geopolitical crises and global disruptions are constant, these approaches may not be enough to face contemporary challenges. The strategy of raising interest rates, for example, although effective in controlling demand inflation, can be counterproductive in an environment of external instability and economic slowdown. Raising interest rates can, in many cases, worsen the recession, as it raises credit costs and restricts consumption and investment (Adrian, 2022). When inflation is driven by external factors, such as energy shortages or the disruption of supply chains, simply controlling the money supply may not solve the underlying problem. In this sense, it is crucial that policymakers adopt a more holistic and integrated approach, considering not only traditional monetary tools, but also fiscal, strategic investment and social support policies (Mishkin, 2011).

Growing global economic interdependence requires greater international cooperation. The global inflationary crisis cannot be solved by national policies alone, as external shocks, such as wars or pandemics, have knock-on effects that affect multiple economies simultaneously. Therefore, the reimagining of monetary and fiscal policies must include a more detailed analysis of global interactions and new forms of economic management that integrate social justice and economic resilience. As highlighted by the International Monetary Fund (2018), cooperation between countries is essential to tackle global imbalances and promote economic stability.

In conclusion, contemporary geo-economic tensions require a thorough review of monetary and fiscal policies. Inflation, exacerbated by geopolitical crises, has serious social implications and challenges traditional approaches to economic control. To build a more resilient and fair economy, a new paradigm is neededthat goes beyond simply manipulating interest rates and takes into account the complexity of global interactions and the needs of the most vulnerable populations (Banco de Portugal, 2023).

2. BIBLIOMETRIC ANALYSIS

With the purpose of mapping scientific publications related to green financing, a bibliometric analysis was carried out based on data obtained from the Clarivate Analytics Web of Science (WoS) and Scopus platforms. The study followed a structured approach in three main stages: planning and execution, data collection, and bibliometric analysis. To answer the central research question, a systematic search was conducted in the aforementioned online databases, followed by a detailed analysis of the collected results.

Bibliometrics, originating from information sciences, uses mathematical and statistical methods to explore bibliographic records available in databases (Linnenluecke, 2017). This methodology makes it possible to identify aspects such as: volume of productions by region; publication periodicity; distribution of research across different fields of knowledge; citation counts related to specific studies; and the impact of a scientific publication, among other factors that assist in organizing results and reducing biases when investigating a given topic. The bibliometric analysis was structured into three main stages — planning, collection, and results analysis — which were developed in an integrated manner to answer the guiding research question: What is the interaction between geoeconomics, inflation control, and fiscal policies, focusing on how these policies impact national economies and global business strategies?

The planning took place in February 2025, the period during which the research was conducted. During this phase, important criteria were defined, such as the exclusive use of electronic databases, excluding physical library catalogs due to the adequate volume of documents available in the chosen sources. Also in the planning phase, search terms were defined: "fiscal policies" AND "inflation control", considering that different variations of expressions fit into the same concept depending on the context in which they are applied. It was decided that the search terms would be entered in the "title, abstract, and keywords" fields, with no restrictions on time, language, or other limitations.

2.1. Results and Discussion

To analyze the bibliometric data from the 5 works in the Scopus database and the 7 in the WoS database, we started the analysis by referencing the global growth rate of scientific publications. It was found that the first publication occurred in 1959 (as shown in Figure 1), titled "Taxation and Inflation," published in the Annals of the American Academy of Political and Social Science. It is believed that this publication emerged because, in that year, the international economy was in a period of recovery. The recession, which had already eased in the second half of

1958, particularly in the United States, gave way in 1959 to a clearly upward trend in almost the entire Northern Hemisphere and also in several agricultural countries in the Southern Hemisphere, except for those whose main products experienced anomalous price drops.

In the WoS database, the first publication appeared in 1998, titled "International Monetary and Financial Arrangements: Present and Future." This publication addresses a wide range of topics under the umbrella of the international monetary system: exchange rate agreements, the structure of the International Monetary Fund, the history and functioning of the European Monetary Union, monetary policy and fiscal policies adopted in recent years by different countries, with special emphasis on central bank independence and inflation control, capital flows, and cross-border asset growth and its influence on financial stability, as well as policy proposals to enhance financial stability. Figure 1 shows the distribution of publications over the years, demonstrating that in both databases, there was a significant increase in publications in 2024, with three publications in the area.

Figure 1. Distribution of publications over the years - Scopus and WOS

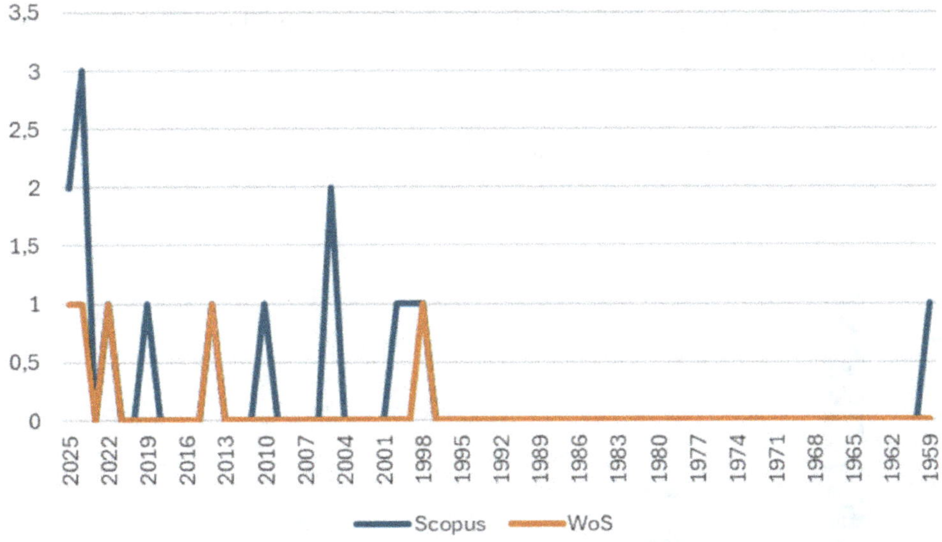

Source: Authors, 2025

Another analysis conducted related to the identification of authors. It was found that in the Scopus database, there are 28 authors publishing on this topic, while in the WoS database there are 9 authors. There are no reference authors in the field, as shown in Figure 2.

Figure 2. Most relevant Scopus and WoS authors

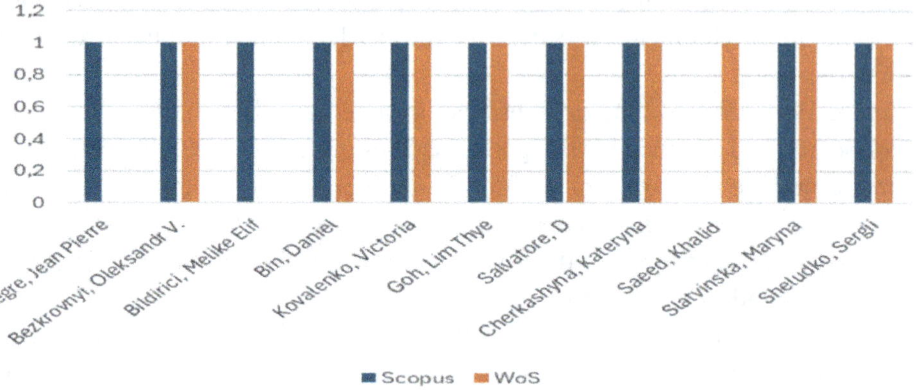

Source: Authors, 2025

Analyzing the countries with the most publications in the area, it was found that the USA stands out with an average of 50% of total publications in the Scopus database and 33% in the WoS database, totaling 5 publications in Scopus and 2 in WoS. Figure 3 demonstrates the main countries highlighted in publications in both databases.

Figure 3. Distribution of Scopus and WoS papers by country

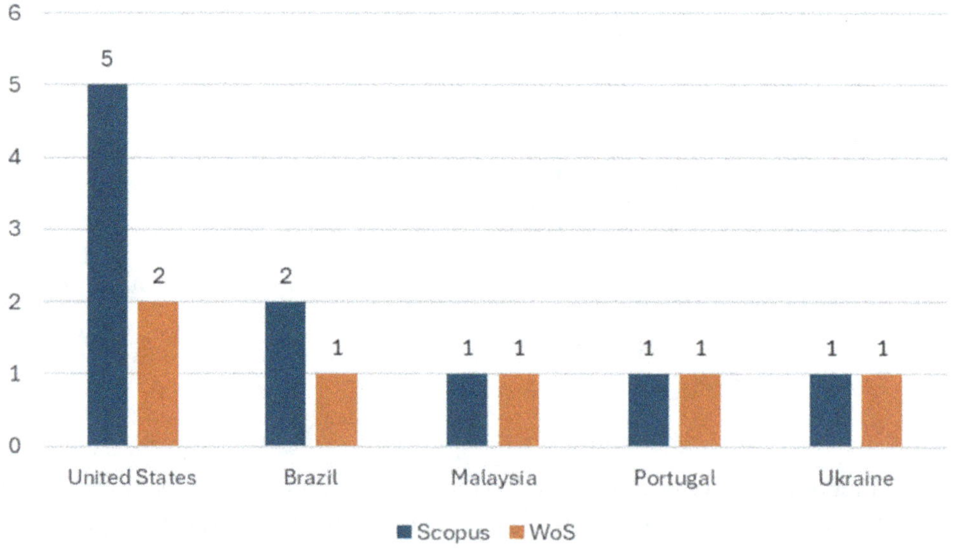

Source: Authors, 2025

Based on the presented results, it is possible to conclude that the interaction between geoeconomics, inflation control, and fiscal policies constitutes an emerging and multifaceted field of study, with direct impacts both on national economies and global business strategies. The bibliometric analysis revealed that, although there is still a geographical concentration of publications, mainly in the United States, the relevance of the topic has grown substantially, especially since 2024, indicating a trend of greater integration between global political economy and corporate strategies. The increase in publications also demonstrates a growing recognition of the interdependence between fiscal policies, monetary stability, and economic sustainability in a globalized context marked by successive crises. Thus, the results reinforce the importance of a holistic and interdisciplinary approach in the formulation of public policies and business strategies, considering the challenges and opportunities emerging from the complex dynamics between geoeconomics and global economic governance.

3. UTILITARIANISM AND ECONOMIC POLICY

3.1. The Ethical Framework of Utilitarianism and Its Implications for Economic Decision-Making

Since its inception, utilitarianism has played a crucial role in the formulation of economic policies, offering an approach to evaluating and justifying decisions based on the results achieved. The fundamental principle of utilitarianism, which aims to maximize well-being and general happiness, was first proposed by Jeremy Bentham (1789) and later extended by John Stuart Mill (1863). In the context of economic policies, utilitarianism provides a framework for evaluating policies based on their outcomes, favoring those that produce the greatest overall value (Becchetti, Castriota, & D'Alessandro, 2020). Santos (2020) refers to utilitarianism as a current of moral philosophy that is dedicated to reflecting on the ethical dilemmas related to disparities in income distribution, highlighting the consequences that such inequalities generate for collective well-being. By prioritizing the maximization of social welfare, utilitarianism significantly influences economic decision-making. In welfare economics, policies are evaluated through cost-benefit analysis to ensure the efficient use of resources (Fleurbaey & Maniquet, 2008). However, measuring personal value and ensuring equity in distribution present considerable challenges (Sen, 1973). In addition, recent advances in behavioral economics question the viability of strictly utilitarian policies, since human preferences and decision-making biases do not always correspond to traditional utility maximization assumptions (Sunstein, 2020). One of the central criticisms of approaches that prioritize aggregate utility maximization in economic policymaking lies in their tendency to neglect distributive justice and the rights of marginalized groups. Alternative perspectives have stressed that focusing exclusively on overall gains can camouflage deep inequalities, perpetuating structural disadvantages. This conflict between promoting efficiency and ensuring equity is a recurring tension in public policy design. In addition, empirical studies suggest that high levels of inequality can not only compromise social cohesion, but also hinder economic growth itself. Galbraith and Kum (2002), for example, show that there is a robust statistical relationship between high inequality and lower economic performance, suggesting that ignoring the distribution of wealth can harm long-term objectives, even from the point of view of efficiency. The adoption of purely utilitarian criteria in the formulation of public policies has been increasingly questioned, especially when considering persistent economic inequality and imperfections in the markets. The traditional utilitarian approach, focused on maximizing aggregate well-being, often overlooks the structural disparities that limit equitable access to economic opportunities. In response, it is essential to design fiscal policies that not only redistribute income, but also promote sustainable incentives for individual and collective development. In this context, recent analyses based on intra-generational accounting models show that, even with a progressive tax system, redistributive impacts can be less effective than expected, depending on how taxes and transfers are structured throughout the life cycle of individuals (Auerbach, Kotlikoff & Koehler, 2016). Thus, policy design must balance distributive justice and intertemporal efficiency, aiming for lasting and inclusive results. Utilitarian approaches continue to exert significant influence on the formulation of public policies aimed at environmental sustainability. The logic of maximizing collective well-being has guided measures such as carbon pricing and the creation of ecological taxes, reflecting an attempt to align social and environmental interests through economic incentives. In recent years, the discussion on the ethical foundations of utilitarianism has intensified, especially in contexts that require complex choices and involve conflicts between efficiency and social justice. This perspective is particularly relevant in economic policies that demand trade-offs between productivity and distributive equity. In addition, the application of utilitarian principles in models such as the circular economy has shown potential to promote sustainable practices by encouraging decisions aimed at long-term collective benefits. In this scenario, Bowden (2009) argues that utilitarianism offers a rational and pragmatic basis for ethical decision-making, especially in situations that require weighing up consequences and principles. His defense of utilitarianism highlights the value of moral consistency and impartiality, suggesting that such qualities are essential for public policies that seek not only effectiveness but also ethical legitimacy. When considering normative approaches to guiding public policy, certain modern versions of utilitarianism offer important practical advantages. In contexts where policymakers face complex choices from an unbiased initial perspective, utilitarianism can serve as an effective tool for maximizing aggregate well-being, without necessarily sacrificing the protection of the most vulnerable groups. This approach, which prioritizes efficiency and global well-being, can be particularly useful in situations of economic instability or asymmetric shocks, as demonstrated by Cashin et al. (2014), who show how oil demand and supply shocks have distinct impacts on global economic growth, requiring adapted and flexible policy responses.

Furthermore, in an environment characterized by persistently low interest rates, as analysed by Greenwald et al. (2022), wealth disparities tend to widen, affecting social cohesion and economic stability. An adjusted utilitarianism, which considers not only immediate well-being but also the intertemporal sustainability of wealth distribution, can help mitigate these growing inequalities by focusing on solutions that promote the common good without ignoring structural imbalances. Thus, by integrating these macroeconomic concerns with normative principles, contemporary utilitarianism reveals itself as an ethical framework with the potential to guide public decisions in a more responsive and just way.

3.2. The Role of Diminishing Marginal Utility in Shaping Fiscal and Monetary Policy Decisions

One of the central foundations of economic analysis is the idea that the subjective value attributed to a good tends to decrease as its quantity increases. In other words, the more you own or consume of something, the less pleasure you get from additional units. This phenomenon is often observed in everyday decisions - such as when the first piece of cake is much more appreciated than the third or fourth. However, research in the field of psychology suggests that this perception of decreasing value may be deeply rooted in moral and cognitive intuitions. Greene and Baron (2000), for example, showed that people often apply the principle of diminishing marginal utility intuitively even in distributive judgments, showing a preference for a more equitable allocation of resources based on an implicit expectation that the first gains are more valuable than the next. This suggests that the idea of diminishing utility is not just an economic abstraction, but also reflects a human psychological tendency with ethical and social implications. According to Santos & Sousa (2021), the so-called law of diminishing marginal utility - which comes from the utilitarian perspective - suggests that human beings gain additional satisfaction with each new unit of a good consumed, but this extra satisfaction tends to progressively decrease as consumption increases, until it reaches a point where the increase in well-being becomes smaller and smaller. The way in which individuals attribute value to additional income has profound implications for the design of economic policies, especially with regard to taxation and the redistribution of wealth. The concept of diminishing marginal utility suggests that each additional unit of income brings less satisfaction the higher the person's income. This principle justifies a progressive tax structure, since the negative impact of higher taxation is relatively smaller for those with higher incomes, while the benefits of transfers to lower incomes tend to be substantially greater in terms of well-being. In this context, public spending on areas such as health and education is particularly effective, as it significantly improves the marginal utility of individuals in lower income brackets. This strategy not only contributes to greater social equity, but also maximizes efficiency in the allocation of public resources. As Easterlin (2005) noted, although the marginal utility of income decreases as income rises, the benefits of public policies aimed at lower-income individuals tend to be more pronounced in terms of well-being.

In addition, empirical studies show that monetary policies, such as quantitative easing, tend to have asymmetric effects on the distribution of wealth and income. During the implementation of such measures in the eurozone, it was found that increases in asset values disproportionately benefited wealthier households, exacerbating inequality (Lenza & Slacalek, 2018). This finding highlights the need to coordinate fiscal and monetary policies in order to mitigate unwanted redistributive effects.

On the other hand, recent research indicates that the degree of diminishing marginal utility is not uniform among individuals and can vary according to cultural and contextual factors (Kimball et al., 2015). This heterogeneity reinforces the importance of public policies that are sensitive to the specific characteristics of each socio-economic group, in order to ensure greater distributive justice and economic efficiency. In formulating monetary policy, diminishing marginal utility (DMU) plays a crucial role in setting interest rates and inflation control strategies. When prices rise and real incomes fall, lower-income households suffer disproportionately, as they assign a higher marginal value to each additional unit of income. This forces central banks to weigh up the distributive effects of their decisions, thus avoiding the worsening of economic inequalities.

Changes in interest rates directly affect consumption and savings decisions, since marginal utility influenced by future uncertainty shapes financial behavior. The theory of permanent income suggests that consumers make decisions based not only on current income, but also on expectations of future income, which implies that one-off economic stimulus measures may have limited impact if they are not accompanied by a perception of long-term stability. When considering the effectiveness of fiscal policy, it becomes clear that consumers' perception of the sustainability of public debt can moderate the effects of government spending on aggregate consumption. If there is an expectation of future tax increases to cover deficits, individuals are likely to react with restraint in their current spending. In this regard, Stark (2004) discusses how tax progressivity can influence citizens' expectations about income redistribution, which in turn affects their consumption and savings behavior in the face of more or less redistributive tax policies.

Furthermore, macroeconomic analysis shows that fluctuations in output and unemployment are not entirely explained by cyclical shocks, but also by the asymmetric response of economic agents to variations in aggregate demand, as discussed by Prachowny (1993). His revision of Okun's Law highlights that the impact of changes in economic policy depends not only on the level of production, but on its composition and efficiency in generating employment.

In the international context, US monetary policy tools have significant implications for the exchange rates of the main European currencies, thus affecting inflationary dynamics and capital flows. As evidenced by Mohd Sofian et al. (2023), the manipulation of US interest rates can provoke immediate responses in the foreign exchange markets, altering the behavior of investors and consumers at a global level. This phenomenon highlights the importance of a coordinated monetary policy, especially in an increasingly interconnected economic scenario.

Maximizing present utility and the limitations imposed by future economic constraints require a well-planned fiscal approach. The concept of diminishing marginal utility (DMI) can be applied to the provision of public goods, where governments need to optimize social welfare by properly distributing resources. Along these lines, investment in areas such as infrastructure, health and education ensures that limited resources are allocated in a way that maximizes their marginal benefits for society. UMD-based fiscal strategies help improve the efficiency of social security systems and labor markets, ensuring that public policies address not only immediate needs, but also long-term equity requirements. As noted by Kimball et al. (2015), the application of the UMD principle revisited offers a more detailed perspective on how changes in preferences and income distribution affect the effectiveness of public policies, especially in contexts of limited resource allocation.

However, as noted by Neville et al. (2021), in inflationary times, it is necessary to rethink resource allocation strategies in order to maintain a balance between growth and cost control. The use of progressive fiscal policies can not only help mitigate the impacts of inflation, but also ensure that changes in work and income structures do not compromise fiscal equity. In fact, as Sanchirico (2008) argues, the progressivity of the tax system can be adjusted to reflect changes in work patterns, so as to ensure that people with greater ability to pay are adequately taxed, promoting social justice and efficiency in the tax system.

In summary, the combination of utilitarian theory and UMD in economic policymaking requires a balance between welfare-optimizing strategies and the consideration of ethical issues related to justice and equity, with an increasing focus on how technological advances and insights from behavioral economics can help refine these principles for contemporary challenges.

4. THE PRINCIPLE OF DIMINISHING MARGINAL UTILITY AND TAX PROGRESSIVITY

It should be remembered at this point, in line with the idea put forward by Santos (2020), that the principle of diminishing marginal utility indicates that applying an extra unit of a given good adds utility to its total utility. However, this extra utility tends to get smaller and smaller as the application increases, until it reaches a point where the additional benefits gradually diminish.

In contemporary societies, characterized by an unequal distribution of wealth and complex economic challenges, the discussion about creating fair and efficient tax systems has become extremely important. The connection between the concept of diminishing marginal utility and tax progressivity serves as a solid basis for formulating public policies that seek to balance economic efficiency with social justice.

In a global scenario where income inequalities have increased substantially, the application of this concept to tax policies becomes even more relevant. The COVID-19 pandemic and subsequent inflationary shocks have accentuated economic disparities, highlighting the urgent need for progressive tax systems. As noted by Ozili and Arun (2020), the crisis caused by the pandemic has exacerbated inequalities, disproportionately affecting the most vulnerable populations and widening the gap between the richest and the poorest. In this sense, tax progressivity not only makes it possible to generate the revenue needed to fund essential public services, but also offers a means of mitigating social disparities, which, if not dealt with properly, can be sources of economic and social instability.

Furthermore, as highlighted by Duncan and Sabirianova (2008), tax progressivity can play a crucial role in reducing income inequalities, by ensuring that citizens with greater contributory capacity pay a greater share of taxes, while the poorest are protected from an excessive tax burden. This tax adjustment not only contributes to equity, but also ensures that resources are distributed more effectively to benefit society as a whole.

The theoretical foundation of tax progressivity is based precisely on the notion that the marginal utility of income decreases as the level of income increases. This non-linear relationship between income and individual well-being has profound implications for the design of redistributive policies. When applied to the fiscal context, it suggests that the transfer of resources from the wealthiest to the neediest segments of society can increase aggregate well-being, even while keeping the economy's total income constant. Auerbach et al. (2016) expand on this idea by analyzing tax progressivity in the United States, highlighting that progressive tax policies can in fact improve equity without significantly compromising economic efficiency.

It should be noted that this approach is not without controversy. Critics such as Feldstein (2008) argue that high levels of progressivity can discourage productivity and innovation. However, recent empirical studies, such as those by Piketty et al. (2018), show that, when properly calibrated, fiscal progressivity does not significantly compromise economic growth and can even strengthen social and political stability - crucial factors for sustainable economic development.

In the case of Portugal, this discussion takes on particular contours. As a peripheral Eurozone economy, with a GDP per capita significantly below the European average (75% of the EU-27 average in 2021, according to Eurostat), but with inequality levels close to the EU average (Gini coefficient of 0.32), Portugal faces the dual challenge of promoting economic growth while ensuring a more equitable distribution of its fruits. The current Portuguese tax system, considered by the OECD (2024) to be one of the most progressive in Europe, reflects this attempt to balance efficiency and equity.

In this context, the following analysis seeks to elucidate how the principle of diminishing marginal utility informs the design of progressive tax systems (point 4.1) and how these principles materialize in contemporary tax structures (point 4.2). Through an approach that combines economic theory, empirical evidence and public policy analysis, this chapter aims to contribute to the debate on the role of fiscal policy in promoting fairer and more economically resilient societies.

4.1. Understanding Diminishing Marginal Utility as the Foundation for Progressive Taxation

The principle of diminishing marginal utility is one of the fundamental pillars of modern economic theory, with profound implications for the design of fiscal and redistributive policies. Rooted in the utilitarian philosophy of Jeremy Bentham and John Stuart Mill, this principle, as analyzed above, postulates that the satisfaction or utility derived from the consumption of each additional unit of a good or service decreases as the total quantity consumed increases. In this context, and regarding the differences in income distribution between countries, Easterlin (2005) notes that "comparing across countries, it is true that income and hapiness are positively related and the marginal utility falls with higher income" (p. 243).

The inverse relationship between quantity consumed and marginal utility has significant practical consequences. When applied to the context of household income and consumption, it reveals that:

1. The first units of income are allocated to basic needs (food, housing, health), generating an extremely high marginal utility;
2. As disposable income increases, additional units are directed towards less essential goods and services, with progressively lower marginal utility;

3. There is a saturation point beyond which additional consumption generates virtually no additional utility. This is a numbered term.

To illustrate this phenomenon, consider the following theoretical example (Table 1), which compares consumption patterns between families in different income brackets. It is important to note that utility cannot be measured quantitatively. It is only possible to order preferences. In any case, for purely academic purposes and for the purposes of this chapter, utility values are assigned to each eu spent on the different levels of consumption:

Table 1. Caption should be sentence case with no ending punctuation if only one sentence

Consumption Level (c)	Marginal Utility / € (Low Incomes)	Marginal Utility / € (High Incomes)	Δ%
1 (Food)	1,200	1,200	-
2 (Clothing)	1,185	1,185	-1.3
3 (Housing)	1,165	1,165	-1.7
4 (Household utilities)	1,140	1,140	-2.1
5 (Public transportation)	1,110	1,110	-2.6
6 (Preventive health)	1,075	1,075	-3.2
7 (Basic education)	1,035	1,035	-3.7
8 (Communications)	990	990	-4.3
9 (Cultural leisure)	940	940	-5.1
10 (Basic leisure)	910	910	-3.2
11 (Premium leisure)	-	860	-5.5
12 (Luxury goods)	-	800	-7.0

Source: Authors, 2025

Analyzing the results:

1. Low-income families (up to level 10) achieve a total utility of 10,750 utility units.
2. High-income families (up to level 12) achieve 12,410 units of total utility
3. The average utility per euro spent is significantly higher in the low-income group (1,075 vs. 1,034 units).

This disparity demonstrably justifies the adoption of progressive tax systems, in which:

- Taxpayers with greater ability to pay (and lower marginal utility of income) bear higher tax rates;
- Essential incomes are protected by lower rates or exemptions;
- The state obtains revenue to finance public goods that maximize collective well-being.

4.2. How Tax Systems in Modern Economies Reflect Utilitarian Principles of Fairness and Equity

According to the theoretical framework that precedes this point, generally speaking, contemporary tax systems incorporate three fundamental mechanisms that reflect the utilitarian logic:

1. Progressivity in Direct Taxes.

For example, the Personal Income Tax (IRS) in Portugal follows a clearly progressive structure. It is, in fact, one of the most progressive of the 27 Member states of the European Union, with nine brackets:

- Tax bracket up to €7,479: 14.5%;
- €7,480-€11,284 bracket: 21%;
- ...
- Bracket above €80,882: 48%.

This structure ensures that:

- Basic needs are practically exempt;
- Average incomes are taxed moderately;
- High earners contribute proportionally more.

2. Selectivity in Indirect Taxes.

VAT differentiates rates according to the essentiality of the goods:

- Reduced rate (6%): essential foodstuffs;
- Intermediate rate (13%): restaurants, some services;
- Standard rate (23%): luxury and superfluous goods.

3. Socially-oriented tax benefits.

Specific deductions for:

- Education and health;
- Permanent housing;
- Maintenance pensions.

In the context of this chapter and the impact on reducing inequalities that it is intended to mitigate, it should be noted that empirical studies (Duncan & Sabirianova, 2008; OECD, 2023; INE, 2022) show that:

- Around 20% of the richest contribute around 55% of total personal income tax revenue;
- Around 40% of the poorest only account for around 8% of revenue;
- The Gini coefficient is reduced by approximately 15% after taxes and transfers.

Figure 4. Diminishing marginal utility and tax progressivity

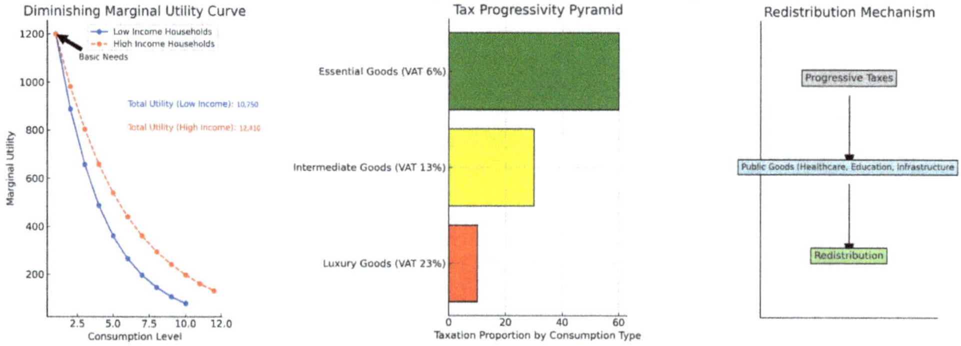

Source: Authors, 2025

Thus, according to all the above framework, the principle of diminishing marginal utility provides a robust ethical and scientific basis for progressive tax systems. In a context of geo-economic tensions and inflation, it is possible to conclude that taking this approach into account will make it possible to:

1. Protect the purchasing power of the most vulnerable;
2. Maintain incentives for economic activity;
3. Financing essential public goods;
4. Promote social cohesion and macroeconomic stability.

Harmonizing economic efficiency and social justice remains a central challenge in the reform of fiscal policies in the 21st century.

5. UTILITARIAN CRITIQUE OF MONETARY POLICY AS A TOOL FOR INFLATION CONTROL

Against a backdrop of geo-economic tensions exacerbated by the war in Ukraine and the global energy crisis, central banks face the classic dilemma of balancing price stability and social equity. The application of fiscal and monetary policies, such as tax increases or interest rates, can have profound effects on income inequalities and economic dynamics. For example, Abdul-Salam (2022) highlights the impact of specific fiscal policies, such as the windfall tax in the UK oil and gas sector, which affects not only the distribution of resources, but also investor behavior and the development of new energy fields. Similarly, Batchelder and Kamin (2019) explore the options of progressive taxation on the richest, arguing that higher taxation can not only improve social equity, but also help fund policies that sustain collective welfare in times of crisis. This type of approach, which considers the redistribution of resources as a crucial tool to mitigate the effects of global economic shocks, is in line with utilitarian philosophical ideas of maximizing collective well-being, as proposed by Bentham and Mill. However, the application of these policies continues to generate controversy, especially when their impact on economic efficiency is questioned. For Friedman (1968), with the use of counter-cyclical monetary policy, "monetary growth, it is widely held, will tend to stimulate employment; monetary contraction, to retard employment" (p. 7). Therefore, the calibration of this type of monetary policy always generates a great deal of discussion and distrust as to its cost-benefit.

In fact, Santomero & Seater, in 1978, already observed that the interconnection between unemployment and inflation raised many doubts about the co-effectiveness of contractionary monetary policies.

The post-pandemic inflationary crisis created an unprecedented economic paradox: while inflation reached historic levels (10.6% in the Eurozone in October 2022, Eurostat, 2022), conventional control mechanisms proved to be socially regressive (OECD, 2023). As the Portuguese case shows - where 70% of mortgage loans are indexed to variable rates (Banco de Portugal, 2023) - middle and low-income families suffer a double impact: loss of purchasing power due to inflation and financial strangulation due to the increase in housing payments (DECO, 2023). This phenomenon goes against the principle of diminishing marginal utility (Piketty, 2014), according to which the same monetary changes have different impacts on well-being depending on the level of income.

The following analysis is developed along two complementary axes, examining the intrinsic limitations of conventional monetary policy (point 5.1) and then exploring policy alternatives that reconcile anti-inflationary effectiveness with social justice (point 5.2). Using a utilitarian theoretical framework, we argue that the current economic policy paradigm urgently needs to be reconfigured in order to meet the challenges of the 21st century.

5.1. Assessing the Limitations of Contractionary Monetary Policies in Addressing Inflation

The strategy used by the European Central Bank (ECB) to fight inflation by raising interest rates very aggressively reveals, in terms of impact, profound social asymmetries when analyzed from a utilitarian perspective. As shown in Table 1, where low-income households achieve an average utility of 1,075 units per euro spent (vs. 1,034 units for high-income households), uniform monetary policy ignores the principle of diminishing marginal utility, disproportionately penalizing the most vulnerable households.

The study by Domanski et al. (2016) in the BIS Quarterly Review demonstrates how these policies widen inequalities: while the increase in interest rates increases debt for 70% of Portuguese households with housing loans (OECD, 2022), it paradoxically benefits holders of financial assets. As Greenwald et al. (2022) warn, this dynamic accentuates the heterogeneity in financial rates of return, deepening social divides.

Figure 5. Differential impact of rising interest rates on family well-being

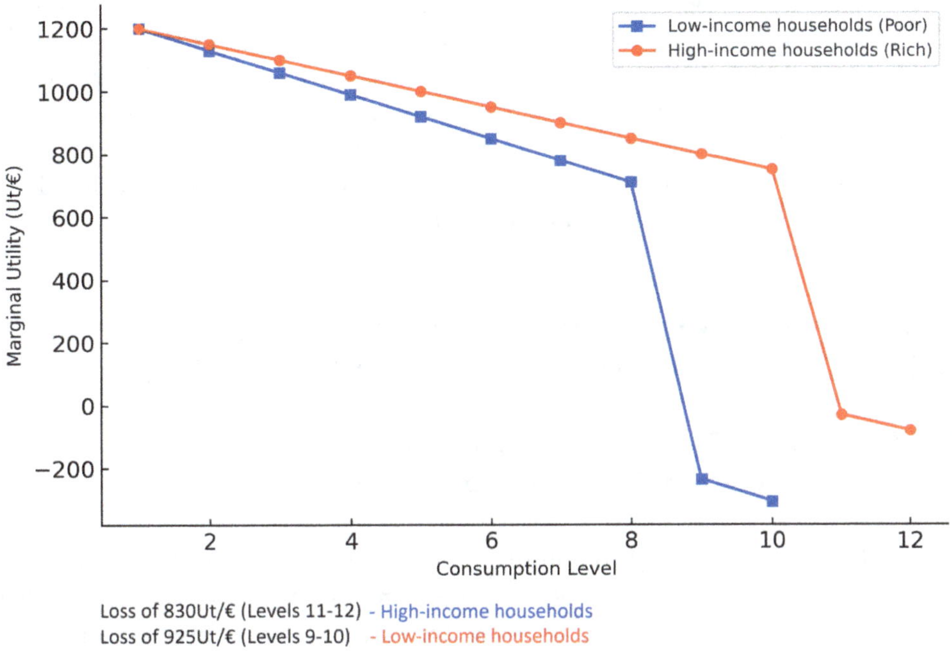

Source: Authors, 2025

Figure 5 illustrates the difference in economic impact between families of different income levels, represented by two distinct lines. The red line refers to the richest households, showing an average loss of utility of 830 units per euro at levels 11 and 12. On the other hand, the blue line represents the poorest households, with an average loss of 925 units of utility per euro at levels 9 and 10. The legend highlights that low-income households suffer a penalty approximately 10% higher, reinforcing the regressive nature of certain policies when applied uniformly, without redistributive adjustments.

5.2. Examining Alternative Approaches Through the Lens of Utilitarianism and Social Equity

Utilitarian theory, as developed by Bentham and Mill, suggests alternative solutions that would maximize collective well-being:

1. Progressive taxation of bank profits: As documented by Brandão-Marques et al. (2023), Portuguese banks made an additional €255 million/month in profits

from raising rates (DECO, 2023). A solidarity tax, along the lines proposed by Piketty (2014) in Capital in the 21st Century, could finance direct compensation;
2. Differentiated indexation mechanisms: Lenza & Slacalek (2018) propose models where credit updates vary according to family income, protecting the lower brackets - a solution successfully implemented in Belgium after 2011;
3. Countercyclical fiscal policy: Galbraith & Kum (2002) show how the combination with public investment in essential sectors (energy, food) can reduce inflationary pressures without social costs.

6. THE ROLE OF FISCAL POLICY IN PROMOTING SOCIAL JUSTICE DURING INFLATIONARY CRISES

6.1. The Role of Fiscal Policies in Distributing the Economic Burden of Inflation More Fairly

Fiscal policy plays a key role in distributing the economic costs of inflation. During inflationary crises, lower income groups are disproportionately affected due to the erosion of their purchasing power and the increase in the prices of essential goods (Brandao-Marques et al., 2023). The recent increase in interest rates by the European Central Bank, in response to rising inflation, has significant repercussions on households with greater exposure to credit, namely those with variable-rate home loans. Although this strategy is effective in controlling inflation, its effects are asymmetrical, disproportionately penalizing borrowers and exacerbating existing economic inequalities. Furthermore, the redistributive effects of monetary policy tend to benefit holders of financial assets, whose wealth increases in certain contexts of expansionary policy or changes in interest rates, perpetuating the concentration of wealth (Domanski, Scatigna, & Zabai, 2016). The absence of adequate compensation mechanisms thus contributes to accentuating the disparity between different socio-economic groups, raising questions about the distributive justice of these measures.

The introduction of complementary tax measures can mitigate these adverse effects. Measures such as positive discrimination through tax cuts for low-income families and temporary increases in the tax contribution of better-off households can create a fairer distribution of economic effort (Celasun et al., 2004). In addition, mechanisms such as targeted subsidies for essential goods and tax deductions associated with housing, health and education expenses can mitigate the inequality resulting from contractionary policies.

6.2. The Role of Fiscal Policies in Distributing the Economic Burden of Inflation More Fairly

Inflation has profound impacts on the socio-economic structure, disproportionately affecting vulnerable populations. Studies indicate that lower-income households are less able to adjust to the rising cost of living, resulting in reduced access to essential goods and services (Dollar, 2007). Inflation on essential goods such as food and energy has a regressive impact, exacerbating economic disparities.

Worsening living conditions can result in increased job insecurity, reduced social mobility and growing social tensions. In particular, the increase in interest rates, by raising the cost of credit, reduces the capacity of families to invest and consume, resulting in an economic contraction that worsens the unemployment rate. In addition, fluctuations in monetary policies, especially those in the US, influence exchange rates and can intensify the negative effects on European economies (Mohd Sofian & Mohd Redzuan, 2023). Thus, the implementation of mitigating fiscal policies, such as the temporary exemption of taxes on essential goods or the creation of targeted social transfers, is key to protecting the most fragile segments of society.

6.3. Windfall Profits, Social Instability, and the Public Perception of Economic Justice

The perception of economic justice plays a central role in social stability. In contexts of inflationary crises, the accumulation of extraordinary profits by specific sectors, such as the financial and energy sectors, can generate social dissatisfaction and increase distrust in institutions (Auerbach et al., 2016). The application of extraordinary taxes on exceptional profits, as a form of fiscal redistribution, is an effective instrument to mitigate these inequalities and reinforce the perception of equity in society.

Measures such as the introduction of additional taxes on companies that benefit from external shocks can finance social support programs, alleviating the impact of inflation on the most disadvantaged groups. The experience with extraordinary taxes, such as those applied to the mining and energy sectors, highlights their potential for redistribution and fiscal stability (Ng'ambi, 2010; Abdul-Salam, 2022). Furthermore, fiscal transparency and public communication on the use of collected revenues are essential to reinforce the population's confidence in economic justice and the efficiency of public policies.

To illustrate the importance of a differentiated tax policy for low-income families, Figure 1 is presented. This figure is based on the data in Table 1, highlighting the impact of tax relief on the marginal utility of different income levels. The objective is to demonstrate how targeted tax relief can minimize economic disparities and promote a fairer distribution of the economic effort needed to contain inflation, and with gains in overall efficiency, as can be seen in the following paragraphs, which explain the figure. It is true that the Laffer Curve will have a say here, as discussed earlier in this chapter, but it is also true that this differentiated fiscal policy, which already adds to the natural fiscal progressivity, is to be used in exceptional times, such as inflationary surges, for example.

Figure 6. Benefits of a discriminatory positive tax policy

Consumption Level (c)	Marginal Utility / € (Low Incomes)	Marginal Utility / € (High Incomes)	Δ%
1 (Food)	1,200	1,200	-
2 (Clothing)	1,185	1,185	-1.3
3 (Housing)	1,165	1,165	-1.7
4 (Household utilities)	1,140	1,140	-2.1
5 (Public transportation)	1,110	1,110	-2.6
6 (Preventive health)	1,075	1,075	-3.2
7 (Basic education)	1,035	1,035	-3.7
8 (Communications)	990	990	-4.3
9 (Cultural leisure)	940	940	-5.1
10 (Basic leisure)	910	910	-3.2
11 (Premium leisure)	-	860	-5.5
12 (Luxury goods)	-	800	-7.0

Consumption levels penalized by the tax burden

Consumption level subject to fiscal policy, in addition to being progressive, also differentiated

Consumption level penalized due to differentiated fiscal policy

Source: Authors, 2025

Discriminatory tax policy benefits low-income families by reducing their tax burden, allowing them to maintain a minimum level of essential consumption. According to the data in Table 1, without tax measures, low-income families reach a level of consumption where marginal utility is already compromised at the 9th level (940 Ut/€1 spent) and at the 10th level (910 Ut/€1 spent). However, with the €1 tax relief, these families are able to better preserve essential levels of consumption, avoiding such a significant loss in their total utility.

Without tax relief and with the effect of contractionary monetary policy:

- Average penalty on utility: [(940Ut/€1 spent + 910Ut/€1 spent) / 2] = 925Ut/€1 spent.

With the effect of the differentiated tax policy (tax relief of €1), the penalty on the utility achieved is set at 910Ut/€1 spent. The overall balance is positive at 15Ut/€1 spent (925Ut/€1 spent - 910Ut/€1 spent).

This means that, with the positive tax policy, low-income families lose less marginal utility, ensuring that their basic expenditure continues to generate the maximum possible well-being.

For higher-income families, the differentiated and progressive tax policy increases the tax burden on the higher consumption brackets. Analyzing the data, before the tax change, the average penalty on the utility of these families was 830Ut/€1 spent (11th and 12th consumption levels), but after the tax reconfiguration, it becomes 857Ut/€1 spent [(910Ut+860Ut+800Ut)/3], plus a 27Ut penalty on average for each €1 spent. Even so, the exchange is clearly positive in terms of economic efficiency achieved. Families with lower incomes narrow the difference in terms of average utility lost for each €1 paid in tax burden, from (925Ut/€1 spent - 830Ut/€1 spent) to (910Ut/€1 spent - 857Ut/€1). This differentiated tax policy allows the most vulnerable families to have access to essential goods without drastically compromising the balance of the anti-inflationary policy and with the advantage that the effect on the efficiency of resource management corresponds to an additional 12Ut//€1 in aggregate terms [(925 + 830) - (910 + 857) = +12Ut//€1]. According to Santos and Sousa (2021), it is this conception present in the theoretical framework that underpins, above all, the actions of governments in the redistribution process. The clearest evidence of this influence is the predominance of the logic of tax progressivity in current tax systems.

Once again, it is true that, in this particular case, the Laffer Curve would have a say. The Laffer Curve relates the tax burden to the tax revenue collected by the States. There is a decrease in tax revenue from a certain level of tax burden, due to the drop in productivity (and output) resulting from the disincentive to work that the increased tax burden constitutes. Furthermore, in a study published in 2008, Takáts and Papp observe that modest reductions in tax rates can cause significant changes in taxpayers' behavior. In particular, these changes can considerably increase people's willingness to declare their income in a more transparent and truthful way.

However, it is also true that this type of differentiated application of taxes is designed for exceptional situations. This is the case of inflationary or hyperinflationary outbreaks, whose contractionary monetary policy to combat them will negatively affect families with mortgages indexed to variable interest rates much more than other parts of society. This circumstance creates a situation of profound social injustice, causing the direct effort to combat inflation to fall disproportionately more on families that have taken out mortgage loans indexed to variable interest rates.

In any case, because it is considered very pertinent for reflection purposes, it is possible that productivity will fall with increases in the tax burden on higher-income classes. This is the reasoning formulated by Takáts and Papp (2008), who analyzed the relationship between cuts in tax rates and government revenue, highlighting that the reduction in rates can, paradoxically, lead to an increase in public revenue.

This occurs because lower taxes tend to encourage greater compliance on the part of taxpayers, reducing tax evasion and expanding the tax base.

In practice, when the total tax burden — especially on labor — becomes excessive, what prevails is a lack of motivation to produce. And the opposite is also true: tax reductions can stimulate productivity. Even more skeptical scholars, such as Trabandt & Uhlig (2011), recognize that tax cuts are hardly cost-free, but they emphasize that a significant part of these costs can be offset by the efficiency gains that such measures provide to the economy.

Nevertheless, in the context of this chapter, the logic of exceptionality explained in the first paragraphs of this point applies strictly in the same way to the "savings policy" duly explained in the following point.

7. PROPOSING A "SAVINGS POLICY" LED BY THE EUROPEAN CENTRAL BANK (ECB)

7.1. The Objectives and Potential Benefits of a "Savings Policy" in the Current Economic Climate

The macroeconomic instability resulting from successive crises – from the COVID-19 pandemic to the energy crisis triggered by the conflict in Ukraine – has revealed structural weaknesses in the Eurozone economies. The global spread of the effects of the pandemic, in particular, has demonstrated how health shocks can quickly transition into economic shocks, disrupting value chains, financial markets and public policies on a global scale (Ozili & Arun, 2020). In this context, a "Savings Policy" promoted by the European Central Bank (ECB) can play a crucial role in economic stabilization, containing inflation and promoting social justice. The concept of this policy would be based on the creation of direct and indirect incentives for private and institutional savings, acting as a complementary mechanism to conventional monetary policy.

The imposition of savings levels, with the aim of reducing the liquidity of money in circulation (as is intended with the contractionary monetary policy), would be defined according to criteria very similar to those used to define income brackets for tax collection purposes.

One of the main advantages of this approach is its ability to moderate aggregate demand without resorting exclusively to increasing interest rates, which disproportionately penalizes the most indebted economic agents (Santos et. al, 2024). With a policy to encourage savings, it would be possible to remove part of the excess liquidity from the economy without resorting to excessively restrictive measures, mitigating the recessive effects associated with the increase in the cost of credit.

In addition, a "Savings Policy" can act as an instrument of economic redistribution and social protection. Studies show that families with lower incomes face greater difficulties in building up financial reserves, becoming more vulnerable to inflationary shocks (Mody & Sandri, 2012). Thus, the creation of financial products encouraged by the ECB, such as deposits with guaranteed returns or savings accounts with tax benefits, could allow greater financial resilience for economically fragile families.

Another fundamental benefit is related to financial stability. A more robust banking system, fuelled by increased savings, reduces dependence on interbank credit and exposure to external shocks, ensuring greater solidity for the European financial sector (Pegano, 2014). Furthermore, higher domestic savings can contribute to the sustainable financing of productive investments, strengthening competitiveness and innovation in the Eurozone.

7.2. How Such a Policy Can Complement Fiscal Strategies and Promote Economic Recovery While Ensuring Social Equity

The complementarity between "Savings Policy" and fiscal strategies can generate a synergistic effect capable of driving a sustained and socially equitable economic recovery. Fiscal policy traditionally has a redistributive role, channeling resources towards reducing inequalities and financing essential public goods. However, its effectiveness can be enhanced when combined with an innovative monetary strategy that simultaneously promotes savings and economic stability.

One of the main challenges of fiscal policies during periods of high inflation is the need to adjust public expenditure levels without compromising social protection. Incentives to save can act as an adjustment cushion for households, reducing the need for state intervention and mitigating pressure on public budgets (Draghi, 2014). The creation of specific savings instruments, with attractive remuneration rates and protected from inflationary erosion, can act as a viable alternative to simple wage indexation, which can have adverse inflationary effects.

Furthermore, a "Savings Policy" can have a positive impact on the structure of the capital market. By encouraging liquidity retention in the financial system, the financing capacity for strategic investments, such as the energy transition and the digitalisation of the European economy, is strengthened. The use of savings funds for public investment and infrastructure can reduce dependence on excessive sovereign debt, allowing a better balance between macroeconomic stability and sustainable growth (Reinhart & Rogoff, 2010).

At the social level, this approach can be designed to correct structural inequalities. For example, specific savings incentive programmes for low-income families can be introduced with state co-financing schemes, in which the government contributes an additional percentage of the amounts saved. Similar models have already been successfully implemented in developed economies, such as Individual Development Accounts (IDAs) in the United States, which have shown positive effects in reducing poverty and increasing financial inclusion (Sherraden, 1991).

Furthermore, the introduction of incentivised savings accounts for small and medium-sized enterprises (SMEs) could contribute to their capitalisation and resilience, reducing the need for debt in times of economic crisis. SMEs represent more than 99% of the European Union's business fabric and are particularly vulnerable to financial shocks, making them priority candidates for this type of intervention (European Commission, 2025).

A key argument is that an ECB-led "Savings Policy" can strengthen confidence in the European economy by demonstrating a commitment to long-term stability and financial inclusion. Creating a savings culture can reduce the impact of future crises by reducing the volatility of aggregate demand and promoting a more balanced and sustainable economic recovery. This approach would allow the ECB to play a more active role in promoting inclusive growth, going beyond the traditional dichotomy between monetary and fiscal policy, and positioning itself as a catalyst for the European Union's economic and social resilience.

8. CONCLUDING THOUGHTS

This chapter has explored the complex interactions between geo-economic stresses, monetary and fiscal policies, and their impacts on inflation, social justice and economic resilience. In a context marked by successive crises - from the COVID-19 pandemic to the war in Ukraine and global energy shocks - it has become clear that traditional approaches to combating inflation, based predominantly on contractionary monetary policies, are insufficient and often socially regressive. The analysis has shown that aggressive increases in interest rates, although effective in controlling inflation, disproportionately penalize the most vulnerable households, exacerbating inequalities and undermining social cohesion.

A central contribution of this chapter lies in the articulation between the principle of diminishing marginal utility and the design of progressive fiscal policies. As evidenced, the marginal utility of income decreases as income increases, which scientifically justifies tax systems that tax proportionally more taxpayers with greater contributory capacity. In Portugal, for example, the progressive structure of the personal income tax and the selectivity of the VAT reflect this logic, protecting essential consumption and redistributing resources to finance public goods. However, challenges remain: excessive taxation can discourage productivity, while insufficient progressivity exacerbates disparities. The solution requires a delicate balance, calibrated on the basis of empirical evidence and sensitive to specific economic contexts.

The utilitarian critique of conventional monetary policies has highlighted the need for innovative alternatives. The proposal for a "Savings Policy" led by the ECB emerges as a complementary mechanism, capable of reducing liquidity in circulation without resorting exclusively to interest rate hikes. By encouraging private and institutional savings - with instruments such as interest-bearing accounts or tax benefits for low-income families - this approach could mitigate the recessionary effects and promote equity. Furthermore, coordination with redistributive fiscal policies, such as solidarity taxes on extraordinary bank profits or public investment in strategic sectors, would strengthen economic resilience and social justice.

The international examples analysed, from Individual Development Accounts in the US to differentiated indexation policies in Belgium, illustrate the potential for solutions adapted to different realities. However, the effectiveness of these measures depends on coordinated multilateral governance. In an economically interconnected world, external shocks require global responses. Cooperation between central banks, governments and international institutions is essential to harmonise macroeconomic stability and social protection, avoiding unilateral measures that could exacerbate imbalances.

Indeed, this chapter has shown how recent geo-economic tensions have exposed the limitations of conventional approaches to combating inflation, highlighting the urgent need for innovative policies that reconcile economic efficiency with social justice. The analysis carried out shows that strategies based exclusively on restrictive monetary policies are not only socially unbalanced, but can also exacerbate structural inequalities, with particularly severe impacts on the most vulnerable households.

Among the proposed solutions, the "Savings Policy" led by the ECB emerges as a promising instrument for the economic challenges of the future. This innovative approach has critical advantages:

1. Economic stabilisation without excessive social costs;
    - Unlike interest rate hikes, which penalise indebted individuals in particular, savings policies can reduce liquidity in circulation through structured incentives, minimising recessionary effects.
    - Example: Savings accounts with guaranteed returns for low-income families could act as "social shock absorbers" during inflationary crises.
2. Financial resilience for the most vulnerable;
    - Co-financing programmes (such as the Individual Development Accounts in the US) have shown that savings incentives can reduce poverty and increase financial inclusion.
    - In the EU, applying this model to SMEs (99% of the business community) would reduce their dependence on credit in times of crisis.
3. Sustainable financing for strategic priorities;

- Savings funds geared towards the energy transition and digitalisation could boost investment without burdening public debt.
- Studies cited (Pagano, 2015; Reinhart & Rogoff, 2010) show that this approach strengthens the stability of the financial sector.

As for future prospects, this chapter can outline three pillars of action:

1. Institutionalization of savings policy costs;
    - Creation of a European regulatory framework for incentivized savings products, with.
        - Progressive tax benefits (greater for low incomes).
        - Integration with social protection systems (e.g. savings accounts linked to unemployment benefits).
2. Innovation in financial instruments;
    - Development of "resilient savings bonds" issued by the ECB, indexed to inflation targets and with crisis protection clauses.
    - Experiences such as that of Belgium with differentiated indexed credits (Lenza & Slacalek, 2018) offer valuable lessons.
3. Continuous monitoring and adaptation;
    - Implementation of distributional indicator dashboards to assess in real time the impact of savings policy on inequalities.
    - Partnerships with academic institutions and think tanks to model scenarios, as suggested by Santos et al. (2024).

In conclusion, savings policy is not just a complementary tool, but a strategic pillar for post-crisis economic governance. By combining inflation control with the promotion of equity, this approach embodies the utilitarian principles of maximizing collective well-being. Its adoption will require political will and supranational coordination, but the potential benefits - from reduced inequalities to greater resilience in the face of future shocks - fully justify this path.

REFERENCES

Abdul-Salam, Y. (2022). Examining the effect of the UK oil and gas windfall tax on the economics of new fields in the UKCS province. *SSRN*. DOI: 10.2139/ssrn.4220963

Adrian, T. (2022). Interest rate increases and volatile markets signal rising financial stability risks. International Monetary Fund. https://www.imf.org/en/Blogs/Articles/2022/10/11/interest-rate-increases-volatile-markets-signal-rising-financial-stability-risks

Atkinson, A. B., & Stiglitz, J. E. (2015). *Lectures on public economics: Updated edition*. Princeton University Press.

Auerbach, A. J., Kotlikoff, L. J., & Koehler, D. (2016). U.S. inequality and fiscal progressivity: An intragenerational accounting (NBER Working Paper No. 22032). National Bureau of Economic Research. https://ssrn.com/abstract=2747187

Balteanu, I., & Viani, F. (2023). The energy dependency of the EU and Spain. Banco de España. *Economic Bulletin*, *2023*(Q3). https://ssrn.com/abstract=4488293

Banco de Portugal. (2023). Financial stability report 2023. https://www.bportugal.pt/sites/default/files/documents/2024-02/ref_11_2023_pt.pdf

Barro, R. J. (1981). Output effects of government purchases. *Journal of Political Economy*, *89*(6), 1086–1121. DOI: 10.1086/261024

Batchelder, L. L., & Kamin, D. (2019). Policy options for taxing the rich. In M. Kearney & A. Ganz (Eds.), Maintaining the strength of American capitalism (pp. 183–210). The Aspen Institute. https://ssrn.com/abstract=3634117

Becchetti, L., Bruni, L., & Zamagni, S. (2020). The utilitarian view of welfare economics. In *The microeconomics of wellbeing and sustainability* (pp. 227–269). Springer. DOI: 10.1016/B978-0-12-816027-5.00008-2

Becchetti, L., Castriota, S., & D'Alessandro, S. (2020). *The utilitarian view of welfare economics*. SpringerLink., DOI: 10.1016/B978-0-12-816027-5.00008-2

Bentham, J. (1789). *An introduction to the principles of morals and legislation*. Oxford University Press. DOI: 10.1093/oseo/instance.00077240

Blanchard, O. (2017). *Macroeconomics* (7th ed.). Pearson.

Borghi, R. A. Z. (2024). Challenges of the global economy in the face of escalating armed conflicts in the post-pandemic era. Jornal do Economista. https://www.corecon-rj.org.br/anexos/5CAA993B73E3D62F8845C563ECB1D711.pdf

Bowden, P. (2009). In defense of utilitarianism. *Annual Conference: Australian Association for Professional and Applied Ethics*. DOI: 10.2139/ssrn.1534305

Brandao-Marques, L., Casiraghi, M., Gelos, R. G., Harrison, O., & Kamber, G. (2023). Is high debt constraining monetary policy? Evidence from inflation expectations (IMF Working Paper No. 2023/143). https://ssrn.com/abstract=4501248 or https://doi.org/DOI: 10.5089/9798400249822.001

Cashin, P., Mohaddes, K., Raissi, M., & Raissi, M. (2014). The differential effects of oil demand and supply shocks on the global economy. *Energy Economics*, *44*, 113–134. DOI: 10.1016/j.eneco.2014.03.014

Celasun, O., Gelos, G., & Prati, A. (2004). Obstacles to disinflation: What is the role of fiscal policy? *IMF Staff Papers*, *51*(3), 1–24. https://www.imf.org/external/pubs/ft/wp/2004/wp04111.pdf

Chung, H. (2023). When utilitarianism dominates justice as fairness: An economic defence of utilitarianism from the original position. *Economics and Philosophy*, *39*(2), 308–333. DOI: 10.1017/S0266267122000098

Cui, T., Jia, S., & Lavastida, T. (2023). From stream to pool: Pricing under the law of diminishing marginal utility. arXiv. https://arxiv.org/abs/2305.03689

DECO. (2023). The impact of rising cost of living on household budgets. DECO Proteste. https://deco.pt/protecao-financeira/o-impacto-do-aumento-do-custo-de-vida-nos-orcamentos-familiares/

Dollar, D. (2007). Poverty, inequality, and social disparities during China's economic reform (Policy Research Working Paper No. 4253). World Bank. https://documents1.worldbank.org/curated/en/182041468241155669/pdf/wps4253.pdf

Domanski, D., Drehmann, M., & Juselius, M. (2016). Wealth inequality and monetary policy. BIS Quarterly Review. https://www.bis.org/publ/qtrpdf/r_qt1603f.htm

Domanski, D., Scatigna, M., & Zabai, A. (2016). Wealth inequality and monetary policy. BIS Quarterly Review, March 2016. https://ssrn.com/abstract=2744862

Draghi, M. (2014, August 22). Unemployment in the euro area. European Central Bank. https://www.ecb.europa.eu/press/key/date/2014/html/sp140822.en.html

Duncan, D., & Sabirianova Peter, K. (2008). Tax progressivity and income inequality (Andrew Young School of Policy Studies Research Paper Series No. 08-26). SSRN. DOI: 10.2139/ssrn.1260860

Easterlin, R. A. (2005). Diminishing marginal utility of income? Caveat emptor. *Social Indicators Research*, *70*(3), 243–255. https://www.jstor.org/stable/27522165. DOI: 10.1007/s11205-004-8393-4

Erb, C. B., & Harvey, C. R. (2013). The golden dilemma. *Financial Analysts Journal*, *69*(4), 10–42. https://ssrn.com/abstract=2078535. DOI: 10.2469/faj.v69.n4.1

European Parliament. (2025). Small and medium-sized enterprises. Factsheets on the European Union. https://www.europarl.europa.eu/erpl-app-public/factsheets/pdf/pt/FTU_2.4.2.pdf

Eurostat. (2021). Income and living conditions - Income distribution and poverty. https://ec.europa.eu/eurostat/web/income-and-living-conditions

Eurostat. (2022). European Union annual inflation was 10.6% in October 2022. https://ec.europa.eu/eurostat/documents/2995521/15265521/2-17112022-AP-EN.pdf/b6953137-786e-ed9c-5ee2-6812c0f8f07f

Feldstein, M. (2008). The effects of taxes on economic behavior (NBER Working Paper No. 13745). National Bureau of Economic Research. https://www.nber.org/system/files/working_papers/w13745/w13745.pdf

Fleurbaey, M., & Maniquet, F. (2008). Utilitarianism versus fairness in welfare economics. In Fleurbaey, M., Salles, M., & Weymark, J. A. (Eds.), *Justice, political liberalism, and utilitarianism: Themes from Harsanyi and Rawls* (pp. 263–280). Cambridge University Press. DOI: 10.1017/CBO9780511619595.012

Fleurbaey, M., & Zuber, S. (2021). Fair utilitarianism. *American Economic Journal. Microeconomics*, *13*(2), 370–401. DOI: 10.1257/mic.20170234

Friedman, M. (1957). *A theory of the consumption function*. Princeton University Press. DOI: 10.1515/9780691188485

Friedman, M. (1968). The role of monetary policy. *The American Economic Review*, *58*(1), 1–17. https://www.jstor.org/stable/1831652

Galbraith, J. K., & Kum, H. (2002). Inequality and economic growth: Data comparisons and econometric tests (University of Texas Inequality Project Working Paper No. 21). https://ssrn.com/abstract=315699 or DOI: 10.2139/ssrn.315699

Greene, J. D., & Baron, J. (2000). Intuitions about declining marginal utility. *Journal of Behavioral Decision Making*, *14*(3), 243–255. DOI: 10.1002/bdm.375

Greenwald, D., Leombroni, M., Lustig, H. N., & Van Nieuwerburgh, S. (2022). Financial and total wealth inequality with declining interest rates. Stanford University Graduate School of Business Research Paper, Columbia Business School Research Paper. DOI: 10.2139/ssrn.3789220

Hausman, D., McPherson, M., & Satz, D. (2017). *Economic analysis, moral philosophy, and public policy*. Cambridge University Press.

Ikegbu, E. A., & Diana-Abasi, F. I. (2017). Utilitarianism as a veritable vehicle for the promotion of a just society. *LWATI: A Journal of Contemporary Research, 14*(2), 121–137.

Instituto Nacional de Estatística. (2023). Rendimento e condições de vida: 2023 – versão retificada em 13/12/2023. Instituto Nacional de Estatística. https://www.ine.pt/ngt_server/attachfileu.jsp?look_parentBoui=638979246&att_display=n&att_download=y

International Monetary Fund. (2018). Addressing global imbalances requires cooperation. https://www.imf.org/en/Blogs/Articles/2018/07/24/blog-addressing-global-imbalances-requires-cooperation

Kammer, A. (2022, April 22). The war in Ukraine is a serious setback to Europe's economic recovery. International Monetary Fund. https://www.imf.org/en/Blogs/Articles/2022/04/21/blog042222-eurreo-war-in-ukraine-is-serious-setback-to-europe-economic-recovery

Kimball, M. S., Ohtake, F., Reck, D., Tsutsui, Y., & Zhang, F. (2015). Diminishing marginal utility revisited. *SSRN*. DOI: 10.2139/ssrn.2592935

Lenza, M., & Slacalek, J. (2018). How does monetary policy affect income and wealth inequality? Evidence from quantitative easing in the Euro area (ECB Working Paper No. 2190). DOI: 10.2139/ssrn.3275976

Li, X., & Hsee, C. K. (2021). The psychology of marginal utility. *The Journal of Consumer Research, 48*(1), 169–188. DOI: 10.1093/jcr/ucaa064

Lin, C.-C., & Peng, S.-S. (2019). The role of diminishing marginal utility in the ordinal and cardinal utility theories. ERN: Other Macroeconomics: Employment. Academic Press.

Linnenluecke, M. K. (2017). Resilience in business and management research: A review of influential publications and a research agenda. *International Journal of Management Reviews, 19*(1), 4–30. DOI: 10.1111/ijmr.12076

Marshall, A. (1890). *Principles of economics*. Macmillan.

Menzl, V. (2021). Alternative views on the link between risk aversion and diminishing marginal utility of wealth. *European Financial and Accounting Journal, 16*(2), 51–72. DOI: 10.18267/j.efaj.255

Mill, J. S. (1863). Utilitarianism. Longmans, Green, Reader, and Dyer.

Mishkin, F. S. (2011). Monetary policy strategy: Lessons from the crisis (NBER Working Paper No. 16755). National Bureau of Economic Research.

Mody, A., & Sandri, D. (2011). The Eurozone crisis: How banks and sovereigns came to be joined at the hip (IMF Working Paper No. 11/269). https://www.imf.org/external/pubs/ft/wp/2011/wp11269.pdf

Mohd Sofian, D. R., & Mohd Redzuan, D. M. (2023). The impact of US monetary policy tools on exchange rates of major European currencies: Tools or games? *SSRN*. DOI: 10.2139/ssrn.4497922

Moral-Muñoz, J. A., Herrera-Viedma, E., Santisteban-Espejo, A., & Cobo, M. J. (2020). Software tools for conducting bibliometric analysis in science: An up-to-date review. *El Profesional de la Información, 29*(1), e290103. DOI: 10.3145/epi.2020.ene.03

Narens, L., & Skyrms, B. (2020). *The pursuit of happiness: Philosophical and psychological foundations of utility*. Oxford University Press. DOI: 10.1093/oso/9780198856450.001.0001

Nelson, E. (2007). Milton Friedman on inflation. Economic Synopses, 1, Federal Reserve Bank of St. Louis. https://files.stlouisfed.org/files/htdocs/publications/es/07/ES0701.pdf

Organisation for Economic Co-operation and Development. (2023). Economic policy reforms 2023: Going for growth. OECD Publishing. https://www.oecd.org/content/dam/oecd/en/publications/reports/2023/10/economic-policy-reforms-2023_6ffe1e12/9953de23-en.pdf

Organisation for Economic Co-operation and Development. (2023). Revenue statistics 2023. https://www.oecd.org/en/publications/revenue-statistics-2023_9d0453d5-en.html

Organisation for Economic Co-operation and Development. (2024). Tax and benefit policy descriptions for Portugal 2024. OECD Publishing. https://www.oecd.org/content/dam/oecd/en/topics/policy-sub-issues/incomes-support-redistribution-and-work-incentives/TaxBEN-Portugal-latest.pdf

Ozili, P. K., & Arun, T. (2020). Spillover of COVID-19: Impact on the global economy (March 27, 2020). *SSRN*. DOI: 10.2139/ssrn.3562570

Pagano, M. (2015). Lessons from the European financial crisis. In Faia, E., Hackethal, A., Haliassos, M., & Langenbucher, K. (Eds.), *Financial regulation: A transatlantic perspective* (pp. 23–48). Cambridge University Press. DOI: 10.1017/CBO9781316026649.004

Piketty, T. (2014). Capital in the twenty-first century. In L. W. R. (Ed.), The economics of inequality (pp. 23–45). Harvard University Press. https://www.jstor.org/stable/j.ctt6wpqbc

Piketty, T. (2020). *Capital and ideology*. Harvard University Press.

Piketty, T., Saez, E., & Zucman, G. (2018). Distributional national accounts: Methods and estimates for the United States. *The Quarterly Journal of Economics, 133*(2), 553–609. DOI: 10.1093/qje/qjx043

Prachowny, M. F. J. (1993). Okun's law: Theoretical foundations and revised estimates. *The Review of Economics and Statistics, 75*(2), 331–336. DOI: 10.2307/2109440

Quiambao, J. E. A. (2022). Thinking ethically: The utilitarianism approach in moral decision making. *International Journal of Multidisciplinary Research and Growth Evaluation, 3*(3), 602–604. DOI: 10.54660/anfo.2022.3.3.30

Rawls, J. (1971). *A theory of justice*. Harvard University Press. DOI: 10.4159/9780674042605

Reinhart, C. M., & Rogoff, K. S. (2010). Growth in a time of debt. *The American Economic Review, 100*(2), 573–578. DOI: 10.1257/aer.100.2.573

Santomero, A. M., & Seater, J. J. (1978). The inflation-unemployment trade-off: A critique of the literature. *Journal of Economic Literature, 16*(2), 499–544. https://www.jstor.org/stable/2722879

Santos, J. R. (2020). *Economia indispensável*. Lisbon International Press.

Santos, J. R., de Bem Machado, A., Sousa, M. J., & Fonseca, R. B. (2024). War in Ukraine and inflation in the Eurozone: Combining monetary and fiscal policies with a new "savings policy" as a more utilitarian solution to combat the inflationary surge. In New Research on Leadership Styles and Performance (pp. 273–292). DOI: 10.52305/ZKQP3465

Santos, J. R., & Sousa, M. J. (2022). Public administration and new information: Increasing utility. In A. Ullah, S. Anwar, Á. Rocha, & S. Gill (Eds.), Proceedings of International Conference on Information Technology and Applications (Lecture Notes in Networks and Systems, Vol. 350). Springer. DOI: 10.1007/978-981-16-7618-5_33

Sen, A. (1997). Welfare economics, utilitarianism, and equity. In *On economic inequality* (pp. 1–19). Clarendon Press. DOI: 10.1093/0198281935.003.0001

Sherraden, M. (1991). *Assets and the poor: New American welfare policy*. M.E. Sharpe.

Stark, K. J. (2004). Fiscal federalism and tax progressivity: Should the federal income tax encourage state and local redistribution? *SSRN*. https://ssrn.com/abstract=546584

Stiglitz, J. E. (2012). The price of inequality: How today's divided society endangers our future. W. W. Norton & Company. https://business.columbia.edu/sites/default/files-efs/imce-uploads/Joseph_Stiglitz/Price%20of%20Inequality%20for%20Sustainable%20Humanity.pdf

Stiglitz, J. E. (2020). *People, power, and profits: Progressive capitalism for an age of discontent*. W. W. Norton & Company.

Stiglitz, J. E. (2022). The causes of—and responses to—today's inflation. Roosevelt Institute. https://rooseveltinstitute.org/publications/the-causes-of-and-responses-to-todays-inflation/

Sunstein, C. R. (2020). Behavioral welfare economics. *Journal of Benefit-Cost Analysis*, *11*(1), 1–25. DOI: 10.1017/bca.2020.14

Takáts, E., & Papp, T. K. (2008). Tax rate cuts and tax compliance: The Laffer curve revisited (IMF Working Paper No. 08/7). *SSRN*. https://ssrn.com/abstract=1087186 DOI: 10.5089/9781451868692.001

Tan, L., & Zhang, Y. (2015). Optimal resource allocation with principle of equality and diminishing marginal utility in wireless networks. *Wireless Personal Communications*, *84*(1), 671–693. DOI: 10.1007/s11277-015-2655-0

Tideman, N., & Plassmann, F. (2019). Utilitarianism as a criterion for state action. In Congleton, R. D., Grofman, B., & Voigt, S. (Eds.), *The Oxford Handbook of Public Choice* (Vol. 1, pp. 365–384). Oxford University Press.

Todorova, T. (2021). Diminishing marginal utility and the teaching of economics: A note. [JRES]. *Journal of Research in Educational Sciences*, *12*(14), 25–31. DOI: 10.14505/jres.v12.14.02

Tooze, A., & Odendahl, C. (2022). Economic consequences of the war: How the Ukraine crisis is reshaping Europe's economic agenda. Centre for European Reform. https://www.cer.eu/publications/archive/policy-brief/2022/economic-consequences-war

Trabandt, M., & Uhlig, H. (2011). The Laffer curve revisited. *Journal of Monetary Economics, 58*(4), 305–327. Advance online publication. DOI: 10.1016/j.jmoneco.2011.07.003

Tukiran, M., Candra, T., & Hendri, K. (2023). The ethics of utilitarianism in a circular economy. *Jurnal Filsafat, 33*(2), 270–289. DOI: 10.22146/jf.74664

Usher, D. (2016). A utilitarian measure of economic growth. Queen's University Economics Department. *Working Paper, 1356*, 1–14.

Varian, H. R. (2014). *Intermediate microeconomics with calculus: A modern approach*. W. W. Norton & Company.

Yang, T., Dong, Q., Du, M., & Du, Q. (2023). Geopolitical risks, oil price shocks and inflation: Evidence from a TVP–SV–VAR approach. *Energy Economics, 127*, Part B. DOI: 10.1016/j.eneco.2023.1070.99

Chapter 3

Trade Policy and International Business Dynamics at the Time of Increasing Geoeconomic Challenges

Anna Karhu
https://orcid.org/0000-0003-2205-0108
University of Turku, Finland

ABSTRACT

This chapter explores the interconnected development of trade policy and international business. Trade policy has developed from the creation of the multilateral governance system to the increasing influence of sustainable development, digitalization, and security. At the same time, the ways of conducting international business have evolved from the rise of multinational companies to global value chains binding together highly specialised companies. By highlighting some of the key developments and related challenges, this chapter provides multiple perspectives to explore the possible future developments of the dynamics of trade policy and international business environment. The chapter highlights ongoing and expected changes in international business environment and their interconnections with geoeconomic developments.

INTRODUCTION

This chapter examines the interconnection between trade policy and international business. Trade policy has evolved from the establishment of the multilateral gov-

DOI: 10.4018/979-8-3373-7907-4.ch003

ernance system to the growing influence of sustainable development, digitalisation, and security. At the same time, the ways of conducting international business have evolved from the rise of multinational companies to global value chains binding together highly specialised companies. Current global changes include long-term development paths, such as the environmental crisis, the diversification of economic power and digitalisation, as well as more sudden disruptions, such as the 2008 financial crisis, the COVID-19 pandemic and wars in Ukraine and the Middle East. These events challenge prevailing multilateral structures and question the global balance of power, business practices, decision-making bases and beliefs about the right ways of acting and goals to pursue. The chapter aims to understand the interconnections of trade policy and international business development. Understanding these dynamics can provide new perspectives on our current challenges.

The increasing geopolitical tension and geoeconomic transformations are changing the international business environment. The past two decades have witnessed an increase in protectionism and nationalistic policies. These developments have been enhanced by the multiple crises from the 2008 financial crisis that halted trade, to COVID-19 that paused economic growth and highlighted the vulnerabilities of the interdependencies between economies, and the more recent Russia-Ukraine war and conflicts in the Middle East, as well as the unpredictability of the US international and trade policies. In addition, the global climate crisis has created a rush of new regulations on trade, investments and doing business to boost the sustainability transition. This transition alters the power balances as sustainable energy production and critical materials change the attractiveness of nations and regions. The rapid development of new technologies and, particularly, Artificial Intelligence (AI) creates new power balances between state actors and private businesses as well as tensions between regions as they compete over power. These changes will influence the power balances also in global value chains. The global economy has been led by the developed nations, but the balance is changing towards developing economies. The growth of population and workforce of the future, economy, investments and innovation capabilities have been increasingly located in developing economies, especially in Asia. (Ghauri, Strange & Cooke, 2021)

Geoeconomics refers to the strategic interactions between state actors and business actors to enhance the power position of states in the contemporary global system (Csurgai, 2018). This interaction is related to issues such as controlling trade routes, gaining access to natural resources and conquering markets, therefore having a direct influence on the international business environment (Csurgai, 2018). The new rise of geopolitical and geoeconomic tendencies differs from the earlier protectionist eras as the race to global leadership is not only searched through military and state-centered forms of 'hard' power disputes, but rather the emphasis is on more economic, network-centered, and complex forms of confrontation, competition, and cooperation

(Babić, Dixon & Liu, 2022). This geoeconomic turn creates space for powerful actors beyond state actors, including firms, social groups, international institutions, think tanks, and others that take part in the global rivalries across different spheres of our societies at the local, national, and transnational levels. However, this does not mean that the 'hard' power should be forgotten. The same industrial capacity that produces the goods for consumers can be used to supply military purposes. Thus, the two means for seeking global power are interconnected (Lind, 2019).

These multiple challenges create a polycrisis, the emergence of multiple challenging and wide-scale changes, that will change the international business environment and demand new strategies and business models from firms. This chapter focuses particularly on the impact of geoeconomics and geopolitics on the international business environment and the influences on how business organisations operate, influencing trade flows, investment decisions, supply chains, and market opportunities. To do this, I will examine the changing international business environment at the intersection of two developments: trade policy and international business operations. The aim is to highlight the connections between the different levels of change from firm to policy.

Here, trade policy is viewed as a changing part of a complex international business environment rather than focusing solely on economic, political or legislative perspectives. Thus, building on academic literature, this chapter explores two interconnected changes that influence the international business environment developments: the development of trade policy and international business organisations (see Figure 1). Global trade has grown rapidly since the two World Wars and has increasingly influenced economic growth and nation-state developments, highlighting the role of geoeconomics (Goldberg & Reed, 2023). Trade policy as a governance mechanism for global trade has developed from creating more opportunities for trade to include more environmental and human rights goals (Aunesluoma, 2022). International business operations have evolved through the possibilities provided by industrialisation, developed communication technologies, and the opening up of new markets (Ghauri, Strange & Cooke, 2021). These two development spheres are explored in two temporal phases: *the growth of globalisation* from the two world wars to the 2008 Financial crisis, and *the emerging polycrisis* from the Financial crisis to today. Earlier studies have identified the 2008 Financial crisis, Russia's invasion to Georgia and WTO challenges becoming more evident as a turning point (WEF, 2023). From that point forward, we have faced a cluster of distinct crises that interact in ways that reinforce each other and the influences they have on our societies, labelled as a polycrisis (Helleiner, 2024; WEF, 2023).

The aim is to describe and examine the interconnected development of trade policy and international business. By examining the past and ongoing changes in these two spheres, we gain further understanding of the interconnections between the developments unfolding. This provides insights into what role international business has in these developments and how international business research could contribute to advancing our understanding of these dynamics. We need to search for new ways of working together across national borders in spite of our different value bases and be able to find, recognise and create shared goals and opportunities. International business research has the potential to provide new perspectives to these discussions.

Figure 1. The two spheres for international business environment developments.

The chapter begins by looking back on how we got here. It examines the development of trade policies since the World Wars, the growth of global trade, and the evolution of international business operations. This examination helps us to understand our current challenges. Next, the chapter turns to more recent events, exploring the influences of the ongoing polycrisis on trade policy and international business operations. This sub-chapter focuses on the developments since the 2008 financial crisis that acted as a turning point in global trade governance and economic development. Highlighting some of the historical key transitions and the emergence of polycrisis provides multiple perspectives for exploring possible future developments in the international business environment. The third sub-chapter focuses on these ongoing and expected changes in the international business environment and their interconnections with geoeconomic developments. The concluding chapter highlights key development paths and gives recommendations for further research.

THE GROWTH OF GLOBALISATION

The Strengthening of the Multilateral Trade Governance

International trade as we understand it today, with its multinationals, global value chains, global governance structures and multilateral governance system supporting open trade, has its roots in the Bretton Woods agreement negotiated in 1944 in the turmoil of the two World Wars. This agreement stemmed from the widely shared will between the different counterparts of the war to gain world peace (Lagarde, 2014). The leading economic minds of the time had presented ideas that more could be gained through comparative advantage, meaning that nations could focus on producing things they produce relatively more efficiently than other nations, and rely on other nations regarding other goods. Thus, the simplified logic was that if we increase economic interdependencies between countries, they would be more hesitant to go to war (Lind, 2019). This assumption provided the value base for the development of the multilateral trade system.

The multilateral trading system was first formally established in 1947 to promote sustainable peace and greater prosperity through increased cross-border commerce underpinned by globally agreed-upon rules (Thrasher, 2021; Koopman et al., 2020). One of the key agreements is the General Agreement on Tariffs and Trade (GATT), which was established in the early post-war period to promote international trade by reducing tariffs and other trade barriers. This period was characterised by the hegemonic influence of the United States, which played a crucial role in shaping the trade regime (Yang, 2011; Murphy & McLarney, 2017; Barton et al., 2010). The geopolitical context of the Cold War also influenced the development of GATT, as international trade was seen as a means to foster prosperity and peace (Barton et al., 2010). These new arrangements focused on global coordination of tariffs, quotas, etc., that would ease the cross-border trade. The global trade and economic development then witnessed a long period of growth between the end of the 1940s and the 1970s.

This new take on international relations and trade, together with rapid economic growth and technological and scientific developments, created remarkable trade growth. Thus, today trade volume is about 45 times what is was in 1950 (WTO, 2025). After the two World Wars, the global economy was divided into Eastern and Western blocs, leading to different trade trajectories until the early 1990s. While inter-bloc trade remained subdued, intra-bloc trade flourished on both sides. However, the share of underdeveloped countries in global trade declined, except Western Asia, which benefited from the expansion of the oil industry. These developments of trade mirrored broader changes in global production structures. Although primary commodities remained central to trade—even among industrialised nations—the most significant growth occurred in manufacturing trade, which had collapsed during the 1930s but rebounded strongly within both blocs. The growth consisted not only of increasing volumes, but also of the increase in different types of goods that were traded as industrialisation made mass production possible and technological development improved transportation. During this period, the emphasis in global trade transformed from primary goods and raw materials to more value-added goods. This transition, however, did not happen equally. There were clear differences between the developed economies and the developing economies. (WESS, 2017)

However, economic growth slowed down towards the 1980s: the tariffs and quotas were already low and did not boost the growth any more, and the challenges for international companies emerged in other areas. Therefore, a new set of experts sat down in a new meeting, the Uruguay Round, in 1986. This round took multiple years and concluded in 1994, and set the ground for establishing the WTO in 1995. The multilateral system had evolved from a US-led system to one with a more heterogeneous power structure, accommodating shifts in relative economic power (Gnangnon, 2017). The establishment of the World Trade Organization (WTO) in 1995 marked a significant milestone in the global trade regime, providing a framework for countries to exchange trade policy commitments and establishing a mechanism to make these enforceable (Koopman et al., 2020). The WTO succeeded GATT, expanding its mandate to include services, intellectual property, and dispute resolution mechanisms. This transition marked a significant shift towards a more comprehensive and rules-based international trading system (Yang, 2011; Murphy & McLarney, 2017; Pomfret, 2021). Despite its initial success, the WTO has faced challenges such as the stalling of the Doha Development Agenda and the rise of new trading powers, which have necessitated continuous adaptation of its rules and practices (Pomfret, 2021; Dong & Whalley, 2010).

Now the focus of agreements was not only on crossing the border, but rather on entering the market. The WTO, with strong, well-enforced rules that continue to adjust to promote competition and a level playing field, remains critical in anchoring the global trading system (Woolcock, 2016). The WTO reduces uncertainty about trade policy, promotes trade and investment, and locks in beneficial reform, fostering trade with non-members (Low, 2022). The multilateral framework with the WTO as its core, along with beneficial components of regional and plurilateral trade agreements, is seen as the optimal way to reconstruct and innovate international economic and trade rules at multiple levels (Kireyev & Osakwe, 2017). For example, when a product from country A entered country B, although the tariffs or quotas were minimal, the foreign company could face unfair competition as host country governments, for example, might unfairly subsidise local producers. To overcome these challenges, the discussion turned to global trade productivity and included a new set of rules and standards. This changed the game, as now these agreements were not only influencing tariffs and quotas on borders, but the national regulations and laws needed to be aligned with the globally agreed-upon standards.

Thus, the deepening of the agreements aimed at creating fair playing field and inclusion of all the WTO member nations to global economy and trade (Alessandrini, 2010). There were stronger focus in WTO to solve the challenges of the developing economies through the regulation supporting open trade and creating economic growth (Panagariya, 2013). The impacts have been both positive and negative, but the multilateral trade governance system did play its part in enabling the rapid economic growth (Head, 2021). The emergence of more open global markets and increasing freedom of access to global flows of capital, goods, information, services, and people is unlocking new opportunities for collaboration and shared prosperity. These developments empower businesses, civic organisations, individuals, and societies to engage more dynamically in the global arena. From a systemic perspective, interdependence fosters greater sensitivity and responsiveness among international actors (Fjäder, 2018). As nations become more interconnected, they are more likely to consider each other's interests, which can enhance mutual understanding and reduce the likelihood of conflict. This dynamic has been recognised as a foundation for sustained peace, stability, and prosperity, as articulated in the theory of complex interdependence by Keohane and Nye (1998). This vision of a world shaped by reciprocal relationships across multiple policy areas and actors suggests a shift toward a global order where security is increasingly maintained through cooperation rather than force.

After the Soviet Union collapsed and a number of new nations opened up for global trade, a period of "hyperglobalization" began in the 1990s, creating remarkable economic progress (Goldberg & Reed, 2023). During this period, extreme poverty fell dramatically, and living standards rose across the globe. Consumers in open economies benefited from access to an unprecedented variety of affordable goods from around the world. Technological advancements from smartphones to computers and other electronics boosted productivity and created new industries and opportunities for international services. While multiple factors contributed to these improvements, openness to trade and market-oriented policies played a crucial role (Goldberg & Reed, 2023). Trade with the low-wage countries helped keep goods prices and inflation low in advanced economies, benefiting consumers there while supporting job creation in exporting nations. Additionally, the Western world experienced an unusually long period of peace, which further supported global prosperity. The deep interconnectedness of the late 20th century arguably helped maintain this peace, as the economic costs of conflict—especially disruptions to global supply chains—became too high for most to bear (Goldberg & Reed, 2023)

The negotiating within the multilateral frame and in WTO became more difficult as rapidly growing emerging markets (particularly BRIC countries) gained more economic power and wanted to be heard when discussing these global rules increasing the diversity of the value base and perspectives. These developments increased the competition and the need for efficiency in international business. The system faced numerous challenges, including a fundamental mismatch between global trade rules and the political and economic factors influencing domestic policy-making (Hoekman, 2018). Members were frustrated with the slow pace of negotiations, and concerns about strategies and behaviours of other members created unprecedented stress on the system of rules and commitments, leading to questions about the system's potential terminal decline (Koopman & Madell, 2023). The rise of predominantly bilateral preferential trade and investment agreements has raised concerns about the undermining of the multilateral system (Gnangnon, 2017).

The growth of trade and investments together with economic growth sifted gradually towards developing countries, particularly Asia and China during the 1980 towards the end of 2000s. This development has influenced to the "traditional" economic and trade balance of developed economies as the source of innovation and growth, and developing economies as a source for resources and market to products (Horner, 2016). In addition, the trade in services and intermediary goods has increased towards the end of this period from 1980s to end of 2000s. The declining transportation costs and technological developments have enabled new forms of trade and made the international market more accessible to different types of companies.

To summarize, during this period of global economic and trade growth, the multilateral trade policy system has evolved significantly since its establishment in 1947, facing various challenges and shaping global economic development. Multilateral trade liberalisation has been found to promote economic development (Zhao, 2023). The WTO has played an important role in supporting globalisation by providing a framework for countries to exchange trade policy commitments and establishing a mechanism to make these enforceable (Koopman et al., 2020). The rise in unilateral protectionist trade measures around the world is seen as endangering the prospects of further multilateral trade liberalisation and ultimately undermining countries' prospects of economic development (Zhao, 2023). The WTO has remained as a key actor in the global trading system. However, the rise of regional trade agreements, bilateral preferential trade agreements and concerns about the system's potential decline pose significant challenges to the multilateral trade policy system.

Globalisation has deepened interdependence not only economically but also culturally and technologically. The prevailing view has been that global flows benefit all participants, creating a more integrated and resilient international community

(Milner 2009). While these connections are vital to national economies and can be perceived as vulnerabilities, they also serve as powerful incentives for maintaining peaceful and stable relations, since disruption would be costly for all involved. Even as some realist perspectives highlight the risks of asymmetric interdependence—where one party may hold more leverage—this very asymmetry can also motivate actors to seek balanced, cooperative relationships to avoid coercion and instability. The distinction between sensitivity and vulnerability interdependence helps clarify that not all interdependence is equal, and that positive interdependence—where benefits are shared and mutual harm is minimised—can be a force for good (Keohane and Nye, 1998).

Moreover, the strategic use of economic tools in international relations, when viewed through a broader lens, reveals that geoeconomics can support geostrategic goals beyond mere power projection. An eclectic approach that blends realist and liberal perspectives allows for a more nuanced understanding of how economic interdependence can be harnessed to promote global cooperation, resilience, and peace. Thus, in a complex international environment, interdependence has been recognised as a strategic asset. When managed wisely, they can enhance national security, foster innovation, and build a more interconnected and peaceful world (Fjäder, 2018). However, the current events with rising tensions in the international system, and the visible return of geoeconomics, global interdependence can also be viewed as a national security issue and a potential concern. Thus, interdependence is increasingly perceived as vulnerability interdependence, which tends to become securitised as vulnerability dependence from a national security perspective (Aaltola et al., 2014).

The Expansion of International Business Organisation

The multinational enterprises (MNEs) were at first in the early 20th century, engaged in international trade and market through export and import activities as well as through economic, political and regulatory factors affecting these (Boddewyn and Goodnow, 2020). As global trade grew and trade policy development created more liberal trade rules and stability to the markets, the emerged new organisation of an MNE spread to multiple industries and markets. MNEs operate both in their home and host countries, and therefore influence policy development as well as markets in multiple contexts. Therefore, MNEs challenged trade policy making. As an example of home market influence, the labour unions and businesses in the United States had supported free trade policies together. The rise and growth of MNEs led the labour associations to consider risks such as taking the jobs, technology and capital out of the United States (Guisinger, 1973). However, these risks were considered to provide no ground for trade restrictions as trade policies were considered not to interfere with domestic employment generation. In a host country context, especially related to developing countries, the MNEs were considered to enhance the development of nations through creating competition and bringing know-how and new technologies (Moore, 1974).

At first MNEs were seen as an efficient way to manage resources and grasp the benefits of international presence. Thus, MNEs could take advantage of opportunities and strengths in different locations (Sölvell & Zander, 1995). Thus, MNEs are considered to have strategic advantage in relation to local companies. MNEs affect domestic firms in host countries by changing competition dynamics and productivity levels. While the presence of MNEs can improve productivity, it can also crowd out domestic firms. Due to this dual impact as MNEs enter the foreign market it is necessary to have other type of trade policy tools in use than just tariffs at the border. The trade policies need to balance the benefits of foreign direct investment with the protection of domestic industries (Contractor et al., 2020). For example, the aim of the host country government might be to increase its competitiveness and independence, and to be able to increase competitiveness requires openness of markets, which creates interdependencies rather than national indecency. Thus, MNEs with their global networks create a paradox that by accepting a higher degree of policy interdependence concerning individual sectors may ultimately increase the overall independence of the country, as only the country which uses its resources efficiently will be able to elevate the well-being of its citizens (Moore, 1974). However, MNEs need a supportive political environment to overcome strongly entrenched protectionist forces to secure easy, cheap and secure trade if the production is to be sold in the world market (Ducker, 1974).

As the trade policies developed deeper covering broader set of aspects of trade, the MNEs need to adapt their strategies and structures in response to these multilateral trade rules (Lawton et al., 2009). Thus, the WTO's decision-making process influences MNEs' strategic choices, requiring them to adjust to the formulation, implementation, and enforcement of trade rules (Anderer, Dür & Lechner, 2020). MNEs may trade off less efficient entry and exit regulations for stronger contract enforcement, highlighting the importance of regulatory environments in attracting foreign direct investment (Lawton et al., 2009). This interplay between MNEs and trade policy development is complex and multifaceted. MNEs influence trade policies through lobbying, integration in global networks, and adaptation to multilateral trade rules. Conversely, trade policies shape MNEs' strategic decisions and investment patterns, emphasising the need for balanced regulatory frameworks that support both economic growth and social equity.

For instance, U.S. multinational corporations' foreign direct investments can lead to increased lobbying for trade protection by U.S. upstream sectors that depend on these multinationals for goods sales. As MNEs shift their input procurement to host-country suppliers, U.S. suppliers experience negative demand shocks, prompting them to lobby for protective trade measures (Lee, 2014). The globalisation of production has changed the political economy of trade policymaking. Traditional supporters of free trade, such as exporters, have now been joined by companies needing intermediaries from abroad for their production processes. MNEs, due to their extensive involvement in international trade, play a crucial role in lobbying for trade liberalisation, influencing trade policy outcomes across industries based on their degree of integration in global networks (Hanousek, Kočenda & Vozárová, 2020).

During the period, the increased international competition pressured companies to focus their operations. The growing competition together with the development of communication technologies, decreasing transportation costs and development of open global markets, MNEs developed increasingly networked structure (Parkhe et al., 2003). The networked MNE was able to more efficiently take advantage of the resources, assets and capabilities of its subsidiaries to create competitive advantage at the international markets (Meyer et al., 2011). Thus, as MNEs are increasingly visible in the international markets and multiple industries and sectors, further instruments have been developed such as Preferential Trade and Investment Agreements (PTIAs) (Miroudot & Rigo, 2022). These agreements facilitate MNE operations by integrating trade and investment issues, which has led to concerns over state sovereignty and the need for rebalancing regulatory power. NGOs and civil society groups advocate for policies that curb corporate excesses and promote distributive justice, social solidarity, and sustainable development (Muchlinski, 2016).

The interaction between MNEs and trade regulations can also lead to conflicts due to differing objectives and complex regulatory frameworks. The globalisation of economic activities has led to the extraterritorial application of national economic regulations, creating tensions among nation-states over jurisdictional boundaries. This often results in conflicts that need resolution through international cooperation and public international law (Chaisse, 2017). Foe example, the enforcement of national regulations on MNEs can be seen as an infringement on the sovereignty of other states, leading to disputes over the demarcation of national jurisdictions (Chaisse, 2017; Avi-Yonah, 2003). MNEs aim to achieve corporate goals on a global scale, while national governments focus on national interests. This inherent conflict generates tensions that are difficult to resolve completely (Bagheri & Jahromi, 2016). Even when policies between home and host governments are supportive, disagreements can arise over the distribution of benefits from activities such as foreign direct investment (FDI), leading to conflicts (Calzolari, 2004). MNEs often face conflicts with national regulations designed to protect the environment. Different countries have varying environmental laws, and MNEs may resist stringent regulations, leading to disputes (Napshin & Brouthers, 2015). National regulations on public health, occupational safety, and environmental protection are often seen as barriers to free trade and investment by MNEs, causing conflicts (Root, 2019).

MNEs may also use their economic power to influence national regulations in their favour, which can lead to regulatory capture and conflicts with national authorities (Grosse, 2005). Changes in MNE investment motives, such as the increased use of intermediary products, can affect national trade balances and lead to conflicts over trade policies (Lundan & Dunning, 2011). There is a notable absence of comprehensive multilateral legal frameworks governing FDI, unlike trade, which is governed by agreements like GATT. This lack of regulation leads to difficulties in managing conflicts between MNEs and national laws (Digdowiseiso & Sugiyanto, 2020). The involvement of state-owned enterprises in cross-border trade and investment raises suspicions about national security and competitive interests, leading to conflicts with private firms and national regulations (Lense, 2016).

In addition to the vast growth of MNEs' presence in international business, the opening up of new markets, the stability brought by the multilateral trade framework, and the technological advancement have opened up opportunities also for small and medium companies (SMEs). The Internet affected international trade growth and provided new types of business opportunities at the end of the period (Freund & Weinhold, 2004). Together with decreasing transportation and travelling costs, engaging in international business has become a valid opportunity for SMEs and different types of new services (Mathews & Healy, 2008). SMEs are more vulnerable to these barriers than the large international companies (Fliess & Busquets, 2006).

To summarise, the dynamics between international business organisations and trade regulations are multifaceted, involving jurisdictional disputes, divergent interests, regulatory challenges, economic and political pressures, legal gaps, and security concerns. However, the development of trade policies towards more open trade and the development of international business organisations have, on a general level, enhanced each other's development. The interdependencies stemming from the global company networks have been supported by trade policy developments. The development of MNEs as networked organisations and the increasing international business opportunities for SMEs created the emergence of global value chains, together with the interdependence driving the multilateral trade governance system. Thus, at the end of the 2000s, there was still strong support for the multilateral trade governance system, although challenges were evident. The interdependencies were still seen as a guarantee for global peace, and international markets were expected to grow and open further.

THE EMERGING POLYCRISIS

Return of geopolitics and Trade Policy Turmoil

The challenges of the multilateral trade governance system have created space for the new emergence of geopolitics and the renaissance of protectionist policies. The prevailing system has been unable to adequately respond and develop as the global trade and international business organisations have evolved. The simultaneous stagnant growth of developed economies, the multiple disruptions and needs for systemic renewal stemming from the climate crisis and stronger integration of new technologies in both businesses and governments have supported the return of geopolitics. This cluster of crises created multiple complex challenges to solve.

This polycrisis period has been considered to begin around the financial crisis in 2008, which caused a massive drop in global trade. In many countries, trade collapse was more severe than the Great Depression of 1930 (Gawande, Hoekman & Cui, 2011). It showed the fragility of the interconnected economic systems and global value chains, as well as pointed out the need to renew our global governance systems. Russia's invasion of Georgia in the same year, and the WTO challenges initiated this polycrisis period (Helleiner, 2024; WEF, 2023). The US–China trade war that escalated for the first time in 2018 also had some of its root causes in the inadequacy of the global governance systems built in the WTO framework. The COVID-19 pandemic, in addition to the enormous healthcare and economic challenges, boosted the increase in protectionist policies. Russia's invasion of Ukraine in 2014 and 2022, and the crisis in the Middle East, even further challenge the global interconnectivity and pressure towards global decoupling, a shift to "two globalizations" – one organised around the US, and the other around China (Darie, Miron & Ciurea, 2024).

The global governance system was meant to create a neutral framework of rules that would bring productivity and efficiency gains. However, it seems that the system has increasingly been applied as a tool in power struggles in international relations. As the global governance began to serve additional values than only increasing interconnections in trade, meaning more socially desirable goals like human rights and environmental goals, it also became a battlefield for the multiplicity of values inherited in the 193 countries in the world. Therefore, it now seems that the global governance system is open to change (Babić, Dixon & Liu, 2022). This means that the choices made by a country or a set of countries can influence and reshape the rules, potentially moving the entire system in favour of some powers rather than others. Thus, it seems we are breaking out from the universalism of the previous order, where common rules govern trade.

During this period the WTO and the multilateral system began to lose their power. Although the WTO's 12th Ministerial Conference in June 2022 marked a positive outcome for global cooperation on trade issues, it highlighted the need for the WTO to adapt and reform to address contemporary challenges such as inequality and geopolitical shocks (Drieghe, 2020). There had been a marked increase in free trade agreements, particularly bilateral ones, which have created consolidated areas of economic integration (Koopman & Madell, 2023). These agreements often complement multilateral efforts but also pose challenges to the traditional multilateral approach. Efforts to integrate development dimensions into multilateral trade negotiations have become increasingly crucial, aiming to address the marginalisation of low-income countries and ensure equitable distribution of benefits (Hufbauer, 2013). The WTO needs to be updated and reformed to address new global challenges, including inequality and the need for enhanced coordination across trade, tax, environment, and health areas (Drieghe, 2020). These milestones reflect the dynamic and evolving nature of the multilateral trade policy system, highlighting both its achievements and the ongoing need for adaptation and reform to meet contemporary global challenges. However, multiple challenges contest the multilateral WTO-led trade governance system.

Pursuing a global agenda for environmental goals, digital trade, etc., is incompatible with a fragmented global economy that now seems to be emerging. The rapid development of information and communication technologies has led to new challenges and opportunities in digital trade. The WTO has struggled to keep pace with these changes, while regional agreements have increasingly incorporated e-commerce provisions (Song & Agarwal, 2023; Barton et al., 2010). Trade policy is increasingly influenced by environmental considerations, with proposals for carbon-free trade areas and other environmentally motivated trade arrangements (Lekić & Osakwe, 2017).

The public discussion seems to be developing towards a perspective that an ideological struggle between democracies and autocracies is taking hold. However, it is necessary to remember that many of the recent crises brought up the challenges in the global governance system rather than a clear conflict between the different ruling systems. The rise of China and other emerging economies has shifted the balance of power in global trade, leading to increased geopolitical competition and the need for new trade policies (Barton et al., 2010). The growth of Asian and South American countries has challenged the development led by Western nations. Thus, there is potential for the emergence of competing blocks if these different groups do not find common ground.

The emergence of polycrisis highlighted the challenges of the interconnectedness of economies. The 2008 financial crisis led to increased coordination among major economies through forums like the G-20, which supplanted the G-7 as the premier forum for international economic coordination. This shift was necessary to address the global economic downturn and foster cooperation among a more diverse group of countries (Bernal, 2011; Chandra & Hanim, 2013). The COVID-19 Pandemic disrupted global trade, highlighting the resilience of certain sectors like agri-food trade, which proved more robust compared to others. This event underscored the importance of maintaining stable trade flows even during global crises (Nelson, 2010). Economic downturns often lead to protectionist policies as countries attempt to safeguard domestic industries. These measures can distort trade and challenge the principles of the WTO, which aims to prevent such practices and promote liberalisation (Allee, 2012; Weber & Grosz, 2009). Structural problems and trade conflicts have escalated, contributing to the current crisis in the multilateral trade system.

Resolving the complex challenges requires multilateral cooperation and gradual de-escalation of conflicts (Das, 2009). Already in the mid-1980s, developing economies had increasingly participated in the multilateral trading system, significantly influencing negotiations like the Doha Round. Their involvement aims to address imbalances and promote development-focused trade policies (Scherrer, 2004). Due to stalled multilateral negotiations, countries have pursued regional and bilateral trade agreements to maintain competitiveness and advance economic reforms (Maśniak & Jędruchniewicz, 2024). Since the late 1990s, there has been a notable increase in regional and bilateral trade agreements. These agreements often provide preferential trade terms among member countries, which can sometimes undermine the multilateral system (Pomfret, 2021; Willemyns, 2020; Kireyev & Osakwe, 2017). The proliferation of RTAs has created a complex landscape where multilateral and regional agreements coexist. While RTAs can complement multilateral efforts, they also pose challenges such as trade diversion and discriminatory practices (Pomfret, 2021).

The challenges arising from the interdependencies have been discussed in literature on deglobalization and decoupling (Witt et al., 2023; Cui et al., 2023). Deglobalization is broadly understood as the weakening of interdependence among nations (Witt, 2019), while decoupling refers more specifically to the erosion of interdependence between particular nations or blocs. Unlike deglobalization, which operates at the global level, decoupling is dyadic and selective—nations may simultaneously reduce ties with some partners while deepening them with others. While interdependence spans multiple dimensions, this discussion centres on economic interdependence, which has historically underpinned the global strategies of MNEs. These firms have long operated under the assumption that economic integration is both beneficial and irreversible. However, recent events have exposed this assumption as a strategic vulnerability.

Empirical evidence indicates that deglobalization and Sino-U.S. decoupling have been unfolding for over a decade, though this is still debated due to definitional ambiguities. The COVID-19 pandemic starkly revealed the fragility of globally optimised supply chains, which, while efficient, proved brittle under stress (Delios et al., 2021; Li, 2020; Shih, 2020). The Russian invasion of Ukraine further intensified these vulnerabilities, highlighting how geopolitical shocks can disrupt deeply embedded economic ties (Simchi-Levi & Haren, 2022). These developments underscore a critical insight: interdependence, once seen as a stabilising force, now constitutes a source of systemic risk. The very structures that enabled globalisation—complex supply chains, cross-border investments, and integrated markets—have become potential liabilities in an era of geopolitical fragmentation and technological upheaval.

Traditional metrics of interdependence, such as trade and foreign direct investment (FDI), reflect this shift. Trade patterns, shaped by decisions made decades ago, exhibit structural inertia. In contrast, FDI flows are more responsive to current perceptions of opportunity and risk. Since the mid-2000s, both trade and especially FDI have declined relative to global GDP, signalling a retreat from globalisation (Witt et al., 2023). This trend mirrors historical episodes of deglobalization, such as during the Great Depression and World War II, suggesting it may not be a temporary aberration.

The COVID-19 crisis catalysed a reassessment of globalisation's risks, particularly the over-reliance on China for critical inputs—from pharmaceuticals to battery components (Cui et al., 2023). Western governments, led by the U.S., have increasingly viewed this dependence as a strategic threat. The Biden administration has explicitly criticised the prevailing globalisation model for prioritising efficiency over resilience, advocating instead for a new economic order based on shared values and strategic autonomy (Herszenhorn, 2021). This shift represents a fundamental challenge to the legitimacy of globalisation's existing logic. China's economic growth and rapid development have challenged the US's power as a global leader (Forgey & Kine, 2022), thus becoming the focal point of efforts to reconfigure global economic ties. The resulting institutional realignment—endorsed by the G7 and other allies—has introduced a new logic of globalisation that prioritises security and resilience over cost-efficiency.

However, this transition is fraught with tension. Macro-level data suggest that the economic costs of decoupling from China are prohibitively high for both sides. Micro-level evidence from MNEs operating in China reinforces this view, revealing a reluctance to abandon established systems despite political pressures (Witt et al., 2023). As a result, the global economy is caught between two competing logics: the entrenched model of globalisation and an emerging paradigm of strategic decoupling (Witt, Välikangas & Lewin, 2021). The more recent tariff increases and changes in the US foreign and trade policy highlight these contradictions. This unresolved tension creates a volatile and uncertain institutional environment. For International business organisations, it necessitates a fundamental rethinking of strategy—one that acknowledges interdependence not as a guarantee of stability, but as a potential threat to operational continuity and geopolitical risk exposure.

Due to the more central role of economics as part of nations' international relations, the trade policy tools have been increasingly applied to serve a much wider set of purposes than just regulating free and fair trade. Thus, as the economic relations have become part of the policy set to strengthen the nation state's position in the global arena, the role, for example, of trade policy has changed. This has created space for geopolitics where multiple state actors have an increasing interest in matters of trade. The trade policy means can be applied in both periods of peace and war against countries to weaken their economy, to reduce their political and military powers, or pressure behavioural change (Csurgai, 2018). The instruments used range from boycotts and sanctions to tariff discrimination and prohibition of investment and other capital flows (Csurgai, 2018). Economic rivalries had often resulted in geopolitical competition and led to different types of conflicts, including military ones, bridging the economy-related policy making to security policies (Csurgai, 2018; Lind 2019).

Development of Global Value Chains

The global economic growth has increasingly moved from the developed to the developing countries. In particular, some of the developing countries have grown rapidly and have drawn the attention of businesses by providing increasing business opportunities (e.g. BRIC countries: Brazil, Russia, India, and China). These rapidly developing nations have increased global competition. Creating pressure to increase efficiency to cut costs, and focus on core competencies to be able to create a competitive advantage. The emergence of new technologies reduces trade costs and enables more efficient global production networks (Song & Agarwal, 2023; De Ville, 2022; Yang et al., 2020). Together with advances in technology, particularly in information and communication technology, and increasing competition, have driven the formation and evolution of global value chains (GVCs) that can include both small and large firm. The majority of firms are engaged in global GVCs that span multiple regions, countries and industries. These value chains are difficult to coordinate as they include a wide variety of business actors, as well as non-market actors in the form of different types of agencies.

GVCs, MNEs and international business more generally influence the distribution of economic benefits and risks in global trade relationships through various mechanisms. They create jobs, improve production efficiency, contribute to national and global economic growth, and increase the trade balance deficit, but also increase the income elasticity of demand for exports and imports (Nanto, 2011; Pandian, 2024). However, they also create risks through possible imbalances in the distribution of economic benefits or weaker integration opportunities for developing countries into GVCs (Nato, 2011; Jangam & Rath, 2021). The globalisation of production has exacerbated income inequality, particularly in developing countries, by stretching wage distributions and heightening the skill premium in the manufacturing sector (Chepeliev et al., 2025).

GVCs have led to greater interdependence among countries, as production processes are fragmented across borders. This has resulted in a rise in trade in intermediate goods, changing the nature of trade flows and increasing the volume of global trade overall. Countries that were previously not major players in global trade have become integral parts of GVCs, leading to the emergence of new trade relationships and partnerships. This has diversified trade patterns and created new opportunities for economic growth, particularly in developing countries. These new interconnections have influenced trade policies. Changes include reducing tariffs on intermediate goods and implementing policies that facilitate trade, such as trade agreements that focus on reducing non-tariff barriers and enhancing regulatory cooperation (Song & Agarwal, 2023; Bacchetta et al., 2024).

The GVC's are in many cases built around MNEs, but not only around MNEs from developed economies, but also around emerging market MNEs (Alvstam et al., 2019). Especially MNE's from China and India have been rising to drive GVCs. For example, Chinese MNE Zhejiang Geely Holding Group (ZGH) rose to a remarkable global position through acquisitions of western firms such as the Volvo Car Corporation (Alvstam et al., 2019).

Trade policies are increasingly focused on enhancing national competitiveness within GVCs. This includes investing in infrastructure, education, and technology to ensure that domestic industries can effectively participate in global production networks (Zagashvili, 2021). The fragmentation of production across borders has created a complex regulatory environment, where compliance with multiple national regulations can be challenging for firms. This has led to calls for harmonisation of standards and regulations to facilitate smoother trade flows. The rise of GVCs has raised questions about corporate governance and accountability, particularly regarding labour standards and environmental regulations. Trade policies are increasingly incorporating provisions that address these issues, reflecting a shift towards responsible business practices within GVCs.

Traditional trade policies aimed at reducing border barriers tend to increase economic efficiency, but global supply chains may affect the incidence or impact of these policies. Policies promoting GVC engagement and strengthening domestic fundamentals are essential for countries to benefit from trade. For example, the shift from multilateral to preferential trade agreements has been driven by geopolitical competition and changing comparative advantages (Zagashvili, 2022). Stable political environments are essential for countries to effectively participate in GVCs. Political instability can disrupt trade flows and deter investment (Zagashvili, 2021).

In addition, the push for sustainable development is influencing GVCs. Firms and countries are increasingly incorporating environmental considerations into their trade policies and production processes (Song & Agarwal, 2023; Bacchetta et al., 2024). There is a growing emphasis on corporate accountability, which includes responsible sourcing and production practices. This trend is reshaping GVCs by promoting ethical and sustainable business practices (Song & Agarwal, 2023). The COVID-19 pandemic has highlighted the need for resilient supply chains. It has led to diversification of supply sources and increased attention to essential goods, although it is unlikely to result in significant reshoring of manufacturing activities. Also, the digitisation of trade, including the implementation of digital trade rules, significantly impacts GVCs, especially in the service sector. These rules promote service trade along GVCs and influence the depth and scope of international trade agreements (Zhan, 2021).

GVCs play a pivotal role in shaping the distribution of economic benefits and risks in global trade relationships. While they offer significant advantages in terms of job creation, economic growth, and trade efficiency, they also pose challenges related to income inequality, external shocks, and imbalanced benefits among countries. Effective policy measures are crucial to harness the benefits of GVCs while mitigating their risks and ensuring inclusive development. Technological advancements are reshaping GVCs by enhancing efficiency, competitiveness, and necessitating new trade policies. These changes offer both challenges and opportunities, requiring dynamic and adaptable strategies to harness the benefits of digital transformation in global trade.

THE FRAGILE FUTURE OF THE INTERNATIONAL BUSINESS ENVIRONMENT

The grand challenges strongly influencing international business and trade policies are the increasing multipolarity of power, the technological transition, and the climate crisis. The multipolarity of global power is witnessed in the increasing geopolitical tensions and application of strong geoeconomic strategies. The technological transition includes the digitalisation of our societies and the integration of AI. The climate crisis has boosted the global call for action to transition towards a more sustainable world. Figure 2 summarises the main characteristics of the presented two phases and highlights key aspects for the future.

Figure 2. The past, present and future of the two spheres of the international business environment.

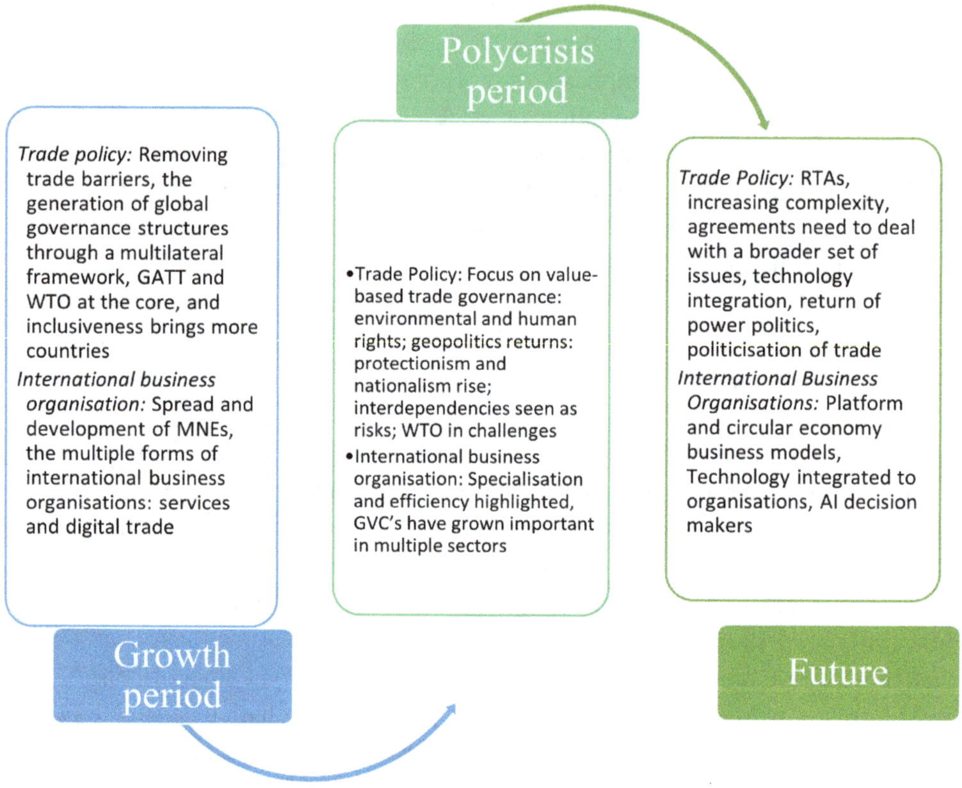

The return of geopolitics with increasing protectionism has challenged the objectives of free trade and broad trade agreements. This trend is exacerbated by geopolitical events such as the COVID-19 pandemic and the Russian invasion of Ukraine, which have disrupted global value chains and questioned the liberal worldview traditionally favoured by Western economies (Curran, 2017). The EU has shifted from multilateral liberalisation through the WTO to more politically attractive bilateral agreements due to these geoeconomic changes (Curran, 2022). The challenges in transatlantic relations have just highlighted the lack of hegemony and breakdown of interdependencies as support for welfare growth and peace. Thus, the multipolarity has created challenges and questioned the prevailing multilateral trade system and creating further competition and challenges in the international business environment. The integration of different policy spheres from trade, environmental, to security creates challenges for policy making. Already, the changed trend in trade policy and the increasing amount of environmental regulations have challenged companies and halted investments, as it is unclear in which direction companies will develop their operations. The integration of security policy issues to respond to the risks stemming from geopolitical and geoeconomic strategies creates further complexity.

The technological transition is significantly transforming international trade, impacting economic development and competitiveness. Between more developed nations, competition over supremacy in technology causes friction. For example, the Sino-U.S. trade friction, particularly in high-tech sectors like rare earth elements, highlights the strategic importance of technological resources and their impact on international trade dynamics (Haaja & Karhu, 2022). On the other hand, developed countries benefit more from digitalisation due to improved infrastructure, while the least developed countries face barriers such as limited internet access and inadequate e-commerce legislation. Technological progress has induced international production fragmentation, allowing higher efficiency and competitiveness. This necessitates proactive trade policies to consider the new reality of business structured around GVCs 4. Industry 4.0 technologies like IoT, AI, and big data analytics are redefining supply chain management, enhancing efficiency, sustainability, and resilience in industries (Liu et al., 2024). These technologies have the potential to restructure global trade by altering the prevailing trade structures (Palmunen et al., forthcoming 2025). They could radically change value chains by creating opportunities for new collaborations, but at the same time create risks of new types of technology-based boundaries that can create further inequalities. Therefore, this integration of technologies more widely in our societies has challenged the multilateral trade governance system and created powerful private companies that aim to dictate the development path.

Stemming from the global climate crisis, the EU is integrating sustainability concerns into its trade policies, balancing economic needs with environmental protection. This shift complicates the development of clear business and policy attitudes due to varying impacts across sectors (Cui, Guo & Bian, 2023). International trade has significant environmental costs, including air pollution from transportation and industrial production. Trade agreements like the Uruguay Round have contributed to increased emissions, highlighting the need for adequate policy responses (Gallagher, 2006). Addressing global challenges like climate change and digitalisation requires large-scale cooperation among businesses, governments, and international organisations. This cooperation is essential for effective trade governance and policy development (Haaja & Karhu, 2022). Thus, the climate crisis has brought multiple stakeholders together globally, and different-level agreements on common goals and actions needed have been established. A functioning multilateral system would support this development. However, the current geopolitical geoeconomic developments do not support the joint investment efforts for sustainable development. The US withdrew from the Paris Agreement and the UN. This has already caused uncertainties to the markets as what will be the future direction of the sustainability transition.

To address contemporary challenges, there is a need for intensive policy actions to reinvigorate the multilateral trading system. This includes updating obsolete rules, adopting new ones to reflect current realities, and ensuring that trade multilateralism works for all. Efforts to integrate development dimensions into multilateral trade negotiations are crucial to address the disparities between developed and developing countries. The WTO and related institutions face calls for systemic restructuring to remain relevant amidst changing global trade dynamics. This includes addressing the theoretical basis of trade regulation and accommodating the growing role of political economy and institutionalism. Modern trends necessitate interdisciplinary research to better understand and manage the spillover effects of trade policies, ensuring that multilateral cooperation remains effective (Ahearn, 2010).

CONCLUSION

In this chapter, I have explored the development of the trade policy system, the international business operations, and their dynamics since the two World Wars. This exploration highlights critical developments and clear changes in the assumptions related to trade policy, thereby altering the goals and beliefs of how to govern global trade. These changes have altered the playing field for international business firms that have innovated new operation modes and ways of conducting their business in the changing international business environment.

The first phase after WWII witnessed declining tariffs and harmonisation of the rules for trading goods. These changes opened up new possibilities for a wider range of companies to engage in international business and created an international business environment where MNEs were able to gain a competitive advantage. Within multiple sectors, from specialised industries like pharmaceutical manufacturing to the production of technical machines such as cars, these large multinationals began to dominate these industries. This was enabled by the technological as well as scientific advancements that made industrial production possible. Together with the opening up of the international business environment and the stability brought by the global level agreements on monetary and trade policies. The scope of the trade policy-based governance and harmonisation widened to include services, and the number of countries included grew. This opened yet new opportunities for MNEs and boosted the spread of Western lifestyles through globalising retail and fast food chains. It seemed that globalisation created a newer stream of opportunities and possibilities for the growth of welfare and wealth through increasing interconnectedness and increasing living standards through consumption of the middle class.

This phase also witnessed challenges related to the growing globalisation, brought in the form of inequalities and severe environmental and human rights challenges, enabled by the more open global market. Yet, there continued to be strong support for the multilateral system, now led by the WTO, to find solutions to these challenges. Thus, the regulations and guidelines increasingly moved from lowering tariffs and harmonising trade rules of goods and services to broader regulations on regulating cross-border business. In addition, the members in the WTO had increased throughout the year, now including most countries. The strong growth of emerging markets, especially China, has given these countries more power in the multilateral system. Through these two developments, deepening of the regulations to include multiple topics from agriculture to data transfer and the increased versatility of voices due to the increased number of countries involved in decision making, the ability to reach decisions on further steps and ways of improving regulations within the WTO framework became increasingly difficult. However, although the multilateral system faced increasing challenges, the international business environment created growing competitive pressures, and due to the stability created by the system, companies were able to find competitiveness through focusing on efficiency. This created a tendency to focus operations around core competencies, and the global value chains emerged. Thus, production of goods was increasingly done in GVC's taking advantage of efficiency brought by narrow expertise and locational benefits.

The second phase highlights the emerging challenges. The financial crisis in 2008 halted trade, and was a historical setback for global trade since the Great Depression in 1930. It was the beginning of multiple crises that continued to challenge the interconnected global trade. Thus, the assumption of economic interdependencies creating stability, growth and peace was increasingly challenged. The US–China trade war in 2018, COVID-19, the Russia–Ukraine war and the developments in the US during Trump's second term of presidency have just highlighted the risks inherited in the economic interdependencies. Changes in trade policy strategies in the EU, the US, and China have been clear, and the use of protectionist trade policy tools has been on the rise. The challenges in the multilateral WTO system that escalated when the US blocked the conflict resolution system have created the emergence of increasing RTAs. The global trade governance framework has become more complex and has been described as a spaghetti bowl, creating challenges in the form of uncertainties, ambiguity and complexity. These challenges revealed the vulnerabilities in GVCs and in the MNE networks. As the challenges emerged, companies discovered that there were clear dependencies related to some resources that a particular company could have a global monopoly over. Thus, companies began to build strategies that would spread their value chains to create resilience for crises. This strengthened the trade policy development and merged trade, technology and sustainability more closely with security policies.

The currently unfolding geopolitical and geoeconomic developments challenge the multilateral trade policy system, creating uncertainty in international markets and changing the rules of the game. Thus, looking forward and anticipating what next year might bring is a challenging task. However, what seems to be clear is that the playing field of international business will change. This change is pushed by the geoeconomic developments, climate crisis and the integration of AI into businesses and our societies. These developments will have an impact on the boundaries companies face in the international business environment. In addition to the traditional national and regional boundaries creating trade blocks, technology-enabled blocks may create a new type of boundaries that companies need to be able to strategise over. These boundaries are not necessarily governed by nation states or multilateral global agreements, but by a group of private companies or individual private actors. Thus, the role of trade policy as a governance mechanism of global trade will have different forms and roles than it has had in the past. It seems that it is highly lightly that the polycrisis will merge different policy spheres even more, and challenge decision making and possibly create multipolarity of power.

These developments call for stronger multidisciplinarity of research and integration of different types of actors from AI-based decision makers to nature as an agent in developing the international business environment. In addition, the different boundaries create further contextual complexity in addition to the regional, national and industry levels. Thus, conceptual as well as theoretical development and rethinking are needed. The impacts of the polycrisis are wide, and the changes needed in trade governance systems, as well as more broadly the activities of international businesses, would require global collaboration. However, the current geopolitical and geoeconomic developments seem to diminish these opportunities, and even deteriorate the already achieved collective understandings to respond to the climate crisis.

The changes call and enable new types of research methods as well as types of data that can be used to create an understanding of the complex and interconnected grand challenges of our time. The traditional research methods applied in international business studies are largely based on past data, and thus, in the context of current rapid developments, hold limited evidence of the way forward. Future studies' methods provide new avenues to explore the emerging phenomenon and possible different development trajectories. Thus, I encourage international business researchers to challenge the prevailing assumption and critically examine the way we understand international business and the different actors involved. The emerging new realities require new perspectives.

REFERENCES

Aaltola, M., Käpylä, J., Mikkola, H., & Behr, T. (2014). *Towards the Geopolitics of Flows: Implications for Finland, FIIA Report No. 40*. The Finnish Institute of International Affairs. Available at www.fiia.fi/en/publication/towards-the-geopolitics -of-flows

Ahearn, R. J. (2009, March). *The global economic downturn and protectionism*. Congressional Research Service, Library of Congress.

Alessandrini, D. (2010). *Developing countries and the multilateral trade regime: The failure and promise of the WTO's development mission*. Bloomsbury Publishing.

Allee, T. (2012). The role of the United States: A multilevel explanation for decreased support over time. Academic Press.

Alvstam, C., Ivarsson, I., & Petersen, B. (2020). Are Multinationals and Governments from Emerging Economies Configuring Global Value Chains in New Ways? *International Journal of Emerging Markets*, *15*(1), 111–130. DOI: 10.1108/IJOEM-02-2017-0055

Anderer, C., Dür, A., & Lechner, L. (2020). Trade policy in a "GVC World": Multinational corporations and trade liberalization. *Business and Politics*, *22*(4), 639–666. DOI: 10.1017/bap.2020.4

Aunesluoma, J. (2022). Global Trade Policy Regimes and Previous Crises. In *Global Trade and Trade Governance During De-Globalization: Transforming Trade Policy for Not-So-United World* (pp. 19–30). Springer International Publishing. DOI: 10.1007/978-3-031-13757-0_2

Avi-Yonah, R. S. (2003). National regulation of multinational enterprises: An essay on comity, extraterritoriality, and harmonization. *Colum. J. Transnat'l L.*, *42*, 5.

Babić, M., Dixon, A. D., & Liu, I. T. (2022). Geoeconomics in a changing global order. In *The political economy of geoeconomics: Europe in a changing world* (pp. 1–27). Springer International Publishing. DOI: 10.1007/978-3-031-01968-5_1

Bagheri, M., & Jahromi, M. J. G. (2016). Globalization and extraterritorial application of economic regulation: Crisis in international law and balancing interests. *European Journal of Law and Economics*, *41*(2), 393–429. DOI: 10.1007/s10657-012-9351-2

Barton, J. H. (2006). *The Evolution of the Trade Regime: Politics, Law, and Economics of the GATT and the WTO*. Princeton University Press.

Boddewyn, J. J., & Goodnow, J. D. (2020) A Short history of the Academy of International Business. https://www.aib.world/about/history/

Calzolari, G. (2004). Incentive regulation of multinational enterprises. *International Economic Review*, *45*(1), 257–282. DOI: 10.1111/j.1468-2354.2004.00125.x

Chaisse, J. (2016). Untangling the triangle: issues for state-controlled entities in trade, investment, and competition law. In *International Economic Law and Governance: Essays in Honour of Mitsuo Matsushita* (pp. 233-258). Oxford University Press.

Contractor, F. J., Dangol, R., Nuruzzaman, N., & Raghunath, S. (2020). How do country regulations and business environment impact foreign direct investment (FDI) inflows? *International Business Review*, *29*(2), 101640. DOI: 10.1016/j.ibusrev.2019.101640

Csurgai, G. (2018). The increasing importance of geoeconomics in power rivalries in the twenty-first century. *Geopolitics*, *23*(1), 38–46. DOI: 10.1080/14650045.2017.1359547

Cui, V., Vertinsky, I., Wang, Y., & Zhou, D. (2023). Decoupling in international business: The 'new'vulnerability of globalization and MNEs' response strategies. *Journal of International Business Studies*, *54*(8), 1562–1576. DOI: 10.1057/s41267-023-00602-5 PMID: 36846272

Curran, L. (2017). EU trade policy after the GFC: The geoeconomics of shifting EU trade policy priorities. In *Advances in Geoeconomics* (pp. 132–140). Routledge. DOI: 10.4324/9781315312132-11

Curran, L. (2022). Future challenges to trade policy in support of international business. In *Global trade and trade governance during de-globalization: Transforming trade policy for not-so-united world* (pp. 161–179). Springer International Publishing. DOI: 10.1007/978-3-031-13757-0_10

Darie, F. C., Miron, A. D., & Ciurea, I. C. (2024). Geoeconomic Dynamics in a New Economic Global Order from West to East. In *Proceedings of the International Conference on Business Excellence* (Vol. 18, No. 1, pp. 469-481). Sciendo. DOI: 10.2478/picbe-2024-0041

Das, D. K. (2006). The Doha Round of multilateral negotiations and the embellishing role of the developing economies. *The International Trade Journal*, *20*(3), 307–354. DOI: 10.1080/08853900600784070

Delios, A., Perchthold, G., & Capri, A. (2021). Cohesion, COVID-19 and contemporary challenges to globalization. *Journal of World Business*, *56*(3), 1–8. DOI: 10.1016/j.jwb.2021.101197

Digdowiseiso, K., & Sugiyanto, E. (2020). The effects of multinational companies on deforestation: The building block or stumbling block. *Journal of Environmental Management and Tourism, 11*(1 (41)), 5. DOI: 10.14505//jemt.v11.1(41).01

Dong, Y., & Whalley, J. (2010). Carbon, trade policy and carbon free trade areas. *World Economy, 33*(9), 1073–1094. DOI: 10.1111/j.1467-9701.2010.01272.x

Drieghe, L. (2020). The first Lomé Convention between the EEC and ACP group revisited: Bringing geopolitics back in. *Journal of European Integration, 42*(6), 783–798. DOI: 10.1080/07036337.2019.1682566

Drucker, P. F. (1974). Multinationals and developing countries: Myths and realities. *Foreign Affairs, 53*(1), 121. DOI: 10.2307/20039495

Dunning, J. H., & Lundan, S. M. (2011). The changing political economy of foreign investment: Finding a balance between hard and soft forms of regulation. *The evolving international investment regime: Expectations, realities, options*, 125-52.

Fjäder, C. O. (2018). Interdependence as dependence: Economic security in the age of global interconnectedness. In *Geo-economics and power politics in the 21st Century* (pp. 28–42). Routledge. DOI: 10.4324/9781351172288-3

Fliess, B., & Busquets, C. (2006). The role of trade barriers in SME internationalisation. OECD Papers, 6(13).

Forgey, Q., & Kine, P. (2022). Blinken calls China 'most serious long-term' threat to world order. https://www.politico.com/news/2022/05/26/blinken-biden-china-policy-speech-00035385

Freund, C. L., & Weinhold, D. (2004). The effect of the Internet on international trade. *Journal of International Economics, 62*(1), 171–189. DOI: 10.1016/S0022-1996(03)00059-X

Gawande, K., Hoekman, B., & Cui, Y. (2011). Determinants of trade policy responses to the 2008 financial crisis. *World Bank Policy Research Working Paper*, (5862).

Ghauri, P., Strange, R., & Cooke, F. L. (2021). Research on international business: The new realities. *International Business Review, 30*(2), 101794. DOI: 10.1016/j.ibusrev.2021.101794

Goldberg, P. K., & Reed, T. (2023, June). Growing threats to global trade. *Finance & Development.*

Grosse, R. (Ed.). (2005). *International business and government relations in the 21st century.* Cambridge University Press.

Haaja, E., & Karhu, A. (2022). Conclusions: The Future of Trade Policy in the Not So United World. In *Global Trade and Trade Governance During De-Globalization: Transforming Trade Policy for Not-So-United World* (pp. 197–202). Springer International Publishing. DOI: 10.1007/978-3-031-13757-0_12

Hanousek, J., Kočenda, E., & Vozárová, P. (2020). Impact of multinational enterprises on competition, productivity and trade spillovers across European firms. *KIER Discussion Paper*, 1028, 1-44.

Head, J. (2021). *The future of the global economic organizations: an evaluation of criticisms leveled at the IMF, the multilateral development banks, and the WTO* (Vol. 5). BRILL.

Helleiner, E. (2024). Economic globalization's polycrisis. *International Studies Quarterly*, *68*(2), sqae024. DOI: 10.1093/isq/sqae024

Herszenhorn, D. M. (2021). Biden's team wants EU allies to get real on 'strategic autonomy'. https://www.politico.eu/article/joe-biden-us-eu-strategic-autonomy-brussels-g20/

Horner, R. (2016). A New Economic Geography of Trade and Development? Governing South–South Trade, Value Chains and Production Networks. *Territory, Politics, Governance*, *4*(4), 400–420. DOI: 10.1080/21622671.2015.1073614

Karhu, A., & Haaja, E. (2022). Lessons from Trade Policy Research. In *Global Trade and Trade Governance During De-Globalization: Transforming Trade Policy for Not-So-United World* (pp. 3–18). Springer International Publishing. DOI: 10.1007/978-3-031-13757-0_1

Keohane, R., & Nye, J. S. (1998). Power and Interdependence in the Information Age. *Foreign Affairs*, *20*(5), 81–94. DOI: 10.2307/20049052

Kireyev, A., & Osakwe, C. (2017). Making Trade Multilateralism Work for All: The Role of WTO Accessions. *Trade Multilateralism in the Twenty-First Century: Building the Upper Floors of the Trading System Through WTO Accessions*, 1.

Lagarde, M. C. (2014). *A new multilateralism for the 21st century*. International Monetary Fund.

Lawton, T. C., Lindeque, J. P., & McGuire, S. M. (2009). Multilateralism and the multinational enterprise. *Business and Politics*, *11*(2), 1–26. DOI: 10.2202/1469-3569.1274

Lee, H. S. (2014). Outward Foreign Direct Investment, Interindustry Networks, and US Trade Politics. *Guoji Maoyi Wenti*, *28*(2), 140–168.

Lekić, M., & Osakwe, C. (2017). WTO rules, accession protocols and mega-regionals: Complementarity and governance in the rules-based global economy. *Trade Multilateralism in the Twenty-First Century: Building the Upper Floors of the Trading System Through WTO Accessions.*

Lesne, J. (2016). On the necessity of requiring international free trade agreements to provide stronger protection of human health and the environment. *Environnement, Risques & Santé : ERS, 15*(3), 238–247.

Li, P. P. (2020). Organizational resilience for a new normal: Balancing the paradox of global interdependence. *Management and Organization Review, 16*(3), 503–509. DOI: 10.1017/mor.2020.30

Lind, M. (2019). The return of geo-economics. *National Interest*, (164), 12–18.

Liu, Y., Zhang, Y., Jiang, R., Cheng, J., & Dai, J. (2024). Limiting heterogeneity in cross-border data flow: Impact on domestic value chains stability and the role of innovation. *PLoS One, 19*(8), e0308716. DOI: 10.1371/journal.pone.0308716 PMID: 39159215

Maśniak, J., & Jędruchniewicz, A. (2024). Foreign Trade as a Channel of Pandemic Transmission to the Agricultural Sector in Poland. *Sustainability (Basel), 16*(16), 7072. DOI: 10.3390/su16167072

Mathews, S., & Healy, M. (2008). 'From garage to global': The internet and international market growth, an SME perspective. *International Journal of Internet Marketing and Advertising, 4*(2-3), 179–196. DOI: 10.1504/IJIMA.2008.017021

Meyer, K. E., Mudambi, R., & Narula, R. (2011). Multinational enterprises and local contexts: The opportunities and challenges of multiple embeddedness. *Journal of Management Studies, 48*(2), 235–252. DOI: 10.1111/j.1467-6486.2010.00968.x

Milner, H. (2009). Power, Interdependence, and Nonstate Actors in World Politics: Research Frontiers. In Milner, H. V., & Moravcsik, A. (Eds.), *Power, Interdependence, and Nonstate Actors in World Politics* (pp. 3–28). Princeton University Press. DOI: 10.2307/j.ctt7t8fk.6

Miroudot, S., & Rigo, D. (2022). Multinational production and investment provisions in preferential trade agreements. *Journal of Economic Geography, 22*(6), 1275–1308. DOI: 10.1093/jeg/lbab031

Moore, R. M. (1972). The Role of International Firms in Latin American Automotive Industry. *Journal of International Business Studies, 3*(1), 51–67. DOI: 10.1057/palgrave.jibs.8490741

Muchlinski, P. (2021). *Multinational enterprises and the law*. Oxford University Press. DOI: 10.1093/law/9780198824138.001.0001

Murphy, J. P., & McLarney, C. (2018). Regionalism and the Multilateral Trading System: The Role of Regional Trade Agreements. In *Geopolitics and strategic management in the global economy* (pp. 1-18). IGI Global Scientific Publishing.

Napshin, S., & Brouthers, L. E. (2015). Intermediary products: FDI strategies, imports, exports, and trade balances in developed economies. *Thunderbird International Business Review*, *57*(4), 311–322. DOI: 10.1002/tie.21673

Nelson, R. M. (2010). *G-20 and International Economic Cooperation: Background and Implications for Congress*. DIANE Publishing.

Palmunen, L.-M., Pelto, E., & Karhu, A. (forthcoming). Blockchain technology and the consequences for trust in international business relations. *European Journal of International Management*.

Panagariya, A. (2013). Challenges to the multilateral trading system and possible responses. *Economics*, *7*(1), 20130010. DOI: 10.5018/economics-ejournal.ja.2013-10

Pomfret, R. (2021). 'Regionalism'and the global trade system. *World Economy*, *44*(9), 2496–2514. DOI: 10.1111/twec.13155

Root, F. R. (2019). Independence and Adaptation: Response Strategies of US-Based Multinational Corporations to a Restrictive Public Policy World. In *Controlling Multinational Enterprises* (pp. 101-110). Routledge.

Scherrer, C. (2004). Global governance: From fordist trilateralism to Neoliberal constitutionalism. In *New rules for global markets: Public and private governance in the world economy* (pp. 109–129). Palgrave Macmillan UK. DOI: 10.1057/9780230524361_6

Shih, W. C. (2020). Global supply chains in a post-pandemic world. *Harvard Business Review*, *98*(5), 82–89.

Simchi-Levi, D., & Haren, P. (2022). How the war in Ukraine is further disrupting global supply chains. https://hbr.org/2022/03/how-the-war-in-ukraine-is-further-disrupting-global-supply-chains

Sölvell, Ö., & Zander, I. (1995). Organization of the dynamic multinational enterprise: The home-based and the heterarchical MNE. *International Studies of Management & Organization*, *25*(1-2), 17–38. DOI: 10.1080/00208825.1995.11656650

Song, L., & Agarwal, V. (2023). The Future of Multilateralism in the Post-pandemic World. *China & World Economy*, *31*(1), 62–87. DOI: 10.1111/cwe.12459

Weber, R. H., & Grosz, M. (2009). Governments' Interventions into the Real Economy under WTO Law Revisited: New Tendencies of Governmental Support of the Automobile Industry. *Journal of World Trade*, *43*(5).

WEF. (2023). This is why 'polycrisis' is a useful way of looking at the world right now. https://www.weforum.org/stories/2023/03/polycrisis-adam-tooze-historian-explains/

Willemyns, I. (2020). Agreement forthcoming? A comparison of EU, US, and Chinese RTAs in times of plurilateral e-commerce negotiations. *Journal of International Economic Law*, *23*(1), 221–244. DOI: 10.1093/jiel/jgz048

Witt, M. A. (2019). De-globalization: Theories, predictions, and implications for international business research. *Journal of International Business Studies*, *50*(7), 1053–1077. DOI: 10.1057/s41267-019-00219-7

Witt, M. A., Lewin, A. Y., Li, P. P., & Gaur, A. (2023). Decoupling in international business: Evidence, drivers, impact, and implications for IB research. *Journal of World Business*, *58*(1), 101399. DOI: 10.1016/j.jwb.2022.101399

Witt, M. A., Li, P. P., Välikangas, L., & Lewin, A. Y. (2021). De-globalization and decoupling: Game changing consequences? *Management and Organization Review*, *17*(1), 6–15. DOI: 10.1017/mor.2021.9

WTO. (2025). Evolution of trade under the WTO: handy statistics. WTO webpages. Available: https://www.wto.org/english/res_e/statis_e/trade_evolution_e/evolution_trade_wto_e.htm

Young, A. R. (2013). The rise (and fall?) of the EU's performance in the multilateral trading system. In *The Performance of the EU in International Institutions* (pp. 117–131). Routledge.

KEY TERMS AND DEFINITIONS

Geoeconomics: Geoeconomics refers to set of actions that are strategically apply economic power to gain advantage over other nations or actors or influence their behaviour.

Geopolitics: Geopolitics refers to influence of geography on politics and international relations.

Global Value Chains, GVC: GVC refers to a set of companies that are interconnected to create added value and bring a product or service from idea to the customers.

International Business Environment: International business environment refers to the complex context in which international business actors operate. It crosses national borders and covers political, economic, legal, technological, and cultural aspects that impact a company's international expansion and operations.

Multinational Enterprise, MNE: MNE refers to companies operating in more than two countries that are networked organization, and actively engaging in international business.

Sustainability Transition: Sustainability transition refers to a set of actions, investments and policies that aim to create a society that does not harm nature or humans.

Technological Transition: Technological transition refers to actions that support the wider integration of technologies in our societies. Especially the transition is focused on the new emerging technologies and their applications, investments and policies.

Trade Policy: Trade policy refers to a set of rules and regulations that aim to govern international trade.

Chapter 4
The BRICS Influence:
Reshaping Global Monetary Systems Amid Geoeconomics Shifts

Surjit Singha
https://orcid.org/0000-0002-5730-8677
Kristu Jayanti University, India

ABSTRACT

This chapter considers the development of BRICS (Brazil, Russia, India, China, and South Africa) as one of the most interesting and efficient agents of reforming the global currency system in the late neoliberal era in the context of changing geoeconomics and geopolitical conditions. It examines how BRICS projects—such as the New Development Bank, the Contingent Reserve Arrangement, and currency swaps—undermine conventional reserve currencies' supremacy and shape a multi-polar financial order. The study illuminates the strategic response of BRICS to trade wars, sanctions, systemic inequities, digital currency innovations, and sustainable development. The chapter ends by examining future perspectives for world financial governance as influenced by BRICS-led reforms and institutional options.

INTRODUCTION

With international power relations changing and the world becoming more economically integrated, the BRICS-Brazil, Russia, India, China and South Africa have proved to be a force in contesting the nature of international finance. As forces for global expansion, they account for an overwhelming majority of the world's population, wealth, resources, and economic growth potential. Their consolidated

DOI: 10.4018/979-8-3373-7907-4.ch004

position in the reform of global financial governance has made them protagonists of the debate on monetary realignment and economic sovereignty (Ferragamo, 2024). Critics argue that the Western-dominated global financial architecture has perpetuated economic asymmetries and constricted the sovereign agency of emerging and developing countries. BRICS advocates for a multipolar, equitable financial system centered on inclusion and autonomy (De Freitas, 2025). With growing geopolitical friction and economic sanctions, BRICS' currency plans have surged into the spotlight. In trying to work towards bilateral currency swaps, regional payment structures such as BRICS Pay, and cooperation for digital currency, the aim is to strengthen monetary autonomy and robustness (Freidin, 2024). Geoeconomics calculations underpin them to offset the strategic leverage of old powers and allow economic cooperation on an equal footing.

This chapter investigates how BRICS are reconfiguring global monetary systems in geoeconomic terms. It will explore the political-economic logic, institutional drivers, and geopolitical determinants of the economic policies of the bloc. It will also consider the potential long-term impact of BRICS' changing strategy, including developing a multipolar financial order, social inclusion and the redefinition of international business standards. From this perspective, BRICS represents a regional bloc and a possible designer of a new global financial model.

Based on prior critical scholarship on BRICS in global financial governance, this contribution further considers how the BRICS portrays itself as a challenger and possible alternative to the current Western-dominated financial order. Aydın (2025) highlights that this broadening and strengthening of BRICS membership poses fundamental questions regarding its potential to challenge the traditional leadership of the IMF and World Bank. If BRICS is an alternative model or a systemic challenger, Aydın responds thematizing the internal diversity of the grouping and the strategic coordination it leads to determine the former.

In this respect Aydın (2025) identifies key three dimensions, that is, BRICS' founding motivations and challenges, its increasing economic and geopolitical capability, notably in the context of the Chinese factor, and in the end, the changing posture of BRICS as it develops an alternative financial system by challenging the normative authority of Western governance institutions. The present chapter builds on these early insights by questioning how BRICS are transforming global currency systems in instruments such as the NDB, CRA and CBDCs, and how the organization of these instruments express larger ideals of multipolarity, financial sovereignty and institutional reform.

New studies of world trade over long periods suggest that the BRICS coalition—comprised of Brazil, Russia, India, China and South Africa—has become far more critical in the make-up of the world's economic activity. Kumar et. al. (2025) analyzes trends in international trade and openness of the economy of BRICS countries from

1971 to 2020, using World Bank databases and panel data analysis in RStudio. The research found that trade engagement continued to increase, especially between 2004 and 2014, with significant increases in exports and imports. However, as expansions go, the study also found significant volatility in net trade balances and terms of trade adjustments, signifying that intra-block trade dynamics remained complex and highly unbalanced. These results also highlight the increasing footprint of BRICS in global trade rehearsals and suggest long-term structural changes towards the international economic order led by emerging economies.

Studies of the changing dynamics of world trade have pointed to the situational response of the developing BRICS+ economies amid geopolitical upheavals. Krishna E. S. et. al. (2025) examine changes in trade volumes and patterns between Russia and its BRICS+ partners—Brazil, India, China, South Africa, and select members—after and before the Russia-Ukraine conflict. Leveraging secondary sources from Bloomberg, the World Trade Organization (WTO), and national trade databases, the analysis examines trade patterns in the pre-conflict period (2018-21) relative to those seen post-2022. The results suggest a significant growth in trade between Russia and some BRICS+ groups after the conflict, which emphasizes the group's dynamic and ability to reorient economic cooperation in a crisis. Moreover, compared with some traditional blocks like the European Union, a differentiated response to global crises is also displayed. The findings of this study provide important policy implications to inform BRICS+ countries in their manoeuvring of the global trade landscape, which is increasingly complex through cooperation and restructuring.

In the context of the BRICS, the convergence of geopolitics and sustainability has received empirical and theoretical attention, especially in tourism studies. In their research, Sailesh (2025) examines how economic cooperation within BRICS impacts sustainable tourism through several determinants of sustainable tourism, such as infrastructure growth, cultural enrichment, environmental control, political soundness and technological advancement. The study concludes that although BRICS countries have great potential to be leaders in sustainable tourism, they also face specific inequalities, policy coherence issues, and environmental management challenges. Mapping barriers and new niches, by both obstacles and emerging opportunities, the chapter reiterates the need for coordinated actions to enhance inclusive and environmentally friendly tourism among BRICS countries. The paper ends with a prospective agenda, urging policymakers and actors in the industry to incorporate sustainability at the heart of tourism planning and international cooperation among the member countries.

Sönmez et. al. (2025) examines whether the BRICS, vis-à-vis Western nations, successfully fulfilled one of its founding objectives: increasing the global economic role of emerging economies. Formed in 2010 to bring together its five large developing nations — Brazil, Russia, India, China and South Africa — BRICS was designed to promote a more equal and competitive global economic power. Based on macroeconomic data cued from the World Bank's database WDI (World Bank-2024), cross-national economic trends in member nations of BRICS are compared over two distinct periods of the pre-(2000–2009) and post-establishment (2010–2023) phases. The study suggests a significant increase in the economic and global performance of the BRICS, led by China in the group's performance. The findings highlight the increasing significance of BRICS as a key factor in forming the world economy, despite internal growth and development discrepancies.

BACKGROUND

The development of the global monetary system has been influenced by the economic stranglehold of several leading powers in the world who possess the globe's reserve currencies. International financial governance has been dominated by institutions such as the International Monetary Fund (IMF) and World Bank, based on the Bretton Woods system, since the end of World War II. However, these bodies have been frequently criticized of perpetuating structural inequalities, constraining the policy space of developing countries, and centralizing financial decision-making authority in advanced Western countries (Desai & Vreeland, 2014). In response to these imbalances, the emerging countries have started to arrange themselves into coalitions that question the old financial hierarchy. The BRICS is one of the leading such coalitions.

BRICS emerged as a coalition of rapidly ascending economies intending to challenge the post–Cold War Western economic order and advocate for a fairer, more inclusive global financial architecture. Over time, BRICS institutionalized its aims by creating the New Development Bank in 2014 and the Contingent Reserve Arrangement in 2015—both designed to lessen reliance on Western-led institutions like the IMF and World Bank (Ferragamo, 2025). BRICS financial aspirations have acquired greater urgency against the backdrop of escalating geopolitical frictions, trade wars, economic sanctions and mounting financial militarisation on the global level. These shocks have revealed the fault lines of a dollar-centric monetary system and pushed BRICS countries to look for alternatives, such as agreements in local currencies, the development of digital currencies, and the creation of a shared reserve currency (Pistilli, 2025). The group has reacted to all technological breakthroughs by considering its use of blockchain, Central Bank Digital Currencies (CBDCs) and other new technologies to create financial systems that are more efficient and automatic (Helmy, 2025). The role of BRICS in global financial governance has provided a growing field of relevance and interest for academia. In its efforts to promote a multipolar monetary system, the bloc has faced the challenges of breaking the dominance of current financial powerhouses, linking different economic systems, and creating sustainable institutions. Although ambitious, the BRICS initiative illustrates a broader shift in the balance of power in the world. It is a strategic move by developing economies to exercise a greater say in their economic destinies.

It seeks to explore how BRICS is reconfiguring the world's monetary arrangements through geoeconomics cooperation, institutional innovation, and strategic financial reforms. By scrutinizing the bloc's initiatives—the NDB and CRA, digital currency experiments, and efforts towards reserve diversification—the chapter makes a valuable contribution to our understanding of BRICS and its transformative potential and future international financial governance direction. McDowell (2021) finds that aggressive use of financial sanctions creates *"political risk"* for reliance on the U.S. dollar, prompting targeted states to pursue de-dollarization. He documents cases in Russia, Venezuela, and Turkey, where American sanctions sparked policies to reduce dollar exposure (e.g., shifting reserves or trading away from USD). Geopolitical friction (sanctions, trade wars) drives emerging economies to seek monetary alternatives. It provides empirical backing for the notion that overusing dollar sanctions may undermine the dollar's dominance.

THEORETICAL FRAMEWORK

Three main theoretical frameworks underpin this chapter, explaining the examination of the place of the BRICS in the transformation of the global monetary system:

Hegemonic Stability Theory (HST): HST argues that the world's economic stability can only be ensured when a single hegemonic power enforces economic order and rules. However, BRICS has made and continues to make, against the backdrop of the US-imposed unipolar financial system, a statement supporting a move to a multipolar financial system. The term is here employed critically to weigh the transition from hegemonic monetary order to decentralized financial governance (Kindleberger, 2013).

Institutionalism in International Political Economy: Institutionalism in IPE Institutionalism posits that global economic outcomes are affected by the rules and norms promulgated by formal institutions. BRICS has established the New Development Bank and the Contingent Reserve Arrangement, representing an institutionalist strategy of reordering global financial norms and creating alternatives to or alternatives for the Bretton Woods institutions (Keohane, 1984).

Geoeconomic Theory: Geoeconomics emphasizes deploying economic instruments (trade, investment, finance) to attain political ends. This theoretical approach can be helpful to account for how BRICS uses financial instruments such as currency swaps and digital currencies not only as a means to achieve economic advantages but also as tools of strategic autonomy and opposition to external pressure (i.e., sanctions) (Luttwak, 1990).

CONCEPTUAL FRAMEWORK

THE RISE OF BRICS IN THE GLOBAL ECONOMY

The rise of BRICS in the world economy represents a significant redistribution of power from established Western economies to emerging ones. During the last two decades, the BRICS countries (Brazil, Russia, India, China, and South Africa) have increased their economic presence and reinforced their political collaboration to change international settings and institutions. Their ascent reflects a common reaction to longstanding structural imbalances in international institutions and a joint aspiration to foster a more representative and inclusive global order (Gupta, 2025).

Economic and Political Synergy within BRICS

With different political systems, geographical locations, and economic development categories, the BRICS countries are finding a strategic game in some fields. Economically, the five countries encompass about a quarter of the world's GDP and over 40% of the population. This population and economic clout endow BRICS with considerable political weight on the global stage. Politically, these countries have a common interest in reforming global governance organizations, such as the IMF and the World Bank, to better represent what the 21st-century world is like (Ferragamo, 2024).

Their complementarity also emanates from economic cooperation: China's manufacturing capability, India's services sector and pool of human capital, Russia's energy reserves, Brazil's agricultural prowess and South Africa's mining and regional reach. This diversity has also helped reinforce the bargaining power and stimulate economic complementarities amongst BRICS, thus consolidating stronger intra-BRICS cooperation in trade, investment, and development finance (Gupta, 2025).

Strategic Motivations Behind BRICS' Collaboration

At the centre of BRICS cooperation is an understanding that there is strategic value in the BRICS process. The creation and follow-up to the bloc are motivated by the necessity of promoting a lessened dependence on Western-dominated global financial institutions, a balanced power against reserve currencies such as the U.S.

dollar, and shielding their economies from outward threats such as sanctions, market volatility and speculative jamming of the system (Pistilli, 2025).

BRICS is also intended to serve as a vehicle for currency and reserve system reform to influence the global economic order. The group seeks to pave alternative development paths less interfered with by the developed countries' geopolitical considerations by prioritizing South-South cooperation and mutual development. Their focus on sovereignty, mutual respect, and non-interference strikes a chord in many developing countries, making BRICS an attractive leader in the Global South. It is symbolic and about actively forming alliances and labouring to create economic models that serve inclusion, sustainability, and autonomy. BRICS has stepped up cooperation with countries in Africa, Latin America and Southeast Asia, providing those countries with development aid, trade pacts and investments that do not always come with the strings attached to traditional Western organizations.

Further, BRICS interventions indicate a movement away from traditional development models from the rest of the world, perpetuating dependence on foreign aid towards capacity and knowledge transfer initiatives between equals. EAC supports economic cooperation models based on common experience in post-colonial development, structural inequality and financial marginalization. Since they are rooted in the principles of non-alignment and multipolarity, BRICS provides an image of global governance that resonates in decentralizing power, institutional empowerment at the regional level, and enhancing collective bargaining for emerging economies.

This aspiration is also evidenced in plans for a BRICS currency, expansion of the NDB's lending powers to non-members, and mechanisms such as BRICS+ to widen its diplomatic and economic horizons. These initiatives, if consolidated, could reshape the normative order of international finance and generate a different future for the world – one in which the world is not ruled by a few players to its general disadvantage but through inclusive and multilaterally agreed-upon negotiations.

CHALLENGES IN THE CURRENT GLOBAL MONETARY SYSTEM

The international monetary system has always been one of unequal structures that favour a couple of powerful countries, including the ones whose currencies are the world's. This structure offers stability and liquidity to global trade and finance, but has also made systemic fragility and continuing economic inequality more likely. Such challenges for developing countries, including the BRICS, highlight the necessity of a more diversified and inclusive international monetary and financial system.

Dominance of Reserve Currencies: USD and Euro

Now let us reiterate the essence of the current financial system, which is a coproduct of the U.S.'s glorious victory in WWII, namely, the ruthless U.S. dollar hegemony and the rule by the Euro with a large gap. As an international currency, central banks and commercial banks predominantly use the dollar for global trade and commodities for their foreign exchange reserves, cross-border invoices, and financial settlements. It has enabled cross-border trade and investment and given the United States disproportionate influence over international economic matters. The "exorbitant privilege" of being able to print the world's reserve currency permits the U.S. to run permanent current account deficits and levy extraterritorial sanctions that resonate across the globe.

For the BRICS and many other developing countries, this dollar dependency inflates the risk of exchange rate volatility, interest rate variations, and geopolitical uncertainties. The Euro, being less potent, is affected by similar deranged balances, specifically in the economic policy structures of the EU. Such overdependence on a few currencies, however, not only centralizes global financial power; it also impedes the room for manoeuvre for policies in emerging markets.

Systemic Vulnerabilities and Inequities

The macroeconomic system of the world is a scalar hierarchy, not unlike a perovskite, and we have again and again witnessed its crisis-proneness, from the 1997 Asian crisis to the 2008 global crisis and the sudden global economic crisis that was the result of the COVID-19 pandemic. It has exposed the vulnerability of a system utterly dependent on a small number of core financial centres and currencies. During times of crisis, capital fleeing from emerging markets to presumed "safe havens" such as the U.S. increases the turmoil and limits access to much-needed liquidity.

Plus, global finance is highly unequal in terms of access. In addition, people had to pay more to borrow when they were not in control of their economic affairs, opened up most countries in developing nations are required to acquire loans if they are in trouble through conditional loans given by multilateral institutions, such as the IMF and the World Bank, or their voice and votes for decisions to influence the world of finance either in the IMF or in the World Bank, we also wanted. These injustices impede development and entrench historic inequalities in the international system.

Despite their increasing share of global output, the continued marginalization of the emerging economies in financial governance discussions means that a dissonance between economic realities and institutional representation exists. This gap intensifies the demand for reforms and a reorientation toward a more equilibrated system.

The Need for Diversification and Inclusivity

To meet these challenges, a consensus is emerging among BRICS nations, particularly that the global monetary system needs to be adjusted to the increasingly multipolar nature of the current economy. De-linking from a U.S. dollar-centric world order is critical to strengthening monetary resilience, promoting financial autonomy, and mitigating the risks of external shocks.

Efforts to establish other reserve currencies, regional payment means, and local currency settlements are already being made. Furthermore, the incorporation of the currency of the Internet and financial technologies provides alternative means for inclusive financial participation, particularly for regions that have historically been left out of formal financial systems.

Inclusivity also requires reform in governance mechanisms to give emerging and developing economies a more decisive say in shaping global financial standards and rules. Modernizing the voting and representation of countries in institutions such as the IMF (International Monetary Fund), advancing capacity-building efforts, alongside reforms in the areas of trade and investment, are significant strides to creating a just, fair and responsive global system to serve the interests of all.

Structural hegemony, systemic vulnerabilities, and institutional injustice continue to persist, and they require immediate reform. BRICS is uniquely positioned, as a bloc, to propose and drive these changes that will contribute to a financial ecosystem for shared prosperity and development worldwide.

BRICS' INSTITUTIONAL CONTRIBUTIONS TO MONETARY REFORM

For a long time, the world monetary arrangement has comprised structural imbalances that disproportionately favour some big economies, a few economies, and, in particular, those using their currency as a reserve. That framework has facilitated the global trade and finance system, but has also revealed systemic weaknesses and long-term imbalances. For developing countries like the BRICS countries, the problems underline the necessity of a more diverse and balanced global financial system.

Dominance of Reserve Currencies: USD and Euro

Beneath the present monetary exploit is the U.S. dollar and the Euro's ascendancy at a long distance. The dollar is used in international trade, as a reserve, and for financial settlement. That has helped lubricate global commerce but has also given the United States an outsized influence over the economic affairs of other nations. The one-two punch of "exorbitant privilege" and a dollar deepening shed from the currency-issuing hegemon enables the U.S. to run chronic current account deficits and to extend sanctions extraterritorially with outsized consequences globally (Desai & Vreeland, 2011).

For BRICS and other emerging economies, this dollar dependence makes them more vulnerable to exchange rate shocks, interest rate spreads and geopolitical tensions. The Euro is also less dominant but demonstrates similar discrepancies, especially between guiding economic policy at the European Union level. This excessive reliance on a handful of currencies concentrates international financial power and constrains policy autonomy in emerging markets (Gupta, 2025).

Systemic Vulnerabilities and Inequities

The world's financial system has repeatedly shown its vulnerability, from the 1997 Asian Financial Crisis through the 2008 Global Financial Crisis to the economic implosion of the COVID-19 pandemic. This has exposed the brittleness of a system hugely dependent on a handful of key financial centres and currencies. During crises, the evacuation of capital from emerging markets and flight toward safe havens, such as the U.S., are among the things that magnify economic destabilization and reduce access to the emergency liquidity needed (Kindleberger, 2013).

In addition, global finance is woefully imbalanced. Emerging countries usually shoulder higher borrowing costs, along with conditional loans from multinational organizations, and have only a limited voice in global finance decisions at the IMF and World Bank. Such imbalances impede growth and perpetuate the old hierarchies of the international system (Keohane, 1984).

The continued exclusion of emerging market economies from financial governance discussions despite their increasing shares of global output indicates a disconnect between economic facts and institutional arrangements. This disconnection is increasing the requests for reform and re-equilibration towards a more equilibrated system (Ferragamo, 2024).

The Need for Diversification and Inclusivity

To tackle this, BRICS members have increasingly agreed that the global monetary system needs to change to fit the multipolar nature of the modern economy. Winding public and private input markets and, from a strategy perspective of differentiating from a monopolar dependence on the U.S. dollar (Alesina, 1988), is thought to be a necessary move for increasing monetary resilience, promoting financial independence, and minimizing susceptibility to external shocks (Luttwak, 1990).

Attempts to encourage other reserve currencies, regional payment systems and local currency settlements are already being made. Furthermore, combining cryptocurrencies and fintech options provides avenues for financial inclusion, particularly for countries left out of the mainstream financial systems (Helmy, 2025).

Inclusivity also implies reforming governance mechanisms through which emerging and developing countries have a more robust opportunity to inform global finance norms and policies. Rationalizing the voting rights systems of institutions such as the IMF, ensuring greater representation of the Global South, and supporting capacity-building initiatives are necessary to create a fair, transparent and responsive system to the needs of all economies (Desai & Vreeland, 2011).

The current system of global money is in a predicament. Moreover, it is precisely because of the continued structural dominance, systemic fragility, and institutional discrimination that there is a crying need for reform. The BRICS group is in an extreme position to push for such structural changes and seeks to create a global financial system that will serve common development and sustainable growth.

THE IMPACT OF GEOECONOMICS AND GEOPOLITICS ON BRICS' STRATEGY

BRICS' strategic trajectory is not determined in a vacuum —it is impacted by the larger trends of geoeconomics and geopolitics in the international system. When economic instruments are weaponized and geopolitical tensions escalate, BRICS member states have repositioned their policy stances to protect their financial sovereignty and promote regional cooperation to construct a resilient economic architecture. Trade wars, sanctions, regional alliances, and the reconfiguration of global power have all influenced the development of the BRICS' joint strategies in monetary reform and international relations.

Trade Wars, Sanctions, and Their Influence on BRICS Policies

Trade wars, particularly the trade war between the U.S. and China, and expanding recourse to economic sanctions as an instrument of foreign policy have combined to drive significant changes in the BRICS orientation to global finance. These events have highlighted the weaknesses of the current financial infrastructure, in particular, dependence on Western financial infrastructure and reserve currencies.

That includes sanctions applied to the BRICS countries, which have spurred BRICS to ramp up its de-dollarisation and financial decoupling course. In reaction to Western sanctions, one response has been for Russia to increase its gold reserves, promote ruble settlement in trade and expand its economic relations with fellow BRICS states. China has been expanding the currency swap-based internationalization of the yuan and the geographical network of its currency swaps.

Indeed, in response to these challenges, BRICS has been investing in alternative trade mechanisms, local payment systems (CIPS for China, SPFS for Russia), and standard digital currency platforms as countermeasures to the global hotspots of financial pressure. These policy responses illustrate how geoeconomic shocks drive BRICS toward greater monetary cooperation.

Geopolitical Alignment and Its Implications for Monetary Reforms

The geopolitics is shifting with the decline of unipolarity and the rise of regional multilateral power centres. As a group of strong but diverse political communities, BRICS are organized around sovereignty, non-intervention and equitable development.

This coincidence in geopolitics makes the BRICS more determined to change the current global monetary governance system. For instance, they have been able to rhetorically frame their foreign policy talk around ideas of solidarity and economic sovereignty, which BRICS members have used to collectively challenge the Political and Legal question "logic" of Western-centric multilateral institutions. This strategic stance informs their demands for more voting rights at the IMF and fairer representation in international regulatory bodies (Ferragamo, 2024).

Moreover, the political-military coordination of BRICS, expressed in their joint statements, summit communiqués and even institutionalization, indicates a common purpose to influence a new world financial order that would be less open to political manipulation and more attuned to current economic facts. This convergence presents the geopolitical coherence required to move forward with unified monetary reforms and systemic alternatives.

Regional Cooperation and Its Global Spillover Effects

All members of BRICS are regionally influential, and they use this not just for their national advantage but also to project BRICS' global presence. Their regional involvements—in the case of actors such as the African Union, MERCOSUR, the Eurasian Economic Union, ASEAN and the Shanghai Cooperation Organisation – are nodes in global economic integration and opportunities for diplomatic presence.

These regional linkages could pave the way for spreading BRICS-originated financial ideas and institutions, including the New Development Bank's reach to non-BRICS, local currency financing arrangements, and regional monetary cooperation. For example:

- India's engagement in South Asia and Africa through development finance and trade facilitation.
- China's Belt and Road Initiative complements BRICS monetary strategies by promoting yuan-based financing.
- South Africa's role in advancing continental integration via the African Continental Free Trade Area (AfCFTA), where BRICS financial tools can be deployed to support infrastructure and digital payment systems.

The offshoot of such regional initiatives is the emergence of a 'counter-veiling' financial network which threatens the hegemony of Western-led institutions and promotes the notion of financial pluralism. These regional encounters extend the space of influence of the BRICS economies and legitimize their alternative frameworks in heterodox economic environments.

The driving force of geoeconomics and geopolitics is becoming increasingly more critical in determining the BRICS strategic currency agenda. Trade disruptions, sanctions, alliances and local diplomacy changes contributed to the bloc's resolve to develop sturdier, more inclusive and self-reliant financial systems. Against this background of continued global instability and unsustainable trends, the BRICS coherent response applying institutional innovation and geopolitical solidarity to their collective pursuit of prosperity is a game-changing reshape of global economic relations with justice, sovereignty and sustainability at its core.

THE ROLE OF BRICS IN FOSTERING A MULTIPOLAR FINANCIAL ORDER

In this ongoing " de-dollarisation background," the discussion about creating a joint payment system between the BRICS countries – Brazil, Russia, India, China, and South Africa – continues. Additionally, their manoeuvres encompass measures to build new economies, chase a shared reserve currency, and employ digital and digital currency systems.

Transition from Unipolar to Multipolar Global Systems

The world's financial system has been mostly unipolar, with everything based on the U.S. dollar and its institutions (the IMF, the World Bank). This focus has empowered some countries to dominate world economic policies unduly. For its part, the BRICS has called for a more equitable system that mirrors the varied economic facts of life in the 21st century. Creating the NDB and the CRA is a concrete commitment that can serve as a basis for avoiding financial relationships focusing on equality and mutual advantage between member nations (Ferragamo, 2024).

Potential of BRICS' Own Reserve Currency Initiatives

BRICS have even ventured to explore a common reserve currency, which is said to be the most audacious of initiatives undertaken by the group. They added that such a currency is designed to cut dependence on the U.S. dollar and protect national economies from outside pressure. The talks covered a currency to be backed by a basket of currencies of the BRICS member states, which is expected to be similar to a common currency, such as gold. Although it is far from certain that a single currency will be feasible — it will require an alignment of money management policies between disparate economies — the proposal reflects BRICS's focus on financial sovereignty and resilience.

Recent empirical evidence supports BRICS's evolving efforts toward reserve diversification through mechanisms such as local-currency trade and discussions of a potential common currency. Fliagin & Abdulganiyu (2025), in a dynamic panel analysis covering the period from 2006 to 2022, found that increased intra-BRICS trade conducted in national currencies has indeed contributed to a short-term reduction in the share of U.S. dollars held in member states' foreign exchange reserves. However, the study also reveals that these de-dollarization effects tend to diminish over time, suggesting that while national currency-based trade can alleviate dollar dependence temporarily, achieving durable reserve diversification remains a complex and long-term challenge. This nuanced result provides a strong empirical basis for the strategic monetary cooperation that is taking place within the BRICS. It underscores the futility of de-dollarization without deeper structural and institutional convergence.

Integration of Digital and Cryptocurrency Strategies

BRICS countries are leading the innovation in the state by using digital currencies for the financial system. They are all at their respective points in their own Central Bank Digital Currencies (CBDCs) journey to improve the quality of payments and financial inclusion and reduce payment costs. China, for example, has been experimenting with the digital yuan, and Russia is proposing the digital ruble to make cross-border transactions easier and less dependent on traditional payment systems.

BRICS has also introduced its decentralized payment system, which has been promoted to accelerate the crediting of cross-border transactions between member countries. These networks would facilitate quicker payments and a level playing field for global financial flows, loosening the grip of today's Western-controlled financial networks (Pistilli, 2025).

This is consistent with broader global movements of monetary innovation, for example, the BRICS group embracing digital financial architecture, from the digital BRICS Pay system to the Central Bank Digital Currencies (CBDCs). Laboure et al. (2021) extensively study cryptos and CBDC, stressing how these technologies are restructuring international monetary exchanges. Their analysis points to several factors propelling experimentation with digital currencies, including gains in payment system efficiency, better access to financial services and strategic autonomy from Western-dominated networks. Crucially, it illustrates how prospective national CBDC deployments will likely undermine current financial hierarchies and expedite monetary decentralization, with this accelerating particularly in Asia and Europe. Including these perspectives also reinforces the portrait that BRICS' digital projects are not so much isolated experiments as part of the worldwide drive to reshape cross-border payments and mitigate systemic dependence on entrenched reserve currencies. By incorporating these regional viewpoints, the chapter highlights that the fintech aspirations of BRICS reflect international reform pathways and are part of a more plural financial order.

The BRICS countries are redefining the institutional framework of global finance by practising institutional innovation, trying to build a common reserve currency, and encouraging the development of digital finance. These common efforts aspire for a fairer, representative, multipolar financial architecture that favours developing countries with reduced systemic risk.

FUTURE PROSPECTS OF BRICS IN GLOBAL FINANCIAL GOVERNANCE

Naturally, with the transformation of the world economic configuration in which deepening geopolitical contradictions, digitalization, and systematic trade and finance changes coexist, BRICS is bound to play an even more critical role in forming global financial governance. With growing capabilities and political alignments, the bloc is finding it easier to challenge established power structures and offer viable alternatives based on equality, diversity and sustainability. However, a long and winding road of complex institutional challenges and opportunities will shape the impact of BRICS as a transformative force.

SCENARIOS FOR GLOBAL MONETARY STABILITY

In the next couple of years, the degree to which BRICS will be able to affect international monetary stability will be associated with its internal integration and the need to articulate a clear vision of the current financial system. Stroke said three types of situations were likely.

De Facto to a Multipolar Reserve System: BRICS initiatives (local currency trade settlements, currency swaps, diversification of reserves) would gradually reduce dependence on the global dollar and Euro. The former could help stabilize the financial system and spread global liquidity risks, while providing developing economies with insurance against exogenous shocks.

BRICS Reserve Currency: If BRICS can develop a joint reserve currency or a standard digital payments system, it can alter the global dynamics of financial power equations. This would help to stabilize trade within — and outside of — the bloc, shield against sanctions and enhance the robustness of international financial flows.

Enhanced Crisis Management Tools: With instruments such as the CRA, BRICS could continue to develop as a viable alternative response in the face of a crisis. By expanding the speed, reach and access to such facilities, the BRICS can underpin wider global monetary stability, especially in the Global South.

Moreover, in each of these cases, the capacity of BRICS to offer a counter-cyclical balance while mitigating a monopoly risk inherent to a unipolar currency regime will be instrumental in bringing about a new shape of international finance.

ROLE IN SUSTAINABLE ECONOMIC DEVELOPMENT

BRICS has recently promoted sustainable development as a part of its financial governance strategy. The NDB has emerged as a key infrastructure and green growth financing instrument in member and non-member countries. Its project pipeline includes renewable energy, water sanitation, transport, and urban resilience, all aligned with the UN's Sustainable Development Goals (SDGs).

Key contributions that BRICS can make to sustainable economic development include the following:

Mobilizing climate finance and promoting a just energy transition, particularly in Africa, Latin America and Southern Asia.

Facilitating sharing and pooling of green technology and investment among BRICS countries supported by BRICS-owned knowledge platforms and innovation centres.

Providing 'bankable' infrastructure finance to everyone (including the local community), and not quite abiding by global standards, without that meaning that the contractual obligations to be met are precisely the same as those that the traditional lenders want.

This will fill a substantial funding gap and recast development finance in line with the new values of mutual respect, inclusion and ecological soundness.

CHALLENGES AND PROSPECTS FOR FURTHER INTEGRATION

Even as BRICS may look toward the future with hope, the road to deeper integration is fraught with challenges. One of the main problems is the striking diversity, massive economic and political differences, various macroeconomic policies, regulatory regimes and strategic interests of its members. This diversity makes establishing consensus decision-making and policy coherence hard to achieve. The problem is compounded by the lack of an institutional mechanism or permanent secretariat to coordinate and consolidate the efforts among the bloc. And there are, in addition, external pressures, including those arising from the imposition of sanctions on member states during the Ukraine crisis, financial markets that have gone haywire, and the changing logistics of international politics, all of which undermine the coherence of the EU and put its strategic discipline and unity to the test in an increasingly uncertain world.

When other emerging economies like Africa, Latin America or the Middle East are invited to become BRICS in, the impact and credibility of BRICS will be dramatically increased. Such expansion, when integrated digitally through interoperable CBDCs, blockchain and AI-based Fintechs, can bring efficiency, transparency, and scale to the BRICS financial system. In addition, more closely aligned responses from member states would allow BRICS to promote better systemic reforms in major multilateral fora such as the G20, the IMF and the WTO. Strategically, BRICS could also gain from the crafting of a full-fledged financial architecture covering trade and investment settlement, investment safeguard, development financing and macroeconomic surveillance, which could serve as a nucleus that evolves to greater institutionalization and coherence in governance. The BRICS's aspirational future in global financial governance is bold and increasingly realistic. The EU can credibly contribute to an era of monetary rebalancing, resilience and sustainability via innovative, inclusive cooperation and reform-minded activism. At a time when the world requires credible alternatives to a failing and unjust financial system, BRICS is at a historic crossroads; BRICS is not only joining global economic governance, but also charting its path with a view to future generations.

The Union faces institutional fragmentation, geopolitical diversity and no formal mechanism to coordinate national policies. BRICS sees the need to build capacity by bridging the global South and North gap. To develop their potential into actionable policy items. Global money is the foundation of some of the distortions plaguing the world economy today, the collapse of the USSR and the growth of globalization; we are still very much in the dollar era. Leveraging their influence, the BRICS-Plus moment must overcome internal differences, create institutions and navigate complex geopolitics via diplomacy to realize its de-dollarization aims and systemic monetary reform agenda. While bodies such as the Contingent Reserve Arrangement (CRA) have been put in place and the talk of a shared reserve currency continues, efforts might fail without enough institutional trust and operational cooperation. Conflicting national interests, different economic capacities, and a lack of a central coordinating mechanism also limit the capacity of the country to act in unison. Establishing a permanent secretariat/a BRICS Financial Coordinating Office is a crucial move towards institutional maturity that will help BRICS harmonize strategies and policy coordination and guarantee the credibility and sustainability of the bloc's monetary experiments.

RECOMMENDATIONS AND SOLUTIONS

For BRICS to reach its goals and make the shaping of the world monetary system sustainable and inclusive, it requires a more multidimensional and forward-looking strategy which strengthens its internal solidarity, deepens its monetary cooperation, and ensures its long-term financial robustness. Given the gain in the economic and geopolitical stakes that Brazil, Russia, India, and China are achieving, the bloc has a timely role to play in this way, such that they may take the lead in changing global financial governance.

Still, overcoming institutional fragmentation and geopolitical diversity within the organization is no mean feat. One key initial step would be establishing a permanent secretariat or coordination institution – possibly a central BRICS Financial Coordination Office – to help coordinate policies, oversee the implementation of joint financial projects and design a common strategy. It would normalize intra-bloc operations and consolidate the BRICS financial identity as a stable and proactive international financial presence.

No less significant is the rapid realization that an outright BRICS reserve currency is advancing, which will reduce dependence on key reserve currencies such as the U.S. dollar and the Euro. This currency, which could be linked to a weighted basket of BRICS member currencies and supported by member countries' strong domestic and digital infrastructure, would be beneficial, as it would not only improve financial independence but also ease intra-BRICS trade and investment. A special high-level task force comprising central bank heads, financial gurus, and economists should be responsible for researching, modelling and piloting this initiative, leveraging the wisdom from regional currency unions and digital monetary innovations.

In tandem with financial diversification, BRICS should invest adequate resources in digital financial infrastructure, namely interoperable Central Bank Digital Currency (CBDC) and blockchain payment platforms. These technologies have the potential to revolutionize cross-border transactions, reducing their time and cost while making them more transparent and less dependent on financial intermediation by Western-controlled institutions. A BRICS Digital Clearing System based on a secure distributed ledger technology and accommodating the national CBDCs could become a game changer in settling trade transactions and digital asset operations across the bloc and other countries.

In light of this, BRICS should expand the developmental fruits of its financial institutions to other developing countries, especially those in the South. This can be done by devising an "Associate Membership" framework, enabling non-member countries to avail themselves of the NDB and CRA terms on mutually agreed terms. By extending its financial hegemony, BRICS can increase its power and emphasize South-South cooperation, which would challenge Anglo-American multilateral institutions.

Besides financial inclusion, BRICS must prioritize local currency trade and economic literacy projects to wean the member countries from foreign currencies. International currency swap maintains the liquidity and credibility between national currencies for global business. Such initiatives must be accompanied by a complete financial literacy campaign at the political, business, and public levels to explain the positive features of local currency and digital finance tools.

BRICS must develop an intense macroeconomic surveillance and early warning mechanism to protect against vulnerability to external shocks, including sanctions, volatility in commodity prices and global financial instability. "The establishment of a BRICS Economic Stability Observatory would help in tracking risk indicators such as inflation, capital flows and currency volatility and enabling timely coordinated policy action among BRICS countries," he added.

Creating a BRICS Financial Innovation Academy as a capacity-building platform would provide policymakers, regulators, and financial practitioners with adequate capabilities to deal with new technologies, regulatory issues, and evolving global economic developments. The academy could be a training, research and innovation hub in areas like blockchain, AI in finance, digital identity, and ESG-aligned investment.

Together, these strategic policies, suggestions, and practical recommendations are formulated to maximize the role of BRICS as a transformative factor in reforming the world of finance. Through institutionalized cooperation, financial innovations and inclusive development, BRICS could transform from a regional bloc into a driver of a new, multipolar and equitable international monetary system based on the principles of addressing the systemic disorders and vulnerabilities that have plagued the global financial order for decades.

FUTURE RESEARCH DIRECTION

The BRICS countries are starting to play a more substantial role in affecting the governance of the global economy, and future research needs to go beyond descriptive and increasingly become a solid base of empirical evidence that can inform policy and strategy development. The transformation of BRICS from a political-economic coalition to the architect of a BRICS-type multipolar monetary order presents the international relations scholar with a to-do list of future research projects. Multiple future research lines will enable a broader overview of this developing framework.

First, one of the most pressing areas to be investigated is the possibility and implications of creating a single BRICS reserve currency. Although plans for such a currency, backed by a basket of national currencies and perhaps commodities, have received attention, academic studies must rigorously explore its potential consequences. Future investigations should focus on the macroeconomic convergence needed, the political desire among the BRICS members, and the operation of such a system. Based on experiences like those of the Eurozone or regional currency boards, researchers can make comparative studies and simulations of the consequences of inflation, trade balance, monetary sovereignty, and systemic stability. Such studies would provide relevant information to governments contemplating adopting some form of common currency.

Second, the digital currency and techno-interoperability of the BRICS countries need to be studied in depth. As individual member countries advance at varying speeds in developing their Central Bank Digital Currencies (CBDCs), increasing attention must be paid to how these digital systems can be made compatible. Further research using the use-case example should be dedicated to the technical specification of cross-border blockchain-based clearing systems and digital financial ecosystems associated regulatory, privacy, and cybersecurity aspects. Furthermore, the legal and regulatory aspects of transnational DCEP use (e.g., jurisdiction and compliance issues, data localization, etc.) should be investigated to guarantee harmonizing regulations among the BRICS.

Another crucial research study is about the BRICS multilateral cooperation model, more specifically, the institutional performance of the NDB and CRA. Academics could review these institutions' performances, governance, and transparency compared with well-established institutions such as the International Monetary Fund (IMF), the World Bank, and the Asian Infrastructure Investment Bank (AIIB). Through such comparative institutional analysis, one can recommend best practices, narrow areas for improvement , and suggest improvements that enhance the credibility and global status of BRICS in DF.

Furthermore, the regional and international spillover effects of BRICS monetary strategies are also worth attention. BRICS is also growing in its influence through regional currency swap agreements and Internet payment plans, so it is necessary to measure how these changes affect neighbouring economies, such as those in Africa, Latin America, Southeast Asia, and other parts of the world. It is recommended that future studies assess the implications of BRICS-initiated projects for trade diversity, debt sustainability and financial inclusion in these countries. By doing so, these dynamics would provide a global context in which BRICS can be an economic generator for the Global South.

Relevant studies should also examine the geoeconomic and geopolitical risks of BRICS monetary cooperation. In an era of sanctions, trade disruptions, and rapidly changing loyalties, scenario-based modelling can be helpful to preclude surprises and inform the development of contingencies. Researchers also need to develop the theory and tools of risk analysis to assess how changes in global politics impact BRICS' financial strategies and resilience.

Another less studied dimension is the behavioural and political economy of currency adoption. The success of BRICS financial instruments requires policy, infrastructure, and public and institutional confidence. Studies that cut across behavioural economics, psychology, and political science may shed light on attitudes, resistance, and diffusion processes related to sponsoring BRICS currencies on financial instruments.

Since ESG (Environmental, Social, Governance) principles are increasingly relevant to global finance, future research could examine how BRICS financial institutions integrate ESG metrics in project selection, funding decisions, and performance monitoring. Research in this space could consider alignment with the UN Sustainable Development Goals (SDGs), climate financing mechanisms, and social impact assessments.

Addressing these key research gaps would allow for greater nuance and empirical insight into the evolution of BRICS' role(s) in global finance and how they vary across members. This understanding will be critical in navigating future policy and institution building and creating an inclusive, sustainable and resilient BRICS-led financial order in an uncertain world.

DISCUSSION

The transformation of BRICS as a collective force in global financial governance is a significant challenge to the arcane world of Western-dominated currency systems that have ruled the roost for centuries. However, the BRICS countries – despite how they are characterized in terms of the political regimes, paths of economic development, and regional interests – support a more inclusive, equitable and multipolar financial regime, as this chapter has argued. From the launch of the NDB, the CRA, and new local and digital currency frameworks, their strategic chess pieces have dramatically moved in favour of increased monetary sovereignty and cooperation among South nations.

The ability of BRICS countries to coordinate their monetary policies to reach currency swaps and future standard reserve mechanisms is the bloc's attempt to handle systemic risks better and gain more independence from the global financial system. These are economic strategies and geoeconomics tools to deal with global financial vulnerabilities (sanctions, trade wars, geopolitical realignment, etc.).

At the same time, introducing digital financial instruments and technologies - e.g. Central Bank Digital Currencies (CBDC) and distributed ledger technology (DLT) based settlement infrastructures - creates various opportunities and challenges. On the contrary, these mechanisms can enhance the efficiency of transactions and enlarge the financing scope of cross-border transactions inside and outside the BRICS region. To ensure that trust and stability are not undermined, these must be managed with sensitivity in the face of concerns over regulatory fragmentation, cybersecurity and data sovereignty.

The discussion also highlights the geopolitics of BRICS exchange rate policies. The BRICS countries have stepped up efforts to build alternatives, with traditional powers using sanctions and weaponizing finance with increasing frequency. These responses are not reactive because they endeavour to build a new normative foundation for financial governance that seeks a trade-off between bilateralism and multilateralism and one that emphasizes sovereignty, development and win-win rather than conditionality and dependency.

BRICS, though, has its share of problems even as it grows as a force to reckon with. The lack of institutional focus, with members varying widely in terms of economic importance and strategic interests, and the lack of a standing secretariat or apparatus of joint enforcement also limit the organization. Furthermore, it is questionable whether such a thing as a common reserve or a standard financial system could exist without a much greater degree of economic or even political convergence.

BRICS has shown itself capable of influencing global financial discourse ever-increasingly. BRICS is reacting to changing imbalances and shaping the future of international monetary politics. They're a reminder that diversification, regional cooperation, and innovation for an inclusive global economy are key to such system building.

It clarifies that BRICS is a 'subjective' force in the global economy and an agency that wants to impact international financial relations. An Expanded World of Geopolitical Uncertainty and All, as BRICS underlined- alternative institutions, technologies and methodologies would ensure a more multipolar world with a more equilibrated global monetary system, which is much nearer to everywhere.

CONCLUSION

Guiding world monetary systems for decades have proven rigid frameworks, and our changing world of international finance needs dynamic, inclusive and resilient alternatives. This is where BRICS enters, not as a loose coalition of emerging markets but as a bargaining player wanting to restructure the foundations of international monetary governance. Through institutions such as the New Development Bank and the Contingent Reserve Arrangement, BRICS demonstrated the ability to be a credible alternative for development financing and monetary stability outside a few reserve currencies.

The united efforts of the block to diminish the dependence on dollar transactions, the promotion of local currencies in bilateral trade, the quest for a common reserve currency, and the endless rehearsals of digital currency rollout show us its broader goal to foster a fair, independent and cooperative (multipolar) world economic order. The BRICS bloc is a group of institutional strong vitality, geographical expansion, strategic homogeneity, but also suffers from different economic development, domestic and foreign geopolitical friction, fragmentation trends, surface global Asia, and Africa force covers up the problem.

BRICS is enlarging its membership, which has sparked new interest in the changing role of the bloc in global financial governance. De Carvalho et al. (2025), writing from a South African standpoint, pose the question of whether this enlargement constitutes an adaptation to reality or reflects a deliberate, programmed attempt to create these new norms of world governance. Their analysis sets out a central tension: BRICS may either reinforce its power by working within the existing international system or confront and transform it by creating alternative and more inclusive structures. The uncertainty raises questions about the bloc's ability to get beyond symbolic opposition and push for structural change. Moreover, as BRICS expands, its strategic direction — reformist incrementalism versus wholesale systemic transformation — will have profound implications for the global distribution of economic power and its effect on the prospects of emerging and developing countries in the Global South. As BRICS continues to develop, financial diversity, inclusion, and sustainable development will play an essential part in the BRICS agenda of building a more equitable world economy. The direction of the bloc's evolution appears ineluctably toward reform and a radical reimagining of global trade and finance for the 21st century.

REFERENCES

Aydın, F. (2025). BRICS: The archetype of 21st century international cooperation alternative or challenge? In Yazdani, E. (Ed.), *Implications, prospects, and challenges in China's Global South strategy* (pp. 207–232). IGI Global. DOI: 10.4018/979-8-3373-0938-5.ch008

De Carvalho, G., Anand, J., & Naidu, S. (2025). BRICS expansion: Adaptive response or proactive restructuring of global governance? *The South African Journal of International Affairs*, 1–24. DOI: 10.1080/10220461.2025.2525312

De Freitas, M. V. (2025). *BRICS: A new framework for New South inclusiveness*. Policy Center for the New South. https://www.policycenter.ma/publications/brics-new-framework-new-south-inclusiveness

Desai, R. M., & Vreeland, J. R. (2011). Global governance in a multipolar world: The case for regional monetary funds. *International Studies Review*, *13*(1), 109–121. DOI: 10.1111/j.1468-2486.2010.01002.x

Ferragamo, M. (2024). From dollar dependency to BRICS autonomy: Legal and economic impacts on global trade governance. *Acta Universitatis Danubius Oeconomica*, *20*(6), 21–38. https://www.researchgate.net/publication/387275679_From_Dollar_Dependency_to_BRICS_Autonomy_Legal_and_Economic_Impacts_on_Global_Trade_Governance

Ferragamo, M. (2025). *What is the BRICS group and why is it expanding?* Council on Foreign Relations. https://www.cfr.org/backgrounder/what-brics-group-and-why-it-expanding

Fliagin, D., & Abdulganiyu, M. (2025). Impact of intra-BRICS trade on the share of United States dollar in international reserve composition. *BRICS Journal of Economics*, *6*(2), 5–20. DOI: 10.3897/brics-econ.6.e143810

Freidin, E. (2024). *BRICS Pay as a challenge to SWIFT network*. Lowy Institute. https://www.lowyinstitute.org/the-interpreter/brics-pay-challenge-swift-network

Gupta, P. (2025). BRICS vs G7: The data behind the new global economic power shift. *Medium*. https://medium.com/@guptaprashant0999/brics-vs-g7-the-data-behind-the-new-global-economic-power-shift-b2ef15f7c12b

Helmy, N. (2025). BRICS' game-changing blockchain payment system: The future of global transactions. *Modern Diplomacy*. https://moderndiplomacy.eu/2025/03/27/brics-game-changing-blockchain-payment-system-the-future-of-global-transactions/

Keohane, R. O. (1984). *After hegemony: Cooperation and discord in the world political economy*. Princeton University Press. DOI: 10.2307/j.ctt7sq9s

Kindleberger, C. P. (2013). *The world in depression, 1929–1939*. University of California Press. https://www.ucpress.edu/books/the-world-in-depression-1929-1939/paper

Krishna, E. S. A., Tom, A., & Joseph, D. (2025). Evaluating the impact of BRICS+ trade policies: A comparative analysis before and after the Russia-Ukraine conflict. In Mbandlwa, Z., Netswera, F. G., & Smirnov, S. A. (Eds.), *Analyzing the impact of BRICS+ nations' trade policies on global economies* (pp. 123–144). IGI Global. DOI: 10.4018/979-8-3693-7969-1.ch005

Kumar, S., Menon, V. A., Kumar, S. T. K., Gupta, A., Shivani, A., Thomas, L. P., & Thomas, J. (2025). Evolving trade patterns in BRICS: An examination of export, import, and GDP trends from 1971 to 2020. In Mbandlwa, Z., Netswera, F. G., & Smirnov, S. A. (Eds.), *Analyzing the impact of BRICS+ nations' trade policies on global economies* (pp. 31–52). IGI Global. DOI: 10.4018/979-8-3693-7969-1.ch002

Laboure, M., Müller, M. H.-P., Heinz, G., Singh, S., & Köhling, S. (2021). Cryptocurrencies and CBDC: The route ahead. *Global Policy, 12*(5), 98–110. DOI: 10.1111/1758-5899.13017

Luttwak, E. N. (1990). From geopolitics to geoeconomics: Logic of conflict, grammar of commerce. *National Interest*, (20), 17–23. https://www.jstor.org/stable/42894676

McDowell, D. (2023). *Bucking the buck: U.S. financial sanctions and the international backlash against the dollar*. Oxford University Press. DOI: 10.1093/oso/9780197679876.001.0001

Pistilli, M. (2025). How would a new BRICS currency affect the U.S. dollar? *Investing News Network*. https://investingnews.com/brics-currency/

Saaida, M. (2024). BRICS Plus: De-dollarization and global power shifts in new economic landscape. *BRICS Journal of Economics, 5*(1), 13–33. DOI: 10.3897/brics-econ.5.e117828

Sailesh, B. (2025). Bridging geopolitics and sustainability: BRICS' impact on global tourism. In Mbandlwa, Z., Netswera, F. G., & Smirnov, S. A. (Eds.), *Analyzing the impact of BRICS+ nations' trade policies on global economies* (pp. 219–262). IGI Global. DOI: 10.4018/979-8-3693-7969-1.ch008

Sönmez, A., Uysal, D., & Amirzai, F. R. (2025). Importance of BRICS countries in the world economy. In Gedikli, A., Erdogan, S., & Çalışkan Terzioğlu, H. (Eds.), *Changing the global political economy: BRICS countries and alternative relations strategies* (pp. 1–48). IGI Global. DOI: 10.4018/979-8-3693-7393-4.ch001

KEY TERMS AND DEFINITIONS

Digital Currencies: Digital currencies refer to currencies that are only available in electronic or digital form, consisting of decentralized cryptocurrencies, such as Bitcoin, and centralized Central Bank Digital Currencies (CBDCs). They allow instant transactions and transfer of ownership across borders, without the need for cash or banks.

Geoeconomics: Geoeconomics is the strategic use of economic instruments to accomplish geopolitical ends. It includes tactics in which countries use trade, investment, energy supplies, and financial tools to shift global power structures and advance national interests.

Geopolitics: Geopolitics is a field of study examining how geography, political borders, and strategic interests impact nations' relationships and power structures. It shows how certain countries wield diplomatic leverage, military force, and/or alliances to dominate global affairs.

Global Monetary Systems: The international monetary system is the institutional arrangement supporting conducive economic activities within and among countries. It is a medium for trade, investment, and economic stability between nations, and it is mainly dominated by currencies such as the U.S. dollar and the Euro.

New Development Bank (NDB): The New Development Bank is a multilateral development bank established by the BRICS countries in 2014 to finance infrastructure and sustainable development projects in EMDCs. It is meant to be an alternative for Western-dominated institutions such as the World Bank and the IMF, with the group concentrating on sovereignty, inclusivity and lending in local currency.

Reserve Currencies: National banks and other major financial institutions hold a reserve currency in significant quantities as part of their foreign exchange reserves. The U.S. dollar, the Euro, and more recently, the Chinese yuan, are used in international transactions, investments and global trade settlements primarily because they are more stable and liquid.

Chapter 5
Economic Disruptions and Business Risks:
The Role of Regional Conflicts in Global Trade

Rismawati Rismawati
https://orcid.org/0000-0001-8046-6764
Universitas Muhammadiyah Palopo, Indonesia

S. Sumarni
https://orcid.org/0000-0003-0021-0721
Universitas Wira Bhakti, Indonesia

Baso R.
https://orcid.org/0000-0003-2894-4735
Universitas Wira Bhakti, Indonesia

Himani Thakur
Chandigarh Group of Colleges Jhanjeri, Mohali, India

ABSTRACT

Increasing geopolitical conflicts cause formerly unheard-of disruptions in global trade. This chapter looks at how regional conflicts—including the Russia-Ukraine war, US-China trade tensions, and Middle East instability—affect international trade, energy markets, supply chains, and corporate risk policies. Financial volatility brought on by economic penalties, protectionist policies, and trade realignment has driven multinational companies (MNCs) to embrace diversification, nearshoring, and digital transformation plans. To improve corporate resilience, the chapter looks at risk management strategies including geopolitics forecasting, artificial intelligence-driven analytics, and policy changes. Furthermore, under examination

DOI: 10.4018/979-8-3373-7907-4.ch005

is how international organizations like the WTO and IMF help to reduce trade conflicts. Understanding the changing link between geoeconomics and business risks will help governments and companies to apply flexible trade models to properly negotiate world uncertainty.

1. INTRODUCTION

1.1 Characterizing Economic Disruptions in a Globalized Economy

While many geopolitical risks are global in scope, firms respond to them differently depending on their size, industry affiliation, and geographic exposure. Multinational corporations with diverse supply chains typically invest more in proactive risk management systems, whereas small and medium-sized enterprises (SMEs) often adopt reactive strategies due to limited resources. For example, MNCs may establish regional risk committees, hedge currency exposure, or relocate sensitive operations, while SMEs tend to rely on ad-hoc adaptation or local partnerships.

Industrial context also plays a critical role. Energy and mining firms operating in politically unstable regions may face threats to asset security, requiring intensive political risk insurance and government engagement strategies. In contrast, service-oriented or digital firms may focus more on cyber threats, digital sovereignty, or regulatory fragmentation. Additionally, geography matters: firms based in emerging economies are typically more vulnerable to abrupt regulatory shifts and often lack institutional support compared to firms in OECD countries.

Recognizing this heterogeneity is essential for developing tailored resilience strategies. Future business models must account not only for geopolitical risk per se, but also for how firm characteristics condition their capacity to respond, adapt, or transform under systemic uncertainty. Economic disruptions denote substantial disturbances in the operation of markets, financial institutions, and trade networks, frequently instigated by external shocks such as geopolitical conflicts, economic crises, or governmental changes (Bednarski et al., 2024). In international trade, economic disruptions occur via supply chain bottlenecks, currency volatility, trade embargoes, and investor fear. The increase in global interconnection has intensified the effects of these disruptions, enabling localized conflicts to generate extensive instability across several economic sectors.

The influence of global interconnection on economic stability is seen in the configuration of contemporary supply chains. Multinational corporations (MNCs) function within a highly interconnected network where raw materials, manufacturing processes, and distribution channels traverse multiple geopolitical regions.

Disruptions in a specific region—such as armed war, political sanctions, or trade restrictions—can reverberate throughout the global economy, impacting firms, employment rates, and national economic performance (Herold & Marzantowicz, 2023 & Duong et al., 2024). The COVID-19 pandemic underscored the vulnerability of global supply systems, as lockdowns and trade restrictions resulted in shortages of key supplies, heightened transportation costs, and inflationary pressures globally. Likewise, the Russia-Ukraine conflict led to escalating energy costs, interrupted agricultural exports, and increased volatility in financial markets.

Historically, economic volatility resulting from geopolitical wars has been a persistent occurrence. The two World Wars resulted in significant disruptions to global trade, culminating in economic collapse and enduring changes in industrial output. The Gulf War (1990-1991) significantly influenced global oil markets, resulting in price instability and energy insecurity. The U.S.-China trade war, initiated in 2018, impacted global trade dynamics, resulting in supply chain alterations and policy modifications by multinational firms. These examples highlight the profound vulnerabilities inside the global economic system, where political and military conflicts yield substantial financial and commercial repercussions. As regional conflicts intensify globally, businesses, policymakers, and international organizations must create solutions to alleviate economic disruptions (Yu et al., 2021 & Rabbi et al., 2023). By examining historical precedents and comprehending the mechanisms by which geopolitical conflicts influence commerce and markets, stakeholders may formulate robust economic policies and corporate strategies to manage risks in an increasingly linked world.

1.2 The Ascendancy of Regional Conflicts and Their Global Economic Consequences

The rising prevalence of regional wars has emerged as a significant catalyst for instability in the global economy, disrupting trade flows, financial markets, and industrial supply chains. In recent decades, global geopolitical tensions have escalated, with conflicts in the Middle East, Eastern Europe, and Asia-Pacific markedly impacting economic stability (Kuhla et al., 2023; Chen & Zhao, 2023; Estrada & Koutronas, 2022). In contrast to previous localized battles, contemporary regional disagreements have worldwide implications owing to the significant economic interconnectedness among countries. Elements such as trade sanctions, military involvement, and interruptions to critical industries intensify the economic ramifications, resulting in inflationary pressures, labor shortages, and diminished investment confidence.

A significant effect of regional conflicts is the alteration of economic alliances and international trade blocs. Historically, free trade agreements and multinational entities like the World Trade Organization (WTO) and the European Union (EU) have promoted open markets and international economic collaboration (Gereffi et al., 2021; Mariotti, 2022; Meyer et al., 2023). Nonetheless, the escalation of geopolitical tensions has led numerous countries to emphasize economic nationalism and protectionism, culminating in trade realignments. The U.S.-China trade conflict has compelled nations to reassess their supply chain linkages, resulting in the diversification of trade alliances and enhanced regional economic collaboration beyond conventional Western-dominated frameworks. The Russia-Ukraine conflict has compelled European countries to diminish their reliance on Russian energy, expediting the shift towards renewable energy sources and alternative suppliers.

Numerous case studies underscore the significant economic repercussions of regional wars on international trade. The Russia-Ukraine conflict, initiated in 2022, interrupted essential supply routes, especially in the energy and agricultural sectors. Russia is a main provider of oil and natural gas, whilst Ukraine is a significant exporter of wheat and corn. The battle resulted in escalating oil prices, worldwide food insecurity, and inflationary pressures on both emerging and established countries. Conflicts in the Middle East, such the Saudi-Yemen war and the Israel-Palestine dilemma, have influenced oil markets, resulting in price volatility and supply interruptions. The persistent tensions in the South China Sea, characterized by territorial disputes among China, Taiwan, and other nations, threaten global trade routes, especially with maritime logistics and semiconductor manufacturing (Abdelsalam, 2023; Fasanya et al., 2021). As regional conflicts persist in influencing the global economic framework, enterprises and governments must adjust to the evolving geopolitical environment. Comprehending the economic ramifications of these conflicts is crucial for formulating resilience solutions that alleviate risks and guarantee economic stability in an increasingly unpredictable environment.

1.3 Geopolitical Risks as a Business Challenge in the Twenty-First Century

The 21st century has experienced a notable transition from economic integration to economic fragmentation, propelled by increasing geopolitical concerns and regional conflicts. The globalization period, marked by open markets and unobstructed international trade, is increasingly confronted with protectionist measures, trade conflicts, and security apprehensions. Numerous countries are emphasizing national interests at the expense of economic collaboration, resulting in a decrease in multilateral agreements and a reorganization of supply networks (Luo, 2024). The U.S.-China trade war, Brexit, and Russia's geopolitical seclusion resulting from the Ukraine conflict exemplify the transformation of global commerce through economic fragmentation. Enterprises that formerly depended on secure international trade accords must now maneuver through an erratic landscape characterized by tariffs, penalties, and political uncertainty that undermine conventional business models. In reaction to geopolitical uncertainty, regulatory and policy changes have emerged as a crucial strategy for governments to protect national security and economic sovereignty (Luo, 2024 & Edler et al., 2023).

Countries are implementing more stringent trade rules, investment limitations, and export regulations to alleviate dangers linked to hostile states. The European Union's Carbon Border Adjustment Mechanism (CBAM) and the United States' CHIPS and Science Act, designed to diminish dependence on Chinese semiconductor production, illustrate how governments are reconfiguring industries to safeguard vital economic interests. Moreover, economic sanctions—like those enacted against Russia—have estranged significant entities from the global financial system, compelling impacted enterprises to pursue alternate markets and suppliers. These policy modifications compel firms to reevaluate their risk exposure and compliance measures to avert regulatory penalties and guarantee business continuity (Wilhelm, 2024). Corporate reactions to changing geopolitical concerns have become essential to strategic planning. Businesses are progressively implementing risk mitigation methods, including supply chain diversification, nearshoring, and digital transformation, to diminish reliance on politically problematic areas (Settembre-Blundo et al., 2021 & Giuffrida et al., 2021).

Multinational corporations (MNCs) are relocating production from high-risk regions to more stable economies, thereby enhancing their capacity to respond to abrupt geopolitical disruptions. Many global technology companies have diminished their dependence on China for production and have redirected their investments towards Southeast Asian and Indian markets. Moreover, enterprises are utilizing sophisticated data analytics and artificial intelligence to observe geopolitical changes in real time, facilitating more responsive decision-making. As geopolitical risks persist in disrupting global company operations, organizations must implement robust policies that guarantee stability in the face of uncertainty. Adapting to economic fragmentation, ensuring compliance with legislative changes, and executing proactive risk management strategies will be crucial for sustained success in a progressively turbulent global economy.

2. GEOPOLITICAL SHOCKS AND BUSINESS VULNERABILITIES

2.1 Disruptions in the Supply Chain: Immediate and Prolonged Consequences

In a time of intensified geopolitical instability, global supply chains are increasingly vulnerable to both short-term and long-term disruptions. These disruptions arise from various interconnected sources, including operational failures at essential trade chokepoints, the enforcement of sanctions and trade limitations, and alterations in regulatory frameworks. This section integrates these dimensions by initially exploring the characteristics and ramifications of supply chain disruptions, subsequently assessing the impact of sanctions and export controls, and ultimately delineating corporate strategies designed to maintain continuity and resilience amid geopolitical uncertainty.

Global supply chains depend on interconnected trade networks and essential transport routes to enable the efficient movement of goods and raw materials. Nonetheless, regional conflicts have progressively interrupted these vital supply chains, resulting in economic instability across all sectors. Critical trade routes and chokepoints, like the Suez Canal, the Strait of Hormuz, the Panama Canal, and the Malacca Strait, are essential to global commerce. Any interruption in these corridors—whether from military wars, blockades, or sanctions—can significantly affect the movement of commodities, resulting in supply shortages, elevated transportation costs, and postponed production cycles. The 2021 Suez Canal blockade, resulting from a grounded vessel rather than a battle, underscored the susceptibility of global trade to interruptions in essential waterways, incurring billions of dollars in damages within days(Yu et al., 2021 & Bednarski et al., 2024).

Regional conflicts significantly influence raw material availability, logistics, and worldwide production, impacting sectors reliant on geographically concentrated resources. Numerous critical raw materials, including oil, gas, rare earth metals, and agricultural commodities, are extracted from politically volatile areas. The Russia-Ukraine conflict has interrupted global supply of wheat, corn, and fertilizers, intensifying food security issues and escalating inflation in underdeveloped nations (Ben Hassen and El Bilali, 2022; Nasir et al., 2022). Likewise, conflicts in the Middle East, including those in Yemen and the Persian Gulf, have consistently jeopardized global oil and gas exports, resulting in fluctuating energy prices and supply instability for industrial output globally. The interruption of logistics infrastructure—such as ports, trains, and air freight facilities—exacerbates these difficulties, hindering organizations' ability to sustain constant operations.

Numerous case studies demonstrate the immediate and prolonged impacts of supply chain disruptions resulting from regional wars. The global semiconductor shortage that commenced in 2020 was exacerbated by geopolitical tensions, notably U.S.-China trade restrictions and the Taiwan Strait dispute, disrupting supply chains for businesses dependent on microchips, including automobiles and consumer electronics (Hamdani & Belfencha, 2024). Likewise, apprehensions over food security have intensified due to conflict-induced export prohibitions, resulting in price increases and shortages in at-risk countries. The energy scarcity problem resulting from Russia's invasion of Ukraine has compelled European nations to reevaluate their energy dependencies, hastening the transition to renewable sources and alternative suppliers.

As disputes persist in disrupting global trade networks, enterprises and policymakers must design robust supply chain policies. By diversifying sourcing areas, utilizing technological improvements, and enhancing regional trade alliances, economies can reduce the risks associated with geopolitical instability and assure improved supply chain continuity throughout time.

2.2 Sanctions, Trade Restrictions, and Export Regulations

Economic sanctions, trade obstacles, and export controls have become as potent geopolitical instruments that profoundly impact multinational corporations (MNCs) and global supply chains. Governments implement these measures in reaction to regional conflicts, human rights abuses, or national security issues (Le et al., 2022; Meyer et al., 2023; Le & Bach, 2022).

Nevertheless, although designed to exert pressure on specific states, these measures frequently result in unforeseen economic repercussions, disrupting global trade and supply systems. Sanctions imposed on Russia after to its incursion into Ukraine exemplify recent measures that curtail its access to global banking networks, immobilize assets, and impede commerce in energy, raw resources, and technology. This has compelled global corporations to either exit the Russian market or reorganize their supply chains to adhere to new laws. Sanctions imposed on Iran and North Korea have restricted their access to international financial systems, impacting businesses dependent on essential raw commodities like oil, gas, and rare metals.

The emergence of protectionist policies and reshoring movements has significantly altered global trade and industrial output. As countries endeavor to diminish dependence on antagonistic nations, numerous have enacted strategies to reshore (repatriate manufacturing to domestic territories) or nearshore (transfer production to proximate, allied states) (Van and Dobrzykowski, 2021; Tsai and Urmetzer, 2024). The U.S.-China trade war expedited the United States' initiatives to diminish reliance on Chinese manufacturing, resulting in heightened investments in American semiconductor and technology production under the CHIPS and Science Act. The European Union has likewise sought further autonomy in vital sectors including energy, medicines, and defense. Although these policies bolster national security and economic sovereignty, they concurrently elevate manufacturing costs, disrupt established supplier networks, and compel enterprises to adjust to new regulatory frameworks (Miró, 2023 & Schmitz and Seidl, 2023).

Export restrictions—particularly on essential resources and sophisticated technologies—constitute a substantial threat to supply chain stability. The U.S. and its allies have imposed restrictions on semiconductor shipments to China, disrupting the global electronics industry and resulting in shortages and increased costs for manufacturers. Likewise, restrictions on rare earth mineral exports from China—crucial for electronics, batteries, and renewable energy technologies—have heightened apprehensions regarding the durability of supply chains in the long run. Nations impacted by these restrictions are currently investing in alternative sources and supply chain diversification measures; nonetheless, the transition is both costly and time-consuming.

With economic penalties, trade obstacles, and export controls influencing global commerce, organizations must formulate proactive plans to manage geopolitical risks, diversify supply chains, and adhere to changing trade regulations. Ensuring resilience in this swiftly evolving environment necessitates vigilant observation of policy changes, prompt decision-making, and investment in regional collaborations to mitigate shocks and sustain competitiveness.

2.3 Strategic Business Responses to Supply Chain Vulnerabilities

In a time of escalating global instability, enterprises must implement strategic measures to alleviate supply chain risks and guarantee operational resilience. Supplier diversification and nearshoring techniques have become essential for firms seeking to mitigate reliance on high-risk areas (Fernández-Miguel et al., 2022 and Merino et al., 2021).

Historically, global supply chains depended on economically advantageous sourcing from a limited number of primary centers, such China for manufacturing and the Middle East for oil. Nonetheless, regional crises, trade barriers, and escalating geopolitical tensions have compelled firms to reevaluate these dependencies. Numerous multinational corporations (MNCs) are currently adopting multi-sourcing techniques, distributing production across various geographical zones to mitigate interruptions. Furthermore, nearshoring—shifting production closer to consumer markets—is gaining momentum. U.S. and European companies are progressively relocating manufacturing operations from Asia to Mexico and Eastern Europe, respectively, to mitigate vulnerability to trade barriers and political volatility.

The digitalization of supply chains and the implementation of blockchain technology are transforming the management of supply chain risks by organizations. Digital solutions offer immediate insight into supply chain operations, enabling companies to foresee problems and enhance logistics networks. Technologies including artificial intelligence (AI), predictive analytics, and Internet of Things (IoT) sensors empower firms to monitor shipments, identify risks, and enhance inventory management. Blockchain significantly improves supply chain transparency, security, and efficiency by establishing immutable transaction records and verifying the legitimacy of items (Hellani et al., 2021). Companies in the pharmaceutical and food sectors are progressively employing blockchain technology to authenticate the provenance and distribution of products, thereby mitigating the danger of counterfeit items and regulatory infractions. Through the utilization of digitization, enterprises may improve their agility and responsiveness in the face of geopolitical disruptions that jeopardize supply chains (Abdallah & Nizamuddin, 2023; Suresh et al., 2022; Panda & Satapathy, 2021).

To address geopolitical unpredictability, firms are adopting corporate mitigation strategies aimed at long-term resilience. Organizations are creating risk assessment models that integrate geopolitical intelligence, enabling them to foresee and address possible disruptions. The strategic accumulation of essential resources, especially in sectors like semiconductor fabrication and energy generation, has emerged as a critical strategy. Moreover, companies are reinforcing collaborations with local suppliers and investing in regional trade agreements to circumvent politically risky areas. Governments are actively providing incentives for enterprises to develop self-sufficient domestic production capabilities in critical sectors such as semiconductors, pharmaceuticals, and defense (Moschieri et al., 2024; Gooding et al., 2022). In light of ongoing regional conflicts affecting global supply chains, firms that aggressively diversify their suppliers, use digital innovations, and execute adaptable risk management methods will be optimally equipped to manage unpredictability and sustain a competitive advantage in the international market.

3. FINANCIAL VOLATILITY AND MARKET RISKS DURING REGIONAL CONFLICTS

3.1 Currency Volatility and Capital Exodus

Regional conflicts significantly influence foreign exchange markets, resulting in increased volatility, currency devaluation, and capital exodus from impacted economies. Geopolitical instability diminishes investor confidence, leading firms and financial institutions to retract their capital from high-risk areas.

This abrupt change in financial flows leads to currency volatility, causing impacted countries to undergo significant devaluations, while safe-haven currencies—such as the U.S. dollar, Swiss franc, and Japanese yen—appreciate in value. Fluctuations in exchange rates elevate transaction costs for multinational corporations (MNCs), disrupting trade agreements and cross-border financial activities. Governments frequently implement monetary interventions, like the utilization of foreign exchange reserves or modifications to interest rates, to stabilize their currencies (Hashmi et al., 2021).

Strategic responses to supply chain vulnerabilities significantly differ based on firm characteristics. Large multinational corporations (MNCs), possessing significant financial assets and extensive global supply chains, frequently implement proactive strategies, including the establishment of alternative production sites across various continents, investment in predictive technologies, and the procurement of long-term agreements with key suppliers (Fernández-Miguel et al., 2022; Settembre-Blundo et al., 2021). Conversely, medium- and small-sized firms (SMEs) typically depend more on operational flexibility and regional collaborations due to their constrained capital and bargaining leverage (Giuffrida et al., 2021).

Sector-specific dynamics further influence these reactions. The energy and mining sectors generally emphasize the procurement of raw materials and the safeguarding of physical assets in high-risk areas (Ben Hassen & El Bilali, 2022; Abdelsalam, 2023), while the technology sector concentrates on data security, adherence to cross-border regulations, and the diversification of suppliers for essential components like semiconductors (Hamdani & Belfencha, 2024; Hellani et al., 2021). The agri-food sector, significantly vulnerable to price fluctuations and logistical constraints, frequently focuses its strategies on long-term supply agreements and the diversification of production sources across various climatic regions (Nasir et al., 2022; Bednarski et al., 2024).

The geographic location is also a crucial factor. Companies in advanced economies, leveraging strong logistical infrastructure and substantial policy backing, typically demonstrate enhanced resilience to geopolitical disruptions (Moschieri et al., 2024), whereas companies in developing economies often depend more on assistance from international organizations or integration into regional trade blocs to alleviate risks (Akizhanov, 2023; Alfaro & Chor, 2023). These variances suggest that supply chain risk mitigation solutions must be tailored to the individual situation, corresponding to the firm's risk profile and organizational capabilities. The varied nature of these strategy approaches highlights the necessity of accounting for firm-specific characteristics when developing supply chain risk mitigation strategies. Table X presents a comparative analysis of business responses based on company size, industrial sector, and geographic location, thereby elucidating the contextual components of geopolitical risk management.

Table 1. Variations in Corporate Strategic Responses to Geopolitical Supply Chain Risks

Characteristic	Response Patterns	Illustrative Examples / Emphasis	References
Firm Size	**Large MNCs**: Proactive measures, multi-continent production facilities, investment in predictive technologies, long-term supplier contracts.	Enhanced capacity to absorb shocks due to diversified assets and capital strength.	Fernández-Miguel et al. (2022); Settembre-Blundo et al. (2021)
	SMEs: Operational flexibility, reliance on regional partnerships, adaptive sourcing within limited budgets.	More reactive strategies due to constrained capital and bargaining power.	Giuffrida et al. (2021)
Industry	**Energy & Mining**: Securing raw materials, physical asset protection in high-risk areas.	Risk concentration in resource extraction and transportation corridors.	Ben Hassen & El Bilali (2022); Abdelsalam (2023)
	Technology: Data security, compliance with cross-border regulations, diversification of critical component suppliers (e.g., semiconductors).	Protection of intellectual property and technological assets.	Hamdani & Belfencha (2024); Hellani et al. (2021)
	Agri-food: Long-term supply contracts, diversification across climatic zones, logistics risk mitigation.	Sensitivity to commodity price fluctuations and transportation bottlenecks.	Nasir et al. (2022); Bednarski et al. (2024)
Geographic Location	**Advanced Economies**: Greater resilience through strong infrastructure, policy support, and institutional capacity.	Ability to leverage domestic policy measures and technology adoption.	Moschieri et al. (2024)
	Developing Economies: Dependence on international aid, integration into regional trade blocs to mitigate risks.	Collaborative arrangements to access larger and more stable markets.	Akizhanov (2023); Alfaro & Chor (2023)

3.2 Commodity Price Disturbances and Inflationary Pressures

Regional conflicts significantly impact commodity prices, especially in the energy, food, and raw materials sectors. Numerous critical resource-producing regions globally are also geopolitical flashpoints, rendering them susceptible to disruptions from armed wars, economic sanctions, and political instability. Energy markets are significantly impacted, as wars in key oil-producing countries can result in supply shortages and price surges. The Russia-Ukraine conflict precipitated a significant increase in global oil and gas prices as a result of sanctions on Russian energy exports, compelling European nations to pursue other suppliers.

Likewise, conflicts in the Middle East, particularly those involving Saudi Arabia, Iran, and Yemen, have consistently induced volatility in the global oil market, as any disruption to the Strait of Hormuz—a critical conduit for global oil shipments—can cause prices to surge.

The food industry is acutely responsive to geopolitical turmoil. Numerous nations depend on agricultural imports, and disturbances in vital food-producing areas can result in supply deficiencies and price escalations. The Russia-Ukraine conflict profoundly affected global wheat and corn exports, given that both nations are leading grain exporters worldwide. Sanctions, blockades, and compromised infrastructure intensified worldwide food insecurity, resulting in price surges and economic pressure, especially in developing countries. Likewise, conflicts in Africa and the Middle East have impeded the exportation of cocoa, coffee, and other essential commodities, resulting in increased pricing in global markets (Orhangazi and Yeldan, 2021).

A direct correlation exists between geopolitical instability and global inflation, as supply chain interruptions, trade restrictions, and heightened transportation costs elevate production expenses for enterprises. Escalating commodity prices induce cost-push inflation, whereby augmented raw material costs result in elevated consumer prices. This inflationary pressure impacts various areas, including manufacturing, construction, retail, and consumer goods. Central banks frequently react by elevating interest rates to mitigate inflation; nonetheless, this concurrently results in diminished economic growth, decreased investment, and heightened financial dangers for enterprises (Orhangazi and Yeldan, 2021).

The influence of escalating commodity prices on multinational business operations is significant, impacting production costs, profit margins, supply chain stability, and pricing strategies. Organizations reliant on energy-intensive production or specialized raw materials from conflict-affected areas must formulate hedging measures, pursue alternative suppliers, and invest in sustainable energy solutions to mitigate financial volatility. In light of ongoing geopolitical tensions influencing global markets, businesses must exhibit adaptability by employing proactive risk management measures to effectively address inflationary pressures and fluctuations in commodity prices.

3.3 Risk Mitigation Strategies for Financial Stability

The volatility of financial markets amid regional conflicts poses considerable hurdles for enterprises, investors, and policymakers. To alleviate the risks linked to currency volatility, capital exodus, and commodity price disruptions, enterprises and financial organizations utilize diverse risk management measures to provide stability and resilience (Elsayed & Helmi, 2021). Efficient financial risk management is essential for firms functioning in conflict-prone areas, as it protects assets, preserves liquidity, and guarantees long-term viability.

A prevalent risk mitigation strategy is hedging against currency risks. Currency volatility can result in significant financial losses for enterprises involved in international trade, especially when interacting with emerging countries influenced by geopolitical instability. Businesses employ forward contracts, options, and currency swaps to mitigate exchange rate volatility and safeguard their revenues (Pellegrino et al., 2024; Harvey & Rabetti, 2024). Multinational businesses (MNCs) in politically unstable nations frequently denominate contracts in stable currencies such as the U.S. dollar or euro to mitigate the risk of local currency devaluation. Furthermore, diversifying revenue sources across various markets mitigates losses in high-risk areas by leveraging profits from more stable economies.

The function of central banks and international financial institutions in stabilizing markets is essential during times of geopolitical instability. Central banks engage in foreign exchange market interventions to stable national currencies by interest rate adjustments, capital restriction measures, or the utilization of foreign exchange reserves to mitigate speculative assaults on their currency (Koziuk, 2023; Wang et al., 2022).

The Russian Central Bank significantly increased interest rates in reaction to sanctions imposed after the 2022 invasion of Ukraine, with the objective of averting capital flight and stabilizing the ruble. Likewise, central banks in emerging economies experiencing political turmoil frequently employ monetary policy instruments to regulate inflation and sustain investor confidence. Globally, entities such as the International Monetary Fund (IMF) and World Bank offer financial aid, policy advice, and economic relief to countries experiencing instability due to conflicts (Sahling, 2023 & Zenchenko et al., 2022). Corporations operating in conflict-prone locations must manage financial risk by diversifying investment portfolios, formulating contingency plans, and implementing flexible pricing. Companies do stress testing and scenario planning to evaluate the financial implications of prospective geopolitical concerns. Forming regional alliances, obtaining alternate supply chains, and investing in insurance products to mitigate political risks are more methods by which firms protect their financial interests. In light of ongoing global economic volatility influenced by regional wars, corporations must implement a proactive financial risk management strategy, utilizing hedging tactics, central bank interventions, and strategic diversification to secure long-term financial stability.

4. BUSINESS STRATEGIES IN TURBULENT GEOPOLITICAL LANDSCAPES

4.1 Scenario Planning and Risk Evaluation in Volatile Regions

In a time when regional conflicts increasingly hinder global trade and economic stability, scenario planning and risk assessment have become vital instruments for multinational corporations (MNCs) functioning in high-risk settings. Businesses must proactively recognize geopolitical risks, evaluate their possible effects, and formulate adaptable solutions to reduce financial losses, safeguard supply networks, and sustain operational resilience (Grosse et al., 2021).

Geopolitical risk forecasting is a crucial element of corporate risk management, entailing the observation of political events, regulatory alterations, and economic trends that may impact business operations. Organizations employ sophisticated analytics, artificial intelligence (AI), and geopolitical intelligence services to monitor risk indicators including trade barriers, governmental stability, and regional crises. Numerous companies collaborate with geopolitical consulting firms, industry associations, and think tanks to acquire immediate insights into new dangers. AI-driven solutions assist firms in analyzing extensive data to forecast political turmoil, economic penalties, or trade disruptions. Firms in energy and commodities markets meticulously observe global diplomatic relations to predict supply chain weaknesses and price variations (Aljohani, 2023 & Javaid et al., 2023).

Evaluating risk exposure in various international markets is essential for organizations aiming to develop or maintain operations in volatile areas. Organizations use risk-mapping assessments to analyze potential threats, classifying markets into low-risk, moderate-risk, and high-risk categories according to criteria such as regulatory environments, economic stability, and security risks. Numerous companies utilize political risk insurance (PRI) to protect investments from expropriation, civil turmoil, and currency inconvertibility. Furthermore, enterprises evaluate their reliance on high-risk markets and pursue strategies to mitigate vulnerabilities by diversifying suppliers, creating alternative industrial centers, or utilizing trade agreements to access more stable regions.

To effectively minimize risks, firms employ scenario-based strategies that equip them for many situations. Best-case, moderate-case, and worst-case scenario models enable organizations to strategize responses to varying degrees of geopolitical volatility. During the Russia-Ukraine crisis, European enterprises who had proactively diversified their energy sources and transportation routes were better equipped to endure disruptions than those largely dependent on Russian supplies (Lambert et al., 2022). Likewise, companies in the technology industry formulate contingency strategies for possible U.S.-China trade conflicts, securing alternate supplies for semiconductors and rare earth elements.

Through the integration of geopolitical forecasting, thorough risk assessments, and scenario planning, global firms may formulate agile and adaptive corporate strategies that bolster resilience against political and economic crises. In a progressively unstable world, enterprises that actively mitigate geopolitical risks will preserve their competitive edge and ensure enduring prosperity.

4.2 Strategies for Diversification and Investment Reallocation

In reaction to increasing regional instability, multinational companies (MNCs) are restructuring their global operations by diversifying investments and relocating manufacturing facilities to mitigate risks. Geopolitical wars, economic sanctions, and regulatory modifications have made specific countries less favorable for business, leading firms to transfer production facilities, create alternative supply chains, and investigate new markets (Meyer & Li, 2022). This tendency is especially evident in industries like semiconductors, automobiles, energy, and medicines, where reliance on a singular country or region may lead to considerable disruptions (Yu et al., 2021; Althaf & Babbitt, n.d.).

Diversification is a prevalent strategic technique, however its implementation differs markedly among various types of organizations. Large multinational corporations frequently possess the financial resources and organizational capabilities to implement multi-location manufacturing strategies, create redundancy in essential processes, and invest in predictive analytics for market entry decisions (Fernández-Miguel et al., 2022). Conversely, small and medium-sized firms (SMEs) often depend on strategic alliances, franchising, or licensing to penetrate new markets due to their constrained capital resources and risk aversion (Giuffrida et al., 2021).

Sector-specific factors also affect diversification and investment reallocation methods. Energy and mining companies typically prioritize relocating operations to resource-abundant and politically stable areas, whereas technology firms focus on safeguarding intellectual property, ensuring data security, and maintaining secure semiconductor supply chains (Hamdani & Belfencha, 2024; Hellani et al., 2021). In the agri-food business, geographic diversification of production locations across several climate zones acts as a safeguard against geopolitical and environmental disturbances (Nasir et al., 2022; Ben Hassen & El Bilali, 2022).

The geographic location further influences strategic decisions. Companies based in developed economies frequently utilize robust institutional frameworks, governmental incentives, and regional trade agreements to enable relocation and mitigate exposure to high-risk markets (Alfaro & Chor, 2023). Conversely, companies in emerging economies may rely more significantly on integration into regional trade blocs, concessional financing from multilateral institutions, or collaborations with foreign investors to facilitate investment reallocation (Akizhanov, 2023).

Regional trade agreements (RTAs) are crucial for facilitating investment relocation by mitigating geopolitical risks and promoting economic stability. Agreements like the Comprehensive and Progressive Agreement for Trans-Pacific Partnership (CPTPP), the United States–Mexico–Canada Agreement (USMCA), and the African Continental Free Trade Area (AfCFTA) provide preferential tariffs, investment safeguards, and dispute resolution frameworks that entice companies in search of stable operational conditions. Amid escalating U.S.–China tensions, numerous firms have relocated production to Vietnam and Malaysia, capitalizing on their involvement in regional agreements that ensure regulatory stability and market access (Amul et al., 2022).

By customizing diversification and investment reallocation plans according to company size, industry dynamics, and regional factors, firms may bolster resilience against geopolitical disruptions and ensure long-term competitiveness in a progressively fragmented global economy.

4.3 Technological and Digital Soluti1ons for Organizational Resilience

In a time of escalating geopolitical instability, enterprises are utilizing technical and digital solutions to bolster resilience, reduce risks, and maintain operational continuity in conflict-affected areas. The amalgamation of artificial intelligence (AI), big data, cybersecurity protocols, and digital transformation enables multinational corporations (MNCs) to foresee disruptions, safeguard assets, and adjust to changing business landscapes (Belhadi et al., 2024 & Browder et al., 2024).

Artificial intelligence and big data are among the most potent instruments for risk management in crisis prediction. Advanced data analytics empowers enterprises to analyze extensive geopolitical, economic, and social data to discern trends indicative of impending conflicts, trade restrictions, or supply chain disruptions. AI-driven forecasting algorithms evaluate historical trends and real-time data, enabling organizations to assess risks, anticipate currency swings, and formulate contingency plans. Global banks and financial organizations employ AI-driven risk assessment tools to analyze political stability before to making overseas investment decisions. Logistics companies utilize predictive analytics to modify shipping routes and inventory levels in response to expected disruptions from regional conflicts.

Cybersecurity threats during periods of geopolitical conflict present a substantial challenge to enterprises functioning in high-risk settings. Cyberattacks frequently intensify during conflicts, as state-sponsored hacking collectives focus on financial institutions, supply chain systems, and essential infrastructure (Gulyas and Kiss, 2023). Cyber warfare can result in data breaches, financial losses, and operational disruptions, especially in sectors dependent on digital transactions and cloud-based infrastructures. To mitigate these attacks, organizations must establish comprehensive cybersecurity frameworks, incorporating end-to-end encryption, artificial intelligence-based threat detection, and multi-factor authentication. Furthermore, enterprises must educate personnel on cybersecurity protocols and establish incident response strategies to alleviate the consequences of such breaches. The emergence of blockchain technology has facilitated a secure and transparent method for safeguarding supply chain integrity (Al-Farsi et al., 2021) enabling firms to monitor transactions and authenticate origins of raw materials, hence mitigating the danger of cyber manipulation.

Integrating AI-driven forecasting, cybersecurity protocols, and digital transformation enables organizations to substantially improve their resilience in high-risk settings. These technology capabilities are most effective when integrated into a comprehensive strategy framework that aligns business responses to geopolitical threats with the unique characteristics of the firm. Figure X illustrates a conceptual synthesis based on the strategies outlined in Sections 2–4, delineating the connection between geopolitical disruptions, critical corporate risk domains (supply chain, financial and market, institutional/regulatory), and strategic responses (supply chain diversification, financial hedging, institutional adaptation). The framework additionally includes moderating variables—firm size, industry sector, and geographic location—that influence the prioritization and execution of strategies (Fernández-Miguel et al., 2022; Giuffrida et al., 2021; Abdelsalam, 2023; Hamdani & Belfencha, 2024; Nasir et al., 2022; Moschieri et al., 2024). This comprehensive viewpoint provides managers and policymakers with a clear framework for customizing risk mitigation strategies to particular organizational environments, thereby improving resilience amid ongoing global uncertainty.

5. POLICY RECOMMENDATIONS AND THE FUTURE OF INTERNATIONAL TRADE

5.1 The Function of International Institutions in Conflict Resolution

International institutions are essential for preserving global trade stability and alleviating economic disturbances resulting from regional wars. Entities such as the World Trade Organization (WTO), International Monetary Fund (IMF), World Bank, and regional economic organizations function as principal arbiters in adjudicating trade disputes, enforcing economic penalties, and offering financial aid to economies impacted by conflict (Hitt et al., 2021). These institutions establish rules-based frameworks that encourage free trade, enhance economic cooperation, and offer ways to mitigate geopolitical concerns. Nonetheless, their efficacy is frequently undermined by political intricacies, enforcement constraints, and opposition from significant global powers (Short, 2021; Bei & Celata, 2023; Ritala, 2024).

The WTO is pivotal in maintaining free and predictable trade, especially under geopolitical crises. The WTO facilitates the resolution of trade disputes among nations, preventing the need for retaliatory economic actions. Recent global trade conflicts, like the U.S.-China trade war and issues about subsidies, have underscored the WTO's constrained enforcement authority, as certain nations circumvent its rules in favor of unilateral trade policy (Drabek, 2024). Likewise, the IMF and World Bank offer financial assistance and policy direction to countries impacted by geopolitical wars, aiding them in stabilizing their economies, executing structural changes, and obtaining emergency funds for infrastructure reconstruction. These groups have played a crucial role in aiding Ukraine, Afghanistan, and post-conflict African nations in achieving financial stability and economic recovery.

Economic diplomacy serves as an essential instrument in mitigating global conflicts. Governments can mitigate economic complaints by cultivating bilateral trade agreements, establishing economic partnerships, and engaging in diplomatic negotiations before these issues grow into full-scale confrontations. The European Union (EU) has utilized economic diplomacy to enhance commercial links and foster stability in adjacent regions. Likewise, the ASEAN (Association of Southeast Asian Nations) Free Trade Area has assisted member states in alleviating geopolitical tensions through enhanced economic collaboration and the promotion of collective wealth. Nonetheless, economic diplomacy encounters challenges when political antagonisms, economic sanctions, and national interests supersede diplomatic resolutions.

Numerous case studies underscore the function of international institutions in mitigating trade disputes. During the U.S.-China trade war, the WTO endeavored to resolve tariff disputes; nevertheless, its power diminished as both nations resorted to unilateral retaliatory actions. The IMF significantly contributed to stabilizing Argentina's economy amid financial crises, fostering market confidence and facilitating international investment. The G20's unified reaction to the 2008 global financial crisis highlighted the efficacy of international organizations in mitigating economic shocks (Akizhanov, 2023). International institutions are essential for trade stability and conflict resolution; nevertheless, their efficacy relies on global collaboration, enforcement mechanisms, and flexibility to new geopolitical threats. Enhancing their functions via reforms, augmented finance, and improved dispute resolution processes would be crucial for establishing a more stable and robust global trading system.

5.2 Toward a More Resilient and Adaptive Global Trade System

As geopolitical tensions continue to disrupt global trade, policy reforms, sustainable business practices, and adaptive trade models are essential to creating a more resilient global economy. Governments, multinational corporations (MNCs), and international institutions must work together to develop trade policies and frameworks that mitigate risks, ensure supply chain continuity, and promote long-term stability in global markets.

One of the most critical steps in ensuring trade resilience is policy reform to safeguard supply chains and trade flows. Governments and trade organizations must develop contingency plans, diversify trade partnerships, and establish stronger economic alliances to reduce overdependence on high-risk regions. Policies promoting nearshoring and friendshoring—relocating supply chains to politically stable and economically aligned nations—have gained traction as businesses seek to reduce vulnerability to geopolitical shocks. Additionally, trade facilitation agreements can help streamline customs procedures, enhance transparency, and ensure efficient cross-border trade even during crises. For example, the Comprehensive and Progressive Agreement for Trans-Pacific Partnership (CPTPP) has provided member nations with a robust framework to maintain trade stability amid global uncertainties (Alfaro & Chor, 2023).

Another crucial aspect of resilience is the implementation of sustainable and ethical business practices in geopolitical risk management. MNCs must integrate Environmental, Social, and Governance (ESG) principles into their global trade strategies to enhance long-term stability (Gündoğdu et al., 2023 & Linnenluecke, 2022). Ethical sourcing, fair labor practices, and compliance with international regulations help companies navigate complex trade landscapes while maintaining corporate responsibility. Additionally, businesses must focus on sustainable supply chain diversification, prioritizing environmentally friendly logistics, reducing carbon footprints, and investing in renewable energy sources. For instance, the European Union's Green Deal has set new standards for sustainable trade, encouraging businesses to adopt climate-conscious policies. By embedding sustainability and ethics into trade strategies, companies can not only comply with regulations but also strengthen their brand reputation and secure long-term market access.

To navigate future economic uncertainties, businesses must embrace adaptive trade models that emphasize flexibility, digital transformation, and regional cooperation. Companies that integrate AI-driven risk analytics, blockchain for supply chain transparency, and predictive modeling can anticipate trade disruptions and respond proactively. Governments can support businesses by fostering multilateral trade agreements that provide market access stability and legal protections. Additionally, trade digitalization, including e-commerce expansion and cloud-based logistics, can help businesses remain agile in volatile environments.

By implementing policy reforms, sustainability-driven risk management, and innovative trade models, global economies can develop a more resilient and adaptive trade system, ensuring economic growth and stability amid rising geopolitical challenges.

5.3 Future Outlook: The Developing Nexus Between Geoeconomics and Business Risks

As geopolitical tensions persist, the global economic landscape necessitates the evolution of trade patterns, regionalization tendencies, and corporate strategies to effectively manage uncertainty. The future of global commerce will be characterized by economic fragmentation, technological progress, and evolving geopolitical alliances, necessitating that corporations and policymakers implement proactive policies to ensure stability and competitiveness (Papadopoulos et al., 2023; Luo, 2024; Seong et al., 2024).

Forecasts for International Trade Dynamics in Light of Escalating Geopolitical Strains

In the forthcoming years, global trade patterns are expected to transition towards more regionalization and strategic realignments. The epoch of hyper-globalization, characterized by corporations favoring efficiency above resilience, is yielding to a more risk-aware strategy in supply chain management. Governments and firms are anticipated to diversify their sourcing, diminish dependence on antagonistic economies, and enhance trade links with politically stable countries. Trade accords like the Regional Comprehensive Economic Partnership (RCEP) and the USMCA will become increasingly important as companies pursue stable, rules-based trade frameworks to alleviate geopolitical concerns. Furthermore, friendshoring and nearshoring methods will increasingly be adopted as corporations relocate operations nearer to domestic markets or allied countries to enhance supply chain security (Witt et al., 2023).

Prolonged Consequences of Regionalization and Economic Fragmentation

The enduring trend of economic fragmentation will transform international commerce, diminishing interdependence among principal economies and promoting the development of regional trade blocs. The U.S.-China trade dispute and the Russia-Ukraine crisis have expedited economic decoupling, compelling states to prioritize national security before economic efficiency. Consequently, international enterprises must adjust to more intricate regulatory frameworks, variable tariffs, and changing trade impediments. This transition may foster opportunities for developing economies to enhance regional alliances, although it also poses a threat to global economic expansion and may elevate expenses for consumers and enterprises alike.

Strategic Business Methods to Maintain Competitiveness in a Volatile Economic Environment

To prosper in a period of increased geoeconomic threats, enterprises must adopt flexible, technology-oriented strategies that bolster resilience. Organizations ought to allocate resources towards digital supply chain management, AI-driven risk evaluation, and blockchain-facilitated trade transparency to enhance operational efficiency and adaptability. Scenario planning, stress testing, and geopolitical risk assessment will be crucial for multinational firms operating in intricate trading situations. Furthermore, enterprises must adopt ESG principles, sustainable sourcing, and regulatory compliance to maintain competitiveness in global marketplaces increasingly shaped by economic nationalism and political realignments (Saeed et al., 2023; Lebepe & Mathaba, 2025). By adjusting to changing trade dynamics, adopting digital transformation, and strengthening regional trade networks, businesses may ensure long-term sustainability and competitiveness in a swiftly expanding global economy.

5.4 Comparative Analysis of Major Geopolitical Conflicts and Their Business Implications

The Russia–Ukraine conflict constitutes a high-intensity interstate war with immediate global ramifications in oil and agricultural markets. Russia, a prominent supplier of oil, natural gas, and essential food commodities, has experienced substantial price volatility and inflationary pressures in both developed and developing economies due to its economic isolation from unprecedented sanctions, particularly imposed by the European Union, United States, and United Kingdom (Ba et al., 2024; Saeed et al., 2023). The EU's prompt transition to liquefied natural gas (LNG) imports and investments in renewable energy highlights how energy security apprehensions expedite structural changes in energy systems. Simultaneously, interruptions to Ukrainian grain exports have intensified food instability, necessitating increased production from alternate suppliers like Brazil and Canada. This conflict has accelerated reshoring, supplier diversification, and heightened focus on geopolitical risk assessment in resource-dependent industries from a business strategy standpoint.

The U.S.–China trade tensions represent a prolonged geoeconomic competition, transitioning from tariff conflicts to extensive economic decoupling. The implementation of reciprocal tariffs has disrupted manufacturing supply chains, increased input costs, and encouraged the adoption of "China+1" strategies, which involve relocating production to third countries such as Vietnam, India, and Mexico (Amul et al., 2022; Van and Łasak, 2023). The technology industry has been significantly impacted, since export restrictions on semiconductors and 5G technology have catalyzed rapid domestic innovation in China and heightened dependence on alternative suppliers in Taiwan and South Korea (Hamdani & Belfencha, 2024; Mark & Roberts, 2023). In contrast to the Russia–Ukraine situation, characterized by an abrupt and multifaceted shock, the U.S.–China conflict signifies a gradual structural transformation in global value chains, distinguished by strategic realignment, regulatory fragmentation, and technology bifurcation.

The crises in the Middle East, including the Israeli-Palestinian dispute, the Saudi-Yemen war, and tensions with Iran, illustrate the enduring vulnerability of resource-rich areas. The region's significance as a vital oil and gas provider, coupled with political instability and infrastructure assaults, exemplified by the 2019 drone strikes on Saudi Aramco, has resulted in sudden supply interruptions and worldwide price surges (Hassan et al., 2024; Maftouh et al., 2022). The Strait of Hormuz, a critical juncture for 20% of worldwide oil transport, continues to represent a strategic weakness. In addition to energy markets, regulatory instability and sanctions have hindered foreign investment, compelling companies to pursue joint ventures, diversify suppliers, and increasingly implement digital transformation and remote operations to alleviate physical and political risks (Antwi-Boateng & Al Jaberi, 2022; Hu et al., 2023).

An investigation comparing these three situations uncovers both similarities and differences in their business ramifications. All three settings emphasize the essential importance of supply chain diversity, energy security strategy, and regulatory risk mitigation. Nonetheless, the temporal dynamics and strategic alternatives vary: acute confrontations, such as the Russia–Ukraine situation, prompt swift operational adjustments and urgent sourcing strategies, while enduring rivalry, exemplified by the U.S.–China relationship, encourage gradual yet significant transformations in value chains. Simultaneously, persistent instability in the Middle East necessitates continuous risk assessment and the fortification of resilience rather than singular modifications.

These cases exemplify the interaction between systemic shocks and firm-level adaptation, influenced by characteristics such as industrial reliance on disputed resources, geographic operational distribution, and availability to policy assistance (Gereffi et al., 2021; Luo, 2024). The findings underscore the imperative for governments to implement coordinated energy transition strategies, establish diverse trade agreements, and develop robust dispute resolution systems. Corporate leaders must incorporate geopolitical risk assessment into fundamental strategy planning, utilizing technical tools for scenario modeling, and aligning investment and sourcing strategies with both short-term volatility and long-term structural changes.

The insights from these conflicts indicate that a resilient business environment relies on anticipatory adaptation—establishing flexible, geographically dispersed operations, investing in innovation and renewable resources, and fostering partnerships capable of enduring geopolitical fragmentation. The ability to manage increasing global interdependencies alongside escalating geopolitical rivalry will determine competitive advantage in the next decades. Table II presents a comparative analysis of the essential insights derived from the three case studies, highlighting their distinguishing characteristics, principal economic and market effects, and the strategic solutions implemented by firms. This synthesis facilitates a greater comprehension of both distinct and intersecting patterns across various geopolitical situations, therefore acting as a practical reference for managers and policymakers in formulating adaptive and resilient company strategies.

Table 2. Comparative Overview of Major Geopolitical Conflicts and Business Implications

Conflict	Key Characteristics	Primary Economic/ Market Impacts	Corporate Strategic Responses	References
Russia–Ukraine Conflict	Acute interstate war with global commodity implications; high-intensity sanctions regime.	Energy price spikes (oil peaked at $130/ barrel in 2022), inflationary pressures, disruptions to wheat, corn, sunflower oil exports.	Rapid reshoring, supplier diversification, accelerated renewable energy investment, LNG sourcing from U.S., Qatar, Norway.	Ba et al. (2024); Saeed et al. (2023)
U.S.–China Trade Tensions	Prolonged geoeconomic rivalry; tariff escalation evolving into technological and supply chain decoupling.	Increased manufacturing costs, disrupted trade flows, technology export restrictions (semiconductors, 5G).	"China+1" strategy, relocation to Vietnam, India, Malaysia, Mexico; North American reshoring under USMCA; tech innovation and alternative sourcing.	Amul et al. (2022); Van & Łasak (2023); Mark & Roberts (2023)
Middle East Conflicts	Persistent political instability in a resource-concentrated region; periodic high-intensity events.	Oil/gas supply volatility, Strait of Hormuz chokepoint risks, infrastructure attacks causing price surges.	Diversified energy sourcing, joint ventures with local partners, digital transformation, remote operations to reduce physical exposure.	Hassan et al. (2024); Maftouh et al. (2022); Antwi-Boateng & Al Jaberi (2022)

CONCLUSION

Geopolitical upheavals have transitioned from sporadic aberrations to enduring characteristics of the global economic landscape. The case studies of the Russia–Ukraine conflict, U.S.–China trade disputes, and Middle Eastern conflicts illustrate the various ways in which political instability, economic competition, and resource concentration converge to transform business landscapes. Each scenario has unique catalysts and sectoral impacts—spanning from sudden energy price surges to incremental value chain adjustments—yet they collectively underscore the importance of supply chain diversity, energy security strategies, and adaptive governance in maintaining operations.

These advances substantiate the significance of integrated risk management frameworks that amalgamate scenario preparation, regional diversification, and policy engagement. Companies functioning in high-risk environments must not only respond to disturbances but also foresee them by ongoing surveillance, predictive analytics, and innovation in products and processes. Sector-specific elements—such as resource reliance in energy, technology interconnections in manufacturing, and climate vulnerability in agriculture—further influence the resilience measures accessible to companies.

Policymakers are essential in fostering resilience via coordinated trade agreements, specific investment incentives, and support for energy transition projects. Aligning business and policy agendas is crucial for mitigating systemic vulnerabilities and promoting long-term stability in global markets.

The interaction between geopolitical dynamics and corporate strategy necessitates a paradigm shift: resilience should be included as a fundamental strategic objective rather than regarded solely as a crisis-management function. By adopting anticipatory adaptation, investing in renewable and digital technologies, and fostering cross-border alliances, companies can effectively maneuver through an era characterized by increased geopolitical fragmentation and profound economic interconnectedness. The ability to function efficiently inside this dual reality will determine competitive advantage in the forthcoming decades.

REFERENCES

Abdallah, S., & Nizamuddin, N. (2023). Blockchain-based solution for pharma supply chain industry. *Computers & Industrial Engineering*, *177*, 108997. Advance online publication. DOI: 10.1016/j.cie.2023.108997

Abdelsalam, M. A. M. (2023). Oil price fluctuations and economic growth: The case of MENA countries. Review of Economics and Political Science. DOI: 10.1108/REPS-12-2019-0162

Akizhanov, K. B. (2023). Argentina: Entrenching Income Inequality. In *Finance Capitalism and Income Inequality in the Contemporary Global Economy: A Comparative Study of the USA, South Korea, Argentina and Sweden* (pp. 125–152). Springer International Publishing. DOI: 10.1007/978-3-031-21768-5_6

Al-Farsi, S., Rathore, M. M., & Bakiras, S. (2021). Security of blockchain-based supply chain management systems: Challenges and opportunities. *Applied Sciences (Basel, Switzerland)*, *11*(12), 5585. Advance online publication. DOI: 10.3390/app11125585

Alfaro, L., & Chor, D. (2023). Global supply chains: The looming "great reallocation". https://www.nber.org/papers/w31661

Aljohani, A. (2023). Predictive analytics and machine learning for real-time supply chain risk mitigation and agility. *Sustainability (Basel)*, *15*(20), 15088. Advance online publication. DOI: 10.3390/su152015088

Althaf, S., & Babbitt, C. W. (n.d.). Disruption risks to material supply chains in the electronics sector. Resources. https://www.elsevier.com/open-access/userlicense/1.0/

Amul, G. G., Ang, M., Kraybill, D., Ong, S. E., & Yoong, J. (2022). Responses to COVID-19 in Southeast Asia: Diverse paths and ongoing challenges. *Asian Economic Policy Review*, *17*(1), 90–110. DOI: 10.1111/aepr.12362

Antwi-Boateng, O., & Al Jaberi, N. H. S. (2022). The post-oil strategy of the UAE: An examination of diversification strategies and challenges. *Politics & Policy*, *50*(2), 380–407. Advance online publication. DOI: 10.1111/polp.12457

Bednarski, L., Roscoe, S., Blome, C., & Schleper, M. C. (2024). Geopolitical disruptions in global supply chains: A state-of-the-art literature review. *Production Planning and Control*, 1–27. DOI: 10.1080/09537287.2023.2286283

Bei, G., & Celata, F. (2023). Challenges and effects of short-term rentals regulation: A counterfactual assessment of European cities. *Annals of Tourism Research, 101*, 103605. Advance online publication. DOI: 10.1016/j.annals.2023.103605

Belhadi, A., Kamble, S., Subramanian, N., Singh, R. K., & Venkatesh, M. (2024). Digital capabilities to manage agri-food supply chain uncertainties and build supply chain resilience during compounding geopolitical disruptions. *International Journal of Operations & Production Management, 44*(11), 1914–1950. DOI: 10.1108/IJOPM-11-2022-0737

Ben Hassen, T., & El Bilali, H. (2022). Impacts of the Russia-Ukraine war on global food security: Towards more sustainable and resilient food systems? *Foods, 11*(15), 2301. Advance online publication. DOI: 10.3390/foods11152301 PMID: 35954068

Browder, R. E., Dwyer, S. M., & Koch, H. (2024). Upgrading adaptation: How digital transformation promotes organizational resilience. *Strategic Entrepreneurship Journal, 18*(1), 128–164. DOI: 10.1002/sej.1483

Chen, W., & Zhao, X. (2023). Understanding global rice trade flows: Network evolution and implications. *Foods, 12*(17), 3298. Advance online publication. DOI: 10.3390/foods12173298 PMID: 37685236

Drabek, Z. (2024). *Is the WTO terminally ill? Threats to the international trading system.* Asia and the Global Economy. DOI: 10.1016/j.aglobe.2024.100078

Edler, J., Blind, K., Kroll, H., & Schubert, T. (2023). Technology sovereignty as an emerging frame for innovation policy. Defining rationales, ends and means. *Research Policy, 52*(6), 104765. Advance online publication. DOI: 10.1016/j.respol.2023.104765

Elsayed, A. H., & Helmi, M. H. (2021). Volatility transmission and spillover dynamics across financial markets: The role of geopolitical risk. *Annals of Operations Research, 305*(1-2), 1–22. Advance online publication. DOI: 10.1007/s10479-021-04081-5

Estrada, M. A. R. & Koutronas, E. (2022). The impact of the Russian aggression against Ukraine on the Russia-EU trade. Journal of Policy Modeling. tDOI: 10.1016/j.jpolmod.2022.06.004

Fasanya, I. O., Oyewole, O. J., Adekoya, O. B., & Badaru, F. O. (2021). Oil price and stock market behaviour in GCC countries: Do asymmetries and structural breaks matter? *Energy Strategy Reviews, 36*, 100682. DOI: 10.1016/j.esr.2021.100682

Gereffi, G., Lim, H. C., & Lee, J. (2021). Trade policies, firm strategies, and adaptive reconfigurations of global value chains. *Journal of International Business Policy, 4*(4), 506–522. DOI: 10.1057/s42214-021-00102-z

Giuffrida, M., Jiang, H., & Mangiaracina, R. (2021). Investigating the relationships between uncertainty types and risk management strategies in cross-border e-commerce logistics. *International Journal of Logistics Management*, *32*(4), 1406–1433. DOI: 10.1108/IJLM-04-2020-0158

Grosse, R., Gamso, J., & Nelson, R. C. (2021). China's rise, world order, and the implications for international business. *Management International Review*, *61*(1), 1–26. Advance online publication. DOI: 10.1007/s11575-020-00433-8 PMID: 33679004

Gulyas, O., & Kiss, G. (2023). Impact of cyber-attacks on the financial institutions. *Procedia Computer Science*, *219*, 84–90. Advance online publication. DOI: 10.1016/j.procs.2023.01.267

Hamdani, M., & Belfencha, I. (2024). Strategic implications of the US-China semiconductor rivalry. *Discover Global Society*, *2*(1), 67. Advance online publication. DOI: 10.1007/s44282-024-00081-5

Harvey, C. R., & Rabetti, D. (2024). International business and decentralized finance. *Journal of International Business Studies*, *55*(7), 840–863. Advance online publication. DOI: 10.1057/s41267-024-00705-7

Hassan, Q., Viktor, P., Al-Musawi, T. J., Ali, B. M., Algburi, S., Alzoubi, H. M., & Jaszczur, M. (2024). The renewable energy role in the global energy Transformations. *Renewable Energy Focus*, *48*, 100545. DOI: 10.1016/j.ref.2024.100545

Hellani, H., Sliman, L., Samhat, A. E., & Exposito, E. (2021). On blockchain integration with supply chain: Overview on data transparency. *Logistics (Basel)*, *5*(3), 46. Advance online publication. DOI: 10.3390/logistics5030046

Herold, D. M. & Marzantowicz, Ł (2023). Supply chain responses to global disruptions and its ripple effects: an institutional complexity perspective. Operations management research. DOI: 10.1007/s12063-023-00404-w

Hitt, M. A., Holmes, R. M.Jr, & Arregle, J. L. (2021). The (COVID-19) pandemic and the new world (dis) order. *Journal of World Business*, *56*(4), 101210. Advance online publication. DOI: 10.1016/j.jwb.2021.101210

Javaid, M., Haleem, A., Khan, I. H., & Suman, R. (2023). *Understanding the potential applications of Artificial Intelligence in Agriculture Sector*. Advanced Agrochem., DOI: 10.1016/j.aac.2022.10.001

Koziuk, V. (2023). The geopolitical "puzzle" of the central bank's switch to gold. *Economics-Innovative and Economics Research Journal*, *11*(2), 225–243. DOI: 10.2478/eoik-2023-0018

Kuhla, K., Willner, S. N., Otto, C., & Levermann, A. (2023). Resilience of international trade to typhoon-related supply disruptions. *Journal of Economic Dynamics & Control, 151*, 104663. DOI: 10.1016/j.jedc.2023.104663

Lambert, L. A., Tayah, J., Lee-Schmid, C., Abdalla, M., Abdallah, I., Ali, A. H., Esmail, S., & Ahmed, W. (2022). The EU's natural gas Cold War and diversification challenges. *Energy Strategy Reviews, 43*, 100934. DOI: 10.1016/j.esr.2022.100934

Lebepe, P. & Mathaba, T. N. D. (2025). Enhancing energy resilience in manufacturing enterprises: A systematic mapping of challenges to strategies. *Journal of Economy and Technology*. DOI: 10.1016/j.ject.2025.01.002

Linnenluecke, M. K. (2022). Environmental, social and governance (ESG) performance in the context of multinational business research. *Multinational Business Review, 30*(1), 1–16. Advance online publication. DOI: 10.1108/MBR-11-2021-0148

Luiz, J. M., & Barnard, H. (2022). Home country (in) stability and the locational portfolio construction of emerging market multinational enterprises. *Journal of Business Research, 151*, 17–32. Advance online publication. DOI: 10.1016/j.jbusres.2022.06.042

Luo, Y. (2024). Paradigm shift and theoretical implications for the era of global disorder. *Journal of International Business Studies, 55*(2), 127–135. Advance online publication. DOI: 10.1057/s41267-023-00659-2

Maftouh, A., El Fatni, O., Fayiah, M., Liew, R. K., Lam, S. S., Bahaj, T., & Butt, M. H. (2022). The application of water–energy nexus in the Middle East and North Africa (MENA) region: A structured review. *Applied Water Science, 12*(5), 83. DOI: 10.1007/s13201-022-01613-7

Mariotti, S. (2022). A warning from the Russian–Ukrainian war: Avoiding a future that rhymes with the past. *Economia e Politica Industriale, 49*(4), 761–782. Advance online publication. DOI: 10.1007/s40812-022-00219-z

Meyer, K. E., & Li, C. (2022). The MNE and its subsidiaries at times of global disruptions: An international relations perspective. *Global Strategy Journal, 12*(3), 555–577. Advance online publication. DOI: 10.1002/gsj.1436

Miró, J. (2023). Responding to the global disorder: The EU's quest for open strategic autonomy. *Global Society, 37*(3), 315–335. Advance online publication. DOI: 10.1080/13600826.2022.2110042

Mohazzem Hossain, S., Biswas, S., & Raihan Uddin, M. (2024). Sustainable energy transition in Bangladesh: Challenges and pathways for the future. *Engineering Reports, 6*(1), e12752. DOI: 10.1002/eng2.12752

Moschieri, C., Ravasi, D., & Huy, Q. (2024). Why do some multinational firms respond better than others to the hostility of host governments? Proximal embedding and the side effects of local partnerships. *Journal of Management Studies*, *61*(2), 627–685. Advance online publication. DOI: 10.1111/joms.12809

Mueller, M. L., & Farhat, K. (2022). Regulation of platform market access by the United States and China: Neo-mercantilism in digital services. Policy & Internet. https://ssrn.com/abstract=3896517 DOI: 10.1002/poi3.305

Nasir, M. A., Nugroho, A. D., & Lakner, Z. (2022). Impact of the Russian–Ukrainian conflict on global food crops. *Foods*, *11*(19), 2979. Advance online publication. DOI: 10.3390/foods11192979 PMID: 36230055

Orhangazi, Ö., & Yeldan, A. E. (2021). The re-making of the Turkish crisis. *Development and Change*, *52*(3), 460–503. Advance online publication. DOI: 10.1111/dech.12644

Papadopoulos, G. D., Magafas, L., Demertzis, K., & Antoniou, I. (2023). Analyzing global geopolitical stability in terms of world trade network analysis. Information. mdpi.comDOI: 10.3390/info14080442

Pellegrino, R., Gaudenzi, B., & Zsidisin, G. A. (2024). Mitigating foreign exchange risk exposure with supply chain flexibility: A real option analysis. *Journal of Business Logistics*, *45*(1), e12338. DOI: 10.1111/jbl.12338

Rabbi, M. F., Ben Hassen, T., El Bilali, H., Raheem, D., & Raposo, A. (2023). Food security challenges in Europe in the context of the prolonged Russian–Ukrainian conflict. *Sustainability (Basel)*, *15*(6), 4745. DOI: 10.3390/su15064745

Ritala, P. (2024). Grand challenges and platform ecosystems: Scaling solutions for wicked ecological and societal problems. Journal of Product Innovation Management. DOI: 10.1111/jpim.12682

Saeed, S., Altamimi, S. A., Alkayyal, N. A., Alshehri, E., & Alabbad, D. A. (2023). Digital transformation and cybersecurity challenges for businesses resilience: Issues and recommendations. Sensors, 23(15), 6666. DOI: 10.3390/s23156666

Schmitz, L. & Seidl, T. (2023). As open as possible, as autonomous as necessary: Understanding the rise of open strategic autonomy in EU trade policy. JCMS: journal of common market studies. DOI: 10.1111/jcms.13428

Settembre-Blundo, D., González-Sánchez, R., Medina-Salgado, S., & García-Muiña, F. E. (2021). Flexibility and resilience in corporate decision making: a new sustainability-based risk management system in uncertain times. Global Journal of Flexible Systems Management, 22(Suppl 2), 107-132. DOI: 10.1007/s40171-021-00277-7

Short, J. L. (2021). The politics of regulatory enforcement and compliance: Theorizing and operationalizing political influences. Regulation & Governance. DOI: 10.1111/rego.12291

Suresh Kumar, K., Nassa, V. K., Uike, D., Kalra, A., Sahu, A. K., Athavale, V. A., & Saravanan, V. (2022). [Retracted] A Comparative Analysis of Blockchain in Enhancing the Drug Traceability in Edible Foods Using Multiple Regression Analysis. Journal of Food Quality, 2022(1), 1689913. DOI: 10.1155/2024/9837204

Tsai, T. Y., & Urmetzer, F. (2024). A decisional framework for manufacturing relocation: Consolidating and expanding the reshoring debate. International Journal of Management Reviews, 26(2), 254-284. DOI: 10.1111/ijmr.12352

Wang, Y., Lucey, B. M., Vigne, S. A., & Yarovaya, L. (2022). The effects of central bank digital currencies news on financial markets. Technological Forecasting and Social Change, 180, 121715. DOI: 10.1016/j.techfore.2022.121715

Wilhelm, M. (2024). Mandatory due diligence legislation: a paradigm shift for the governance of sustainability in global value chains? Journal of International Business Policy. DOI: 10.1057/s42214-024-00193-4

Witt, M. A., Lewin, A. Y., Li, P. P., & Gaur, A. (2023). Decoupling in international business: Evidence, drivers, impact, and implications for IB research. Journal of World Business. DOI: 10.1016/j.jwb.2022.101399

Yu, Z., Razzaq, A., Rehman, A., Shah, A., Jameel, K., & Mor, R. S. (2021). Disruption in global supply chain and socio-economic shocks: a lesson from COVID-19 for sustainable production and consumption. Operations Management Research, 1-16. DOI: 10.1007/s12063-021-00179-y

Zenchenko, S., Strielkowski, W., Smutka, L., Vacek, T., Radyukova, Y., & Sutyagin, V. (2022). Monetization of the Economies as a Priority of the New Monetary Policy in the Face of Economic Sanctions. Journal of Risk and Financial Management, 15(3), 140. DOI: 10.3390/jrfm15030140

Chapter 6 Reconfiguring Global Trade: The Economic Impact of the Russia–Ukraine Conflict and Strategic Responses

Puneett Bhatnagr
https://orcid.org/0000-0002-9281-1809
Amity University, India

ABSTRACT

The Russia-Ukraine conflict poses a major disruption to global trade flows and therefore changes the economic fortunes of nations worldwide. This study explores the critical obstacles of the conflict on international trade, highlighting adverse impacts and potential benefits in different regions. Based on a mixed-method approach of both statistical data analysis and qualitative insight, this study examines the use of relevant information that is important for global and international organisations' global and regional shifts in trade volumes, GDP, and inflation. Of course, the findings show that the impact was not even. Some of the economies were able to benefit from the reshaping of trade relations—India, Saudi Arabia, and China–while many of the other neighbouring countries of Ukraine, among the other European countries, particularly had a hard hit economically. This will provide policy alternatives that would lessen the adverse effects of trade and build the economic resilience of countries, especially those reliant on Russia and Ukraine for critical imports.

DOI: 10.4018/979-8-3373-7907-4.ch006

1. INTRODUCTION

The global business environment has undergone massive change over the last few decades due to the impacts of globalization, technology, and liberalization of trade policies (Seyoum, 2024; Vlados & Chatzinikolaou, 2024). Increased interdependence has made world trade patterns more complex and susceptible to geopolitical disturbances (Imran-Ur-Rahman et al., 2024; Bednarski et al., 2023). A case in point is the current Russia-Ukraine conflict, which reignited in February 2022 with the Russian invasion of Ukraine (Kizilova & Norris, 2023; Kozyrev, 2024). Resulting in a geopolitical and economic crisis, with huge impacts on international trade, global supply chains, and the economies of several countries (Zhao, 2024; Vargas-Hernández & Vargas-González, 2024; Chatterjee, 2024).

The economic repercussions are global, as Russia and Ukraine both play critical roles in world trade (Boyko et al., 2023; Brosig & Verma, 2024; Zhang et al., 2024). Russia is a significant exporter of crude oil and natural gas (Henderson, 2024; Xia & Li, 2024), while Ukraine supplies various agricultural goods, including wheat and other grains (Devadoss & Ridley, 2024; Balma et al., 2024; Özocakli et al., 2024). Russia and Ukraine war has severely disturbed these exports, leading to price rises in not only energy but also food markets (Ateed, 2023; Bilali & Hassen, 2024; Oyebamiji et al., 2024). This war has also been declared against Russia by Western nations of the world who also have complicated trade dynamics (Jakupec, 2024; Verma & Düben, 2024). The recent spates of imposition of sanctions on Russia and Ukraine have created huge trade reallocation and economic shifts across the world (Thakkar, 2024; Cooper, 2024). While existing literature has looked at the broader geopolitical and economic consequences of the Russia-Ukraine conflict (Hossain et al., 2024; Ozili, 2024; Tosun et al., 2024; Khan et al., 2024; Aizenman et al., 2024), there is a gap in understanding the specific impacts it has on international trade flows (Lohani, 2020; Ma et al., 2023; Lampe & Sharp, 2024; Del Rosal, 2023). However, little attention has been paid to the heterogeneity of impacts, including how there have been gains or losses from trade diversion by different nations (Köseoğlu et al., 2023; Jiang & Chen, 2024; Tong, 2024). Therefore, this study fills this gap by considering the heterogeneous effects of the Russia-Ukraine war on global trade flows, specifically focusing on countries which have suffered compared to those that have benefited from the changes in trade relations. The key research questions guiding this study are as follows:

(1) How has the Russia-Ukraine conflict impacted global trade flows?
(2) What factors have driven the trade reallocations observed during the conflict?
(3) Which countries have been adversely affected, and which have benefited from the trade diversions?

To answer these questions, the current study uses a mixed-method approach using both qualitative and quantitative information. The analysis period covers 2010 to 2022, looking at key economic indicators that show changes in crude oil prices, inflation, and trade volumes across regions. This indicates a complete landscape of impacts, where some countries such as India, Saudi Arabia, and China have been able to realise gains in the economy from trade reallocations, (Nguyen et al., 2024; Cui et al., 2024) while others such as the neighbouring countries of Ukraine and some European nations have suffered serious economic setbacks (Nizhnikau & Moshes, 2024; David & LD, 2024).

Previous research has concentrated on regional disruptions in Europe, specifically GDP losses and inflationary pressures, but has not explored how these economic shocks spread globally, especially in non-European regions (Almazán-Gómez et al., 2023). As previously found, countries heavily dependent on Ukrainian and Russian exports often neglect the bigger effects on global food systems and long-term resilience plans (Jagtap et al., 2022). The research on the conflict's inflationary effects has mostly focused on the short term, with none addressing how these tendencies will evolve over the medium to long term, especially in emerging markets (Maurya et al., 2023). Existing trade sanctions research has shortcomings. Trade sanctions research has mostly concentrated on short-term economic effects and ignored potential changes in global trade networks (Mardones, 2022). Long-term geopolitical upheaval, such as China's commercial links altering owing to the conflict, may explain the research gap in global economic landscapes (Huang, 2022).

An increase in the price of crude oil has negatively affected the performance of global trade, as indicated by the rise in inflation, sourced mostly from sanctions on Russian exports (Moshiri & Kheirandish, 2023). However, countries that could arrange alternative supplies of energy or seize the opportunity for aberrant trade arrangements have been able to mitigate these negative impacts (Wilson et al., 2024; Kashwan & Lee, 2024). This strongly highlights the need for policymakers to consider the differential impacts of geopolitical conflicts on global trade when fashioning their responses (Pushp et al., 2024). Countries overly dependent on Russian and Ukrainian exports should diversify their trade relationships and look for alternative supply chains to be immune to such breakdowns (Balmaceda et al., 2024; Kozielec et al., 2024). The second point concerns the vital necessity of international cooperation in dealing with the economic fallouts of geopolitical conflicts, especially through the global stabilisation of energy and food markets. Such insights shed light on the deeper understanding of how conflicts, like the Russia-Ukraine war, can reshape global trade dynamics and how to shape strategic policy prescriptions so that future risks are tempered.

2. LITERATURE REVIEW

The Russia-Ukraine War, or the Russo-Ukrainian War, broke out in 2014 after the protests of Euromaidan in Ukraine ousted from power the pro-Russian Ukrainian President Viktor Yanukovych (Gunneriusson & Ratsiborynska, 2024). Subsequently, Russia proceeded to annex Crimea in March 2014, a measure that was condemned at the international level but legitimized by a disputed referendum in Crimea (Allison, 2023). After that annexation, Donetsk and Luhansk oblasts of Ukraine also saw pro-Russian separatist movements, which led to the armed conflict between Ukrainian forces and pro-Russian separatists supported by Russia. Thousands died in this conflict, driving millions out of their homes (Bhatnagr et al., 2024). Sporadic fighting persisted despite various cease-fire agreements, such as the Minsk agreements of 2014 and 2015. The situation remained tense but relatively contained until early 2022.

The Russia-Ukraine war, ratcheted by several notches after the invasion of Ukraine by Russia in February 2022, is further located within its complex history of geopolitical tension, cultural narratives, and competing national identities. The deep historical linkage is made with the Soviet era, where Russia still looks at Ukraine as falling within its strategic orbit (Grossfeld, 2024). These tensions drastically peaked during the annexation of Crimea in 2014 and the subsequent conflict in Eastern Ukraine (Locoman & Lau, 2024). Historically, Russia has been trying to legitimize its actions by framing the discourse with World War II and accusations regarding Russian speakers (Zavershinskaia, 2024). Further, more steps have been taken to escalate the conflict. The result has been a massive humanitarian catastrophe—civilians have died in large numbers, and there is a huge displacement crisis (Haque et al., 2022). In addition, the conflict has been very disastrous to Ukrainian infrastructure, economy, and social stability, even when it forms a layer in a greater geopolitical battle between NATO and Russia's imperial ambitions (Malyarenko & Kormych, 2023).

The multi-country involvement in the Russia-Ukraine conflict has given rise to escalated global geopolitical tensions. Many countries have been involved due to their direct or indirect involvement in supporting one of the countries, either Russia or Ukraine (Podgórska et al., 2023). For instance, the United States and the European Union have offered extensive military and humanitarian assistance to Ukraine, whereas countries such as Belarus and Iran have supported Russia with their military help (Håkansson, 2023). This kind of internationalisation has multiplied the effect on the conflict because it initiates a domino effect in Global trade and economic relations (Claessen, 2023; Bhatnagr & Rajesh, 2024). Geopolitical tensions are forcing nations to reevaluate their trade relations, especially with Russia and Ukraine. According to Hossain and Masum (2022), the war has forced other countries not directly involved to take sides, thus complicating the dynamics of international trade.

Such geopolitical shifts in both global supply chains and trading patterns continue to underline the deep consequences of this conflict on international commerce.

Scholars, such as Bhattacharjee et al., (2023), critically established the economic effects of the war between Russia and Ukraine through documented evidence of damage to both economies. The rise in military spending was at a high pace at the inception of 2014 and 2015, which led to decreases in economic activities and GDP in both Russia and Ukraine. From the Russian perspective, the impact of the war was more experienced in the latter part of 2022, when it officially went into recession (Semenenko et al., 2023). Besides the direct damage to the Russian and Ukrainian economies, the war has broader ramifications for the global economy. Chen & Semmler (2024) affirm that the war has led to heavy disequilibria in international markets, leading to lower projections for global GDP growth rates. Moreover, this problem has been compounded by the increasing volatility witnessed in global markets, primarily in oil and agriculture-related industries. Thangavel & Chandra (2024) further go on to posit that most of these studies indicate that dependencies upon Russian and Ukrainian exports have allowed such disruptions to have an exponentially higher level of impact on the global economy since a wide variety of industries and countries are affected.

It has, in turn, increased the price of key export commodities, including oil, metals, and agricultural products. According to Boungou & Yatié (2024), the adverse effects of the war on the global commodity markets have been particularly pronounced, with substantial price hikes realized on major export commodities in oil, metals, and agriculture following production disruptions and sanctions on Russian exports. This is further emphasized by the fact that these sanctions have had a significant impact on Russia's position as a major global oil supplier, resulting in a sharp increase in global oil prices and causing energy markets worldwide to stagnate (Pereira et al., 2022). Specifically, the interruption of Ukrainian exports, particularly of wheat and other essential food commodities, has a severe impact on world food security. Astrov et al. (2022) have calculated that the combined wheat exports of Russia and Ukraine account for over 30% of the global total. The ongoing conflict between the two countries has increased food costs. The Black Sea Grain Initiative, created to make it easy for Ukraine to export grain during the war, was quickly left by the wayside; a set of linked disruptions sent food prices soaring and led to shortages in many countries. (Kormych & Malyarenko, 2022; Bhatnagr, 2024).

While the Russia-Ukraine conflict has wreaked havoc in the economic spheres, not all countries are facing the worst consequences. Such trade disruptions have brought about a significant reallocation of global trade flows, which have provided specific countries with an opportunity to gain more over and above others. Global markets have seen an increase in the demand for exports from countries such as China, India, and Saudi Arabia, which is an adjustment to the loss of supplies from

Russia and Ukraine (Olayungbo et al., 2024). India and China have taken advantage of lower-priced Russian oil and have realised gains from the sanction-induced curtailment of Russian exports to Western countries (Kumar, 2022). Major oil producers, such as Saudi Arabia, have also utilised this opportunity to benefit their energy products. These trade diversions underscore the heterogeneous effects of the war, in which some countries benefit from the reordering of global trade flows, while others lose substantially.

In this context, the existing literature (Table 1) predominantly provides a general understanding of the economic and geopolitical impacts of the Russia-Ukraine conflict; however, there is still a need to detail the effects of differential impacts across regions and industries. Therefore, this study attempts to address this gap by examining both the bad and good outputs of the conflict concerning global trade, focusing on exactly what has been pushing such changes. In conclusion, although the war in Ukraine had disastrous consequences for many countries, it also created new opportunities for others, reshaping the world of global trade in complex and uneven ways. The dynamics, therefore, call for further exploration in this literature review to inform policy response mechanisms that address the negative impacts of the conflict and maximise opportunities.

Table 1. Literature Review in Ukraine Russia War

Citation	Region	Model Used	Study Type	Variables Studied	Findings
Wisniewski, 2023	Europe	Multiple Linear Regression	Quantitative	Energy policy, Russian energy dependence	European countries' varied dependence on Russian energy influences future policy directions, with proximity to Russia being a key determinant.
Sabljic et al., 2023	Western Balkans	Econometric Analysis	Quantitative Study	Financial Performance, Banking Sector	The conflict exacerbates existing vulnerabilities in the banking sector, reducing profitability and financial stability.
Rabbi et al., 2023	Europe	Descriptive Analysis	Literature Review	Food security pillars (availability, access, use, stability)	At stake in the conflict are food security and input costs in Europe, which have continued to rise, thereby impacting food affordability and access.

continued on following page

Table 1. Continued

Citation	Region	Model Used	Study Type	Variables Studied	Findings
Quaglia & Verdun, 2023	Europe	Principal-Agent Framework	Qualitative	Financial sanctions, central banks	European central banks are being dragged into financial warfare that directly impacts the monetary policies of the region, with enormous stress on geopolitical considerations.
Prause et al., 2023	Baltic Sea Region	Fuzzy Real Options Model	Case Study	Ammonia production, energy sector	The conflict is moving in a direction that places regional ammonia production closer to the need to offset energy and fertilizer shortfalls.
Nguyen et al., 2023	Global	Conceptual Framework	Review	Food security pillars, geopolitical conflicts	Russia's war has intensified global food insecurity, as political conflicts give birth to cyclical violence and hunger.
Malyarenko & Kormych, 2023	Ukraine	Process Tracing, Fieldwork	Qualitative	Economy of occupied territories	Russian policies destabilized the Ukrainian territories, leading to their economic de-modernization.
Malhotra et al., 2023	Russia and Wheat-Importing Nations	DCC-GARCH model	Quantitative	Commodity prices, financial market linkages	The involvement of financial markets allows the short-run volatilities created by Russian agricultural commodities to be magnified.
Al-Saidi, 2023	Middle East	Descriptive Analysis	Regional Analysis	Food vulnerability	Dependency on Russian and Ukrainian imports leaves the Middle East facing increased food insecurity. Short-run answers are seen in regional help and diversification of sources for energy revenues.
Serrano & Angosto-Fernández, 2022	Global	Event Study Method	Quantitative	Global equity returns	This affects global equity markets, depending on Russian gas and geopolitical factors.
Pandey & Kumar, 2022	Global	Event Study Method	Quantitative	Tourism sector stocks	The conflict negatively affected tourism sector stocks, with significant variations by region.

continued on following page

Table 1. Continued

Citation	Region	Model Used	Study Type	Variables Studied	Findings
Nasir et al., 2022	Global	Descriptive Analysis	Literature Review	Food production, trade	The conflict disrupted food production in Ukraine, thereby increasing global food prices with threats to food security.
Jagtap et al., 2022	Global	PRISMA Approach	Systematic Review	Food supply chains, logistics	Supply chain disruption in the global food supply led to a major increase in food prices, necessitating alternative supply chain strategies.
Hassen & El Bilali, 2022	Global	Descriptive Analysis	Literature Review	Food security, fertilizer access	The conflict is affecting global food security through impacts on food production, labour, and fertilizers.
Čábelková et al., 2022	Post-Soviet Region	Linear and Hierarchical Regression	Quantitative	International trade	Military conflicts and differences in infrastructure have greatly impacted the sustainability of international trade in the post-Soviet region.

3. RESEARCH METHODOLOGY

This study uses a mixed-method approach of combining both qualitative and quantitative data analyses to find out the complex impacts that the Russia-Ukraine conflict has on world trade flows. The methodology is designed to explore the differential effects across countries and regions, with special attention paid to identifying trade diversion that has both positive and negative impacts on international trade dynamics. It makes possible a full-fledged assessment of the trade pattern both before and after the intensification of the conflict in 2022 using data collected from 2010 to 2022. The world trade data include the World Bank, IMF, and other international relevant economic databases (WITS, 2024; IMF, 2024).

Such studies majorly involve the collection of data regarding big economic indicators such as the price of crude oil, the Consumer Price Index (CPI), changes in GDP, and trade volume as a percentage of GDP. These variables are very important to be understood in conflict and global trade performance (Sharma and Shrivastava, 2021). Crude oil prices are of particular importance because Russia is a major oil exporter (Bagchi et al., 2024), and the sanctions imposed on it have come with significant disruption in global oil markets. The standard proxy for inflation is the

Consumer Price Index (CPI) (Habib & Kayani, 2024), which correlates well with energy price fluctuations (De & Mallik, 2024) and hence their broader economic implications. While trade volume as a percentage of gross domestic product is a measure that directly reflects how much international trade is impacted by the conflict (Nam & Ryu, 2024), therefore GDP changes are studied as indicators of the overall economic health of states and regions.

The study period provides a comparison of the economic conditions before the conflict and after the conflict to isolate the effect of the war on trade dynamics. A combination of statistical methods is used to analyze the collected data. The primary method applied is multivariate regression analysis, the same as used in related studies (Dworschak, 2023; Caso et al., 2023; Tadesse et al., 2024), which tests the relationship between trade performance as a percentage of GDP and a range of independent variables, including changes in GDP, changes in CPI, and fluctuations in the price of crude oil, coupled with a binary post-war indicator that differentiated the pre-war and post-war periods. The regression model further plays a central role in describing both the direct and indirect influences of the conflict between Russia and Ukraine on the developed trade model. The control variable is for the year to account for any time-based trends that would influence the results irrespective of the conflict. Descriptive statistics were carried out, and a Wilcoxon Signed-Rank Test was applied to compare major economic indicators before and after the conflict. It is a non-parametric test, taking the variables assumed to be not normally distributed (Okoye & Hosseini, 2024); hence, it is more appropriate than the traditional parametric tests (Lin et al., 2024). The Wilcoxon test shows the statistical significance of changes in GDP on a global scale, together with inflation and oil prices, providing a sound estimation of how the conflict changed global economic conditions. The core multivariate regression model used in the study is specified as follows:

$$\text{Trade Performance (\% GDP)} = \beta_0 + \beta_1(\text{GDP Change}) + \beta_2(\text{CPI Change}) + \beta_3 (\text{Crude Oil Price Change}) + \beta_4 (\text{Post-War Indicator}) + \beta_5(\text{Year}) + \epsilon$$

Given the global repercussions of the war, the discussion provided is also region-specific. The collected data were segregated further into a region-wise basis as per the categorisation available with the World Bank (Volkov et al., 2024; Bhatnagr et al., 2024a), and the regions considered were East Asia and Pacific (EAP), Europe and Central Asia (ECA), Latin America and Caribbean (LAC), Middle East and North Africa (MENA), North America (NA), South Asia (SA), and Sub-Saharan Africa (SSA). By taking a by-region approach, it was possible to check most appropriately how the world in different parts is affected by the conflict.

A clustered multivariate regression model used in similar studies (Jasinskaja-Lahti et al., 2024; Mohamad, 2024) was developed for each region while considering each cluster as an independent region, which means the identification of region-specific impacts because it points to unique economic conditions and trade dependencies that shape how a conflict will affect different regions. In the case of South Asia, the model reports a significant direct negative effect of conflict on trade performance. In contrast, for Europe and Central Asia, this effect turns out to be more indirect, passing through rising oil prices and inflation. The construction of separate models for each region allows the study to yield richer insights into how the impact of conflict on global trade dynamics varies across regions. In this model, trade performance is also used as a percentage of GDP, and the dependent variable represents GDP change, CPI change, crude oil price change, and the postwar indicator. This means that the year is used as a control variable in the models to represent the possible trends that are not related to the conflict. The model is capable of capturing the multifaceted nature of the conflict's impact on global trade through the inclusion of both direct (e.g. the post-war indicator) and indirect effects (e.g. changes in oil prices and inflation).

4. RESULTS

4.1 Global Economic Disruptions

The most pronounced effects of the Russia-Ukraine war have been noted in dramatic fluctuations in global crude oil prices. The study notes a surge in oil prices in 2022 that was largely attributed to sanctions placed on Russian exports, which went on to cause significant interruptions in the global energy market. Meanwhile, from 2014 to 2016, the price of crude oil fell before the actual full-scale upsurge in conflict, which in itself was a clear reflection of how market forces had become complex and fluid because of geopolitical turmoil. This rise in oil prices and rising global inflation has greatly hampered international trade, whether in imports or exports.

In addition, multivariate regression analysis confirms that these economic disruptions bore a toll on the performance of global trade. Specifically, the study finds that trade in goods and services decreased as a share of world GDP from approximately 59.23% in the pre-war period to 56.4% in the post-war period. This is a statistically significant decrease and thus clearly proves the direct war effect on international trade flows. Moreover, the rate of inflation, as measured by the CPI, also declined tremendously from 3.725% in the pre-war period to 2.23% post-war. From the above results, it is evident that although inflationary pressures were mounted during the war, they were subsequently counterbalanced by the general wider economic changes.

More interestingly, in the case of these disruptions of trade and inflation, no significant changes were observed in global GDP during the post-war period. Apparently, in this context, the war posed a certain level of vehement disruptive force over some economic sectors and regions, while towards general global phenomena, the world economy remained relatively stable in terms of GDP growth. This may be because the diversification of economic activities in various regions helped cushion the overall economic effects of the war. On the other hand, crude oil prices significantly decreased following the outbreak of the war. With an increase of 96.24% before the war, statistics show that this decreased to 57.11% after the war. This decline shows how sensitive energy markets are to what is happening at a geopolitical level and, more importantly, the significant influence that energy supplies have on shaping global economic stability.

Figure 1. Data Distribution of Variables at the Global Level

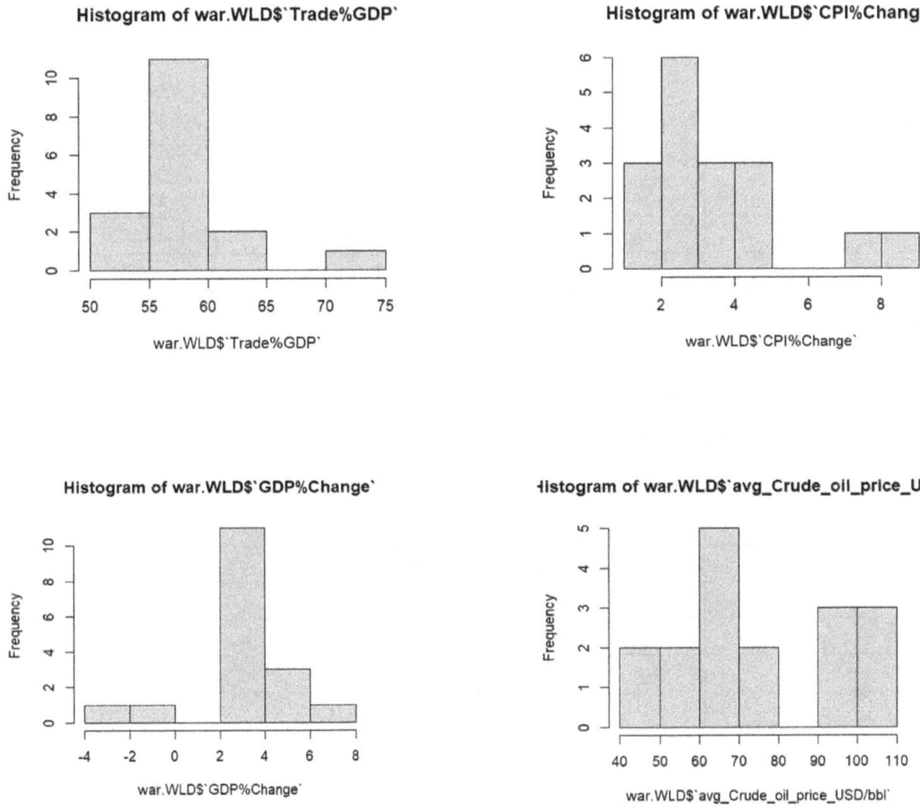

Figure 2. Residual vs Fitted Plot (Left) and Q-Q Plot (Right) of Regression Model

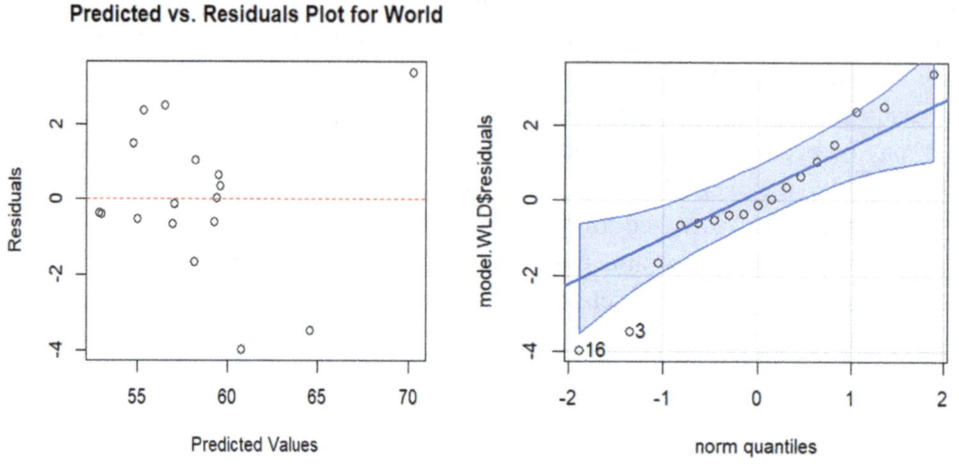

Table 2. Region-Specific Regression Models

Dependent: Trade % of GDP	EAP	ECA	LAC	MENA	NA	SA	SSA
(Intercept)	289.091	-2085.521 ***	-890.701 *	2362.296 *	-73.636	-877.883 *	909.472
	(540.196)	(407.940)	(338.770)	(960.157)	(375.535)	(394.023)	(620.892)
GDP % Change	1.141 *	0.928 **	0.166	-0.428	0.487	0.589 *	0.587
	(0.507)	(0.254)	(0.229)	(0.635)	(0.285)	(0.199)	(0.416)
CPI % Change	1.940 **	1.146 **	1.166 **	0.637	0.613	1.690 **	0.751
	(0.517)	(0.260)	(0.281)	(0.606)	(1.059)	(0.390)	(0.358)
Crude oil price change %	-0.031	-0.052.	0.013	-0.037	-0.026	-0.015	0.013.
	(0.036)	(0.028)	(0.027)	(0.051)	(0.036)	(0.021)	(0.024)
year	-0.118	1.073 ***	0.463 *	-1.133 *	0.052	0.452 *	-0.423
	(0.268)	(0.203)	(0.168)	(0.477)	(0.187)	(0.196)	(0.309)
Post-War	-4.011.	-2.203	1.186	-2.264	-2.970	-5.952 *	-4.163
	(2.060)	(2.014)	(1.594)	(4.289)	(1.767)	(2.389)	(2.252)
R ^ 2	0.925	0.928	0.881	0.816	0.516	0.914	0.916
Adj . R ^ 2	0.892	0.896	0.826	0.733	0.273	0.875	0.847
Num . obs.	17	17	17	17	16	17	12

4.2 Regional Variations in Economic Impact

The regional impacts of the war were analysed in detail in this study. There are large variations in the effect of the Russia-Ukraine War on the performance of trade across the world's regions. Region-specific regression models were developed to consider the effect of the Russia-Ukraine War on trade performance across various regions. The finding on the South Asian region suffers the most severe negative impact on trade performance. The regression analysis showed a large negative effect size for South Asia, which was statistically significant ($B = -5.952$, $p < 0.05$), confirming that the region is vulnerable as a result of disturbances caused by conflict. This may have occurred because South Asia has recently suffered from energy imports from Russia and, more importantly, the economic instability that arises from global inflation. High vulnerabilities to war were also observed in Europe, and Central Asia scored a predictability of 92.8% in the regression model concerning its negative effect on the trade performance of the regions, which mainly passed through an indirect manner as increasing oil prices and inflation made the economic problems more difficult for these countries.

On the other hand, the North American region displayed very low predictability in the regression model ($R^2 = 0.516$), indicating that the factors linked to war explained a few of the trends of trade performance in the United States and Canada. This may be attributed to the relative insulation of the North American economies from the direct impact of the conflict, especially in terms of energy supplies: the U.S. and Canada both have diversified energy sources and strong domestic production capabilities. These results also reflect heterogeneity in other regions. The direct effect of the war on trade performance was weak for the Middle East and East Asia-Pacific regions, with countries in these regions benefiting from altered global trade patterns. The most notable among the countries that registered an increase in trade flows were Saudi Arabia and India, mainly due to the increased demand for oil and access to cheaper Russian crude oil, respectively. China also seized turmoil to gain a greater share of global food markets that had been previously supplied by Ukraine because it was one of the leading suppliers of staple foods.

4.3 Robustness of the Models

Using residual vs. fitted plots and Q-Q plots, an investigation into the robustness of the regression models showed that the East Asia-Pacific, South Asia, Middle East, and North Africa regions had very strong models. These models captured the economic dynamics in these regions and showed the notable impacts of the Russia-Ukraine war on performance in both trade and inflation. However, the models for Central Asia and Europe showed signs of homoscedasticity, implying that the relationship between the independent variables and trade performance could not be constant across the different observations. Therefore, there is a need to further refine the models, particularly for Europe, which was most affected by the conflict. The need for more precise modelling points to the complexity of the impact of the trade war; each region had a different level of economic disruption based on its particular trade links with Russia and Ukraine.

To ensure the reliability of the regression models, we perform several robustness checks. The residuals vs. fitted plot was used to enable us to see if the assumption of homoscedasticity is satisfied, as it shows whether the variance of the residuals is constant across the values of the independent variables. We also have Q-Q plots available for checking normality, as this is one of the central assumptions in the regression analysis. This test for robustness further strengthens the validity of the models because even though it shows some signs of homoscedasticity for the models of Europe and Central Asia, it reveals that further improvement in the models of these regions needs to be done.

The analysis results reveal that the impact of the Russia–Ukraine conflict on worldwide trade flows is broad but rather uneven across the regions. In the global regression model, the barely significant direct negative influence of conflict on trade performance is moderated by changes in crude oil prices and inflation. Country-specific models show a direct negative impact on the South Asian region, whereas in Europe and Central Asia, it is affected by indirect factors such as oil price fluctuations. For the rest of the regions, for example, North America, there is less effect since they do not highly depend on Russia–Ukraine trade. Therefore, this highlights the importance of region-specific analysis in understanding the global impact of the conflict. Although the war has come with its challenges to most of the countries, it has also involved other economies diverting trades to benefit from making up for all the disruptions that have been caused by this political tension between the two economies, more so if all goes wrong and the situation leaves the world oil and food markets facing a lot of uncertainties.

In sum, the findings of this study confirm wide spillovers from the Russia-Ukraine War for global trade and economic stability. This has deeply shaken international energy markets, caused inflationary imbalances, and reversed the flow of international trade. A few regions and countries, such as Saudi Arabia, India, and China, could capture some gains from the changing trade landscape in both aspects. All others have shown negative repercussions, especially in the areas of their trade performance and inflation. In this way, the findings of this study have practical implications for understanding the broader economic consequences attached to geopolitical conflicts, and for which strategic policy responses need to be called up in their mitigation.

5. DISCUSSION

The significance of this study lies in the understanding of global trade disturbances under the Russia-Ukraine conflict, elaborating on the economic factors and regional impacts that have essentially reshaped trade flows. With the first research question, the findings identify the greatly destabilised international trade, particularly in regions and sectors heavily dependent on Russian energy exports and Ukrainian agricultural produce. Global trade volumes, as measured by their contribution to GDP, fell dramatically in the post-war period, when trade performance dropped from 59.23% pre-war to 56.4% post-war. The contraction itself reflects the spillover effects of sanctions against Russian exports, mostly oil, and disruptions in the global supply chains. The ripple effect is felt through decreased trade activity across industries, as countries try to manage inflationary pressures and volatile energy markets. These results were in line with the previous studies (Čábelková et al., 2022; Bhatnagr et al., 2024b; Mardones, 2022).

Second, the study attempts to identify what pushed these trade reallocations through these windows during the conflict. The increased trading costs with the key drivers were identified with the rise in crude oil prices, global inflation, and economic instability due to geopolitical tensions in line with previous studies (Tuzova & Qayum, 2016; Von Below & Vezina, 2016). As shown by the regression analysis, variations in crude oil prices and inflation as leading predictors of changes in global trade performance. This underpins the role of energy markets as catalysts for international trade dynamics during crises. Sanctions on Russian oil have forced many countries to search for alternative sources of energy, leading to the realignment of global trade relationships. Further, the implications of war-induced inflationary pressures are not only felt in the costs of goods production, but also in transportation charges, which have contributed to higher production costs and, therefore, aggravated trade disruptions. These suggest further that, while the models explain much of the variation in trade performance, the political-economic landscape might be so intricate that other factors, such as political alliances and regional security concerns, shape trade flows.

Based on the third question which countries have benefited and which have been lost from trade diversion? This unevenness in the impact of conflict is found in the study by countries most closely involved with Russia and Ukraine, such as Belarus, Tajikistan, and many of those in Central Asia, who experienced sizable economic costs due to their reliance on imports from the two countries. The food and energy crises induced by the war hit these regions, leading to a decrease in their trade volume and economic instability. At the same time, reallocation in world trade found the United States, Saudi Arabia, China, and India to be at the receiving end. Arms exports have gone up into the U.S., and Saudi Arabia leveraged upon demand for their oil triggered by sanctions from Russia. Both China and India have improved their energy security by securing discounted Russian oil and improving their trading performance which is in line with previous studies (Malle, 2017; Røseth, 2017; Bhatnagr et al., 2024c). These results depict an unequal distribution of the economic aftershocks of the conflict, as some countries use the situation to strengthen their positions in the global market.

6. THEORETICAL CONTRIBUTION

The study provides unique theoretical contributions as an empirical study on the detailed effects of the Russia-Ukraine conflict, which has limited attention in the previous literature, on global trade flows (Ma et al., 2023; Larch & Yotov, 2024; Lampe & Sharp, 2024; Tiwari et al., 2024). By employing a robust multivariate regression model (Dworschak, 2023; Caso et al., 2023; Tadesse et al., 2024), this study quantifies the extent to which key economic variables propel trade performance in the context of a major geopolitical conflict impacting crude oil prices, inflation, and changes in GDP. The introduction of region-specific models of regression has also brought in the details by which different parts of the world are affected, and hence, understanding—the dimensions that often escape one's grasp through a more generalised analysis.

This study further addresses the previous literature gaps by primarily focusing on regional disruptions within Europe, particularly concerning GDP losses and inflationary pressures, and addresses insufficient exploration of economic shocks that propagate on a global scale, especially in non-European regions (Almazán-Gómez et al., 2023). Further, food security disruptions in countries dependent on Ukrainian and Russian exports have been studied, the studies address the broader implications for global food systems and the development of long-term resilience strategies which have not been sufficiently theorized (Jagtap et al., 2022). Additionally, existing studies on the inflationary effects of the conflict have primarily offered short-term analyses, this study addresses the lack of evolution in these inflationary trends in the medium-to-long term, particularly in emerging markets (Maurya et al., 2023). Finally, while trade sanctions have been analyzed in terms of their immediate economic impacts, this study addresses the gap in understanding how sanctions might reconfigure global trade networks over time (Mardones, 2022). Finally, this study contributes to the theoretical understanding of how geopolitical shifts, such as China's evolving economic relations due to the conflict, could reshape the global economic landscape in the long run, a topic that has been underexplored in current literature (Huang, 2022).

7. PRACTICAL IMPLICATIONS

This study provides enormous practical implications for policymakers, regulators engaged in cross-border trade, and businesses involved in the global marketplace. The findings emphasise the need to diversify trading relationships and ensure energy supply to minimise the effects of geopolitical crises, such as the Russia-Ukraine War. This will entail that policymakers in regions with very high imports from conflicted countries, such as Central Asia and Europe, establish economic resilience by seeking alternative trading partners and domestic energy production. For countries that have been trading with these reallocations in favour of other countries, the results of the study point to an opportunity to leverage these changes to increase influence in global markets to countries such as Saudi Arabia, China, and India. Furthermore, businesses operating in international markets must understand that they work within the rapidly changing geopolitical landscapes. Their prime interest is to ensure the resilience of their supply chains to explore newer market opportunities that could open up as a result of such disruptions. In general, the current research emphasises the need for strategic thought and a proactive policy agenda to navigate the difficult set of challenges being thrown up by global conflict to ensure sustainable economic development in an uncertain international environment.

8. LIMITATIONS

Despite providing insightful findings, this study has certain limitations. It relies on secondary data and annual metrics, which may overlook short-term fluctuations and the nuanced real-time effects of the Russia-Ukraine conflict on global trade. Furthermore, focusing only on key economic indicators, such as crude oil prices, GDP, and inflation, will not fully reflect other trade-resilience-influencing factors, such as political alliances and technological shifts. However, the regional regression models are robust, but they exhibit signs of homoscedasticity in some regions, such as Central Asia and Europe, indicating the need for model refinement. Furthermore, the long-term implications and adaptations of global trade flow changes necessitate further research, as the present study primarily focuses on short-to-medium-term impacts. Future studies can incorporate more granular real-time data and specifically examine the role of emerging technologies in mitigating trade disruptions. Additionally, case studies or interviews with policymakers would provide further qualitative insights in addition to the existing quantitative research regarding strategic responses to geopolitical conflicts and their effects on trade.

9. CONCLUSION

This study underscores the gravity and variety of the consequences of the Russia-Ukraine conflict on the flow of global trade. It emphasizes how geopolitical disturbances can significantly alter the dynamics of international trade. According to the study, the global volumes of trade have decreased, while the prices of crude oil have increased, leading to inflation and sanctions imposed on Russian exports. Of course, there are disparities in the regions, and nations in Central Asia and Europe suffer more, while others, such as Saudi Arabia, China, and India, benefit from the readjustments of trade. The study is exceptional as it presents a comprehensive empirical examination of how global energy markets, inflationary pressures, and trade dependencies work during geopolitical crises. The application of region-specific regression models in this study provides more accurate results about the diverse impacts across different parts of the world and thus serves as a valuable guide to policymakers and businesses in navigating the complexity of international trade operations during conflicts. This testifies to the importance of economic diversification, energy security, and resilience in the face of serious global geopolitical events, an area that is surely most important for the provision of resources to make strategic planning and policy development into reality.

REFERENCES

Aizenman, J., Lindahl, R., Stenvall, D., & Uddin, G. S. (2024). Geopolitical shocks and commodity market dynamics: New evidence from the Russia-Ukraine conflict. *European Journal of Political Economy*, *85*, 102574. DOI: 10.1016/j.ejpoleco.2024.102574

Al-Saidi, M. (2023). Caught off guard and beaten: The Ukraine war and food security in the Middle East. *Frontiers in Nutrition*, *10*, 983346. Advance online publication. DOI: 10.3389/fnut.2023.983346 PMID: 36895270

Allison, R. (2023). Russia's Case for War against Ukraine: Legal Claims, Political Rhetoric, and Instrumentality in a Fracturing International Order. *Problems of Post-Communism*, *71*(3), 271–282. DOI: 10.1080/10758216.2023.2254915

Almazán-Gómez, M. Á., Llano, C., Pérez, J., & Rauhut, D. (2023). Socioeconomic impacts of Russian invasion of Ukraine: A multiregional assessment for Europe. *Journal of Regional Science*, *64*(2), 333–354. DOI: 10.1111/jors.12676

Astrov, V., Ghodsi, M., Grieveson, R., Holzner, M., Kochnev, A., Landesmann, M., Pindyuk, O., Stehrer, R., Tverdostup, M., & Bykova, A. (2022). Russia's invasion of Ukraine: Assessment of the humanitarian, economic, and financial impact in the short and medium term. *International Economics and Economic Policy*, *19*(2), 331–381. DOI: 10.1007/s10368-022-00546-5 PMID: 40478010

Ateed, E. H. (2023). The impact of Russia-Ukraine war on the global energy crisis. In *Advances in public policy and administration (APPA) book series* (pp. 119–138). DOI: 10.4018/979-8-3693-0440-2.ch007

Bagchi, B., Paul, B., & Ghosh, R. (2024). Dynamic effects of crude oil price shocks on stock markets and exchange rates: Evidence from major oil importing countries amid Russia-Ukraine conflict. *Global Business and Economics Review*, *30*(2), 234–257. DOI: 10.1504/GBER.2024.136424

Balma, L., Heidland, T., Jävervall, S., Mahlkow, H., Mukasa, A. N., & Woldemichael, A. (2024). Long-run impacts of the conflict in Ukraine on grain imports and prices in Africa. *African Development Review*, *36*(S1). Advance online publication. DOI: 10.1111/1467-8268.12745

Balmaceda, M., Högselius, P., Johnson, C., Pleines, H., Rogers, D., & Tynkkynen, V. (2024). Rethinking energy materialities in the shadow of Russia's war on Ukraine. *Energy Research & Social Science*, *117*, 103678. DOI: 10.1016/j.erss.2024.103678

Bednarski, L., Roscoe, S., Blome, C., & Schleper, M. C. (2023). Geopolitical disruptions in global supply chains: A state-of-the-art literature review. *Production Planning and Control*, 1–27. DOI: 10.1080/09537287.2023.2286283

Bhatnagr, P. (2024). Consumer insights on cultural appropriation in fashion: A Douyin analysis. *Asia Pacific Journal of Marketing and Logistics*. Advance online publication. DOI: 10.1108/APJML-07-2024-0893

Bhatnagr, P., & Rajesh, A. (2024). Artificial intelligence features and expectation confirmation theory in digital banking apps: Gen Y and Z perspective. *Management Decision*. Advance online publication. DOI: 10.1108/MD-07-2023-1145

Bhatnagr, P., Rajesh, A., & Misra, R. (2024). Neobank adoption: Integrating the information systems effectiveness framework with the innovation resistance model. *Management Decision*, *62*(10), 3315–3352. Advance online publication. DOI: 10.1108/MD-06-2023-0977

Bhatnagr, P., Rajesh, A., & Misra, R. (2024a). The impact of Fintech innovations on digital currency adoption: a blockchain-based study in India. *International Journal of Accounting and Information Management*. DOI: 10.1108/IJAIM-11-2023-0275

Bhatnagr, P., Rajesh, A., & Misra, R. (2024b). Continuous intention usage of artificial intelligence enabled digital banks: A review of expectation confirmation model. *Journal of Enterprise Information Management*, *37*(6), 1763–1787. DOI: 10.1108/JEIM-11-2023-0617

Bhatnagr, P., Rajesh, A., & Misra, R. (2024c). A study on driving factors for enhancing financial performance and customer-centricity through digital banking. *International Journal of Quality and Service Sciences*, *16*(2), 218–250. DOI: 10.1108/IJQSS-09-2023-0141

Bhattacharjee, A., Gaur, D., & Gupta, K. (2023). Russia–Ukraine war and the impact on Indian economy. *Journal of Economic Studies (Glasgow, Scotland)*, *51*(4), 841–858. DOI: 10.1108/JES-03-2023-0136

Bilali, H. E., & Hassen, T. B. (2024). Disrupted harvests: How Ukraine – Russia war influences global food systems – a systematic review. *Policy Studies*, *45*(3–4), 310–335. DOI: 10.1080/01442872.2024.2329587

Boungou, W., & Yatié, A. (2024). Uncertainty, stock and commodity prices during the Ukraine-Russia war. *Policy Studies*, *45*(3-4), 1–17. DOI: 10.1080/01442872.2024.2302440

Boyko, N., Nes, K., & Schaefer, K. A. (2023). International trade and Ukraine's pursuit of self-determination. *World Economy*, *47*(4), 1460–1477. DOI: 10.1111/twec.13493

Brosig, M., & Verma, R. (2024). The war in Ukraine, the Global South and the evolving global order. *Global Policy*, *15*(4), 740–745. Advance online publication. DOI: 10.1111/1758-5899.13366

Čábelková, I., Smutka, L., Rotterova, S., Zhytna, O., Kluger, V., & Mareš, D. (2022). The sustainability of international trade: The impact of ongoing military conflicts, infrastructure, common language, and economic wellbeing in Post-Soviet region. *Sustainability (Basel)*, *14*(17), 10840. DOI: 10.3390/su141710840

Caso, N., Hilhorst, D., Mena, R., & Papyrakis, E. (2023). Does disaster contribute to armed conflict? A quantitative analysis of disaster–conflict co-occurrence between 1990 and 2017. *International Journal of Development Issues*, *23*(1), 1–23. DOI: 10.1108/IJDI-01-2023-0015

Chatterjee, N. (2024). Impact of economic crises on economic development of developing nations in a globalised world. In *Emerald Publishing Limited eBooks* (pp. 299–313). DOI: 10.1108/978-1-83753-586-620241020

Chen, P., & Semmler, W. (2024). Wage – price dynamics and financial market in a disequilibrium macro model: A Keynes – Kaldor – Minsky modeling of recession and inflation using VECM. *Journal of Economic Behavior & Organization*, *220*, 433–452. DOI: 10.1016/j.jebo.2024.01.012

Claessen, E. (2021). The making of a narrative: The use of geopolitical othering in Russian strategic narratives during the Ukraine crisis. *Media, War & Conflict*, *16*(1), 82–99. DOI: 10.1177/17506352211029529

Cooper, J. (2024). The machine tool industry of Russia at a time of war and sanctions. *Post-Communist Economies*, *36*(5), 1–35. DOI: 10.1080/14631377.2024.2325787

Cui, J., Maghyereh, A., & Liao, D. (2024). Risk connectedness between international oil and stock markets during the COVID-19 pandemic and the Russia-Ukraine conflict: Fresh evidence from the higher-order moments. *International Review of Economics & Finance*, *103470*, 103470. Advance online publication. DOI: 10.1016/j.iref.2024.103470

David, M., & LD, N. (2024). Russia's war on Ukraine: Unbottled emotions and the conditioning of the EU's Russia policy. *Revue D'intégration Européenne. Journal of European Integration*, *46*(5), 661–684. DOI: 10.1080/07036337.2024.2363613

De, U. K., & Mallik, G. (2024). Crude oil price, manufacturing index, and consumer price index: Is there any temporal link in India? *IIMB Management Review*, *36*(2), 137–145. Advance online publication. DOI: 10.1016/j.iimb.2024.03.007

Del Rosal, I. (2023). Trade effects of liner shipping across world regions. *Maritime Business Review*, *9*(1), 2–16. DOI: 10.1108/MABR-06-2023-0040

Delanty, G. (2023). Introduction to the special issue on the Russo-Ukrainian War: A new European war? Considerations on the Russo-Ukrainian War. *European Journal of Social Theory*, *26*(4), 431–449. DOI: 10.1177/13684310231174098

Devadoss, S., & Ridley, W. (2024). Impacts of the Russian invasion of Ukraine on the global wheat market. *World Development*, *173*, 106396. DOI: 10.1016/j.worlddev.2023.106396

Dworschak, C. (2023). Bias mitigation in empirical peace and conflict studies: A short primer on posttreatment variables. *Journal of Peace Research*. Advance online publication. DOI: 10.1177/00223433221145531

Ferrández-Serrano, V., & Angosto-Fernández, P. L. (2022). A Russian carol: Impact and dependence on global equity markets during the Ukraine invasion. *Journal of Economic Studies (Glasgow, Scotland)*, *50*(7), 1399–1412. DOI: 10.1108/JES-06-2022-0364

Grossfeld, E. (2024). Russia's declining satellite reconnaissance capabilities and its implications for security and international stability. *International Journal of Intelligence and CounterIntelligence*, *38*(1), 1–30. DOI: 10.1080/08850607.2024.2330848

Gunneriusson, H., & Ratsiborynska, V. (2024). Geopolitics in the Contested Areas. In *Geopolitics in the Contested Areas* (pp. 1–15). DOI: 10.1007/978-3-031-25399-7_59-1

Habib, A. M., & Kayani, U. N. (2024). Price reaction of global economic indicators: Evidence from the COVID-19 pandemic and the Russia–Ukraine conflict. *SN Business & Economics*, *4*(1), 19. Advance online publication. DOI: 10.1007/s43546-023-00619-w

Håkansson, C. (2023). The Ukraine war and the emergence of the European commission as a geopolitical actor. *Journal of European Integration*, *46*(1), 25–45. DOI: 10.1080/07036337.2023.2239998

Hassen, T. B., & Bilali, H. E. (2022). Impacts of the Russia-Ukraine war on global food security: Towards more sustainable and resilient food systems? *Foods*, *11*(15), 2301. DOI: 10.3390/foods11152301 PMID: 35954068

Henderson, J. (2024). The impact of the Russia-Ukraine war on global gas markets. *Current Sustainable/Renewable. Energy Reports, 11*(1), 1–9. DOI: 10.1007/s40518-024-00232-x

Hossain, A. T., Masum, A., & Saadi, S. (2024). The impact of geopolitical risks on foreign exchange markets: Evidence from the Russia–Ukraine war. *Finance Research Letters, 59*, 104750. DOI: 10.1016/j.frl.2023.104750

Hossain, A. T., & Masum, A. A. (2022). Russian invasion of Ukraine, geopolitical risk, and global financial markets. SSRN *Electronic Journal*. DOI: 10.2139/ssrn.4056137

Huang, Y. (2022). China's changing economic relations with the world: Introduction. *China Economic Journal, 15*(3), 231–234. DOI: 10.1080/17538963.2022.2118458

IMF. (2024). https://data.imf.org/?sk=9D6028D4-F14A-464C-A2F2-59B2CD424B85

Imran-Ur-Rahman, I., Shafi, M., Fauzi, M. A., & Fetuu, E. (2024). Examining trade flow dynamics in the face of deglobalization and decoupling: A comparative analysis of developing and developed nations. *Kybernetes*. Advance online publication. DOI: 10.1108/K-02-2024-0503

Jagtap, S., Trollman, H., Trollman, F., Garcia-Garcia, G., Parra-López, C., Duong, L., Martindale, W., Munekata, P., Lorenzo, J., Hdaifeh, A., Hassoun, A., Salonitis, K., & Afy-Shararah, M. (2022). The Russia-Ukraine Conflict: Its implications for the global food supply chains. *Foods, 11*(14), 2098. DOI: 10.3390/foods11142098 PMID: 35885340

Jakupec, V. (2024). Dynamics of the Ukraine War. DOI: 10.1007/978-3-031-52444-8

Jasinskaja-Lahti, I., Szebeni, Z., Birman, D., Mitikka, E., & Renvik, T. A. (2024). Diasporas during conflict: A mixed-method analysis of attitudes of the Russian-speaking community in Finland towards the Russia-Ukraine war. *Journal of Community & Applied Social Psychology, 34*(4), e2824. Advance online publication. DOI: 10.1002/casp.2824

Jiang, W., & Chen, Y. (2024). Impact of Russia-Ukraine conflict on the time-frequency and quantile connectedness between energy, metal and agricultural markets. *Resources Policy, 88*, 104376. DOI: 10.1016/j.resourpol.2023.104376

Kashwan, P., & Lee, H. (2024). Beyond stakeholder consultations: Red-green coalition democratizes Maine's offshore wind energy policymaking. *Energy Research & Social Science, 116*, 103692. DOI: 10.1016/j.erss.2024.103692

Khan, N., Mejri, S., & Hammoudeh, S. (2024). How do global commodities react to increasing geopolitical risks? New insights into the Russia-Ukraine and Palestine-Israel conflicts. *Energy Economics, 107812*. Advance online publication. DOI: 10.1016/j.eneco.2024.107812

Kizilova, K., & Norris, P. (2023). "Rally around the flag" effects in the Russian–Ukrainian war. *European Political Science*. Advance online publication. DOI: 10.1057/s41304-023-00450-9

Kormych, B., & Malyarenko, T. (2022). From gray zone to conventional warfare: The Russia-Ukraine conflict in the Black Sea. *Small Wars & Insurgencies, 34*(7), 1235–1270. DOI: 10.1080/09592318.2022.2122278

Köseoğlu, S. D., Mercangöz, B. A., Khan, K., & Sarwar, S. (2023). The impact of the Russian-Ukraine war on the stock market: A causal analysis. *Applied Economics*, 1–11. DOI: 10.1080/00036846.2023.2188168

Kozielec, A., Piecuch, J., Daniek, K., & Luty, L. (2024). Challenges to food security in the Middle East and North Africa in the context of the Russia–Ukraine conflict. *Agriculture, 14*(1), 155. DOI: 10.3390/agriculture14010155

Kozyrev, V. (2024). The war in Ukraine and its impact on the US perspective of Europe. In *Global power shift* (pp. 17–43). DOI: 10.1007/978-3-031-48117-8_2

Kumar, S. (2022). Regional organizations and States in international Relations: A study of India's approach towards regional organizations. *Millennial Asia, 15*(2), 259–277. DOI: 10.1177/09763996221105148

Lampe, M., & Sharp, P. (2024). Cliometric approaches to international trade. In *Springer eBooks* (pp. 859–897). DOI: 10.1007/978-3-031-35583-7_8

Larch, M., & Yotov, Y. V. (2024). Estimating the effects of trade agreements: Lessons from 60 years of methods and data. *World Economy*, *47*(5), 1771–1799. Advance online publication. DOI: 10.1111/twec.13569

Lin, K. K., Arya, N., Malik, S., & Diaz, M. (2024). Continuous variable analyses. In *Elsevier eBooks* (pp. 141–145). DOI: 10.1016/B978-0-323-85663-8.00078-7

Locoman, E., & Lau, R. R. (2024). Narratives of conflict: Russian media's evolving treatment of Ukraine (2013–2022). *Media, War & Conflict*. Advance online publication. DOI: 10.1177/17506352241257053

Lohani, K. K. (2020). Trade Flow of India with BRICS Countries: A Gravity Model Approach. *Global Business Review*, *25*(1), 22–39. DOI: 10.1177/0972150920927684

Lohani, K. K. (2020). Trade Flow of India with BRICS Countries: A Gravity Model Approach. *Global Business Review*, *25*(1), 22–39. DOI: 10.1177/0972150920927684

Ma, S., Shen, Y., & Fang, C. (2023). Can data flow provisions facilitate trade in goods and services?—Analysis based on the TAPED database. *The Journal of International Trade & Economic Development*, *33*(3), 343–368. DOI: 10.1080/09638199.2023.2179860

Malhotra, G., Yadav, M. P., Tandon, P., & Sinha, N. (2023). An investigation on dynamic connectedness of commodity market with financial market during the Russia–Ukraine invasion. *Benchmarking*, *31*(2), 439–465. DOI: 10.1108/BIJ-11-2022-0727

Malle, S. (2017). Russia and China in the 21st century. Moving towards cooperative behaviour. *Journal of Eurasian Studies*, *8*(2), 136–150. DOI: 10.1016/j.euras.2017.02.003

Malyarenko, T., & Kormych, B. (2023). Russian policy towards the economy of occupied Ukrainian territories: Crawling de-modernization. *Eurasian Geography and Economics*, *64*(2), 220–237. DOI: 10.1080/15387216.2023.2167097

Mardones, C. (2022). Economic effects of isolating Russia from international trade due to its 'special military operation' in Ukraine. *European Planning Studies*, *31*(4), 663–678. DOI: 10.1080/09654313.2022.2079074

Maurya, P. K., Bansal, R., & Mishra, A. K. (2023). Russia–Ukraine conflict and its impact on global inflation: An event study-based approach. *Journal of Economic Studies (Glasgow, Scotland)*, *50*(8), 1824–1846. DOI: 10.1108/JES-01-2023-0003

Mohamad, A. (2024). Herding behaviour surrounding the Russo–Ukraine war and COVID-19 pandemic: Evidence from energy, metal, livestock and grain commodities. *Review of Behavioral Finance*, *16*(5), 925–957. Advance online publication. DOI: 10.1108/RBF-12-2023-0339

Moshiri, S., & Kheirandish, E. (2023). Global impacts of oil price shocks: The trade effect. *Journal of Economic Studies (Glasgow, Scotland)*, *51*(1), 126–144. DOI: 10.1108/JES-08-2022-0455

Nam, H., & Ryu, D. (2024). Does trade openness promote economic growth in developing countries? *Journal of International Financial Markets, Institutions and Money*, *93*, 101985. DOI: 10.1016/j.intfin.2024.101985

Nasir, M. A., Nugroho, A. D., & Lakner, Z. (2022). Impact of the Russian–Ukrainian conflict on global food crops. *Foods*, *11*(19), 2979. DOI: 10.3390/foods11192979 PMID: 36230055

Nguyen, H. H., Van Nguyen, P., & Ngo, V. M. (2024). Energy security and the shift to renewable resources: The case of Russia-Ukraine war. *The Extractive Industries and Society*, *17*, 101442. DOI: 10.1016/j.exis.2024.101442

Nguyen, T. T., Timilsina, R. R., Sonobe, T., & Rahut, D. B. (2023). Interstate war and food security: Implications from Russia's invasion of Ukraine. *Frontiers in Sustainable Food Systems*, *7*, 1080696. Advance online publication. DOI: 10.3389/fsufs.2023.1080696

Nizhnikau, R., & Moshes, A. (2024). The war in Ukraine, the EU's geopolitical awakening and implications for the "contested neighbourhood.". *Policy Studies*, *45*(3-4), 1–18. DOI: 10.1080/01442872.2024.2306972

Okoye, K., & Hosseini, S. (2024). Choosing Between Parametric and Non-parametric Tests in Statistical Data Analysis. In *springer* (pp. 87–98). DOI: 10.1007/978-981-97-3385-9_4

Olayungbo, D. O., Zhuparova, A., Al-Faryan, M. S., & Ojo, M. S. (2024). Global oil price and stock markets in oil exporting and European countries: Evidence during the Covid-19 and the Russia-Ukraine war. *Research in Globalization*, *8*, 100199. DOI: 10.1016/j.resglo.2024.100199

Oyebamiji, S. I., Ashe, M. O., & Kiyala, K. J. C. (2024). Russia-Ukraine War: Impacts on energy market and food security in Africa. In *˜The œanthropocene: Politik - economics - society - science* (pp. 419–441). DOI: 10.1007/978-3-031-48375-2_19

Ozili, P. K. (2024). Global economic consequences of Russian invasion of Ukraine. In *Advances in human services and public health (AHSPH) book series* (pp. 195–223). DOI: 10.4018/978-1-6684-9467-7.ch010

Özocakli, D., Başar, B. D., Ekşi, İ. H., & Ginn, W. (2024). Effect of Grain Corridor Agreement on grain prices. *International Economic Journal*, *38*(3), 1–18. DOI: 10.1080/10168737.2024.2372764

Pandey, D. K., & Kumar, R. (2022). Russia-Ukraine War and the global tourism sector: A 13-day tale. *Current Issues in Tourism*, *26*(5), 692–700. DOI: 10.1080/13683500.2022.2081789

Pereira, P., Bašić, F., Bogunovic, I., & Barcelo, D. (2022). Russian-Ukrainian war impacts the total environment. *The Science of the Total Environment*, *837*, 155865. DOI: 10.1016/j.scitotenv.2022.155865 PMID: 35569661

Podgórska, K., Jekaterynczuk, A., Yarosh, O., Kuzmuk, O., & Liubchuk, V. (2023). Support for Ukrainian refugees after Russia's invasion of Ukraine: Aid structure and resilience factors. Case studies of Lublin and Lutsk. *European Societies*, 1–25. DOI: 10.1080/14616696.2023.2206892

Prause, G., Olaniyi, E. O., & Gerstlberger, W. (2023). Ammonia production as alternative energy for the Baltic Sea region. *Energies*, *16*(4), 1831. DOI: 10.3390/en16041831

Pushp, P., Sharma, A., & Ahmed, F. (2024). Flexibility in the WTO: Navigating the dynamics of multilateralism using Grounded theory. *Global Journal of Flexible Systems Management*. DOI: 10.1007/s40171-024-00413-z

Quaglia, L., & Verdun, A. (2023). Weaponisation of finance: The role of European central banks and financial sanctions against Russia. *West European Politics*, *46*(5), 872–895. DOI: 10.1080/01402382.2022.2155906

Rabbi, M. F., Hassen, T. B., Bilali, H. E., Raheem, D., & Raposo, A. (2023). Food security challenges in Europe in the context of the prolonged Russian–Ukrainian conflict. *Sustainability (Basel)*, *15*(6), 4745. DOI: 10.3390/su15064745

Røseth, T. (2017). Russia's energy relations with China: Passing the strategic threshold? *Eurasian Geography and Economics*, *58*(1), 23–55. DOI: 10.1080/15387216.2017.1304229

Sabljic, S., Rakovic, T. S., & Vasic, V. (2023). The new challenges of the Western Balkan banking industry during ongoing global crisis. *Journal of Balkan & Near Eastern Studies*, *25*(4), 671–682. DOI: 10.1080/19448953.2023.2167166

Semenenko, O., Sliusarenko, M., Onofriichuk, A., Onofriichuk, V., & Remez, A. (2023). Impact of the Russian–Ukrainian war on the national economy of Russia. *Journal of Interdisciplinary Economics*, *36*(1), 41–57. DOI: 10.1177/02601079231207489

Seyoum, B. (2024). International Trade Policy for growth and Prosperity. In *Palgrave studies in democracy, innovation, and entrepreneurship for growth* (pp. 275–314). DOI: 10.1007/978-3-031-44776-1_7

Sharma, P., & Shrivastava, A. K. (2021). Economic activities and oil price shocks in Indian outlook: Direction of causality and testing cointegration. *Global Business Review*, *097215092199049*. Advance online publication. DOI: 10.1177/0972150921990491

Tadesse, G., Yitayih, S., Gashaw, F., Fentahun, S., Amare, A., Kibralew, G., & Zeleke, T. A. (2024). Magnitude and factors associated with post-traumatic stress disorder among war-affected internally displaced people in northwest Ethiopia, 2022. *SAGE Open Medicine*, *12*, 20503121241259629. Advance online publication. DOI: 10.1177/20503121241259629 PMID: 39086554

Thakkar, C. (2024). Russia-Ukraine War, India, and US grand strategy: Punishing or leveraging neutrality? *Policy Studies*, *45*(3-4), 1–19. DOI: 10.1080/01442872.2024.2302437

Thangavel, P., & Chandra, B. (2024). Impact of sanctions on Russia on global economy. *International Journal of Business Forecasting and Marketing Intelligence*, *9*(1), 1–8. DOI: 10.1504/IJBFMI.2024.135717

Tiwari, M., Ferrill, J., & Allan, D. M. (2024). Trade-based money laundering: A systematic literature review. *Journal of Accounting Literature*. Advance online publication. DOI: 10.1108/JAL-11-2022-0111

Tong, E. (2024). Repercussions of the Russia–Ukraine war. *International Review of Economics & Finance*, *89*, 366–390. DOI: 10.1016/j.iref.2023.07.064

Tosun, O. K., Eshraghi, A., & Vigne, S. A. (2024). Firms entangled in geopolitical conflicts: Evidence from the russia – Ukraine war. *Journal of International Money and Finance*, *103137*, 103137. Advance online publication. DOI: 10.1016/j.jimonfin.2024.103137

Tuzova, Y., & Qayum, F. (2016). Global oil glut and sanctions: The impact on Putin's Russia. *Energy Policy*, *90*, 140–151. DOI: 10.1016/j.enpol.2015.12.008

Vargas-Hernández, J. G., & Vargas-González, O. C. (2024). Global supply, production and value chains. In *Emerald Publishing Limited eBooks* (pp. 277–297). DOI: 10.1108/978-1-83753-586-620241019

Verma, R., & Düben, B. A. (2024). The Russia–Ukraine war and inter-state dynamics in the Indo-Pacific. *International Politics*, *61*(5), 903–922. Advance online publication. DOI: 10.1057/s41311-023-00551-8

Vlados, C., & Chatzinikolaou, D. (2024). The emergence of the new globalization: The approach of the evolutionary structural triptych. *Journal of Global Responsibility*. Advance online publication. DOI: 10.1108/JGR-04-2023-0063

Volkov, A. D., Roslyakova, N. A., Vasilieva, A. V., Averyanov, A. O., Tishkov, S. V., & Nalivaychenko, E. V. (2024). Preferential Regime of the Russian Arctic: Tendencies and First Results from Realization of the World's Largest Special Economic Zone. *Journal of Risk and Financial Management*, *17*(1), 28. DOI: 10.3390/jrfm17010028

Von Below, D., & Vezina, P. F. (2016). The trade consequences of pricey oil. *IMF Economic Review, 64*(2), 303–318. DOI: 10.1057/imfer.2016.3

Wilson, A., Connor, P., & Hardy, J. (2024). Fighting the past to win the future: Regulatory roulette, institutional inertia and the challenge of enabling military energy security. *Energy Research & Social Science, 114*, 103584. DOI: 10.1016/j.erss.2024.103584

Wiśniewski, T. P. (2023). Investigating Divergent Energy Policy Fundamentals: Warfare Assessment of past dependence on Russian energy raw materials in Europe. *Energies, 16*(4), 2019. DOI: 10.3390/en16042019

WITS. (2022). WITS. https://wits.worldbank.org/countrystats.aspx?lang=en

Xia, X., & Li, A. (2024). Global natural gas market and changing trends of natural gas trade. In *Current Chinese economic report series* (pp. 139–152). DOI: 10.1007/978-981-99-7289-0_9

Zavershinskaia, P. (2024). State's Legitimisation of Violence through Strategic Narration: How the Kremlin Justified the Russian Invasion of Ukraine. *The International Spectator, 59*(2), 1–19. DOI: 10.1080/03932729.2024.2327492

Zhang, D., Wang, C., & Wang, Y. (2024). Unveiling the critical nexus: Volatility of crude oil future prices and trade partner's cash holding behavior in the face of the Russia–Ukraine conflict. *Energy Economics, 132*, 107413. DOI: 10.1016/j.eneco.2024.107413

Zhao, C. (2024). Russia and the war in Ukraine: The Chinese perspective on Europe's role. In *Global power shift* (pp. 45–60). DOI: 10.1007/978-3-031-48117-8_3

Chapter 7
Adoption of Green Concepts and Technology in Supply Chains:
Case Study of East Africa

Rehema M. Kiarie
https://orcid.org/0009-0001-3962-7746
Riara University, Kenya

ABSTRACT

Increased international trade has led to interconnection of supply chains across continents and countries. With the disruptions existing in the global economy, the domestic economies of many countries feel the resulting impact whenever there are any major world events that intertwine with the supply chain, for example, the adoption of green supply chain practices, disruption of shipping logistics, and economic trade wars. While the developed countries have made noticeable movements in moving towards green supply chains, countries in Africa and more specifically East Africa are yet to make substantial changes. In this chapter, green supply chain management has exhibited quantifiable benefits that range from reduction in CO2 emissions, reduction in waste, cost savings arising from use of clean energy, incorporation of local sourcing, and sourcing from suppliers who would be classified as disadvantaged from an economic perspective.

INTRODUCTION

Countries around the globe operate on different economic models and the global supply chain is essential for ensuring the movement of goods and information across

DOI: 10.4018/979-8-3373-7907-4.ch007

domestic and international borders and vice versa. With concerns being raised about the sustainability of these global supply chains, players around the globe have to be cognizant of these effects. Major efforts have been launched globally to achieve sustainability through the adoption of green supply chain management. Energy, a key component of global supply chain operations, is utilized in production and logistics processes. The global supply chain significantly contributes to global supply chain operations, with 23% of global carbon emissions equivalent to 6.4 billion tons of carbon dioxide associated with traded goods (Davis, Peters, & Caldeira, 2011). The gradual decline in traditional energy sources such as fossil fuel, carbon and natural gas has led to increased efforts towards renewable energy sources (Zhang, Fu, Tian, & Peng, 2022).

KEY OBJECTIVES

Several East African countries have initiated sustained campaigns to achieve green supply chains, contributing to global efforts to combat CO_2 emissions. As net importers of fossil energy, these countries could significantly reduce imports of a major production factor by adopting green supply chains. GSCM is a key component of achieving organizational success within the triple bottom line (TBL) model. This chapter assesses the mechanisms for achieving green supply chain adoption including the integration of technologies such as artificial intelligence (AI) and examines strategies that have been adopted by various industries and organizations in East Africa. The analysis relies on secondary data using qualitative research methods, with data categorized to derive meaningful insights. The chapter reviews strategies adopted in the use of green supply chains and AI to achieve sustainability in the supply chain, the effects of these strategies on global supply chains, cost implications, challenges posed, lessons learned, and potential research gaps.

LITERATURE REVIEW

The global supply chain encompasses various aspects that enable the flow of raw materials and finished products through interactions between suppliers and buyers worldwide. Companies move raw materials and finished products across countries, relying on international sourcing to achieve low-cost production in countries with lower manufacturing costs. This process involves a complex logistics and warehousing system that must adapt to diverse regulatory requirements across countries. To enable seamless global supply chains, information flow is critical in the interactions among supply chain actors.

Industry 4.0 Concept and Global Supply Chain Management

The fourth industrial revolution, also known as Industry 4.0 is an advancement in industrial activities that involves the incorporation of science and technology into industry leading to digitization of the manufacturing sector. Industry 4.0 relies on advanced technologies that include Internet of Things (IoT) and AI. IoT refers to an interconnection of various devices to the internet resulting in them exhibiting intelligent behaviour and autonomy to perform activities that would otherwise have been performed by humans (Ali, Ali, & Badawy, 2015). In East Africa, the following enabling technologies will play a central role in enabling the region achieve Industry 4.0 in the future; cloud computing, big data analytics, blockchain, IoT, robotics, 3D printing, AI, biotechnology, energy storage and cybersecurity (Travaly & Muvunyi, 2020).

Theoretical Framework for Firms in East Africa seeking to achieve sustainability in their supply chains

a) Institutional Theory

The Institutional Theory posits that the reason leading to firms applying sustainability in their supply chains arises from regulatory pressures to comply and meet societal expectations for achieving sustainability (DiMaggio & Powell, 1983). Within the East African context, a weak regulatory environment for sustainable supply chain practices exists and most firms adopt voluntary measures. However, firms that produce for the export market are forced to conform to the international standards set by the developed countries for them to incorporate sustainability in their supply chains (Adjei-Bamfo, Maloreh-Nyamekye, & Ahenkan, 2019).

b) Stakeholder Theory

This theory asserts that the need to meet the requirements of stakeholders will influence the behaviour of organizations to implement sustainability in their supply chains (Freeman, 1984). Developed countries demand adoption of high sustainability standards by firms exporting horticultural produce to their countries and subsequently, these firms push their suppliers further down the value chain to adopt the same practices. In Kenya, 30% of horticultural firms have been forced to adopt green supply chain management practices due to the demands from the export market (Nasiche & Ngugi, 2014).

CHALLENGES FACED IN ACHIEVING SUSTAINABILITY IN GLOBAL SUPPLY CHAIN MANAGEMENT

Global Supply Chain Management faces various challenges due to the multiple economies, systems and players. Challenges affecting attainment of sustainability in the global supply chain operate in the internal and external environments. Some of the external factors that disrupt attainment of sustainability in the global supply chain include trade wars, currency exchange rates, fluctuations in demand and supplies, logistical disruptions resulting in delivery delays and increased concern toward achieving environmental sustainability and favourable social impacts (Sujatmiko, Krisnanto, Sasmita, & Wahab, 2024).

Green Supply Chain Management

For a product to reach the final consumer, multiple products and processes are utilized to create the final product. During this process, large quantities of carbon dioxide emissions, toxic materials, fossil fuel emissions and discarded packaging materials are produced (Chin, Tat, & Sulaiman, 2015). Green Supply Chain Management originated in the 1970's when the first summit on Human Environment was held by the United Nations resulting in adoption of green supply chain practices from the 1990s followed by research by the academic fraternity from the early 2000's (Ojo, Adeniyi, Ogundimu, & Alaba, 2022). From previous research, the amount of greenhouse emissions has increased rapidly with fossil fuels and industrialization contributing to 78% of the documented emissions (Hejazi, Batati, & Bahurmuz, 2023).

Global Green Supply Chain Management Practices

Globally, many firms recognize that while green supply chain management practices have a cost implication, the long-term benefits outweigh the financial outlay. In developed countries, green supply chain practices have not been left at the discretion of organizations to implement. Environmental legislation has been enacted and is aggressively monitored to ensure compliance. From both practice and legislation, research has shown that green production and logistics have a significant impact on resource usage and performance of the firm which ultimately minimizes environmental impact (Khan & Qianli, 2017).

Environmental, Social and Governance Disclosure

Environmental, Social and Governance Reporting has taken centre stage in the corporate world, whereby corporations are not only preparing annual financial statements but also preparing reports illustrating the extent to which they have practiced ethical, social and sustainable practices with the aim of reducing carbon emissions, optimizing resource utilization and effectively managing waste from their operations (Ab Aziz & Alshdaifat, 2025). ESG disclosure is either made due to mandatory disclosures or voluntary disclosures. From research, limited standards and lack of comparison show that voluntary disclosure faces limitations in comparison to mandatory disclosures which apply consistently within a specific jurisdiction.

GREEN SUPPLY CHAIN MANAGEMENT PRACTICES IN AFRICA

By creating a sustainable supply chain within the African continent, many small and medium enterprises face major constraints in implementing green supply chain management strategies. This is mainly because of lack of adequate finances to implement these strategies, the lack of a culture geared towards sustainable supply chain practices and the voluntary implementation of green supply chain practices. From previous research, a large proportion of green procurement practices are implemented by large manufacturing firms which have adopted various strategies including content restrictions, green specifications, green supply chain audits, design, packaging, re-using, and recycling of waste materials (Mchopa, Kazungu, & Changalima, 2024). According to research, in the Republic of South Africa, the manufacturing sector and by extension the supply chain accounted for 20% of greenhouse emission between 1999 and 2020 (Epoh, Langton, & Mafini, 2024). This shows that the supply chain has a responsibility in ensuring environmental conservation.

COMPARATIVE ANALYSIS OF GREEN SUPPLY CHAIN PRACTICES IN DEVELOPED COUNTRIES VS DEVELOPING COUNTRIES

Concerns for environmental conservation and adoption of green supply chain practices differ among the various countries and this is profound when a comparison is made between the developed countries and developing countries. While the developed countries have significant experience in adoption of green supply chain practices, the developing countries are yet to exert sufficient environmental pressures to compel various industries to adopt green supply practices. The table below provides a comparative analysis of the key green supply chain practices/strategies in developed countries in comparison to developing/African countries.

Table 1. Comparative Analysis of Green Supply Chain Practices in Developed Countries vs Developing/African Countries

Aspect	Developed Countries	Developing/African Countries
Progress of implementation of green supply chain management practices	The adoption is entrenched both socially, culturally and politically making it a way of living and the end consumer holds firms accountable for their practices	Slow implementation of green supply chain management practices (Epoh, Langton, 2024)
Environmental regulations	Implementation of green supply chain management practices is managed by strict regulations on environmental preservation (Abdellatif & Graham, 2019)	Characterized by weak environmental regulations and implementation is on a voluntary basis (Abid, 2016)
Use of technology in adopting green supply chain management practices	These countries have far more advanced technologies e.g. blockchain technology that are critical in achieving green supply chain	Limited technological infrastructure resulting in a partial implementation of green supply chain management practices
Approach to adoption of green supply chain management practices	Developed countries have adopted green supply chain practices as a result of demand from the consumers and regulatory pressure	African countries face supplier resistance especially due to capital limitations by suppliers (Gera, et al., 2021)

In order to give a more detailed focus on firms located in East Africa that are actively engaged in incorporating sustainability in their supply chains, below is a comparative analysis based on previous research studies.

Table 2. Comparative analysis based on previous research studies

Green Supply Chain Management Practice	Kenya	Uganda	Tanzania
Green Purchasing	2	2	2
Eco-design	2	1	2
Green Manufacturing	1	1	1
Reverse Logistics	1	1	1
Green Distribution	2	2	2

Table 3. Color analysis

Color Code	Rating	Interpretation
Green	3	Very high adoption of green supply chain practices
Amber	2	Moderation adoption of green supply chain practices
Red	1	Low adoption of green supply chain practices

Source: Author, 2025

From the analysis above, none of the countries in East Africa has excelled in adoption of green supply chain management practices.

The Republic of Kenya has achieved moderate adoption in green purchasing, eco-design and green distribution practices. The main challenges that have limited full implementation of green supply chain practices include limited financial resources and expert knowledge in incorporating sustainability in the supply chain as well as poor infrastructure (Adjei-Bamfo, Maloreh-Nyamekye, & Ahenkan, 2019).

In the Republic of Uganda, moderate adoption of green supply chain management practices is evident in green purchasing and green distribution. From previous research, this has been propelled by close collaboration with suppliers for products that are sold in the export market. However, low technological expertise and financial constraints have greatly reduced the country's ability to fully embrace green supply chain management practices (Namagembe, Sheila; Ryan, Suzanne; Ramaswami, Sridharan;, 2019).

In the United Republic of Tanzania, green purchasing, eco-design and green distribution take the lead in moderate adoption of green supply chain management practices. The key industries that have taken the lead in adopting green supply chain practices are the horticultural and agricultural sectors that are export oriented. The major factors that have hindered full adoption of sustainability in the supply chain are high cost of adoption, poor infrastructure and limited awareness.

To augment the analysis above, the chart below provides comparative statistics on the rate of adoption of global supply chain management practices in developed vs developing countries.

Table 4. Adoption Rates of Green Supply Chain Management Practices

Green Supply Chain Management Practice	Developed Countries	Developing Countries (including Africa)
Level of Adoption	Exhibit adoption rates of between 60% to 80% (Walker, Di Sisto, & McBain, 2008)	Exhibit low adoption rates of 10% to 20% (Adjei-Bamfo, Maloreh-Nyamekye, & Ahenkan, 2019)
Applicable green supply chain practices	Focus on energy-efficient logistics, green supply chain and Industry 4.0 technologies (Govindan, Azevedo, Carvalho, & Cruz-Machado, 2015)	Focus on waste management, green procurement and eco - designs
Beneficial Measures	15% to 25% reduction in carbon emissions reported by firms & 10% to 20% savings from efficiency (Zhu, Sarkis, & Lai, 2013)	A reduction in carbon emissions between 10% to 15% and 5% to 10% savings from efficiency (Luthra, Vinod, Sanjay, & Haleem, 2016)

Source: Author, 2025

ARTIFICIAL INTELLIGENCE AND GREEN SUPPLY CHAINS

Artificial Intelligence has gained momentum in various fields including supply chain management as a means of reducing the human touch to processes and increasing efficiency. With AI technologies, organizations are able to use predictive analytics in the decision-making process. Previous research has shown that AI can reduce the vulnerabilities associated with the adoption of green supply chains through innovative technologies including, internet of things (IOT), blockchain technology, robotics, fuzzy logic, machine learning and big data analytics (Qu & Kim, 2024).

INTERNET OF THINGS (IOT) AND GREEN SUPPLY CHAINS

IoT is a representation of smart supply chain management that involves integration of a limitless number of devices that are linked to big data, cloud computing and wireless sensory networks. Smart supply chain involves utilization of technology to increase efficiency. The initial IoT application in supply chain was based on the use of RFID in inventory management through the use of a handheld device to track and identify stock items using sensors (Khan, et al., 2022). Previous research has indicated that warehouses are key to logistics operations and these warehouses significantly contribute to CO_2 emissions through lighting, air conditioning, cooling and heating within the warehouse (Singh & Roy, 2020). Research on the role of IoT in achieving sustainability has shown that IoT can reduce 20-30% of CO_2 emission and energy use through monitoring, tracking and optimization of the Triple Bottom Line dimensions (Ding, Ward, & Tukker, 2023). In summary, IoT makes the supply chain smart through instrumentation and collection of massive amounts of information that is collected through sensors, interconnection of devices, business units and products.

BLOCKCHAIN TECHNOLOGY AND GREEN SUPPLY CHAINS

Blockchain technology facilitates the exchange of data across the supply chain in a manner that cannot be altered while ensuring visibility across all the players in the supply chain industry in real time. Block chain technology is a key technology defined in Industry 4.0. It involves the use of a digital data base that is decentralized in a manner that various players in a peer-to-peer network can log in their transactions in a chronological order and create records that are tamperproof and permanent (Treiblmaier, 2018). Access to the blockchain is through IoT devices that are connected to the internet and data is stored by the nodes with certain users given permission to create ledgers once data is stored in the nodes which enables identification of the data in terms of where it is stored, either in countries, institutions or identified sites (Singh, Thakkar, & Jatinder, 2022). From previous research, block chain technology has been shown to reduce risks, increase transparency and enable matching of data in real time while simplifying the audit process to establish the accuracy of data submitted in the network (Dutta, Choi, Somani, & Butala, 2020).

ROBOTICS AND GREEN SUPPLY CHAIN

Robotics involves the integration of mechatronics and automation that mimic human characteristics to make decisions with a great level of autonomy and respond to the environment (Dindorf & Wos, 2024). In the warehouses, robotics is utilized in automated guided vehicles that transport goods from one point to another without human intervention. It is also applied in collaborative robots that are semi-independent and are used to control work operations by serving as adaptable storage containers used to transport orders that have been picked.

FUZZY LOGIC AND GREEN SUPPLY CHAIN

Fuzzy logic is an artificial intelligence technique that is used to solve problems through definition of lower and upper limits of a sample space and integrating a fuzzifier, which determines values of membership for the definition of output or input variables; inference rules that are defined by an expert who understands the business. It also utilizes fuzzy inferences machine that groups the rules using control processes and applies them in scenarios for simulation and a defuzzifier that defines the simulation results (de Moura, Quaresma, & Salum, 2021). Previous research has used fuzzy logic in the chicken meat industry and the results showed that fuzzy logic was effective in evaluating the performance of sustainability in the supply chain (Hasibuan, Yunita, & Zulkarnaen, 2025).

MACHINE LEARNING AND GREEN SUPPLY CHAIN

Machine learning is one of the AI technologies utilized to increase the efficiency of devices to interpret and manage huge quantities of data in the supply chain. Previous studies have shown benefits in the use of machine learning in transport and distribution, manufacturing, supplier selection, inventory control and demand and sales estimates (Kumar, et al., 2022). Through the use of machine learning in complex systems, firms that wish to enhance the capacity of their carbon emission technology can benefit through the use of machine learning to come up with a solution that is optimal based on green transformation and big data in the supply chains (Wu & Zuo, 2023).

BIG DATA ANALYTICS AND GREEN SUPPLY CHAINS

The elements of big data include huge quantities of data that are variable and generated continuously in real time and application of big data analytics enables organizations to utilize technology to process the huge volumes of data, identify gaps and patterns and make decisions that are verifiable through the existing data (Rahman, Saha, Ratul, & Graham, 2024). The focus on big data analytics in green supply chain management involves data mining, statistics, machine learning and optimization which influences green purchasing, internal environment management and customer green cooperation (Jia, 2020).

MODELS FOR ASSESSING GREEN SUPPLY CHAINS

SustainableSCOR Model

SustainableSCOR which replaced the GreenSCOR model is an adaptation of the Supply Chain Operations Reference Model (SCOR). The SCOR model integrates supply chain processes into an organization's overall functions and goals and focuses on 5 major areas, i.e. processes, performance, people, practices and special applications. Six major processes are defined by the SCOR model; plan, source, make and deliver which are procurement functions as well as return and enable (APICS, 2017). SustainableSCOR Model incorporates environmental measures that cover the upstream and downstream activities of a value chain from the conception of a product to its end use (APICS, 2017). It is a tool that enables organizations to achieve efficient operations through integrating green supply chain management tools into organizations' supply chains through considering the environmental and social impacts in the analysis of supply chains.

Life Cycle Assessment (LCA) Model

The LCA model is used to assess the impact of a product's entire life cycle from extraction of raw materials to disposal or recycling of the used product. It focuses on carrying out an inventory analysis and impact assessment of the environment as a result of the product's lifecycle. The LCA model can be used to modify a supply chain with the aim of applying data to improve the environmental performance. LCA is used to assess the environmental impacts of products, processes and materials throughout their lifecycle using four main stages; goal and scope, analysis of inventory, assessment of impact and interpretation. Through these four stages, an entity can be able to assess specific areas where environmental impacts can be minimized (Moutik, Summerscales, Jones, & Pemberton, 2023).

Triple Bottom Line (TBL) Model

The TBL model combines environmental, social and economic aspects towards achieving sustainability in the supply chain. Environmental aspects focus on replacing traditional raw materials and energy with eco-friendly inputs while the social component focus on ensuring conducive working conditions for the labour used in production, while at the same time ensuring positive results arise from these strategies to enable a company generate sufficient revenues that will sustain its operations. Research has shown that the TBL model is useful in building sustainable supply chains and the economic component of building a resilient supply chain is the most important since it is the simplest to achieve and realize thereafter, followed by the environmental component.

SPECIFIC CASE STUDIES FROM EAST AFRICA

East Africa has been identified as one of the regions in Africa that is fastest growing and is made up of three countries located east of the African continent namely, Kenya, Uganda and Tanzania (AfDB, 2025) Economically, the three East African countries are net importers of goods, thereby exposing them to the global supply chain. The selection of the sample size for the case studies was based on the parameters highlighted below;

Table 5. The selection of the sample size for the case studies was based on the parameters highlighted below

Criteria	Description
Location	Firms must be located in East Africa
Type of Evidence	To qualify for the research, firms should have demonstrated application of green supply chain management practices
Industry representation	Firms should be operating in sectors or industries that can be shown to possess significant impact on the environment
Size of the Firm	The selected firms ranged from large firms to SMEs
Sustainability Commitment	There should be a documented commitment by firms to implementing sustainability in their supply chains
Data Accessibility	Since secondary data was utilized, selection was based on firms with readily available information on sustainability
Voluntary/Non-voluntary measures	Firms were selected based on the requirement for them to adhere to sustainability measures or their commitment to implement voluntary measures

Source: Author, 2025

In terms of data collection, the study combined both qualitative and quantitative data. For the secondary data, company reports, certifications and policies on sustainability for the selected firms were used. A template structured to analyze the secondary data collected was developed and utilized for the research.

A large number of firms in East Africa have realized the need to adopt sustainability in their supply chains ranging from green supply chains to environmentally friendly supply chain practices and adoption of technology. For the specific case studies identified, eight organizations were from Kenya, which is the largest economy in East Africa, three were from Tanzania, one was from Rwanda and one company operated in Kenya, Uganda and Tanzania. From the thirteen companies identified, only two were government-owned enterprises. Limitations existed in identifying these firms using secondary sources since only a few firms had documented milestones that they had achieved in implementation of green supply chain management.

Table 6. Analysis of Specific Case Studies from East Africa

#/ Name of Company/ Country	Background	Initiative in relation to Sustainable Supply Chains	Statistics	Analysis based on TBL
1. Safaricom PLC, Kenya	Safaricom PLC is a telecommunications company located in Nairobi, Kenya and founded in 1997 with a customer base of 44 million customers and an annual revenue of $ 2.7 billion as at March 2024. Several key milestones have been undertaken by Safaricom in order to achieve sustainability in their supply chain (ASPK, 2025).	• Elimination of plastic in retail packaging • Planting of 5 million trees in degraded forest reserves • Integrated Waste Management	Statistics in 2019 • Estimated number of people impacted both directly and indirectly is 900,000 • Annual publishing of sustainability report • 2.52 tonnes of plastic eliminated from the supply chain • 8.64 tonnes of paper eliminated from the supply chain • 258,250 kgs of recyclable waste • Savings of $361,218.55 annually (ASPK, 2025) **Statistics in 2023** • 98% of solid waste recycled within 71 facilities • Full implementation of the UN Guiding Principles through the Sustainable Supplier Impact Program (Safaricom, 2025).	• The firm adheres to global voluntary sustainability initiatives, namely the UN Guiding Principles and responsible sourcing principles requirements on sustainability reporting • Significant emphasis on waste management and recycling • Reduction in the use of fossil fuel • Supplier engagement is one of the enablers toward achieving sustainability in the supply chain • Voluntary publishing of ESG reports • Economic benefits of the sustainability efforts visible • Documented statistics on sustainability initiatives in the supply chain

continued on following page

Table 6. Continued

#/ Name of Company/ Country	Background	Initiative in relation to Sustainable Supply Chains	Statistics	Analysis based on TBL
2. Delmonte Kenya Ltd., Kenya	Delmonte is a food processing company founded in 1965 located in Kenya that processes canned pineapples and various juice concentrates. The company brands itself as a vertically integrated organization with the ability to integrate sustainability practices from the farm to the store (Delmonte Kenya Ltd, 2022).	• Reduction of carbon foot print • Sustainable farming practices • Increased efficiency in logistics • Logistics efficiency • Joined the Pacific Coast Food Waste Commitment in 2022 • Reviewed vendor code of conduct • Use of artificial intelligence to establish demand and supply for avocadoes	• Planted 574,800 tress to date • 29.7% of the farms utilized farming practices that were sustainable • Reduced fuel consumption, i.e. more product was transported per load with each container consuming 1.43 tonnes of fuel in the year 2022 in comparison to 1.81 tonnes of fuel in 2019 • Diversion of 93% food waste from landfill • Conducted 72 assessments on suppliers to ensure social compliance (Delmonte Kenya Ltd, 2022) • Reduced product waste through the use of AI and big data analytics to establish a pricing model that was able to match supply and demand	• The firm voluntarily adheres to global commitments towards achieving sustainability • Reduction in CO_2 emissions • Sustainable farming practices • Reduction in fossil fuel consumption • Reduction of waste • Increased social compliance by suppliers • Voluntary publishing of ESG reports • Documented statistics on sustainability initiatives in the supply chain

continued on following page

Table 6. Continued

#/ Name of Company/ Country	Background	Initiative in relation to Sustainable Supply Chains	Statistics	Analysis based on TBL
3. Lori Systems Ltd., Kenya	Lori is an e-logistics company that seeks to coordinate haulage across Africa seamlessly. The firm matches transporters with cargo owners with the aim of lowering the transport cost. The company focuses on diversity, equity and inclusion. Lori has a network of trucks numbering 20,000 and assists in logistics from ports and farms to factories and families (Lori Systems Ltd, 2025).	• Reduction of greenhouse emissions • Empty mile reduction • Adoption of electric vehicles (EVs)	• 10% of emissions from greenhouses emanate from the transport industry • Savings of operating expenditures up to 45% on electric heavy-duty trucks • From empty mile reduction through backhaul optimization, the company has saved 9,000 tons in CO_2 emissions • Electric trucks savings of 45% • 18% savings through the use of the web-based coordination platform (World Economic Forum, 2025)	• Adoption of technology that reduces the carbon footprint, i.e. electric vehicles • Reduction of green house emissions through optimization cargo loads • Documented statistics on sustainability initiatives in the supply chain

continued on following page

Table 6. Continued

#/ Name of Company/ Country	Background	Initiative in relation to Sustainable Supply Chains	Statistics	Analysis based on TBL
4. East African Breweries Ltd., Kenya, Uganda & Tanzania	East African Breweries PLC is an alcohol production and distribution company in Kenya, Uganda and Tanzania that deals with alcoholic and adult non-alcoholic drinks (EABL, 2025)	• Social inclusion through engagement of women and persons with disability as part of the value chain • Environmental sustainability • Pioneer Grain to Glass Sustainability	• Targeted spending amount to $45 million to 700 persons with disability who are part of the 60,000 farmer-partner base & • 40% of the partner base is made up of women • 150,000 small holder farmers provided with resources and agricultural skills • EABL has built a resilient supply chain that assists communities to adapt to climate change and contribute to the bottom line of the business • Aim is to halve the carbon through engagement of suppliers in the supply chain • Increase recycled content in plastic bottles to 35% • $65,600 was spent on forest fencing to enhance security (EABL, 2025) • Annual publishing of sustainability report • Initiative to reduce amount of water used in drinks by 30% by 2030 and replenish more water that is used by 2026	• The firm has laid a lot of emphasis on social inclusion of vulnerable persons in the supply chain • Focus on waste management and recycling of packaging materials • Enhancing environmental conservation through forest conservation initiatives • Voluntary publishing of ESG reports • Incorporating sustainability in the production process through reducing the raw materials used in production, e.g. water • Documented statistics on sustainability initiatives in the supply chain

continued on following page

Table 6. Continued

#/ Name of Company/ Country	Background	Initiative in relation to Sustainable Supply Chains	Statistics	Analysis based on TBL
5. Unilever, Kenya	Unilever is a multinational firm with operations in Kenya. The firm produces, distributes and markets consumer goods in 190 countries	• Social sustainability through local sourcing due to external shocks • Published rules for track and trace identity preservation for tracing sustainable material back to a single point of origin (Unilever, 2025) • Use of AI, IoT and digital technology to help farmers in East Africa handle farming challenges as a result of unpredictable weather	• 49% local sourcing was achieved in 2023 • Intention to invest $68 million in supplier diversity (AMC, 2025) • Partnership with technology innovators to find a solution for farmers through the following; • AquaSpy – an IoT that is cloud-based to assist farmers make informed decisions through understanding soil conditions and seasonal crop conditions • Clean Crop Technologies to assist in increasing crop germination and resistance to diseases • Smart Cloud Farming to assist in monitoring and scanning of soil (Diageo, 2024)	• Voluntary publishing of ESG reports • Providing farmers applications leveraged AI, IOT and Digital Technology • Waste management through separation of sustainable and non-sustainable material • Published Code for Sustainable Sourcing programs • Economic benefit of supply chain sustainability efforts • Documented statistics on sustainability initiatives in the supply chain
6. Tanzania Breweries Ltd., Tanzania	Tanzania Breweries Ltd is the largest and oldest brewery in Tanzania founded in 1933 and is involved in the production, processing and distribution of alcoholic beverages and non-alcohol malt drinks (TBL, 2025)	• Use of returnable or recycled content for primary packaging	• Target to achieve 100% returnable or recyclable material for primary packaging by 2025 • In 2022, a total of 16,109 tonnes of glass bottles and crates were recycled	• Environmental conservation through waste reduction • Voluntary publishing of ESG reports • Water Conservation

continued on following page

Table 6. Continued

#/ Name of Company/ Country	Background	Initiative in relation to Sustainable Supply Chains	Statistics	Analysis based on TBL
7. Leta Kenya, Kenya	Leta is a technology company that offers logistics services through automating the movement of goods in Kenya (Leta, 2025)	• Using AI to select the most suitable vehicle for the specific delivery and come up with an efficient way of handling the goods, e.g. LIFO or FIFO	• Delivery numbers have increased to 4.5 million from 500,000 • Quantity of tons handled has increased to 150,000 tons to 20,000 tons • The number of vehicles managed has increased to 7,400 from 2,000 • Company manages deliveries averaging 10,000 each day (Empower Africa, 2025)	• Application of AI to increase efficiency in handling of good • Documented statistics on sustainability initiatives in the supply chain
8. MarketForce, Kenya	MarketForce is a digital company that enables merchants to place orders, source and make payment for inventory through mobile channels and have the goods delivered by the nearest distributor to their store (Marketforce, 2025)	• Use of AI to optimize inventory for small traders	• No statistics are available	• Application of AI to assist small traders optimize their inventory

continued on following page

Table 6. Continued

#/ Name of Company/ Country	Background	Initiative in relation to Sustainable Supply Chains	Statistics	Analysis based on TBL
9. Viebeg Technologies, Rwanda	Viebeg Technologies provides a one-stop platform for the real-time procurement of medical supplies and equipment. The company utilizes AI for the management of supply chain processes (Viebeg Medical, 2025)	• Use of a B2B procurement platform, VieProcure that is data driven to reduce the risk involved in the procurement of medical equipment and supplies • The Health Demand Simulation Model (HDSM) uses demographic and public health data to enable decision-making (Viebeg Medical, 2025)	• Middlemen have been eliminated from the value chain leading to 40% cost savings for customers • Viebeg products have been used to treat patients • The technology has covered over 1000 healthcare providers in Rwanda, Democratic Republic of Congo and Kenya (AFDB, 2022)	• AI has assisted in proactive management of shocks as a result of civil unrest and climate events • Use of applications that apply big data analytics • Reduce stock outs of medical supplies
10. Cargill Kenya Ltd (CKL), Kenya	Cargill Kenya Ltd, a company that has been in operation since 1948, is involved in the agricultural sector including trade in maize, barley, wheat and bulk grain handling	• Reduction of greenhouse gases • Elimination of deforestation and reduce water used in the organization's operations	• 670,000 metric tons of CO_2 were reduced within the supply chain • 85% implementation of water stewardship in their operations (Cargill, 2025)	• Voluntary publishing of ESG reports • Documented statistics on sustainability initiatives in the supply chain
11. Connected Health AI Network (CHAIN), Tanzania	CHAIN is an AI enabled supply chain technology that uses predictive technology for the delivery of healthcare services and specifically vaccine consumption (PR Newswire, 2020)	• Use of AI to predict the accuracy of vaccine utilization (PR Newswire, 2020)	• 70% forecasting accuracy on vaccine utilization was achieved in 2018 • Use of AI to audit stock (PR Newswire, 2020) • 96% reduction in vaccine wastage (MIT, 2020)	• Reduced stock outs • Vaccines required to increase coverage reduced • Documented statistics on sustainability initiatives in the supply chain

continued on following page

Table 6. Continued

#/ Name of Company/ Country	Background	Initiative in relation to Sustainable Supply Chains	Statistics	Analysis based on TBL
12. Kenya Electricity Generating Company PLC, Kenya	Company was incorporated in 1954 with the mandate of developing, managing and operating power plants to generate electricity	• 1st company in Kenya to benefit under the clean development mechanism • Local sourcing • Actively promoting the participation of disadvantaged groups as part of government action towards promoting these groups to be sustainable in business	• Generation of 984MW of geothermal power • Ranked in the top ten geothermal producing companies globally	• Adoption of international standards and rules in sustainability efforts • Voluntary publishing of ESG reports
13. Mkulazi Holding Company Ltd., Tanzania	A company incorporated in 2016 and involved in the sugar industry, specifically in production of sugar and related bio products including pulp and ethanol. The company is full owned by government entities and is located in Morogoro Town, Tanzania (MHCL, 2025)	• Use of green inputs for production • Reduced waste during disposal by converting waste into bio products e.g. ethanol, pulp	• No statistics	• Increased profitability with reduced waste

KEY FINDINGS AND DISCUSSIONS

Green supply chain management is resource intensive in terms of financial resources, information technology and human capacity. From the thirteen firms identified, only four can be classified as Small and Micro-Enterprises, i.e. Lori Systems Ltd, Leta Kenya, MarketForce and Viebeg Technologies. The other nine firms, Safaricom PLC, Delmonte Kenya Ltd, East African Breweries Ltd, Unilever, Tanzania Breweries Ltd, Cargill Kenya Ltd, CHAIN, Kenya Electricity Generating Company PLC and Mkulazi Holding Company Ltd are large local and multinational companies. Two of the firms identified are either owned by the government or the government has majority shareholding in the entities namely, Kenya Electricity Generating Company PLC and Mkulazi Holding Company Ltd. From the identified firms, eight of them had publicly documented statistics on the extent to which their supply chain was effectively meeting the sustainability requirements namely Safaricom PLC, Delmonte Kenya Ltd, Lori Systems Ltd, East African Breweries Ltd, Unilever, Leta Kenya, Cargill Kenya Ltd and CHAIN. Seven of the firms namely Safaricom PLC, Delmonte Kenya Ltd, East African Breweries Ltd, Unilever, Tanzania Breweries Ltd, Cargill Kenya Ltd and Kenya Electricity Generating Company Ltd, were voluntarily publishing ESG reports. From the companies that were identified, none of them was compelled by their respective governments to publish mandatory ESG reports. Six of the identified firms namely Safaricom PLC, Delmonte Kenya Ltd, East African Breweries Ltd, Unilever, Tanzania Breweries Ltd, Mkulazi Holding Company Limited, had put in place adequate measures to manage waste through either reducing waste, reusing waste through conversation to other products or recycling certain components of the products. Three of the firms that were studied focused their sustainability efforts of reducing greenhouse gases into forest activities, i.e. Safaricom Ltd (Kenya) and Cargill Kenya Ltd had successfully planted trees in forest areas that were degraded while East African Breweries Ltd (Kenya, Uganda and Tanzania) had spent $ 65,600 in forest fencing activities. Six of the companies namely Lori Systems Ltd, Unilever, Delmonte Kenya Ltd, Leta Kenya, MarketForce and Viebeg Technologies had incorporated technology and in particular AI into their green supply chain initiatives. From the six companies that had statistics on adoption of AI for their green supply chain initiatives, only two firms, Delmonte Kenya Ltd and Unilever, were classified as large corporations while the rest were classified as small and micro enterprises. Four of the firms had put in place concrete practices for management of social aspects of sustainability in the supply chain through active engagement of small and micro enterprises and disadvantaged groups as part of their supply base namely, Safaricom PLC, East African Breweries Ltd, Unilever and Kenya Electricity Generating Company PLC. From these four companies, only one company had a statutory requirement to ensure mandatory inclusion of its suppliers as part of the supply base, i.e. Kenya Electricity Generating Company PLC. Only one company had extensively incorporated the use of technology in all its supply chain operations from raw material production to the end user, i.e. Unilever. In the engagement of suppliers as part of implementing the green supply chain, one company had voluntarily adopted a standard for assessing the sustainability of suppliers, i.e. Safaricom Ltd had adopted the UN guiding principles and responsible sourcing principles. In the area of logistics, Lori Systems Ltd had adopted the use of electric vehicles in its operations. Tanzania Breweries Ltd had put in place aggressive waste management practices with a target of achieving 100% return or recycling of primary packaging by the year 2025.

The findings above uncover milestones toward implementation of green supply chain management which can be interrogated to identify gaps that still exist. Due to the visibility of large corporations and their potential impact on both the economy, environment and society, there exists extensive scrutiny from their consumers and also various regulatory bodies. As such, in the interest of meeting one of the sustainable development goals (SDG), SDG 13 on climate action, these firms will be inclined to allocate sufficient resources that will ensure that they have addressed regulatory concerns and have also satisfied their customer base which is increasingly becoming wary of the devastating effect that industries are having on the environment. Furthermore, these firms are keen on meeting both voluntary and mandatory requirements toward attainment of sustainability in their operations including the supply chain. Very few small and medium enterprises have the financial capability to fully implement green supply chain practices and as such the analysis is a good representation of the fact that it is majorly large corporations that will pursue both voluntary and mandatory actions to ensure that they meet their environmental, economic and social requirements within their operations.

From the analysis, another interesting fact emerges in terms of the intentions of various governments in attaining green supply chains. Only two of the firms in the study are owned by the government. A few proponents argue that the government should not engage in commercial undertakings which should be left to the public sector. Therefore, the number of firms that are privately owned and engage in commercial undertakings exceed those that are state owned. This can further be inferred to mean that even fewer firms that are commercial-oriented and owned by the government will be keen to apply green supply chain practices.

An organization's image in the face of both its customers and the government is seen as a means of marketing its brand. A large proportion of the cases studied had publicly documented statistics related to their initiatives in implementing sustainable supply chain management. By publicly disclosing that a firm is complying with initiatives toward sustainable supply chain management, firms were able to win loyalty from their existing customers, attract more customers and reduce regulatory scrutiny.

While the countries in East Africa had provided guidelines on ESG reporting, none of these countries had enacted legislation demanding mandatory publishing of ESG reports. From the analysis, it is the large corporations that were publishing ESG reports in comparison to the small and medium enterprises. This can once again be inferred to be an area where the large corporations would want to increase their brand visibility as being compliant with environmental, social and governance principles.

Our planet, Earth, has a finite surface area and therefore there is a limit to the amount of waste that can be accommodated. Most of the firms that are involved in the production process had put in place measures for the reuse, reduction and recycling of waste. By reducing or eliminating waste, organizations are in a better position to achieve green supply chains.

Greenhouse gases have been linked to degradation of the environment and an increasing number of organizations that are profit oriented are investing in the reduction of green-house gases. One of the ways in which green-house gases can be reduced is through increasing the number of trees on our planet. Huge investments are being made by various companies toward increasing the forest coverage with the aim of reducing the carbon footprint.

The number of firms that were integrating technology into their green supply chain management activities were few and majority of them were small and medium enterprises apart from Unilever and Delmonte kenya Ltd. From the analysis, small and medium enterprises leveraged on technology to keep their overhead costs low in order to get closer to break-even point. In a highly competitive corporate space, firms that enjoy market leadership will rarely reveal the extent of the factors that give them a competitive edge. As indicated earlier, a large number of the firms studied were large corporations and therefore it is likely that while they may possess cutting edge technology which enables them maintain market leadership, they may not be willing to disclose certain aspects of their technological infrastructure that would expose them to their competitors.

In the current business environment, society places corporations that spend more on their social responsibilities on a higher pedestal. As part of sustainable supply chains, four firms were actively engaged in ensuring that small and micro enterprises as well as firms owned by disadvantaged groups were given an opportunity to participate as suppliers.

In the public sector in Kenya, companies owned by the government had a statutory requirement to provide a percentage of their businesses exclusively to firms owned by disadvantaged groups (youth, women and persons with disability). Kenya Electricity Generation Company PLC, a public listed corporation where the government of Kenya owns 70% of its shareholding is under statutory obligation to provide business opportunities to firms that are owned by youth, women and persons with disability.

Adoption of technology has a very high initial investment cost and therefore only one firm had incorporated advanced technology in its entire supply chain from sourcing of raw materials to the finished product, i.e. Unilever.

Adoption of sustainability within the supply chain was optional and many firms were likely to only meet the bare minimum requirements in ensuring that they met the expectations of society considering that the governments in East Africa had no regulatory role. One notable company, Safaricom PLC had gone beyond utilizing its own standards in ensuring that its suppliers implement sustainable practices through the adoption of internationally accepted standards, i.e. UN guiding principles and responsible sourcing principles.

The decline in the use of vehicles powered by internal combustion engines has rapidly taken place in the developed countries. However, in the developing countries which included countries in East Africa, it was noted that one of the firms studied had adopted the use of electric vehicles in its logistics operations.

BENEFITS OF ADOPTING GREEN SUPPLY CHAIN MANAGEMENT

From the key findings and discussions, there were quantifiable benefits for firms that adopted green supply chain management practices. Safaricom PLC, had successfully eliminated use of plastic in its retail packaging which was a considerable step toward reducing the negative impacts on the environment. Many corporations in East Africa were still using fossil fuel in their logistics operations and therefore it was encouraging that Delmonte Kenya Ltd had managed to increase the quantity of product transported per load, therefore more product was transported for each load, resulting in reduced fuel consumption. Artificial Intelligence and Big Data Analytics has also assisted Delmonte Kenya Ltd to reduce waste through the analysis of data to predict price and therefore match supply and demand. Tanzania Breweries Ltd had also been aggressive in its waste reduction initiatives through the use of recycled content or returnable material for primary packaging of its products. In logistics, Lori Systems Ltd had been able to save 45% of its operational expenditures through the use of electric heavy-duty trucks as well as optimizing logistics to ensure that there was minimal empty mile. With these initiatives, less fuel was consumed and there was also reduced CO_2 emissions. Cargill Kenya Ltd had also made significant strides in reducing its CO_2 emissions with an estimated reduction of 670,000 metric tons of CO_2. East Africa Breweries Ltd had been able to recycle 35% of the content in its plastic bottles and therefore ensured less waste being generated. Unilever Kenya had been able to implement measures to ensure 49% of their raw materials and inputs were sourced locally, which reinforced their societal commitment to achieve sustainability in their supply chains.

CHALLENGES IN THE ADOPTION OF GREEN SUPPLY CHAIN MANAGEMENT

For a successful green supply chain, all players in the supply chain must adopt the same practices. As indicated, it is easier for large corporations to adopt green supply chain practices due to their financial strength. However, small and micro enterprises will find it difficult due to limited financial muscle and the need to keep their costs low. Even if the large corporations adopt green supply chain management practices fully, the supply chain will not fully achieve its intended objective if the rest of the players in the value chain do not follow suit.

Many of the green supply chain initiatives that have been identified in the study are voluntary measures and therefore, firms will not be under obligation to implement or fully implement best practices in green supply chain management. It is also notable that the government has also lagged behind in pushing firms to adopt green supply chain management practices.

Technology is rapidly changing and what might work today will not be suitable in the future. There is a cost element with upgrading to new technology and this is an impediment to firms that want to keep up to date with green supply chain practices.

The green supply chain practices will vary from industry to industry and it is not a one size fits all. For example, while some firms may be able to reduce water used in their production processes, it may not be possible for other firms. At the same time, some industries are heavy energy consumers and therefore while they would ultimately wish to get rid of fossil fuels, it may not be possible due to the energy demands. Therefore, it may be difficult to compel firms in various industries to adhere to a single set of standards.

CONCLUSION, GAPS, AND SUGGESTIONS FOR FUTURE RESEARCH

One of the key points from the study is the need to consider developing different sets of standards for different industries that will guide firms in implementing green supply chain practices. While some firms are undertaking voluntary measures to implement green supply chain practices, other firms may not be interested in following suit and therefore it becomes counterproductive for the global supply chains. Governments need to take the lead in ensuring that initiatives toward achieving green supply chain management become mandatory requirements for entities operating within their jurisdictions. For example, governments could enforce the mandatory reporting on ESG operations by firms.

For future research, consideration can be given to documenting standards for adopting green supply chain management practices in different industries. A comparison of other regions in Africa and their green supply chain management practices can also be studied to give comparisons and enrich the studies that have already been undertaken.

REFERENCES

Ab Aziz, N. H., & Alshdaifat, S. M. (2025). ESG Reporting: Impacts, Benefits and Challenges. In Alshurafat, H., Hamdan, A., & Sands, J. (Eds.), *Sustainable Horizons for Business, Education, and Technology* (pp. 69–76). Springer Nature.

Abdellatif, H., & Graham, S. (2019). Green Supply Chain Management Practices in Developing Countries - A Case Study from Jordan. *International Journal of Simulation: Systems, Science & Technology*, 10.1-10.6.

Abid, M. (2016). Does economic, financial and institutional developments matter for environmental quality? A comparative analysis of EU and MEA countries. *Journal of Environmental Management*, 183–194.

Adjei-Bamfo, P., Maloreh-Nyamekye, T., & Ahenkan, A. (2019). The role of e-government in sustainable public procurement in developing countries: A systematic literature review. *Resources, Conservation and Recycling*, 189–203.

AFDB. (2022). *How Rwanda is using Artificial Intelligence to improve healthcare*. Retrieved from African Development Bank: https://www.afdb.org/en/success-stories/how-rwanda-using-artificial-intelligence-improve-healthcare-55309

AfDB. (2025). *East Africa Economic Outlook 2024*. Retrieved from afdb.org: https://www.afdb.org/sites/default/files/documents/publications/reo_east_africa_english_2024.pdf

Africa, E. (2025). *Kenyan Startup Leta Raises $5 Million to Boost AI-Powered Logistics Platform in Africa*. Retrieved from Empower Africa: https://empowerafrica.com/kenyan-startup-leta-raises-5-million-to-boost-ai-powered-logistics-platform-in-africa/

Ahmad, A., Ikram, A., Rehan, M. F., & Ahmad, A. (2022). Going green: Impact of green supply chain management practices on sustainability performance. *Frontiers in Psychology*, 1-12.

Ali, Z. H., Ali, H. A., & Badawy, M. M. (2015). Internet of Things (IoT): Definitions, Challenges, and Recent Research Directions. *International Journal of Computer Applications*, 37–46.

AMC. (2025, 04 20). *Unilever Kenya to Source US $50 million worth of Raw Materials locally by 2025*. Retrieved from African Marketing Confederation: https://africanmarketingconfederation.org/unilever-kenya-to-source-us50m-worth-of-raw-materials-locally-by-2025/#:~:text=According%20to%20Unilever%2C%20the%20company,%2468%2Dmillion%20in%20supplier%20diversity

APICS. (2017). Supply Chain Operations Reference Model. Chicago, Illinois, USA.

ASPK. (2025). *Safaricom Takes A Leap On Its Sustainability Goals in becoming a 'green' organization*. Retrieved from Association of Sustainability Practitioners in Kenya: https://aspkenya.org/general/safaricom-takes-a-leap-on-its-sustainability-goals-in-becoming-a-green-organization/

Barney, J. B. (1991). Firm Resources and Sustained Competitive Advantage. *Journal of Management*, 99–120.

Bashar, A. M., Taher, M. A., Islam, M. K., & Ahmed, H. (2024). The Impact of Advanced Robotics and Automation on Supply Chain Efficiency in Industrial Manufacturing: A Compartive Analysis between the US and Bangladesh. *Global Mainstream Journal of Business, Economics, Development & Project Management*, 2834-2739.

Cargill. (2025). *Impact Report 2024*. Retrieved from Cargill: https://www.cargill.com/sustainability/doc/1432270798723/2024-impact-report.pdf

CCICED. (2021). *Green Recovery with Resilience and High Quality Development*. Springer.

Chin, T. A., Tat, H. H., & Sulaiman, Z. (2015). Green Supply Chain Management, Environmental Collaboration and Sustainability Performance. *Science Direct*, 695-699.

Daily, B. (2023, 10 31). Carbacid joins list of companies ditching KPLC for solar power. Nairobi, Nairobi, Kenya.

Davis, S. J., Peters, G. P., & Caldeira, K. (2011). The supply chain of CO2 emissions. *Proceedings of the National Academy of Sciences*, 18554-18559.

de Moura, A. C., Quaresma, S. F., & Salum, M. I. (2021). Application of Fuzzy Logic to Analyze the Performance of Sustainability Logistics in Industrial Departments. *International Journal for Innovation Education and Research*, 306–327.

Delmonte Kenya Ltd. (2022). *2022 Sustainability Report*. Retrieved from https://freshdelmonte.com/wp-content/uploads/2023/10/FDM_2022_SustainabilityReportFINAL.pdf

Diageo. (2024, 09 05). *Diageo partners with tech innovators to help build resilience in Sub-Saharan African agriculture*. Retrieved from Diageo: https://www.diageo.com/en/news-and-media/press-releases/2024/diageo-partners-with-tech-innovators-to-help-build-resilience-in-sub-saharan-african-agriculture#:~:text=5th%20September%202024%3A%20Diageo,Diageo%20Sustainable%20Solutions%20(DSS)

DiMaggio, P., & Powell, W. (1983). The iron cage revisited: Institutional isomorphism and collective rationality in organizational fields. *American Sociological Review*, 147–160.

Dindorf, R., & Wos, P. (2024). Challenges of Robotic Technology in Sustainable Construction Practice. *Sustainability*, 1–26.

Ding, S., Ward, H., & Tukker, A. (2023). How Internet of Things can influence the sustainability peformance of logistics industries - A Chinese case study. *Cleaner Logistics and Supply Chain*, 1-14.

Dutta, P., Choi, T.-M., Somani, S., & Butala, R. (2020). Blockchain technology in supply chain operations: Applications, challenges and research opportunities. *Transportation Research Part E, Logistics and Transportation Review.*

EABL. (2025). *EABL Sustainability Report 2024.* Retrieved from East African Breweries Ltd: https://www.eabl.com/sites/default/files/2024-10/EABL-2024-Sustainability-Report.pdf

EABL. (2025). *East African Breweries Ltd.* Retrieved from Our Business: https://www.eabl.com/our-business

Epoh, R. L., Langton, I., & Mafini, C. (2024). A model for green supply chain management in the South African manufacturing sector. *Cogent Business & Management.*

Freeman, E. (1984). *Strategic Management: A Stakeholder Approach.* Pitman.

Gera, R., Chadha, P., Nag, M. B., Sharma, S., Arora, H., Parvez, A., & Sergeevna, L. Y. (2021). A systematic review of green supply chain management practices in firms. *Journal of Cleaner Production*, 535–542.

Govindan, K., Azevedo, S. G., Carvalho, H., & Cruz-Machado, V. (2015). Lean, green and resilient practices influence on supply chain performance: Interpretive structural modeling approach. *International Journal of Environmental Science and Technology*, 15–34.

Green, K. W., Zelbst, P. J., Meacham, J., & Bhadauria, V. S. (2012). Green supply chain management practices: Impact on performance. *Supply Chain Management*, 290–305.

Hasibuan, S., Yunita, I., & Zulkarnaen, I. (2025). Evaluating supply chain sustainability and agility using fuzzy logic approach: a case in Indonesian agroindustry. *BIO Web of Conferences.* EDP Sciences.

Hejazi, M. T., Batati, B. A., & Bahurmuz, A. (2023). The Influence of Green Supply Chain Management Practices on Corporate Sustainability Performance. *Sustainability.*

Jia, L. (2020). The role of big data analytics in enabling green supply chain management: A literature review. *Journal of Data, Information and Management*, 75–83.

Khamisu, M. S., & Paluri, R. A. (2024). *Emerging trends of environmental social and governance (ESG) disclosure research.* Cleaner Production Letters.

Khan, S. A., & Qianli, D. (2017). Impact of Green Supply Chain Management Practices on Firms' Performance: An Empiral Study from the Perspective of Pakistan. *Environmental Science Pollution*, 16829-16844.

Khan, Y., Su'ud, M. B., Alam, M. M., Ahmad, F. S., Ahmad, A. Y., & Khan, N. (2022). Application of Internet of Things (IoT) in Sustainable Supply Chain Management. *Sustainability*, 1–14.

Kumar, V., Pallathadka, H., Sharma, S. K., Thakar, C. M., Singh, M., & Pallathadka, L. K. (2022). *Role of machine learning in green supply chain management and operations management. Materials Today: Proceedings*. Elsevier.

Leta. (2025). *Your deliveries,* Retrieved from Leta: https://leta.ai/

Li, F. (2024). Challenges and Opportunities for Sustainable Supply Chain Management. *Frontiers in Business, Economics and Management*, 160–163.

Lori Systems Ltd. (2025). *Transport Empowerment*. Retrieved from Lori Systems Ltd: https://www.lorisystems.com/impact.html#transport

Luthra, K. S., Vinod, K., Sanjay, A., & Haleem, A. (2016). Barriers to implement green supply chain management in automobile industry using interpretive structural modeling technique: An Indian perspective. *Journal of Industrial Engineering and Management*, 231–257.

Maris. (2021). *Meta Electric Partners with Sendy to Provide Cleaner, Cheaper Deliveries*. Retrieved from Marisafrica: https://marisafrica.com/meta-electric-sendy-partnership/

Marketforce. (2025). *Facilitating growth across the African retail ecosystem in a digital age*. Retrieved from Marketforce360: https://marketforce360.com/company.html

Mchopa, A. D., Kazungu, I. E., & Changalima, I. A. (2024). Green Supply Chain Management Among Small and Medium Manufacturing Firms in East Africa: A Review of Practices and Antecedents for Sustainability. *Sustainable Education and Development - Clean Energy* (pp. 243-257). Springer Nature.

Meixell, M. J., & Gargeya, V. B. (2005). Global supply chain design: A literature review and critique. *Transportation Research*, 531–550.

MHCL. (2025). mkulazi.co.tz. Retrieved from About Mkulazi: https://www.mkulazi.co.tz/about

MIT. (2020). *Massachusetts Institute of Technology*. Retrieved from Improving global health equity by helping clinics do more with less: https://news.mit.edu/2020/macro-eyes-vaccine-chain-health-equity-0626

Mohammed, A. (2023). The Utilization of Robotics in Supply Chain Management and its Various Applicatons. *International Journal of Information Technology, Modeling and Computing*, 1-9.

Moutik, B., Summerscales, J., Jones, J. G., & Pemberton, R. (2023). Life Cycle Assessment Research Trends and Implications: A Bibliometric Analysis. *Sustainability*.

Mukwano Industries Ltd. (2025). *Mukwano Industries Uganda Ltd*. Retrieved from https://mukwano.com/about-us/: https://mukwano.com/about-us/

Mwanaumo, E. T., Mwanza, B. M., & Siaminwe, L. (2023). Green Supply Chain Management Practices and Effects on Organizational Performance in the Zambian Beverage Manufacturing Industry . *Logistics and Operation Management*, 15-30.

Namagembe, S., Ryan, S., & Ramaswami, S. (2019). Green supply chain practice adoption and firm performance: Manufacturing SMEs in Uganda. *Management of Environmental Quality*, 5–35.

Nasiche, F., & Ngugi, G. K. (2014). Determinants of Adoption of Green Procurement in the Public Sector: A Case Study of Kenya Pipeline Company. *International Journal of Social Sciences and Entrepreneurship*, 351-372.

Ojo, L. D., Adeniyi, O., Ogundimu, O. E., & Alaba, O. O. (2022). Rethinking Green Supply Chain Management Practices Impact on Company Performance: A Close-Up Insight. *Sustainability*, 2–19.

Oyewo, A. S., Sterl, S., Khalili, S., & Breyer, C. (2023). Highly renewable energy systems in Africa: Rationale, research and recommendations. *Joule*, 1437–1470.

Paiola, M., & Gebauer, H. (2020). Internet of things technologies, digital servitization and business model innovation in BtoB manufacturing firms. *Industrial Marketing Management*, 245–264.

PR Newswire. (2020). Retrieved from Macro-eyes receives $2.2M grant from the Bill & Melinda Gates Foundation to bring AI to low income countries: https://www.prnewswire.com/news-releases/macro-eyes-receives-2-2m-grant-from-the-bill--melinda-gates-foundation-to-bring-ai-to-low-income-countries-300999849.html

Qu, C., & Kim, E. (2024). Reviewing the roles of AI-integrated technologies in sustainable supply chain management: Research propositions and a framework for future directions. *Sustainability*, •••, 6186.

Rahman, M. A., Saha, P., Ratul, S. H., & Graham, G. (2024). Big data analytics capability and supply chain sustainability: Analyzing moderating role of green supply chain management practices. *Benchmarking*.

Raut, R. D., Mangla, S. K., Narwane, V. S., Dora, M., & Liu, M. (2021). Big Data Analytics as a mediator in Lean, Agile, Resilient, and Green (LARG) practices effects on sustainable supply chains. *Transportation Research Part E, Logistics and Transportation Review*.

Safaricom. (2025). *2024 Sustainable Business Report*. Retrieved from safaricom.co.ke: https://www.safaricom.co.ke/images/Downloads/Safaricom-Sustainable-Report-2024-compressed.pdf

Singh, C., Thakkar, R., & Jatinder, W. (2022). Blockchain in Supply Chain Management. *European Journal of Engineering and Technology Research*, 60-69.

Singh, S. K., & Roy, S. (2020). Lecture Notes in Electrical Engineering. In Mandal, V. N. (Ed.), *Lecture Notes in Electriacl Engineering* (pp. 301–313). Springer.

Sujatmiko, Krisnanto, B., Sasmita, H., & Wahab, A. (2024). Global Supply Chain Management: Trends, Challenges, and Strategies. *Vifada Management and Digital Business*, 20-38.

Taj, S., Imran, A. S., Kastrati, Z., Daudpota, S. M., Memon, R. A., & Ahmed, J. (2023). IoT-based supply chain management: A systematic literature review. *Ineternet of Things*.

TBL. (2025). *Welcome to Tanzania Breweries Ltd PLC, Tanzania's Oldest and #1 Brewer*. Retrieved from Tanzania Breweries Ltd: https://www.tanzaniabreweries.co.tz/

Travaly, Y., & Muvunyi, K. (2020). *The future is intelligent: Harnessing the potential of artificial intelligence in Africa*. Retrieved from Brookings: https://www.brookings.edu/articles/the-future-is-intelligent-harnessing-the-potential-of-artificial-intelligence-in-africa/

Treiblmaier, H. (2018). The impact of the blockchain on the supply chain: A theory-based research framework and a call for action. *Supply Chain Management*, 545–559.

Tundys, B., & Wisniewski, T. (2023). Triple Bottom Line Aspects and Sustainable Supply Chain Resilience: A structural equation modelling approach. *Frontiers in Environmental Science.*

Unilever. (2025). *Unilever Sustainable Sourcing Programme for Agricultural Raw Materials.* Retrieved from unilever.com: https://www.unilever.com/files/archive-unilever-sustainable-sourcing-programme-for-agricultural-raw-materials-scheme-rules.pdf

Vaidya, S., Ambad, P., & Bhosle, S. (2018). Industry 4.0 - A Glimpse. *2nd International Conference on Materials Manufacturing and Design Engineering* (pp. 233-238). Amsterdam: Elsevier B.V.

Viebeg Medical. (2025). *Artificial Intelligence.* Retrieved from Viebeg Medical: https://www.viebeg.com/philosophy/ai/

Walker, H., Di Sisto, L., & McBain, D. (2008). Drivers and Barriers to Environmental Supply Chain Management Practices: Lessons from the public and private sectors. *Journal of Purchasing and Supply Management*, 69–85.

World Economic Forum. (2025). *Lori Systems.* Retrieved from weforum.org: https://www.weforum.org/organizations/lori-systems-corp/

Wu, T., & Zuo, M. (2023). Green supply chain transformation and emission reduction based on machine learning. *Science Progress*, 1–15.

Zejjari, I., & Benhayoun, I. (2024). The use of artificial intelligence to advance sustainable supply chain: Retrospective and future avenues explored through bibliometric analysis. *Discover Sustainability.*

Zhang, L., Fu, S., Tian, J., & Peng, J. (2022). A review of energy industry chain and energy supply chain. *Energies, MDPI*, 1-32.

Zhu, Q., Sarkis, J., & Lai, K.-h. (2013). Institutional-based antecedents and performance outcomes of internal and external green supply chain management practices. *Journal of Purchasing and Supply Management*, 106–117.

Chapter 8
Analyzing the Long-Run and Short-Run Impact of GDP on NIFTY 50:
Evidence From ARDL Approach

Shefali Saini
https://orcid.org/0009-0006-7355-6159
Chandigarh University, India

Gurpreet Kaur
https://orcid.org/0000-0003-2903-7117
Chandigarh University, India

ABSTRACT

The chapter examines the long-run and short-run impact of GDP on NIFTY 50 in India using data from April 2011 to July 2024. The study employs ARDL Bounds testing, Granger Causality test, and other econometric tools to explore the relationship. GDP, as the independent variable, and NIFTY 50, as the dependent variable, are transformed into natural logarithms to stabilize the data. Results reveal no long-term cointegration between GDP and NIFTY 50, as indicated by the F-statistic from the ARDL Bounds test. However, Granger causality results suggest that NIFTY 50 influences GDP in the short run, while GDP does not Granger-cause NIFTY 50. The study highlights the significance of these findings for policymakers and investors, suggesting further exploration into stock market dynamics with other macroeconomic variables.

DOI: 10.4018/979-8-3373-7907-4.ch008

INTRODUCTION

The stock market is widely regarded as a barometer of economic health, reflecting a nation's financial health and growth trajectory. According to the International Monetary Fund (2022), 'global stock market capitalization grew from $54 trillion in 2011 to $93 trillion in 2021,' underscoring its role in channelling resources into productive ventures and driving economic growth. Stock markets provide businesses with an essential platform to raise funds, facilitating expansion and innovation (World Bank, 2023). In India, 'the total market capitalization of its stock market reached $3.7 trillion in 2023, ranking it as the fifth-largest globally and accounting for approximately 3.1% of global market capitalization' (World Bank, 2023).

While India's internal reforms—such as the implementation of the Goods and Services Tax (GST) in 2017 and demonetization in 2016—have fundamentally altered the macroeconomic landscape, external factors have also played a significant role in influencing investor sentiment and stock market performance. Events like the U.S. Federal Reserve's interest rate decisions, global oil price fluctuations, and geopolitical tensions have increasingly contributed to capital flow volatility and market corrections in emerging economies, including India. For instance, the 2013 'Taper Tantrum' led to a rapid depreciation of the Indian rupee and caused significant turbulence in the equity markets.

Despite being mentioned in various studies, structural breaks such as COVID-19, demonetization, and global geopolitical events like the Russia-Ukraine war remain under-analyzed in their empirical impact on market dynamics. Incorporating event-study approaches or dummy variables in econometric models can help capture the influence of such disruptions on the GDP-NIFTY relationship. In particular, structural shifts during the pandemic introduced new challenges in interpreting traditional macro-financial linkages, as market recoveries became increasingly driven by central bank liquidity and fiscal expansion rather than just underlying economic output.

The integration of India into the global financial system, coupled with liberalization policies, has expanded the country's exposure to global macroeconomic cycles. This interconnectedness means that India's stock market movements are not only a reflection of domestic economic growth but also of global liquidity trends, trade dynamics, and foreign investor behavior. With a market capitalization of $3.7 trillion in 2023, India ranks among the world's top five equity markets, highlighting the critical role of capital markets in supporting the country's economic development. Moreover, this global exposure necessitates an understanding of how spillovers from major economies—such as interest rate hikes by the U.S. Fed or European energy price shocks—impact domestic investment flows and index performance.

Stock indices, such as the NIFTY 50, are essential proxies for market performance and economic stability. The NIFTY 50, 'which tracks 50 of the largest and most liquid companies across various sectors, represents approximately 65–70% of the total market capitalization of the National Stock Exchange' (OECD, 2021). The index reflects the performance of major industries such as technology, banking, energy, and pharmaceuticals, offering a comprehensive snapshot of the Indian economy. From 2011 to 2021, 'the NIFTY 50 generated an annualized return of 15%, aligning with India's robust economic growth trajectory' (OECD, 2021). Moreover, the OECD notes that 'stock markets act as leading indicators of economic cycles, providing real-time insights into investor sentiment and corporate performance,' which is invaluable for policymakers and investors (OECD, 2021).

The performance of this index has been significantly influenced by recent phenomena such as the digitization of trading platforms, a surge in retail investor participation post-COVID, and the rise of environmental, social, and governance (ESG) investing. These trends have added new dimensions to the traditional GDP-stock market relationship, making it essential to revisit this linkage in light of both structural reforms and shifting investor behavior. The growing influence of algorithmic trading, passive investing, and social media-fueled speculation further complicates the interpretation of index movements in relation to economic fundamentals.

Given the NIFTY 50's responsiveness to macroeconomic developments, it is essential to examine its linkage with Gross Domestic Product (GDP), one of the most critical macroeconomic indicators. GDP measures the monetary value of all goods and services produced in a country. 'GDP directly influences stock market performance by driving corporate revenues and liquidity' (International Monetary Fund, 2024). Between 2011 and 2023, India's GDP grew at a compounded annual growth rate (CAGR) of 6.8%, supported by reforms such as 'the introduction of the Goods and Services Tax (GST) in 2017 and demonetization in 2016,' as well as increased foreign direct investment (FDI) inflows (World Bank, 2023). These changes boosted investor sentiment and corporate profitability, cementing the stock market's role in the Indian economy.

Its relationship with stock market indices like the NIFTY 50 offers valuable insights into the efficiency of capital markets in pricing economic fundamentals. Traditional economic theories, such as the Efficient Market Hypothesis (EMH), posit that 'stock prices reflect all available information, including GDP data,' while behavioral finance theories suggest that robust GDP growth fosters investor optimism, driving markets upward (OECD, 2021). Conversely, 'weak GDP performance often triggers negative investor sentiment, leading to market corrections' (OECD, 2021). Integrating both theoretical perspectives into empirical research strengthens the interpretive depth and allows for reconciliation of contrasting conclusions in literature. Additionally, analyzing GDP's impact in conjunction with corporate earnings growth, which acts as a transmission mechanism between macroeconomic conditions and stock returns, can provide more granular insights.

India's financial landscape has been shaped by globalization and liberalization since the early 2000s. Structural reforms and economic policies have attracted significant foreign investments, boosting stock market growth (Reserve Bank of India, 2023). For instance, 'net FDI inflows into India rose from $22 billion in 2012 to over $49 billion in 2021, contributing significantly to economic growth and enhancing liquidity in the equity market' (World Bank, 2023).

In this context, it becomes imperative to analyze how GDP fluctuations, both in the short and long run, affect stock market behavior. Moreover, recent structural shocks like the COVID-19 pandemic and policy interventions by regulatory bodies such as the Reserve Bank of India (RBI) and the Securities and Exchange Board of India (SEBI) have had profound impacts on market dynamics. For example, during the early months of the COVID-19 pandemic, 'the NIFTY 50 index initially declined by nearly 40% in early 2020 but rebounded rapidly due to timely fiscal stimulus and strong GDP recovery' (International Monetary Fund, 2024). These developments necessitate a policy-oriented discussion that connects empirical findings with regulatory actions. Additionally, the emergence of unconventional monetary policies and liquidity-driven rallies has increased the importance of evaluating stock indices like NIFTY not only as reflections of GDP trends but also as leading indicators of economic expectations.

To capture these dynamics, the study employs Autoregressive Distributed Lag (ARDL) bounds testing, Granger causality analysis, and impulse response functions.

GLOBAL MACROECONOMIC LINKAGES

The relationship between macroeconomic indicators and stock market performance cannot be fully understood without considering the global context in which national markets operate. In India, external factors such as U.S. Federal Reserve interest rate decisions, global commodity price fluctuations, and geopolitical risks significantly influence market behavior. For instance, the 2013 'Taper Tantrum'—when the U.S. Fed announced a reduction in its quantitative easing program—led to capital outflows from emerging markets like India and triggered volatility in the NIFTY 50 index (IMF, 2014).

Similarly, oil price shocks have historically impacted India's trade balance, inflation rate, and investor sentiment, all of which are key drivers of market fluctuations. Given India's dependency on crude oil imports, sudden spikes in Brent Crude prices tend to raise inflation expectations and increase fiscal pressure, thereby dampening market performance (RBI Bulletin, 2022). Additionally, USD–INR volatility plays a role in determining foreign institutional investment (FII) flows. 'During periods of rupee depreciation, FIIs often retreat, exerting downward pressure on equity indices'.

These global macroeconomic linkages suggest that India's equity markets do not function in isolation but are part of an interconnected system influenced by international capital flows, interest rate differentials, and global investor sentiment. 'Integrating these external variables into the analysis enhances the explanatory power of empirical models and provides policymakers with a more holistic understanding of market movements' (World Bank, 2021).

This chapter aims to provide a comprehensive assessment of the long-run and short-run relationship between GDP and the NIFTY 50 index, using advanced econometric tools and a broader macroeconomic perspective. It incorporates global influences, structural breaks, and post-pandemic dynamics to offer a nuanced understanding of the GDP-market interaction in India's evolving financial landscape. Comparative insights from economies like China and Brazil will be used where relevant to contextualize India's experience among emerging markets. The discussion is further enriched by linking findings to retail investor behavior, sectoral trends, and the evolving role of financial market regulators in emerging economies.

REVIEW OF LITERATURE

Fichtner and Joebges (2024) investigate the long-run relationship between national stock market indices and GDP across G7 countries between 1991 and 2019. Using the ARDL bounds testing approach, the study finds limited evidence of a stable long-term cointegration relationship between stock prices and GDP during the entire sample period. However, stronger linkages are observed in the sub-period 2001–2019, particularly in Anglo-Saxon economies and Japan. When a relationship exists, a 1% increase in stock indices leads to a 0.2% increase in GDP within two to three years. The study also examines asymmetric effects, revealing that GDP is more responsive to positive stock price changes than to declines, especially in non-Anglo-Saxon countries. Despite controlling for variables like foreign demand, profit share, and long-term interest rates, the study finds that none of these fully explain the instability of the stock-GDP link. Overall, the findings support the view that while a long-run relationship may be emerging in recent decades, it remains sensitive to structural changes and vary across countries.

Bunjaku (2024) analyzes the long-term relationship between GDP and the stock market in the United States, focusing on its implications for index fund investments. Using a simple linear regression model with nominal GDP as the independent variable and the S&P 500 index as the dependent variable over a 29-year period (1990–2019), the study finds a strong and statistically significant positive correlation. The regression model yields a β coefficient of 0.911 and an R^2 of 0.83, indicating that approximately 83% of the variation in the S&P 500 is explained by changes in

GDP. The findings suggest that over the long term, the S&P 500 and GDP follow similar growth trajectories, reinforcing the idea that GDP can be a valuable predictor for equity market trends. This has important implications for passive investment strategies, such as index fund investing, particularly for long-term investors seeking lower volatility and broad market exposure. The study also supports cross-country consistency in the positive relationship between GDP and stock market performance, aligning with similar findings in the academic literature.

The aim of this study is to explore the relationship between macroeconomic variables, specifically GDP and inflation, and stock market performance. The research spans from 2008 to 2019, employing tools such as descriptive statistics, Pearson's correlation, and multiple regression analysis. Key findings indicate a positive correlation between GDP and stock market indices, while inflation negatively impacts stock prices, highlighting the significance of these macroeconomic factors in predicting stock market movements (Parmar, 2023).

Kushwaha et al. (2023) explores the impact of GDP and inflation on the Bombay Stock Exchange (BSE) index from 1980 to 2021. Using correlation, regression analysis, and ANOVA, the research finds a strong positive relationship between GDP and BSE and a moderate negative relationship between inflation and BSE. The regression model demonstrates that GDP and inflation together explain 88.5% of the variation in the BSE index. Findings indicate that a 1% increase in GDP leads to a 17.08% rise in BSE, while a 1% increase in inflation causes a 2.17% decline. This study underscores the significant role of macroeconomic factors in stock market performance, providing insights for investors and policymakers.

The study examines the impact of GDP on the Indian stock market, focusing on the BSE Sensex and NSE NIFTY 50 indices over the period 2005–2021. Using Karl Pearson's correlation analysis and simple linear regression, the research identifies a strong positive correlation between GDP and both stock indices, with R-squared values of 82.7% and 83.4% for Sensex and Nifty 50, respectively. The findings demonstrate that GDP significantly influences stock market performance in India. This work highlights the critical role of GDP as a predictor of stock market trends while emphasizing the need for further studies on other macroeconomic factors (Saxena, 2022).

The study examines the impact of GDP on stock market movement in India, focusing on NIFTY 50 and SENSEX indices from 2011 to 2020. Using secondary data from sources like RBI and NSE, the paper applies correlation and regression analysis to explore relationships between the variables. It finds a strong positive correlation between GDP and stock market indices, with GDP significantly influencing stock market performance. The research highlights the role of GDP as a macroeconomic driver for stock market trends in India. These findings provide a basis for further investigation into the interaction of GDP with other macroeconomic factors (Vasani, 2020).

The study examines the causal link between GDP, inflation, and Nifty returns from 2007 to 2017 using quarterly data. Employing econometric tools like the Augmented Dickey-Fuller test (ADF), Johansen co-integration test, and Vector Error Correction Model (VECM), the analysis explores both short- and long-term relationships. Findings reveal a lack of significant long-run causality between GDP, inflation, and Nifty returns, but suggest short-term interdependence among the variables. The research highlights that GDP growth positively influences Nifty returns, while inflation has a negative effect. These insights emphasize the complex dynamics of macroeconomic variables and stock market performance (Raju et al., 2018).

Kizys and Pierdzioch (2009) conduct an extensive empirical investigation to explore whether asymmetric macroeconomic shocks explain variations in the international co-movement of stock returns across major industrialized economies from 1975 to 2004. Using a time-varying parameter model estimated with Kalman filtering, they analyze stock return co-movement among G7 nations and model macroeconomic shocks through two VAR frameworks—one based on inflation, industrial production, and short-term interest rates, and the other using open-economy variables like real exchange rates and price ratios. Despite the sophistication of these models, the study finds that asymmetric shocks are not systematically linked to changes in stock return co-movement over time. This result is consistent across both time-series and panel-data regressions and remains robust across subsamples and VAR specifications. The only notable exception is a significant intra-European co-movement in the post-1994 period, potentially linked to EU integration. The findings suggest that monitoring asymmetric macroeconomic shocks may be of limited value for international portfolio diversification strategies based on return comovement.

Binswanger (2004) investigates whether the breakdown in the historically strong relationship between stock returns and real economic activity observed in the United States during the early 1980s also occurred in other G-7 nations. Using quarterly data from 1960 to 1999—including real GDP, industrial production, and stock returns adjusted for inflation—the study applies cointegration tests, OLS regressions, vector error correction models (VECM), and structural break diagnostics such as Chow and CUSUM tests. The findings suggest that similar breakdowns occurred in Japan, Canada, and an aggregate European G-7 economy, while evidence for France, Italy, and the UK was weaker or inconclusive. The paper attributes this decoupling to the rise of speculative bubbles and investor exuberance, which caused stock prices to diverge from macroeconomic fundamentals. These results support the hypothesis that the weakening link between stock markets and real activity was not unique to the U.S. but part of a broader international phenomenon.

Table 1. Literature review

Author(s) & Year	Country/Region	Methodology	Key Variables	Major Findings
Binswanger (2004)	G7 Countries	Cointegration, VECM, Chow Test	Real GDP, Stock Returns	Breakdown in GDP-stock link in U.S., Japan, EU post-1980; speculative bubbles
Kizys & Pierdzioch (2009)	G7 Countries	VAR, Time-Varying Parameters	CPI, Industrial Prod., Interest	No systematic link between asymmetric shocks and comovement
Bunjaku (2024)	United States	Linear Regression	Nominal GDP, S&P 500	Strong long-term correlation ($R^2 = 0.83$); relevant for index fund investing
Fichtner & Joebges (2024)	G7 Countries	ARDL Bounds Test	Real GDP, Real Stock Index	Weak long-term link overall, stronger post-2001 in Anglo-Saxon economies
Parmar (2023)	India	Pearson Correlation, Regression	GDP, Inflation, Sensex	Positive GDP-stock correlation; inflation negative
Kushwaha et al. (2023)	India (BSE)	Regression, ANOVA	GDP, Inflation, BSE Index	1% GDP → 17% BSE rise; inflation dampens index
Saxena (2022)	India (Sensex/ NIFTY)	Pearson Correlation, Regression	GDP, Stock Indices	R^2 ~ 83%; GDP significant predictor
Vasani (2020)	India	Correlation, Regression	GDP, NIFTY, Sensex	Strong positive correlation
Raju et al. (2018)	India (CNX Nifty)	ADF, Johansen Cointegration	GDP, Inflation, NIFTY	Short-run causality only; no long-run link

While existing literature provides a mix of perspectives on the GDP–stock market relationship—ranging from stable long-term correlations in developed markets (Bunjaku, 2024) to evidence of breakdowns or structural variability in global contexts (Binswanger, 2004; Fichtner & Joebges, 2024)—most studies have either focused on developed economies or relied on broad correlation and cointegration frameworks without exploring the full range of domestic structural shifts. Furthermore, Indian studies (e.g., Parmar, 2023; Kushwaha et al., 2023; Saxena, 2022; Vasani, 2020) largely emphasize linear relationships using standard regression tools and limited macroeconomic variables. In contrast, this chapter adds substantial value by contextualizing the GDP–NIFTY 50 relationship within both global and local shocks—such as demonetization and COVID-19—using structural break diagnostics, ARDL modeling, and impulse response analysis. By incorporating high-frequency proxies for GDP, sectoral stock indices, and investor behavior metrics like the India VIX, this study offers a multidimensional and empirically rigorous assessment that not only addresses gaps in the Indian literature but also contributes to the broader debate on whether emerging markets mirror global patterns or chart unique trajectories.

THEORETICAL FOUNDATIONS

- **Fama (1970) – Efficient Market Hypothesis (EMH)**

Fama's (1970) Efficient Market Hypothesis (EMH) is a cornerstone of modern financial theory, positing that financial markets are "informationally efficient," meaning that all available information is fully reflected in asset prices at any given time. Under the EMH, changes in stock prices should only occur due to the arrival of new, unexpected information, implying that consistent excess returns are unattainable through either technical or fundamental analysis. In the context of the GDP–stock market relationship, EMH suggests that expected GDP growth should already be incorporated into current stock prices, and only unanticipated shifts in macroeconomic performance would cause market fluctuations. Therefore, if markets are fully efficient, we should observe little to no systematic correlation between lagged GDP data and future stock returns, a hypothesis that has been tested with mixed empirical results.

- **Shiller (2000) – Behavioral Finance**

In contrast to EMH, Robert Shiller's (2000) behavioral finance framework challenges the notion of rational market behavior by incorporating psychological and cognitive biases into financial decision-making. Shiller argues that investor sentiment, herd behavior, overreaction, and speculative bubbles often drive stock prices away from their fundamental values. His work, particularly highlighted in *Irrational Exuberance*, emphasizes that stock markets can become disconnected from macroeconomic indicators like GDP, especially during boom-and-bust cycles. This perspective is particularly relevant when examining periods of structural breaks such as the 2008 global financial crisis or the COVID-19 pandemic, where markets behaved irrationally relative to underlying economic fundamentals. Behavioral finance thus provides a theoretical lens for understanding why stock prices may respond excessively—or insufficiently—to macroeconomic developments, including GDP trends.

- **Campbell & Shiller (1988) – Valuation Ratios**

Campbell and Shiller (1988) provide a bridge between EMH and behavioral approaches by examining valuation ratios—such as the price-to-earnings (P/E) ratio—as predictors of future stock returns. Their model posits that while markets may be generally efficient, valuation ratios contain information about expected returns and long-term economic performance. In particular, high valuation levels are often associated with lower subsequent returns, suggesting mean reversion tendencies in asset prices. When applied to the GDP–stock market nexus, their findings imply that current stock market valuations may signal future economic activity, and that deviations between GDP growth and valuation metrics could highlight periods of over- or under-valuation. Their work introduces a more nuanced understanding of how financial markets and macroeconomic indicators interact over time.

- **Keynesian View on Market Behaviour:**

Keynes (1936) argued that financial markets are often driven by "animal spirits"—irrational waves of optimism or pessimism—rather than fundamentals. In the Keynesian framework, uncertainty, speculation, and liquidity preferences dominate investment decisions, leading to frequent disconnections between stock prices and real economic indicators like GDP. This perspective explains why market reactions to macroeconomic shifts are often delayed, exaggerated, or contrary to rational expectations, particularly during crises or structural breaks.

- **Shiller's Narrative Economics:**

Building on behavioral finance, Shiller (2021) introduced the concept of "narrative economics", asserting that viral stories and shared beliefs can significantly shape investor behavior and macroeconomic outcomes. These narratives—like India's "Atmanirbhar Bharat" initiative or the "retail investing boom" post-COVID—become self-reinforcing mechanisms that drive investor sentiment, market participation, and price trends, even in the absence of corresponding GDP changes. This lens is particularly relevant in emerging markets where digital media and policy announcements rapidly influence public expectations.

CONCLUSION TO THEORETICAL FRAMEWORK

Together, these theoretical perspectives provide a comprehensive lens through which to interpret the complex and evolving relationship between GDP and stock market performance. Fama's Efficient Market Hypothesis (1970) underscores the foundational belief in rational pricing, implying that only unexpected macroeconomic changes should affect asset values. In contrast, Shiller's (2000) behavioral finance approach and his later work on narrative economics (2021) highlight the psychological and sociocultural dimensions of market behavior, especially in times of crisis or transition. Campbell and Shiller's (1988) focus on valuation ratios offers a middle ground, showing how deviations from economic fundamentals can signal long-term corrections. The Keynesian view further enriches this discussion by emphasizing the role of uncertainty, liquidity preference, and speculative dynamics in driving asset price fluctuations independent of macroeconomic fundamentals. When applied to the Indian context—especially during structurally disruptive events like demonetization and the COVID-19 pandemic—these frameworks collectively explain why GDP and equity markets can at times converge, diverge, or respond asymmetrically. This multi-theoretical foundation thus equips researchers and policymakers with a richer toolkit to decode the economic signals embedded within financial markets.

Primary Objective

The aim of the study is to analyse the impact of GDP on the NIFTY50 in short-run and long-run for the time period 2011 till 2024.

Hypothesis

Null Hypothesis:
H01: There is no long-run cointegration relationship between GDP and NIFTY 50.
H02: GDP do not Granger-cause changes in NIFTY 50 in the short run.
H03: NIFTY 50 do not Granger-cause changes in GDP in the short run.

Data Sources

This study examines monthly time series data spanning from April 2011 to July 2024. Quarterly Gross Domestic Product (GDP) data was sourced from the official Reserve Bank of India (RBI) website and subsequently converted into monthly data using an interpolation technique. Additionally, the monthly price data for the NIFTY 50 Index was retrieved from the National Stock Exchange (NSE) website. To stabilize the data and ensure consistency, all values were transformed into their natural logarithms.

Methodology

The study employed the Augmented Dickey-Fuller (ADF) test to check for unit root and stationarity in the variables. After confirming stationarity at I(1) levels,

Pearson correlation analysis was conducted to measure the strength and direction of the linear relationship between GDP and NIFTY 50, revealing a strong positive correlation. To analyze the long-run relationship, the ARDL Bounds testing technique was applied for the period 2011–2024, but the F-statistic indicated no long-term cointegration. Consequently, the study proceeded with Granger Causality analysis in a multivariate VAR framework to examine short-run causality and direction of influence. Furthermore, Impulse Response Function (IRF) analysis was conducted to visualize the dynamic effects of GDP shocks on NIFTY 50 over a 10-period horizon. All computations were performed using EViews software.

Given the limitation of relying on interpolated monthly GDP values, future iterations of this model could incorporate high-frequency macroeconomic proxies such as the Index of Industrial Production (IIP) or monthly GST collections. These indicators are released on a monthly basis and closely track underlying economic activity, offering a more immediate view of output fluctuations. Their inclusion would serve as a robustness check to validate the consistency and accuracy of the GDP estimates used in the ARDL framework.

Modeling Justification and Assumptions

The choice of the Autoregressive Distributed Lag (ARDL) model in this study is justified by the nature of the data, which includes variables that are a mix of I(0) and I(1) integration orders. According to Pesaran et al. (2001), ARDL is well-suited for such datasets and allows for robust estimation of both long-run and short-run dynamics without requiring pre-testing for unit roots to the same extent as traditional cointegration techniques. Furthermore, the ARDL bounds testing approach provides more flexibility in lag selection and small sample properties, making it a preferred choice for macro-financial studies in emerging markets.

To handle the unavailability of official monthly GDP data, the study uses interpolated monthly estimates derived from quarterly GDP data and complemented with high-frequency proxies such as the Index of Industrial Production (IIP). Previous literature (e.g., Ray & Borah, 2006; Katoch & Sidhu, 2019) supports the reliability of IIP as a leading indicator for economic activity, particularly in industrially driven economies like India. In this context, the interpolation method offers a practical compromise to examine monthly co-movements with financial variables such as NIFTY 50.

Key assumptions underlying this model include the stationarity of first differences for all variables, the absence of serial correlation in the residuals, and the stability of the estimated long-run coefficients over time. Lag length was chosen based on the Akaike Information Criterion (AIC), ensuring optimal model fit and minimizing information loss. Diagnostic tests such as the Breusch-Godfrey Serial

Correlation LM Test and CUSUM tests were conducted to confirm model validity and parameter stability throughout the sample period.

Data Analysis

Figure 1. Trend of Log GDP and Log NIFTY 50 (2011-2024)

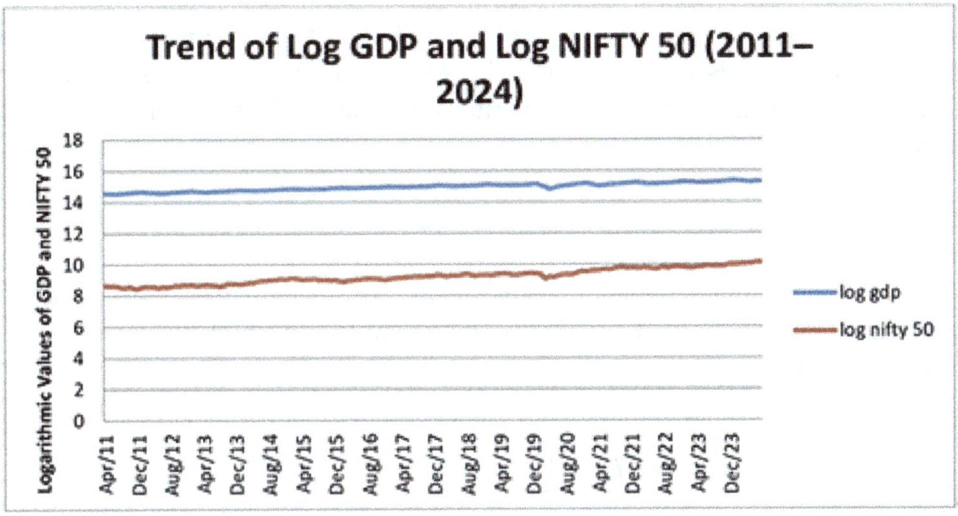

Table 2. Pearson Correlation

	Log GDP	Log NIFTY50
Log GDP	1	0.9610
Log NIFTY50	0.9610	1

Note: 1. The results have been computed by using the Pearson Correlation test using EViews software10.
Source: Computed

The line graph and Pearson correlation results together provide compelling evidence of a strong relationship between log GDP and log NIFTY 50 from 2011 to 2024. The graph illustrates a consistent upward trend in both variables, with log GDP showing steady economic growth and log NIFTY 50 reflecting parallel movement, indicating its sensitivity to GDP changes. This visual alignment is further substantiated by the Pearson correlation coefficient of 0.961078, which signifies a very strong positive linear relationship. The high correlation suggests that as GDP grows, the NIFTY 50 index tends to increase proportionally, highlighting the interconnectedness of economic performance and stock market trends. These findings emphasize the influence of GDP as a key macroeconomic driver for stock market performance in India.

NIFTY 50 is the dependent variable and Gross Domestic Product (GDP) is the independent variable. The regression model of the study is as follows:

$$NIFTY50_t = \alpha_o + \alpha_1\, GDP + \varepsilon_{1t} \text{ -} \qquad (1)$$

Where, α_o is a constant, α_1 is a coefficient of exports and ε_{1t} is the error term in the model which is in the equation (1). All the variables are transformed into their natural logarithms. Therefore, the final description of the model is presented in succeeding equation:

$$LnNIFTY50_t = \alpha_o + \alpha_1\, lnGDP + \varepsilon_{1t} \text{ -} \qquad (2)$$

Firstly, the stationarity of the variables is checked as the ARDL method needs variables to be stationary at either I(0) or I(1) levels. Unit root tests are broadly used to check stationarity

Table 3. Unit Root Table: ADF, lnGDP

Tests	**ADF**
Level (Intercept)	0.8265
Level (Trend and intercept)	0.6401
1st Difference (Intercept)	0.000

Note: 1. The results have been computed by using the ADF test using EViews software10.
2. The symbols *, **, and *** signify statistical significance at the 10%, 5%, and 1% levels, respectively.
Source: Computed

Table 4. Unit Root Table: ADF, lnNIFTY50

Tests	**ADF**
Level (Intercept)	0.9767
Level (Trend and intercept)	0.0567
Level(1st difference)	0.000

Note: 1. The results have been computed by using the ADF test using EViews software10.
2. The symbols *, **, and *** signify statistical significance at the 10%, 5%, and 1% levels, respectively.
Source: Computed

The results from the tests show that lnGDP, lnNIFTY50 stationary at I(1) using ADF, as depicted in Table 2 and 3. The p-value of all the variables are statistically significant at 0.0 by using the ADF test. The results qualify for using the ARDL model to deduce the long-run relationship between the variables. In the next step, the existence of a long-run relationship will be examined using the Bounds test approach. Following is the ARDL equation of the model when NIFTY50 is a dependent variable:

$\Delta\ln(\text{NIFTY50})_t = \alpha 0 + j\Delta\ln(\text{GDP})_{t-1}\ \varepsilon_{1t.}$.

The null hypothesis, H01: ð1 = ð2 = 0, which assumes no co integration, is being tested against the alternative hypothesis, H11: ð1 ≠ ð2 ≠ 0, which suggests the presence of co integration. Table 3 presents the outcomes of the Bounds test.

Table 5. F Bounds Test

Significance	10%	5%	2.5%	1%
I(0)	3.02	3.62	4.18	4.94
I(1)	3.51	4.16	4.79	5.58

F-Statistic 3.4247
Source: Computed

According to the criterion, we accept the null hypothesis if the f-value is lower than the I(0) bound. Suppose the computed f-value is higher than the I(1) bound; in that case, we can reject the null hypothesis and accept the alternative hypothesis, which shows long-run cointegration relationship between the variables. If the f-statistic falls between the bounds, the test is inconclusive. The ARDL Bounds test findings indicate that the f-statistic value, 3.4247, is lower than the I(0) Bound value of 3.62, even at a significance level of 5%. This result strongly supports that there is no long-term relationship between the variables. The subsequent phase will involve the analysis of short-term causation through the utilization of VAR Granger causality.

Short-Run Analysis: VAR Granger Causality

The null hypothesis posits no short-term causal relationship between the variables, while the alternative hypothesis says that there is such a relationship between the variables from 2011-2024. As per the criteria, the null hypothesis is rejected when the p-value is below the 5% threshold.

Table 6. Granger Causality Test

Variables	Excluded Variables	Chi- Square	Degree of freedom	P- Value
Log nifty50	Log GDP	5.584	2	0.0613
Log GDP	Log nifty50	29.742	2	0.000

Here, the results depicted in Table 5 clearly show a no causality running between NIFTY50 and GDP, in the short period at a 5% level of significance, i.e., 0.0613> 5% significance level. Since the p-value (0.0613) is greater than the conventional significance level of 0.05, we fail to reject the null hypothesis. This means that in the short run, changes in the GDP do not Granger-cause NIFTY 50, indicating no significant causal relationship from the GDP to NIFTY50 in the short run. Similarly to check the NIFTY50 granger causes GDP, in this case the p-value (0.000) is less than 0.05, so we reject this null hypothesis. This suggests that NIFTY50 granger causes GDP rate in the short run.

Figure 2.

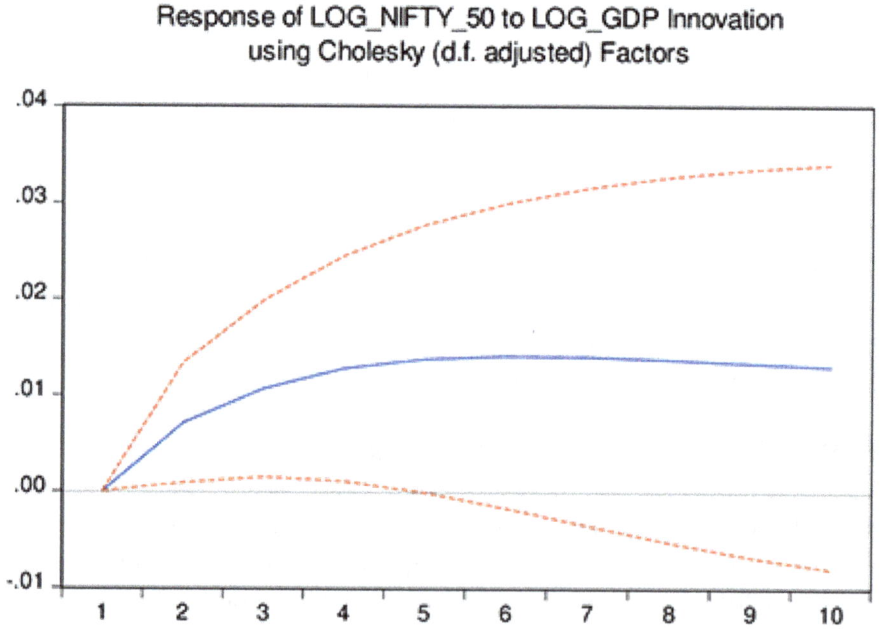

The impulse response function (IRF) demonstrates the impact of a 1-unit shock in LOG_GDP on LOG_NIFTY_50 over a 10-period horizon. Initially, the response is positive but modest, indicating a mild and immediate reaction of the NIFTY 50 index to changes in GDP. Over the subsequent 4–5 periods, the response grows steadily, highlighting a sustained and increasingly positive influence of GDP on the stock market. Beyond the 5th period, the response stabilizes, suggesting that the long-term effect of GDP on NIFTY 50 is both positive and enduring. Confidence intervals further validate the robustness of this positive relationship, although some uncertainty persists in later periods.

Policy Implications and Strategic Relevance

This study offers a range of implications that are of strategic importance to market regulators, investors, and forecasters. For regulatory bodies such as the Securities and Exchange Board of India (SEBI) and the Reserve Bank of India (RBI), understanding the short-run response of the NIFTY 50 to GDP variations can help guide policy calibration and communication. These insights can enhance regulatory preparedness during periods of rapid economic changes or volatile capital flows, allowing institutions to better anticipate and respond to market sentiments and liquidity dynamics.

For retail investors, the results caution against a simplistic interpretation of GDP trends as direct signals for short-term investment decisions. While long-term economic growth supports market fundamentals, the short-run divergence driven by behavioral anomalies—such as herd behavior and overreaction—calls for diversified and sentiment-informed strategies (Shiller, 2000). Incorporating behavioral metrics like the India VIX alongside sectoral indices (e.g., NIFTY Bank, NIFTY IT) may provide a more comprehensive foundation for portfolio management in volatile periods.

The study also has implications for economic analysts and forecasters. The use of ARDL and impulse response functions enables a nuanced understanding of lagged and contemporaneous dynamics between GDP and equity markets. These findings underscore the need for forecasters to move beyond linear macro-financial linkages and adopt flexible models that account for short-term fluctuations, investor behavior, and sectoral heterogeneity.

In sum, the empirical insights of this research can inform more responsive regulatory frameworks, more disciplined investor strategies, and more adaptive macroeconomic forecasting practices.

Key Contributions

This chapter makes several original contributions to the literature on macro-financial linkages in emerging economies. First, it provides a novel application of the ARDL framework in the context of the GDP–NIFTY 50 relationship using interpolated monthly data. Second, the chapter proposes incorporating investor sentiment indicators (e.g., India VIX) and high-frequency economic proxies such as the Index of Industrial Production (IIP) and GST collections, offering a more dynamic representation of real-time economic activity. Third, the study adds conceptual depth by synthesizing theoretical perspectives from the Efficient Market Hypothesis (EMH), behavioral finance, and valuation theory, while embedding comparative international insights from countries like the U.S., China, and Brazil. Lastly, it contributes practical value by outlining policy implications for SEBI and RBI, thereby bridging academic findings with financial market regulation and investment strategies.

LIMITATIONS OF THE STUDY

While this study offers valuable insights into the dynamic relationship between GDP and the NIFTY 50 index using the ARDL framework, several limitations must be acknowledged. First, the reliance on interpolated monthly GDP data, due to the unavailability of official high-frequency GDP figures in India, may introduce estimation errors that affect model precision. Second, although global macroeconomic influences are discussed conceptually, the empirical model focuses solely on domestic variables, excluding direct testing of international spillovers such as U.S. interest rates or oil price shocks. Third, the study does not account for sector-specific performance within the broader index, which may obscure heterogeneous responses among industry groups. Lastly, behavioral variables such as investor sentiment indices and survey-based measures are recognized theoretically but not incorporated empirically due to data constraints. These limitations suggest opportunities for future research to enhance robustness through more granular data and expanded variable inclusion.

SCOPE FOR FUTURE RESEARCH

Building on the findings of this study, future research can explore several avenues to deepen the understanding of macro-financial linkages in emerging markets like India. First, incorporating high-frequency proxies such as GST collections, Index of Industrial Production (IIP), or satellite-based economic indicators can improve the accuracy of monthly GDP estimation and better capture short-term economic fluctuations. Second, expanding the variable set to include global macroeconomic shocks—such as U.S. Federal Reserve policy changes, Brent crude oil prices, and global risk indices—would help quantify cross-border transmission effects on Indian equity markets. Third, a disaggregated analysis of sectoral indices (e.g., NIFTY IT, NIFTY Pharma, NIFTY Bank) could reveal differential sensitivities to macroeconomic shocks, offering more actionable insights for policymakers and investors. Additionally, empirical integration of behavioral metrics—such as India VIX, trading volume by retail vs. institutional investors, or sentiment indices derived from financial news—could further enrich predictive modeling frameworks. Finally, comparative studies with other emerging markets like Brazil, South Africa, or Vietnam could illuminate whether observed patterns are unique to India or part of broader trends across similar economies.

CONCLUSION

This study investigated the long-run and short-run relationship between GDP and the NIFTY 50 index in India from April 2011 to July 2024, employing the ARDL Bounds test, Pearson correlation analysis, Granger causality analysis, and Impulse Response Functions. The results indicate the absence of a long-term cointegration relationship between GDP and NIFTY 50, as the F-statistic from the ARDL Bounds test was below the lower bound critical value. This finding suggests that GDP does not exert a significant influence on the stock market in the long run. Conversely, the short-run analysis revealed a unidirectional causal relationship from NIFTY 50 to GDP, as indicated by Granger causality tests, while GDP did not Granger-cause NIFTY 50. Furthermore, impulse response analysis demonstrated that a shock to GDP results in an initial positive, albeit modest, impact on the NIFTY 50 index, which stabilizes within 4–5 periods. These findings highlight the complex and dynamic interplay between GDP and stock market performance in India.

Picking this topic for study is essential because GDP and stock market indices are two of the most widely tracked indicators of economic health, yet their relationship remains debated, especially in emerging markets like India. While traditional economic theories suggest that economic growth drives stock market performance, this study reveals that the stock market itself plays a more immediate role in influencing economic activity in the short run. Understanding this interaction is crucial for policymakers, investors, and economists, as it helps refine strategies for market regulation, economic forecasting, and investment decision-making. Additionally, India's financial landscape has evolved significantly in the past decade, with increasing foreign investment, rapid technological advancements, and shifts in economic policy, making it vital to reassess how GDP and stock markets interact in this changing environment.

Including the impulse response function (IRF) enhances this research by illustrating how GDP shocks influence NIFTY 50 over time, capturing the magnitude and duration of the effect rather than just correlation. It validates the short-run causality findings, showing that GDP impacts the stock market briefly before stabilizing. This dynamic perspective aids policy decisions, investment strategies, and market efficiency analysis beyond static econometric models. Additionally, the Pearson correlation coefficient of 0.9610 strongly confirms a positive association between GDP and NIFTY 50, reinforcing the short-term impact of GDP fluctuations on stock market performance.

The study's findings have significant implications for policymakers, investors, and researchers. The lack of a long-term relationship underscores the importance of structural factors, global market influences, and other macroeconomic variables—such as inflation, interest rates, and foreign direct investment—in shaping the performance of India's stock market. Policymakers can utilize the NIFTY 50 index as a short-term economic indicator to design timely and responsive fiscal and monetary policies. For investors, the stronger short-term influence of the stock market on GDP provides actionable insights for strategic decision-making, particularly in timing investment decisions based on economic and market cycles. Additionally, given the observed unidirectional short-run causality from NIFTY 50 to GDP, investors and analysts can leverage stock market trends as leading indicators of broader economic performance.

Future research should explore the role of additional macroeconomic variables and structural factors in shaping the relationship between GDP and stock market indices, particularly in emerging markets like India. Additionally, studies incorporating external shocks, such as geopolitical events or global financial crises, could provide a more comprehensive understanding of the dynamics between economic growth and stock market performance. Further analysis using high-frequency data, sector-specific indices, or behavioral finance perspectives could also deepen insights into how investor sentiment and external macroeconomic forces interact with stock market movements over time. By expanding the scope of analysis, future studies can contribute to a more holistic framework for understanding the intricate relationship between GDP and financial markets in India and other developing economies.

REFERENCES

Binswanger, M. (2004). Stock returns and real activity in the G-7 countries: Did the relationship change during the 1980s? *The Quarterly Review of Economics and Finance*, *44*(2), 237–252. DOI: 10.1016/j.qref.2003.07.001

Bunjaku, F. (2024). Decoding the stock market and GDP relationship over the long term: Implications for index fund investments. *International Journal of Management and Applied Research*, *12*(1), 1–13. DOI: 10.5281/zenodo.10654133

Chordia, A., & Gurbani, K. (2021). How is economic growth correlated to index growth? *Journal of Student Research*, *10*(3), 1–12. DOI: 10.47611/jsrhs.v10i3.1775

Fichtner, F., & Joebges, H. (2024). *Does the stock market predict GDP? Revisiting the empirical evidence for G7 countries. IMK Studies, 90*, 1–38. Düsseldorf: Macroeconomic Policy Institute (IMK). https://www.econstor.eu/bitstream/10419/283065/1/p-imk-study-90-2024.pdf

International Monetary Fund. (2022). *Global financial stability report.* https://www.imf.org/

International Monetary Fund. (2023). *Global financial stability report: Market resilience amid tightening global conditions.* https://www.imf.org/en/Publications/GFSR

International Monetary Fund. (2024). *Geopolitics, global trade, and the U.S. dollar: Insights from Gita Gopinath.* https://www.imf.org/en/News/Articles/2024/05/07/sp-geopolitics-impact-global-trade-and-dollar-gita-gopinath

Kizys, R., & Pierdzioch, C. (2009). Changes in the international comovement of stock returns and economic activity: Evidence from the G7 countries. *Journal of International Financial Markets, Institutions and Money*, *19*(2), 289–305. DOI: 10.1016/j.intfin.2008.01.002

Kushwaha, S., Kafle, S. C., & Khanal, B. (2023). Impact of GDP and inflation on stock market in India: A case study of BSE index. *BMC Journal of Scientific Research*, *6*(1), 136–148. DOI: 10.3126/bmcjsr.v6i1.60961

Organization for Economic Co-operation and Development. (2021). *Financial markets and economic cycles.* https://www.oecd.org/

Parmar, Y. (2023). An empirical impact of GDP and inflation on Indian stock market inclusive with Sensex. *International Journal of Creative Research Thoughts*, *11*(2), 688–694. https://www.ijcrt.org/papers/IJCRT2302082.pdf

Rajput, N., & Sufiya, . (2022). Impact of COVID-19 on financial integration: Study on BRICS. *Investment Management and Financial Innovations, 19*(2), 119–129. DOI: 10.21511/imfi.19(2).2022.10

Raju, J. K., Manjunath, B. R., & Pradeep, K. S. (2018). Impact of inflation and GDP on CNX Nifty. *Adarsh Journal of Management Research, 11*(1). Advance online publication. DOI: 10.21095/ajmr/2018/v11/i1/139602

Reserve Bank of India. (2023). *Annual report 2022–2023.* https://www.rbi.org.in/

Rout, B. S., & Das, N. M. (2024). BRICS stock markets performances during COVID-19: Comparison with other economic crises. *Vikalpa, 49*(3), 230–243. Advance online publication. DOI: 10.1177/02560909241264430

Saxena, P. (2022). An empirical study on implications and impact of GDP on the Indian stock market. *NeuroQuantology : An Interdisciplinary Journal of Neuroscience and Quantum Physics, 20*(22), 938–950. DOI: 10.48047/nq.2022.20.22.NQ10070

Vasani, S. V. (2020). Analysis of impact of gross domestic product (GDP) on stock market movement in India. *Global Journal of Management and Business Research: B Economics and Commerce, 20*(8), 35–43. https://globaljournals.org

World Bank. (2023). *Market capitalization of listed domestic companies.* https://www.worldbank.org/

Chapter 9
Reassessing FDI Determinants in Emerging Countries:
A Geoeconomic Perspective via Machine Learning Approach

Ichrak Dridi
ESCT Business School, Manouba University, Tunisia

Mohamed Malek Belhoula
https://orcid.org/0000-0002-2110-3936
ESCT Business School, Manouba University, Tunisia

ABSTRACT

This chapter examines the determinants of foreign direct investment inflows in 23 emerging countries over the period 2004–2023, using three tree-based machine learning models, decision tree, XGBoost, and random forest, to analyze 44 distinct indicators. The study evaluates how crises alter investor priorities by comparing stable and turbulent periods. Results show that during stable periods geopolitical risk, lagged unemployment, and digital infrastructure dominate, while trade openness and geopolitical stability gain prominence during crises, and capital openness and institutional quality become critical post COVID-19. Grounded in institutional and internationalization theories, these findings underscore the context-dependent adaptability of investor behavior. The study provides policy insights for emerging markets, advocating crisis-responsive strategies like digital infrastructure upgrades, trade openness during shocks, and institutional reforms to boost foreign investment and long-term growth.

DOI: 10.4018/979-8-3373-7907-4.ch009

1. INTRODUCTION

The determinants of Foreign Direct Investment (FDI) in emerging economies have gained renewed urgency amid shifting global capital flows and geopolitical realignments. While FDI has long been associated with economic growth and technological transfer (Alfaro et al., 2017), these advantages are conditional and vary significantly depending on host country characteristics (Wiessner et al., 2024; Oberhauser, 2024). This duality highlights the importance of understanding what drives FDI inflows, especially for emerging economies seeking to attract and mitigate risks. Policymakers, particularly in developing economies, require evidence-based insights to design targeted investment frameworks amid volatile conditions (IMF, 2024).

Scholars traditionally emphasize FDI's role in capital formation, employment generation, and knowledge transfer (Borensztein et al., 1998; Kumar et al., 2022). However, critics note that these outcomes depend on host-country absorptive capacity and institutional quality (Ajayi, 2006; Wiessner et al., 2024). Such debates highlight why analyzing determinants, rather than assuming benefits, is critical. Specifically, only by attracting the right type of FDI can countries optimize its developmental impact. Recent data illustrates this complexity, despite global capital flow contractions (IIF, 2023), emerging markets have maintained stable FDI inflows, suggesting that traditional drivers like regulatory quality (Kaushal, 2021) may now interact with new factors such as crisis resilience.

The Institute of International Finance projects a 32% rebound in net capital inflows to emerging economies in 2024, driven largely by FDI (IIF, 2023). Yet this recovery remains fragile, contingent on both external conditions and domestic policy choices. The fragility of these trends highlights the need of empirically assessing how FDI determinants behave under varying macroeconomic conditions.

Yet, research on key determinants of FDI has yielded mixed results. Previous research has demonstrated that various factors influence FDI, such as macroeconomic factors (Ranjan & Agrawal, 2011; Korsah, et al., 2025) and institutional factors (Okara, 2023; Mirkovikj et al., 2024). Furthermore, several theories have been proposed to explain key drivers of foreign investment. Specifically, the theoretical understanding of FDI has emerged through distinct stages, beginning with the neoclassical Rate of Return-on-Investment theory which explained capital flows but overlooked managerial control (Hymer, 1976; Dinkar & Rahul, 2014). Hymer's (1960) seminal work on monopolistic advantages theory introduced a fundamental shift by showing that foreign investors require distinctive capabilities to compete successfully with host-country businesses. Subsequent developments included Location Theory's (Erdal & Tatoglu, 2002) focus on host-country characteristics and Internalization Theory's (Buckley & Casson, 1976) emphasis on transaction cost minimization. Dunning's (1977) Eclectic Paradigm summarized these elements through its tripartite framework of Ownership, Location, and Internalization advantages, later developed by Dunning and Lundan (2008) to incorporate modern globalized production systems and digital transformation.

Despite extensive research, understanding what drives FDI in emerging markets remains challenging, as traditional theories and studies fail to fully explain today's complex investment patterns. Traditional FDI theories, such as the neoclassical model, Hymer's Monopolistic Advantage, and Dunning's OLI Paradigm, focus heavily on economic factors like profits or market size but often overlook critical modern influences like global political tensions, government-led investments, and technological advancements (Blackwill & Harris, 2016; Ohashi, 2018). Likewise, empirical studies have key limitations. Most studies focus on a single country or small sample (Dua & Garg, 2015; Revilla, 2016). Similarly, many do not account for how FDI determinants shift during economic turmoil (Poulsen & Hufbauer, 2011) or only focus on one crisis type's effects on FDI determinants (Ayinde, Fatai, and Adeyemi, 2024; Firdos et al., 2024). Furthermore, studies on FDI determinants rely on traditional econometric methods that struggle to capture complex patterns (Economou et al., 2017). Therefore, the chief objective of this study is to determine and compare the key factors driving FDI across different economic contexts while assessing how crisis periods reshape investor priorities, using advanced machine learning tools for more accurate and insightful outcomes, addressing both theoretical and empirical gaps.

Specifically, this study fills these critical gaps through three key contributions. First, we analyze 23 emerging economies across 2004–2023, examining both stable conditions and two crisis periods, the Global Financial Crisis and COVID-19 pandemic, to identify how FDI drivers vary over time in calm and turbulent periods. Second, we leverage machine learning tools, enhanced by methods to rank key factors (Mean SHAP feature importance), to uncover complex relationships and achieve better predictions than traditional methods permit. Third, by mapping the evolution of FDI determinants across calm and turbulent cycles, we provide policymakers with practical strategies to boost investment attractiveness, equip investors with data-driven insights, and advance academic understanding of FDI's role in sustainable growth. Our machine learning approach not only overcomes methodological limitations but also offers, to the best of our knowledge, the first comprehensive comparison of FDI drivers across stable and crisis conditions in emerging markets. This focus ensures our findings are relevant for economies navigating post-crisis recovery or stable growth, a critical advantage in today's unpredictable global environment.

The remainder of this chapter is structured as follows: the next section presents the literature review done on FDI determinants. The third section is devoted to the theoretical framework. The fourth and fifth sections discuss the data description, the methodology and the results and discussions. The last section stands for the conclusion and policy implications.

2. LITERATURE REVIEW

A wide array of studies and theoretical frameworks has been developed by economists and analysts to elucidate the drivers of FDI, the attributes that enhance a country's attractiveness to foreign investors, and the strategic considerations behind investment modes and entry strategies (Paul & Feliciano-Cestero, 2021). While there is broad consensus that a range of macroeconomic, institutional, and policy variables affect FDI, the specific determinants vary across countries and regions.

Despite it has gained increasing attention in academic and political debate, the concept of geoeconomics is subject to multiple and often divergent definitions, as it is characterized by a diversity of definitions across scholars and policymakers. While certain scholars view geoeconomics strictly as the use of geopolitical or military power to achieve economic outcomes, others extend its scope to encompasses the complex relationship between international economics, geopolitical strategy, and national Policy, albeit at the cost of weakening its theoretical coherence. A third perspective considers that geoeconomics strategy is mainly concerned with trade and industrial policy, emphasizing how governments use economic instruments to boost national competitiveness. These definitional differences reflect wide disagreements over whether geoeconomics presents a tool of state power, a unique policy domain, or a structural feature of international competition (Blackwill & Harris, 2016, p. 19).

In practice, geoeconomics concept denotes the use of economic policy tools including trade, sanctions, and investment to reach broader geopolitical objectives (Luttwak, 1990). This is remarkably evident in the evolving nature of FDI, which is not limited to private-sector profit maximization or market growth. Instead, FDI has become a key instrument of securing long-term geopolitical advantages. Furthermore, strategic and political motivations for FDI, particularly in energy, technology, and infrastructure, have become increasingly prominent alongside market access and cost efficiency objectives.

This evolution illustrates the growing influence of national interests in determining FDI dynamics, frequently aligned with broader geopolitical objectives. For instance, initiatives such as China's Belt and Road (BRI) emphasize the use of outward FDI by China to achieves tow objectives, namely to generate economic benefits and enhance geopolitical positioning, revealing a clear application of geoeconomic principles (Ohashi, 2018). Similarly, the practice of major powers to invest in resource-rich but politically unstable regions illustrates how FDI is used as a tool to secure strategic assets, thus enhancing national influence and geopolitical position along with using it as an economic strategy (Al Mustofa & Risyad, 2025). Therefore, FDI serves as key component of geoeconomics strategy, where economic activities are driven by broader national objectives. The relationship between national power, long-term goals, and geopolitical interests makes FDI a form of geopolitical engagement and not only business decision.

The literature reveals a diverse set of perspectives, with some theories emphasizing economic fundamentals, others focusing on institutional quality, and some examining the role of specific factors such as financial development and governance. This review synthesizes the findings of various studies, grouping them by the relevant categories of determinants they address.

2.1 Economic Factors

A number of studies have highlighted the significance of macroeconomic variables as critical drivers of FDI inflows. For instance, Schneider and Frey's (1985) politico-economic model demonstrated superior explanatory power by incorporating both economic and political factors as compared to other models. Their analysis showed that FDI inflows responds favorably to higher real per capita GNP and negatively with balance of payments deficits. Lee, Kang, and Lee (2024) analyzed FDI inflows from 1996 to 2019 across 178 countries and found that while most FDI targets developed nations, inflows to developing countries are increasing and less volatile. They observed that economic factors such as GDP and trade openness are key drivers of FDI in developing economies. The role of macroeconomic stability is also evident in studies focused on specific countries. Dua and Garg (2015) found that higher domestic returns, a depreciating exchange rate, and improved infrastructure were the key drivers of FDI inflows in India. Similarly, Revilla (2016) found that market attractiveness and infrastructure quality were critical factors for FDI in ASEAN countries, although high taxes and population growth were seen as deterrents.

Furthermore, while focusing exclusively on periods of economic turmoil, Ayinde, Fatai, and Adeyemi (2024) found that during the COVID-19 pandemic, the size of the economy was a primary determinant of FDI attraction in emerging economies with history of high FDI inflows, whereas interest rates and exchange rates played a more significant role in those with history of low FDI receipts. Likewise, Firdos et al. (2024) found that GDP growth rate, control of corruption, and political stability had positive and statistically significant long-run coefficients, indicating these factors enhanced FDI inflows in the South Asian Association for Regional Cooperation region. Conversely, unemployment rate, inflation, exchange rate, and the COVID-19 pandemic showed negative and significant effects. These findings underscore the centrality of economic fundamentals, including market size, infrastructure, and exchange rate policies, in attracting FDI.

2.2 Institutional Quality and Governance

Institutional quality plays a significant role in shaping the attractiveness of developing countries to foreign investors. A growing body of literature suggests that governance-related factors, such as political stability, corruption control, regulatory quality, and the rule of law, have a direct impact on FDI inflows. For instance, Gupta et al. (2024) found a strong positive correlation between institutional quality and inward FDI in India and South Africa, indicating that improvements in institutional frameworks could enhance their attractiveness to foreign investors. Similarly, Saha et al, (2022) and Sinha et al. (2024) highlighted the positive impact of control of corruption and regulatory quality on FDI, though they also noted that other institutional factors such as the rule of law and voice and accountability had negative effects.

Saidi et al. (2023) further stressed that while institutional quality did not show a significant direct link to FDI in their study of 102 developing countries, improving governance structures is still crucial for fostering FDI. The importance of institutional quality in FDI attraction is also highlighted by Dimitrova et al. (2020), who focused on the Middle East and North Africa (MENA) region, though they excluded many African countries. They found that institutional frameworks significantly influence FDI inflows, suggesting that the quality of institutions must be considered when formulating policies to attract foreign investment.

2.3 Financial Development

Financial development is another factor that has garnered attention in recent studies on FDI. An et al. (2023) examined the role of financial development in enhancing the positive effects of FDI on economic growth in emerging and developing Asian countries. They concluded that well-developed financial systems are essential for attracting FDI, which in turn contributes to sustainable economic growth, in line with Sustainable Development Goal 8 (promoting decent work and economic growth). This insight aligns with the work of Mottaleb and Kalirajan (2010), who found that factors such as infrastructure, business climate, and foreign aid, in addition to financial development, positively drive FDI, especially in Asia.

2.4 Regional and Sector-Specific Factors

The significance of region-specific factors has also been noted in various studies. For example, Katenova (2018) found that FDI had a significant positive impact on GDP in Kazakhstan, suggesting that country-specific factors such as economic structure and market openness play a key role in attracting foreign investment. Similarly, Ashurov et al. (2020) highlighted strong positive links between FDI and GDP, labor force, and debt services in Central Asian countries, underscoring the importance of region-specific dynamics. The impact of regional factors is also demonstrated in the study by Lee et al. (2024), which examined 178 countries and found that social factors, including infrastructure and innovation, are more critical in developed economies, whereas economic factors like GDP and trade drive FDI in developing economies. This suggests that while there are broad patterns in FDI determinants, they may be region-specific, with emerging economies relying more heavily on economic fundamentals like GDP and trade openness to attract foreign investors.

2.5 Source-Specific FDI Dynamics

Recent research underscores that the source country of FDI significantly influences its determinants and impacts, particularly through geopolitical and strategic considerations (Chang et al., 2021; Sutherland et al., 2020). Notably, Chinese outward FDI (OFDI), often driven by state-led initiatives such as the BRI, diverges from traditional FDI patterns due to its alignment with geopolitical objectives (Ohashi, 2018). Unlike FDI from developed economies, which typically prioritizes market-seeking or efficiency-seeking motives, Chinese OFDI frequently targets strategic assets, such as infrastructure or natural resources, in emerging markets.

Chang et al. (2021) and Sutherland et al. (2020) find that Chinese OFDI can negatively affect political stability in host countries, particularly in resource-rich or geopolitically sensitive regions. This effect stems from large-scale projects that may raise concerns about debt sustainability, local governance challenges, or perceived foreign influence, potentially exacerbating political tensions. For instance, BRI-related investments have been linked to increased scrutiny of host country institutions, impacting their stability (Oberhauser, 2024). These findings suggest that the source of FDI shapes the relative importance of determinants like political stability and institutional quality, as investors from different countries weigh these factors based on their strategic priorities.

A proper understanding of FDI inflows demands consideration of the theoretical frameworks governing investment determinants, which will be addressed in the next section.

3. THEORETICAL FRAMEWORK

FDI is a key driver of growth in emerging markets, but understanding what attracts it today is complex due to global changes that traditional theories do not fully explain. This study explores what drives FDI in 23 emerging economies from 2004 to 2023, using machine learning to identify key factors across stable and crisis periods. We propose a new framework that combines traditional FDI theories with insights into global politics and technology, addressing why older theories fall short and guiding our analysis of how economic, governance, and technological factors shape FDI.

Traditional FDI theories struggle to explain modern investment flows for three main reasons. First, they focus heavily on economic factors like profits or market size, often ignoring how global political tensions, such as trade disputes or regional conflicts, influence investor decisions (Blackwill & Harris, 2016). Second, they overlook government-led investments, like China's BRI, where countries use FDI to achieve strategic goals beyond profit, such as securing resources or global influence (Ohashi, 2018). Third, they do not account for the growing role of technology, such as digital infrastructure, which is vital in today's digital economy. These gaps make it hard to understand why FDI drivers shift during crises like the Global Financial Crisis or COVID-19, where factors like trade networks or digital capabilities become critical. Our framework addresses these issues by combining economic, political, and technological factors to better explain FDI in emerging markets.

The study of FDI has evolved through several theoretical frameworks, each offering distinct perspectives on what drives cross-border investment decisions. The neoclassical Rate of Return-on-Investment theory suggests that capital flows to countries with higher profits until returns are equal worldwide. This idea assumes investors only seek profits, like buying stocks, but ignores their need to control businesses or navigate local challenges, making it less relevant for FDI (Hymer, 1976). This limitation led Dinkar and Rahul (2014) to note that before the 1950s, FDI was often seen as just another form of investment.

Stephen Hymer's Monopolistic Advantage Theory (1960) addressed this gap by arguing that foreign investors need unique strengths, such as better technology or management skills, to compete with local firms familiar with their markets. This explains why companies invest abroad to use their advantages, but it does not fully consider how global politics or technology shape these choices. Location Theory (Erdal & Tatoglu, 2002) focuses on why certain countries attract FDI, pointing to local advantages like access to resources, markets, or stable governance. However, it often misses how global strategies or digital advancements make a country appealing. Buckley and Casson's (1976) Internalization Theory explains that companies invest abroad to keep their unique strengths in-house, avoiding reliance on external partners. Yet, this idea does not address how government policies or crises affect these decisions.

Dunning's (1977) Eclectic Paradigm (OLI—Ownership, Location, Internalization) combines these ideas, suggesting that FDI occurs when firms have unique strengths (Ownership), find attractive countries (Location), and benefit from controlling operations directly (Internalization). While powerful, this framework struggles to explain FDI driven by government strategies or digital technologies, even with updates noting the rise of emerging economies (Dunning & Lundan, 2008). Our framework builds on this by adding global political and technological factors to better understand today's FDI.

This framework posits that FDI inflows in emerging markets are driven by a dynamic combination of local factors (e.g., market size, trade openness, digital infrastructure), governance quality (e.g., political stability, transparency), and global political factors (e.g., geopolitical risk, government-led investments). These drivers vary in importance across economic contexts, with crises like the Global Financial Crisis and COVID-19 amplifying the role of resilience-related factors, such as financial flexibility and governance trust. Instead of assuming fixed patterns, we use machine learning to explore how these factors interact in complex ways, identifying which are most important in stable periods, the Global Financial Crisis, and the COVID-19 pandemic (Lundberg & Lee, 2017). This exploratory approach is ideal for capturing context-specific patterns that traditional theory miss.

To guide this exploratory analysis, we propose three research questions:

1. What are the primary determinants of FDI inflows in emerging markets during stable economic periods, and how do they reflect geopolitical and technological priorities?
2. How do trade networks and geopolitical risk influence FDI during the Global Financial Crisis?
3. What role do financial openness, governance quality, and digital infrastructure play in attracting FDI during the COVID-19 pandemic?

4. DATA AND METHODOLOGY

This section presents the dataset description, explain the ML methodologies, and analyze their characteristics while highlighting the evaluation metrics used for model selection and the application of mean SHAP values for feature importance analysis.

4.1 Data Description

To achieve the empirical part of this study a sample of twenty-three countries is used. The selection of these countries in the sample is based on the availability of data for FDI inflows and geopolitical indices (see Table A.2). Similarly, the annual sample period (2004–2023) was determined by the availability of data for macroeconomic, financial, institutional quality, and geoeconomic indicators. This 19-year timeframe captures a transformative period marked by major global economic events, including the 2008 financial crisis and the COVID-19 pandemic, offering a comprehensive context to examine the evolving determinants of FDI inflows.

Based on prior empirical studies and established theories on FDI determinants, twenty-two variables (see Table A.1) were included in all machine learning models. To account for temporal dependencies, one-period lagged values of these variables were also considered, resulting in a total of forty-four features (current and lagged). Therefore, the dataset integrates a diverse set of variables organized into five key categories, reflecting the multidimensional nature of FDI drivers. Specifically, these categories include macroeconomic variables, financial variables, institutional indicators, geoeconomic drivers, and uncertainty and geopolitical factors (see Table A.1). Descriptive statistics for these variables are reported in Table A.1

To ensure the dataset was suitable for machine learning analysis, several pre-processing and optimization steps were undertaken. First, missing values in both current and lagged features were addressed using IterativeImputer, a method that leverages a multivariate imputation strategy to estimate missing data based on relationships between features. Following this, all features were scaled using Min-MaxScaler to standardize their ranges and ensure comparability across variables. With the preprocessing complete, the dataset was then split into training (80%) and testing (20%) subsets, with a fixed random state of 42 to guarantee reproducibility of results. To further optimize the performance of the machine learning regressors, hyperparameter tuning was performed using two well-established techniques, namely the Randomized Search Cross-Validation and the Grid Search Cross-Validation, which systematically identify the best model configurations.

4.2 Methodology

Foreign Direct Investment (FDI) inflows are influenced by a mix of economic, political, institutional, and geographic factors. Traditional statistical methods, such as ordinary least squares (OLS) or panel data models, often struggle to capture complex, non-linear relationships and interactions among these factors. They can also be prone to errors if the model is not specified correctly. To overcome these challenges, this study uses tree-based machine learning methods, which are better at detecting complex patterns and interactions in data (Breiman, 2001; Chen & Guestrin, 2016). These methods also excel at identifying the most important factors driving FDI through advanced techniques like the mean SHAP feature importance method (Lundberg & Lee, 2017), which ranks factors based on their impact on predictions. For these reasons, we selected three tree-based machine learning approaches for this study. The following subsections will explain the characteristics of these methods, the evaluation metrics used to choose the best model, and the SHAP technique for ranking key factors.

4.2.1. Decision Tree

Decision trees are a type of machine learning method that predict outcomes by splitting data into smaller groups based on specific features, forming a tree-like structure of rules (Breiman et al., 1996). In this structure, decision points (nodes) use feature values to divide the data, branches show the possible paths, and end points (leaves) provide the final predictions. Many studies have successfully used decision trees for prediction tasks (Mienye, Sun, & Wang, 2019; Yusuf, 2022).

In this study, we use a decision tree model for two purposes: to compare its performance with two other tree-based methods and to identify the best model for predicting Foreign Direct Investment (FDI) inflows in emerging markets. To optimize the model, we use a two-step tuning process. First, we randomly test different settings (50 iterations with 5-fold cross-validation), then we fine-tune with a targeted grid search (3-fold cross-validation). This approach improves efficiency, reducing computational time by 60-80% compared to traditional methods, while keeping the model accurate (Bergstra & Bengio, 2012).

4.2.2. Random Forest

Random Forest is a machine learning method that combines multiple decision trees to make more accurate predictions. Each tree is trained on a random subset of the data, and their results are combined to produce a stronger, more reliable forecast. This approach helps prevent overfitting and handles complex data well. Previous studies, such as Jiménez & Herrero (2019), Horobet et al. (2021), and Esclanda-Lo et al. (2024), have used Random Forest to identify key factors driving Foreign Direct Investment (FDI).

To optimize our Random Forest model, we use a two-step tuning process. First, we conduct a broad search with RandomizedSearchCV (50 iterations and 5-fold cross-validation) to find promising settings. Then, we refine the model with a precise GridSearchCV (3-fold cross-validation) to ensure the best performance.

4.2.3. XGBoost

XGBoost (Extreme Gradient Boosting) is an advanced machine learning method that builds on gradient boosting techniques (Chen & Guestrin, 2016). It improves on traditional methods by using regularization (L1/L2 penalties) to prevent overfitting, automatically handling missing data, and speeding up calculations with parallel processing. Its high accuracy and ability to manage outliers and correlated data make it popular for various applications, including analyzing Foreign Direct Investment (FDI) determinants (Esclanda-Lo et al., 2024).

To optimize the XGBoost model, we use a two-step tuning process. First, we perform a broad search with RandomizedSearchCV (50 iterations and 5-fold cross-validation) to identify effective settings. Then, we fine-tune the model using GridSearchCV (3-fold cross-validation) to achieve the best performance.

4.2.4. Evaluation Metrics

To choose the best machine learning model for this study, we used six standard metrics commonly found in research (Nagelkerke, 1991; Guyon & Elisseeff, 2003; Chai & Draxler, 2014; Esclanda-Lo et al., 2024). These metrics assess how well the model predicts Foreign Direct Investment (FDI) inflows:

Mean Squared Error (MSE): Measures accuracy by averaging the squared differences between predicted and actual values, giving more weight to larger errors.
Root Mean Squared Error (RMSE): Shows the standard deviation of prediction errors, providing a measure in the same units as the target variable.
Mean Absolute Error (MAE): Calculates the average of absolute differences between predicted and actual values, less affected by extreme errors.
Explained Variance Score: Indicates the percentage of variation in the data that the model explains.
R^2 Score: Measures how much of the total variation in the data is explained by the model, showing its overall fit.
Max Error: Identifies the largest single error between predicted and actual values, highlighting the worst-case prediction.

4.2.5. Mean SHAP Feature Importance

To understand which factors most influence Foreign Direct Investment (FDI) inflows, we used the mean SHAP (SHapley Additive exPlanations) technique, based on game theory principles (Shapley, 1953; Lundberg & Lee, 2017). This method, applied with our best-performing tree-based machine learning model, measures how much each factor contributes to predictions by averaging their impact. It offers a reliable way to rank the importance of factors driving FDI.

The SHAP approach stands out for two reasons: it introduces a new way to measure feature importance consistently, and it proves that this method is the only one meeting key theoretical standards. It builds on and improves several existing techniques (Strumbelj & Kononenko, 2010; Lundberg & Lee, 2017). Many studies have used SHAP to interpret machine learning results (Mavruk, 2022; Kovvuri et al., 2023; Liu et al., 2024). In this study, we use mean SHAP to identify and rank the key drivers of FDI in emerging markets.

5. EMPIRICAL RESULTS

5.1 Evaluation Metric Results

Before identifying the key drivers of FDI inflows, we evaluated three tree-based models using standard performance metrics (MSE, MAE, RMSE, R^2, explained variance, and max error) to select the optimal model for our prediction task. Among these, the random forest model demonstrated superior performance (Table 1). We then employed SHAP (SHapley Additive exPlanations) values, an advanced feature importance technique to rank predictors based on their contribution to the model's output. To analyze FDI determinants, we conducted this assessment across three distinct time periods, namely the full sample period (Baseline analysis), the Global Financial Crisis subperiod, and the COVID-19 pandemic subperiod. This approach allowed us to compare how feature importance rankings shifted during stable versus turbulent economic conditions, revealing context-specific FDI drivers.

Table 1. Evaluation metrics

	Random Forest	XGBoost	Decision tree
MSE	0.4627	0.5075	0.8700
MAE	0.5722	0.6042	0.7907
RMSE	0.6802	0.7124	0.9327
R^2	0.5154	0.4685	0.0888
Explained Variance	0.5687	0.5280	0.1377
Max Error	1.6622	1.5689	1.6032

5.2 SHAP Feature Importance Analysis During the Full Sample Period

The SHAP feature importance analysis, conducted using a random forest model, identifies geopolitical risk (GEOPR) as the predominant determinant of FDI inflows in emerging markets (Figure 1 and Table 2). This is followed closely by the lagged unemployment rate (UNEMP LAG (1) = 0.071) and current digitalization infrastructure (DIGI = 0.065), ranking second and third, respectively. The lagged geopolitical risk (GEOPR LAG (1) = 0.063) also features prominently among the top four factors, underscoring the persistent influence of geopolitical stability on investment decisions.

5.2.1 Geopolitical Risk as a Primary Driver of FDI Inflows

Our findings reveal geopolitical risk as the preeminent driver of FDI inflows, surpassing even traditional economic factors in predictive importance. This highlights the critical importance foreign investors place on conflict mitigation and international political stability, where elevated geopolitical risks amplify uncertainty and deter capital flows which is consistent with prior work on political-institutional determinants (Caldara & Iacoviello, 2022). Notably, while political stability (captured in our institutional quality index) reflects domestic governance durability (Okara, 2023), geopolitical risk operates as a distinct external dimension encompassing cross-border tensions and global power dynamics. The centrality of geopolitical risk as the foremost driver of FDI inflows is consistent with a robust body of literature emphasizing the influence of political and institutional factors on investment decisions in emerging markets.

Studies such as Peres et al. (2018) underscore that institutional quality and political stability are critical determinants of FDI attractiveness. Similarly, Petrov et al. (2022) highlight the adverse impact of geopolitical risks, noting their role in elevating uncertainty and discouraging foreign investment. These findings align with the OLI Theory and Location Theory of FDI, which posits that a stable political environment is essential for fostering investor confidence and facilitating FDI inflows (Mahmood et al., 2019). The prominence of both current and lagged geopolitical risk in the SHAP analysis further reinforces the notion that investors prioritize sustained political stability when evaluating emerging markets.

5.2.2 Lagged Unemployment Rate and Labor Market Dynamics

The significant ranking of lagged unemployment rates indicates that investors view historical labor market conditions as a robust proxy for economic stability. High or persistent unemployment signals potential labor market inefficiencies and subdued consumer demand, both of which can undermine long-term investment prospects. The high ranking of the lagged unemployment rate as a determinant of FDI inflows is substantiated by prior research exploring labor market conditions as a macroeconomic driver of investment. Ashurov et al. (2020) emphasize that labor force characteristics, including availability and productivity, are pivotal for FDI attractiveness. However, the negative correlation between labor force participation and FDI inflows, as evidenced in the study's results, suggests that elevated unemployment may signal an uncompetitive or low-productivity labor market, deterring investors (Revilla, 2016). The lagged effect of unemployment, as captured in the SHAP analysis, reflects investors' reliance on historical labor market trends to assess the long-term viability of investment destinations. Persistent unemployment may indicate structural economic challenges, diminishing a market's appeal despite labor availability. This finding resonates with Martinez-Vazquez et al., 2011), who identify labor market conditions, particularly unemployment, labor cost, and total labor force as significant control variables in FDI inflow studies, especially in developing economies.

5.2.3 Digital Infrastructure as a Catalyst for FDI

The high ranking of digitalization infrastructure reflects its growing role as a pivotal determinant of FDI attractiveness (Duran, 1999; Sahoo, 2006). Advanced digital infrastructure, encompassing high-speed internet and communication technologies, enhances a country's global economic integration and competitiveness, thereby shaping investors' long-term strategic decisions. The significance of digitalization infrastructure as a key determinant of FDI inflows aligns with contemporary research highlighting the role of technological readiness in enhancing the investment climate of developing economies. Lee et al. (2024) note that robust infrastructure, particularly digital infrastructure, strengthens a country's integration into the global economy, making it more appealing to foreign investors. Access to high-speed internet and advanced communication technologies, as emphasized by Emako et al. (2022), signals a forward-looking and competitive business environment. The high ranking of DIGI in the SHAP analysis underscores its increasing relevance in emerging markets, where technological advancements are pivotal for attracting FDI. This finding also aligns with the revised version of the Eclectic Paradigm of Dunning and Lundan (2008) along with broader literature on social and innovation-driven factors, which highlight the growing importance of globalization and technological readiness in shaping FDI decisions (Lee et al., 2024).

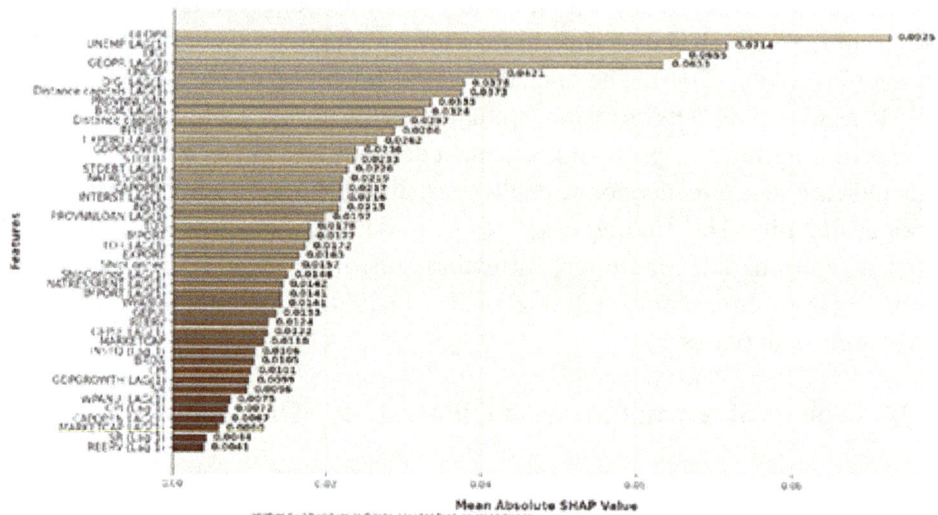

Table 2. Mean SHAP values for the whole period

Feature	Mean SHAP
GEOPR	0,092542
UNEMP LAG(1)	0,071435
DIGI	0,065453
GEOPR LAG(1)	0,063317
UNEMP	0,04211
DIGI LAG(1)	0,037644
Distance capitals LAG(1)	0,037331
PROVNNLOAN	0,033287
BROA LAG(1)	0,032423
Distance capitals	0,029694
INTERST	0,028551
EXPORT LAG(1)	0,026231
GDPGROWTH	0,023634
STDEBT	0,023306
STDEBT LAG(1)	0,022569
NATRESSRENT	0,021949
CAPOPEN	0,021703

continued on following page

Table 2. Continued

Feature	Mean SHAP
INTERST LAG(1)	0,021644
INSTQ	0,021476
PROVNNLOAN LAG(1)	0,019715
TOR	0,017799
IMPORT	0,017706
TOR LAG(1)	0,017192
EXPORT	0,016329
ShipConnec	0,015712
ShipConnec LAG(1)	0,01481
NATRESSRENT LAG(1)	0,014173
IMPORT LAG(1)	0,01413
WPANUI	0,014091
GEPUI	0,0133
REERV	0,012378
GEPUI LAG(1)	0,012183
MARKETCAP	0,011773
INSTQ LAG(1)	0,010623
BROA	0,010526
CPI	0,010113
GDPGROWTH LAG(1)	0,009941
SR	0,009589
WPANUI LAG(1)	0,007487
CPI (Lag 1)	0,007189
CAPOPEN LAG(1)	0,006711
MARKETCAP LAG(1)	0,006043
SR (Lag 1)	0,004391
REERV (Lag 1)	0,004073

5.3 SHAP Feature Importance Analysis During the Global Financial Crisis

The current imports of goods and services (% of GDP) (IMPORT = 0.278) emerges as the most influential determinant of FDI inflows in emerging markets during the Global Financial Crisis period, underscoring the critical linkage between

FDI inflows and a country's reliance on foreign goods (Figure 2 and Table 3). Geopolitical risk (GEOPR = 0.172) ranks second, reflecting heightened investor sensitivity to political instability during periods of economic turmoil.

The prominence of current imports suggests that, amidst the Global Financial Crisis, investors prioritized markets with robust import capacity, perceiving them as more resilient to global supply chain disruptions. This finding indicates that countries with strong trade linkages were viewed as better positioned to weather the crisis, thereby attracting greater FDI inflows. The high ranking of geopolitical risk highlights the amplified role of political stability during periods of economic uncertainty. Elevated geopolitical risks likely prompted investors to redirect capital toward safer regions, as heightened uncertainty increased perceived investment risks. The lagged geopolitical risk (GEOPR LAG (1) = 0.112) and lagged global economic policy uncertainty index (GEPUI LAG (1) = 0.091) further reveal that investors' decisions were shaped by historical conditions rather than immediate shocks, emphasizing the enduring impact of prior-year stability on FDI attractiveness.

Trade openness, as captured by current exports (EXPORT = 0.108) and lagged imports (IMPORT LAG (1) = 0.082), also emerges as a key attractor of FDI inflows during the Global Financial Crisis, reinforcing the importance of global economic integration even in times of stress. Conversely, features with the lowest influence include lagged exports (EXPORT LAG (1) = 0.069), the global economic policy uncertainty index (GEPUI), and real exchange rate volatility (REERV = 0.074). These findings suggest that investors prioritized structural factors, such as trade dynamics and geopolitical stability, over cyclical risks like currency fluctuations or short-term policy uncertainty. This aligns with the notion that, during crises, investors focus on fundamental market characteristics that signal long-term resilience.

Strong institutional frameworks further served as a stabilizing anchor during the Global Financial Crisis, mitigating uncertainties and enhancing FDI attractiveness. Countries with transparent governance and robust institutional quality were better positioned to retain FDI inflows despite global financial instability. This finding is consistent with the Location and OLI Theories of FDI, which emphasizes the role of stable and predictable governance in fostering investor confidence during periods of economic disruption. Collectively, these results highlight the interplay of trade openness, geopolitical stability, and institutional quality as critical determinants of FDI inflows in emerging markets during the Global Financial Crisis, with investors demonstrating a preference for markets exhibiting structural resilience and historical stability.

Table 3. Mean SHAP values for the Global Financial Crisis period

Feature	Mean SHAP
****** Global Financial Crisis period******	
IMPORT	0,277521
GEOPR	0,171568
INSTQ	0,128719
GEOPR LAG(1)	0,112373
EXPORT	0,108422
GEPUI LAG(1)	0,090563
IMPORT LAG(1)	0,081699
REERV	0,073717
GEPUI	0,071407
EXPORT LAG(1)	0,069874

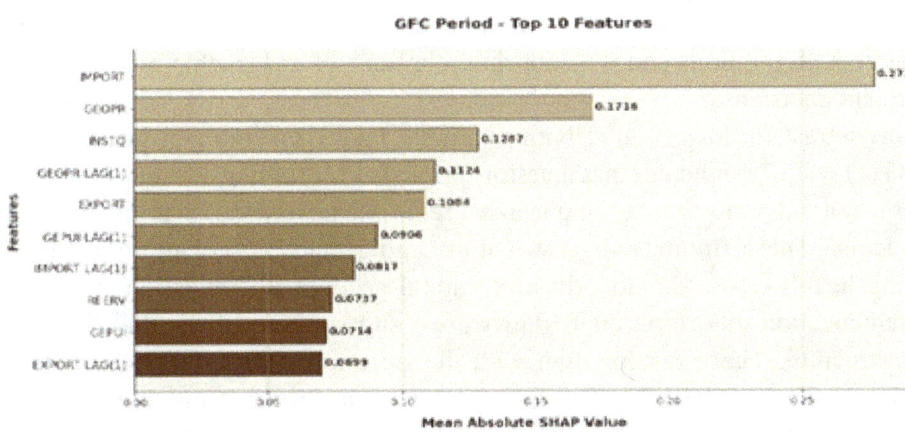

5.4 SHAP Feature Importance Analysis During the COVID-19 Crisis

Capital openness (CAPOPEN = 1.002) emerges as the dominant determinant of FDI inflows in emerging markets during the COVID-19 crisis, highlighting a pronounced investor preference for markets with liberalized capital accounts (Figure 3 and Table 4). This significant weighting suggests that, during the crisis, access to liquidity and ease of capital movement surpassed traditional location-specific advantages, reflecting the need for financial flexibility in an uncertain global environment. The institutional quality composite index (INSTQ = 0.82), ranking second, underscores the critical role of robust institutional frameworks as a stabilizing force, absorbing uncertainty by providing clarity, predictability, and trust in regulatory policies.

Digital infrastructure (DIGI = 0.43), ranked third, signals a pivotal evolution in FDI determinants, as countries with advanced digital capabilities demonstrated greater resilience to pandemic-related disruptions. This finding reflects the growing importance of technological readiness in maintaining economic continuity and attracting FDI during crises. Financial market indicators, notably stock market returns (SR = 0.34) and lagged bank return on assets (BROA LAG (1) = 0.27), ranking fourth and sixth respectively, further highlight investors' focus on financial health as a proxy for a market's ability to withstand crisis-induced shocks. This complies with the neoclassical Rate of Return-on-Investment and Monopolistic Advantage Theories. While geopolitical risk (GEOPR = 0.24) remains relevant, its diminished significance relative to capital flow and institutional factors suggests that pandemic-specific concerns temporarily overshadowed traditional geopolitical considerations. Distance-related variables also retain notable importance, likely reflecting supply chain reconfigurations and the enduring relevance of geographic proximity in investment decisions.

In contrast, the lowest-contributing variable, lagged institutional quality (INSTQ LAG (1) = 0.17), indicates that investors prioritized current institutional conditions over historical performance, emphasizing real-time governance stability during the pandemic. These findings suggest that emerging markets seeking to attract FDI during health crises should prioritize capital account liberalization, transparent communication of institutional frameworks, and sustained investment in digital infrastructure. These results align with the Location and OLI Theories of FDI, which emphasizes the role of strong governance in fostering investor confidence during periods of uncertainty (Mahmood et al., 2019). Additionally, the prominence of digital infrastructure resonates with contemporary theories of globalization and innovation, which highlight technological readiness as a critical driver of FDI in digitally transforming economies (Lee et al., 2024). The findings also complement prior studies, such as Emako et al. (2022), which underscore the role of digital connectivity in enhancing market attractiveness during global disruptions. Collectively, these insights provide a nuanced understanding of how investor priorities adapt to health crises, offering actionable policy implications for emerging markets aiming to shape FDI inflows.

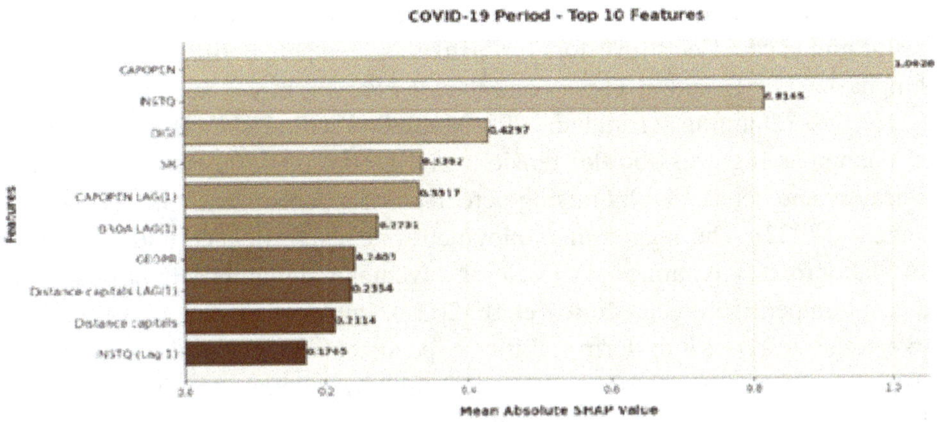

Table 4. Mean SHAP values for the COVID-19 period

Feature	Mean SHAP
******COVID-19 period******	
CAPOPEN	1,002824
INSTQ	0,816467
DIGI	0,429681
SR	0,336231
CAPOPEN LAG (1)	0,331747
BROA LAG (1)	0,273077
GEOPR	0,240292
Distance capitals LAG (1)	0,235398
Distance capitals	0,211362
INSTQ LAG (1)	0,170536

5.5 Discussion

Over the full sample period, encompassing stable and non-crisis conditions, the SHAP feature importance analysis identifies geopolitical risk (GEOPR), lagged unemployment rate (UNEMP LAG(1)), and digitalization infrastructure (DIGI) as the top determinants of FDI inflows in emerging markets. These findings align with the geoeconomic framework, which posits that FDI decisions are shaped by a dynamic interplay of Location advantages (e.g., technological readiness, labor market conditions) and geoeconomic factors (e.g., geopolitical stability). Geopolitical risk's prominence reflects investors' prioritization of stable political environments, as emphasized by Location Theory and the OLI Paradigm's focus on host country attractiveness (Dunning & Lundan, 2008; Mahmood et al., 2019). High geopolitical risk, encompassing cross-border tensions and global power dynamics, increases uncertainty and deters FDI by raising perceived risks, consistent with Caldara and Iacoviello (2022). The lagged unemployment rate's significance underscores the role of labor market dynamics as a Location advantage, signaling economic stability and cost competitiveness (Ashurov et al., 2020). Investors rely on historical labor market trends to assess long-term viability, as persistent unemployment may indicate structural inefficiencies (Revilla, 2016). Digital infrastructure's high ranking highlights its role as an Ownership advantage, enabling firms to leverage technological capabilities in host countries (Lee et al., 2024). This interplay, where geopolitical stability enhances investor confidence in institutional frameworks, which in turn supports technological investments, creates a reinforcing cycle that drives FDI attractiveness in stable periods.

During the Global Financial Crisis (2008–2009), the SHAP feature importance analysis reveals that trade dynamics, particularly imports, and geopolitical risk emerged as the predominant determinants of FDI inflows in emerging markets. This shift reflects the crisis's impact on global capital flows and trade volumes, amplifying the importance of Location advantages like trade openness and geoeconomic factors like political resilience. The prominence of imports suggests investors prioritized markets integrated into global value chains, as robust trade linkages signaled resilience against supply chain disruptions (Duran, 1999; Sahoo, 2006). Geopolitical risk, particularly its lagged effect, underscores the OLI Paradigm's emphasis on stable governance as a critical Location advantage during crises (Mahmood et al., 2019). Investors favored markets with a history of predictable governance, as lagged geopolitical risk reflects long-term structural stability rather than short-term volatility. This interplay between trade dynamics and geopolitical stability explains why investors redirected capital to emerging markets with strong trade networks and institutional reliability during the GFC. The diminished role of cyclical factors like exchange rate volatility (REERV) further supports the geoeconomic framework's focus on structural fundamentals in crisis contexts, as investors prioritized resilience over transient risks.

During the COVID-19 pandemic (2020–2022), the SHAP feature importance analysis identifies capital openness, institutional quality, and digital infrastructure as the primary determinants of FDI inflows in emerging markets. This shift reflects the unique demands of a health-driven crisis, where financial flexibility, governance trust, and technological resilience became paramount, aligning with the geoeconomic framework's emphasis on adaptive Location and Ownership advantages. Capital openness (CAPOPEN) dominated as investors sought markets with liberalized capital accounts to ensure liquidity and flexibility amid global disruptions (Chinn & Ito, 2008). Institutional quality (INSTQ) played a critical role by providing governance transparency and trust, reinforcing the OLI Paradigm's focus on stable institutional frameworks as a Location advantage (Peres et al., 2018). Digital infrastructure's prominence reflects its role as an Ownership advantage, enabling firms to navigate pandemic-related disruptions through technological readiness (Emako et al., 2022). The interplay of these factors, where robust institutions facilitate capital mobility and digital investments enhance operational resilience, explains why emerging markets with these attributes attracted FDI during the crisis. The reduced significance of geopolitical risk suggests that health-specific concerns, such as policy effectiveness and digital adaptation, temporarily overshadowed traditional geopolitical considerations, highlighting the context-specific nature of FDI determinants.

The observed shifts in FDI determinants across contexts can be explained through the geoeconomic framework's integration of economic and geopolitical dynamics. In stable periods, investors prioritize long-term attractiveness, balancing geopolitical stability, labor market health, and technological readiness to maximize Ownership and Location advantages. During the GFC, the collapse of global trade and capital flows heightened the importance of trade networks and political resilience, as investors sought markets with structural stability to mitigate risks. The COVID-19 crisis, characterized by mobility restrictions and digital transformation, elevated capital openness and digital infrastructure, as firms leveraged these to maintain operations in uncertain environments. The ML approach, particularly SHAP analysis, enhances this understanding by uncovering non-linear interactions that traditional theories might miss, such as the reinforcing effect of institutional quality on digital infrastructure investments. This interplay underscores the study's contribution, particularly by combining geoeconomic principles with ML, we reveal how FDI determinants adapt to global volatility, offering a nuanced perspective on emerging markets' attractiveness.

These findings have significant implications for both theory and policy. Theoretically, they extend the OLI Paradigm by incorporating geoeconomic factors like geopolitical risk and state-driven strategies, which are critical in modern FDI flows (Blackwill & Harris, 2016). They also highlight the need to update Location Theory to account for technological readiness as a key determinant in digitalized economies (Lee et al., 2024). For policymakers, the results suggest context-specific strategies, specifically, in stable periods, fostering geopolitical stability and digital infrastructure can enhance FDI attractiveness while during financial crises, strengthening trade openness and institutional reliability is key. Additionally, in health crises, prioritizing capital account liberalization and technological investments can sustain inflows. The interplay of these factors suggests that emerging economies should adopt integrated policies that align institutional reforms with technological advancements to navigate global volatility effectively.

6. CONCLUSIONS AND POLICY IMPLICATIONS

This study employs tree-based machine learning models to examine the determinants of FDI inflows in 23 emerging economies from 2004 to 2023, addressing the dynamic interplay of geoeconomic, institutional, and technological factors across stable and crisis periods. By grounding our analysis in the geoeconomic framework, we uncover novel insights into how FDI attractiveness evolves in response to global economic conditions. Our findings reveal that FDI determinants vary significantly across economic contexts, reflecting the complex interplay of Location and Ownership advantages within a geoeconomic context. In stable periods, geopolitical risk, lagged unemployment rate, and digital infrastructure dominate, underscoring the importance of political stability, labor market health, and technological readiness as key Location and Ownership advantages. During the Global Financial Crisis, trade dynamics (imports) and geopolitical stability emerge as primary drivers, highlighting the resilience of markets integrated into global value chains and with predictable governance. In the COVID-19 period, capital openness, institutional quality, and digital infrastructure take precedence, reflecting investor preferences for financial flexibility, governance trust, and technological adaptation in health-driven crises. These shifts demonstrate how geoeconomic factors, such as geopolitical risk and state-driven strategies, interact with institutional and technological factors to shape FDI decisions, extending the OLI Paradigm by incorporating modern global dynamics.

The study's primary contribution lies in its use of machine learning, specifically SHAP feature importance analysis, to uncover non-linear and context-specific interactions that traditional econometric models often miss. This approach reveals the dynamic nature of FDI determinants, such as the amplified role of digital infrastructure during COVID-19, which reflects the growing importance of technological readiness as an Ownership advantage in digitalized economies. By integrating geoeconomic principles, the study extends traditional FDI theories to account for geopolitical realignments and state capitalism, as seen in initiatives like China's Belt and Road Initiative (Ohashi, 2018). This provides a nuanced understanding of how emerging markets attract FDI under varying conditions, addressing gaps in prior literature that often assumes static or linear relationships. The interplay of factors, where geopolitical stability enhances institutional trust, which in turn supports technological investments, offers a novel perspective on FDI attractiveness, particularly in crisis contexts.

These insights have significant implications for policymakers in emerging economies. In stable periods, fostering geopolitical stability and investing in digital infrastructure can enhance FDI inflows. During financial crises, strengthening trade openness and institutional reliability is critical to maintaining attractiveness. In health crises, liberalizing capital accounts and prioritizing technological resilience can sustain investor confidence. These context-specific strategies, derived from the geoeconomic framework, enable policymakers to align institutional reforms with economic and technological priorities, navigating global volatility effectively.

REFERENCES

Ajayi, S. I. (2006). *FDI and economic development in Africa*. ADB/AERC International.

Ajide, F. M., Osinubi, T. T., Oladipupo, S. A., & Soyode, E. O. (2025). Economic complexity in Africa: The role of Chinese FDI and trade. *Journal of Chinese Economic and Foreign Trade Studies*, *18*(1), 86–108. DOI: 10.1108/JCEFTS-07-2024-0063

Al Mustofa, M. U., & Risyad, M. H. (2025). Geopolitical risk and foreign direct investment: The role of liberalization, institutions and financial markets. *Studies in Economics and Finance*, *42*(4), 730–758. DOI: 10.1108/SEF-09-2024-0621

Alfaro, L. (2017). Gains from foreign direct investment: Macro and micro approaches. *The World Bank Economic Review*, *30*(Supplement_1), S2–S15.

An, T.-H. T., Chen, S.-H., & Yeh, K.-C. (2023). Does financial development enhance the growth effect of FDI? A multidimensional analysis in emerging and developing Asia. *International Journal of Emerging Markets*. Advance online publication.

Anyanwu, J. C. (2012). Why does foreign direct investment go where it goes? New evidence from African countries. *Annals of Economics and Finance*, *13*(2), 425–462.

Ashurov, S., Abdullah Othman, A. H., & Rosman, R. (2020). The determinants of foreign direct investment in Central Asian region: A case study of Tajikistan, Kazakhstan, Kyrgyzstan, Turkmenistan and Uzbekistan (A quantitative analysis using GMM). *Russian Journal of Economics*, *6*(2), 162–176. DOI: 10.32609/j.ruje.6.48556

Ayinde, T. O., Fatai, B. O., & Adeyemi, F. A. (2024). Macroeconomic determinants of foreign direct investment in emerging economies in turbulent times–A case of COVID'19 pandemic. *Transnational Corporations Review*, *16*(4), 200079. DOI: 10.1016/j.tncr.2024.200079

Balasubramanyam, V. N., Salisu, M. A., & Sapsford, D. (1996). Foreign direct investment, trade policy and economic growth. In *Trade and Development: Essays in Honour of Jagdish Bhagwati* (pp. 3–21). Palgrave Macmillan UK. DOI: 10.1007/978-1-349-25040-0_1

Bandekar, B. N., & Sankaranarayanan, K. G. (2017). Trends and determinants of FDI in BRICS countries: A panel data analysis. *ZENITH International Journal of Business Economics & Management Research*, *7*(11), 53–65.

Bénassy-Quéré, A., Coupet, M., & Mayer, T. (2007). Institutional determinants of foreign direct investment. *World Economy*, *30*(5), 764–782. DOI: 10.1111/j.1467-9701.2007.01022.x

Bergstra, J., & Bengio, Y. (2012). Random search for hyper-parameter optimization. *Journal of Machine Learning Research*, *13*(1), 281–305.

Blackwill, R. D., & Harris, J. M. (2016). *War by other means: Geoeconomics and statecraft*. Harvard University Press.

Blomstrom, M., & Kokko, A. (2001). Foreign direct investment and spillovers of technology. *International Journal of Technology Management*, *22*(5-6), 435–454. DOI: 10.1504/IJTM.2001.002972

Borensztein, E., De Gregorio, J., & Lee, J. W. (1998). How does foreign direct investment affect economic growth? *Journal of International Economics*, *45*(1), 115–135. DOI: 10.1016/S0022-1996(97)00033-0

Breiman, L. (1996). Bagging predictors. *Machine Learning*, *24*(2), 123–140. DOI: 10.1023/A:1018054314350

Breiman, L. (2001). Random forests. *Machine Learning*, *45*(1), 5–32. DOI: 10.1023/A:1010933404324

Buckley, P. J., & Casson, M. (1976). *The future of the multinational enterprises*. Macmillan. DOI: 10.1007/978-1-349-02899-3

Buckley, P. J., Clegg, J., Cross, A. R., Liu, X., Voss, H., & Zheng, P. (2007). The determinants of Chinese outward foreign direct investment. *Journal of International Business Studies*, *8*(4), 499–518. DOI: 10.1057/palgrave.jibs.8400277

Budiono, S., & Purba, J. T. (2023). Factors of foreign direct investment flows to Indonesia in the era of COVID-19 pandemic. *Heliyon*, *9*(4), e15429. DOI: 10.1016/j.heliyon.2023.e15429

Caldara, D., & Iacoviello, M. (2022). Measuring Geopolitical Risk. *The American Economic Review*, *112*(4), 1194–1225. DOI: 10.1257/aer.20191823

Calvo, G. A., Leiderman, L., & Reinhart, C. M. (1993). Capital inflows and real exchange rate appreciation in Latin America: The role of external factors. *Staff Papers - International Monetary Fund. International Monetary Fund*, *40*(1), 108–151. DOI: 10.2307/3867379

Calvo, S. G., & Reinhart, C. (1996). Capital flows to Latin America: is there evidence of contagion effects? Available at *SSRN* 636120.

Chai, T., & Draxler, R. R. (2014). Root mean square error (RMSE) or mean absolute error (MAE). *Geoscientific Model Development Discussions*, *7*(1), 1525–1534.

Chen, T., & Guestrin, C. (2016, August). XGBoost: A scalable tree boosting system. In *Proceedings of the 22nd ACM SIGKDD International Conference on Knowledge Discovery and Data Mining* (pp. 785-794).

Chiappini, R., Coupaud, M., & Viaud, F. (2022). Does attracting FDI affect population health? New evidence from a multi-dimensional measure of health. *Social Science & Medicine*, *301*, 114878. DOI: 10.1016/j.socscimed.2022.114878

Chinn, M. D., & Ito, H. (2008). A new measure of financial openness. *Journal of Comparative Policy Analysis*, *10*(3), 309–322. DOI: 10.1080/13876980802231123

Davis, S. J. (2016). *An index of global economic policy uncertainty (No. w22740)*. National Bureau of Economic Research. DOI: 10.3386/w22740

De Castro, P. G., Fernandes, E. A., & Campos, A. C. (2013). The determinants of foreign direct investment in Brazil and Mexico: An empirical analysis. *Procedia Economics and Finance*, *5*, 231–240. DOI: 10.1016/S2212-5671(13)00029-4

De Ville, B. (2013). Decision trees. *Wiley Interdisciplinary Reviews: Computational Statistics*, *5*(6), 448–455. DOI: 10.1002/wics.1278

Dias, M., Dias, J., & Hirata, J. (2014). Foreign Direct Investment in Brazil: The effects of productivity and aggregate consumption. *Journal of Stock and Forex Trading*, *3*(127), 59–73. DOI: 10.4172/2168-9458.1000127

Dimitrova, A., Rogmans, T., & Triki, D. (2020). Country-specific determinants of FDI inflows to the MENA region: A systematic review and future research directions. *Multinational Business Review*, *28*(1), 1–38. DOI: 10.1108/MBR-01-2019-0003

Dinkar, N., & Rahul, C. N. (2014). A selective review of foreign direct investment theories. Asia-Pacific Research and Training Network on Trade, 2-26.

Dua, P., & Garg, R. (2015). Macroeconomic determinants of foreign direct investment: Evidence from India. *Journal of Developing Areas*, *49*(1), 133–155. DOI: 10.1353/jda.2015.0025

Dunning, J. H. (1977). Trade location of economic activity and the MNE: A search of an eclectic approach. In Ohlin, B., Hesselborn, P. O., & Wijkman, P. J. (Eds.), *The international allocation of economic activity*. DOI: 10.1007/978-1-349-03196-2_38

Dunning, J. H. (1993). International direct investment patterns. In *The global race for foreign direct investment: Prospects for the future* (pp. 107–132). Springer Berlin Heidelberg. DOI: 10.1007/978-3-642-78309-8_5

Dunning, J. H., & Lundan, S. M. (2008). *Multinational enterprises and the global economy*. Edward Elgar Publishing.

Durán, J. E. (1999). *Los determinantes de la IED en los países de América Latina y el Caribe: Su impacto sobre el comercio y la integración regional*. ECLAC, Mimeo.

Economou, F., Hassapis, C., Philippas, N., & Tsionas, M. (2017). Foreign direct investment determinants in OECD and developing countries. *Review of Development Economics*, *21*(3), 527–542. DOI: 10.1111/rode.12269

Emako, E., Seid, N., & Mesfin, M. (2022). The effect of foreign direct investment on economic growth in developing countries. *Transnational Corporations Review*, *14*(4), 382–401. DOI: 10.1080/19186444.2022.2146967

Erdal, F., & Tatoglu, E. (2002). Locational determinants of foreign direct investment in an emerging market economy: Evidence from Turkey. *Multinational Business Review*, *10*(1).

Esclanda-Lo, C. G., Masangkay, G. A., Ong, C. A. S., & Reyes, R. S. (2024). *Exploring the evolving determinants of foreign direct investment and the investing country preferences in developing Asian economies using machine learning* (Vol. 62). Bank for International Settlements.

Firdos, R., Subhan, M., Mansuri, B. B., & Alharthi, M. (2024). Unraveling the impact of COVID-19 pandemic on foreign direct investment and its determinants: Empirical insights from SAARC countries. *Journal of Economic Studies (Glasgow, Scotland)*, *51*(6), 1247–1265. DOI: 10.1108/JES-08-2023-0420

Goldstein, I., & Razin, A. (2006). An information-based trade off between foreign direct investment and foreign portfolio investment. *Journal of International Economics*, *70*(1), 271–295. DOI: 10.1016/j.jinteco.2005.12.002

Gondim, I. J. C., Morandier, N., Dias, I. R. R., Couto, C. A. P., & Charotta, T. C. A.GONDIM. (2017). Analysis of domestic factors affecting outward foreign direct investment in Brazil. *Latin American Business Review*, *18*(1), 1–18. DOI: 10.1080/10978526.2016.1251821

Goodspeed, T. J., Martinez-Vazquez, J., & Zhang, L. (2011). *The role of public services and taxes in attracting 'foreign' direct investment (No. 433)*. Hunter College Department of Economics.

Gupta, S., Yadav, S. S., & Jain, P. K. (2024). Does institutional quality matter for foreign direct investment flows? Empirical evidence from BRICS economies. *International Journal of Emerging Markets*, *19*(12), 4431–4458. DOI: 10.1108/IJOEM-11-2021-1713

Hannan, S. A. (2018). *Revisiting the determinants of capital flows to emerging markets—A survey of the evolving literature*. International Monetary Fund.

Horobet, A., Popovici, O. C., & Bela cu, L. (2021). Shaping competitiveness for driving FDI in CEE countries. *Romanian Journal of European Affairs, 21*(2).

Hymer, S. H. (1976). The international operations of national firms: A study of direct foreign investment. Cambridge, MA: The MIT Press. (Original publication 1960)

IIF. (2023). The Institute of International Finance, https://www.iif.com/publications/capital-flows

IMF. (2024). Emerging Markets Show Resilience Despite Global Monetary Tightening, https://www.imf.org/en/Blogs/Articles/2024/07/12/emerging-markets-show-resilience-despite-global-monetary-tightening

Jiménez, A., & Herrero, Á. (2019). Selecting features that drive internationalization of Spanish firms. *Cybernetics and Systems, 50*(1), 25–39. DOI: 10.1080/01969722.2018.1558012

Katenova, M. (2018). Foreign direct investment and gross domestic product in Kazakhstan. International Journal of Economics. *Business and Management Studies, 5*(1), 40–45. DOI: 10.20448/802.51.40.45

Kaushal, L. A. (2021). Impact of institutional and regulatory quality on FDI inflow: Case of a developing Indian economy. *Cogent Economics & Finance, 9*(1), 1985201. DOI: 10.1080/23322039.2021.1985201

Khamphengvong, V., Xia, E., & Srithilat, K. (2018). Inflow determinants of foreign direct investment. *Human Systems Management, 37*(1), 57–66. DOI: 10.3233/HSM-17229

Korsah, E., Amanamah, R. B., & Gyimah, P. (2025). Drivers of foreign direct investment: New evidence from West African regions. *Journal of Business and Socio-economic Development, 5*(1), 3–19. DOI: 10.1108/JBSED-12-2021-0173

Kovvuri, V. R. R., Fu, H., Fan, X., & Seisenberger, M. (2023). Fund performance evaluation with explainable artificial intelligence. *Finance Research Letters, 58*, 104419. DOI: 10.1016/j.frl.2023.104419

Kumar, N., & Singhal, N. (2022). Role of outward foreign direct investment in economic growth of India: Evidence from non-linear ARDL approach. *Jindal Journal of Business Research, 11*(2), 187–204. DOI: 10.1177/22786821221127670

Kumari, R., & Sharma, A. K. (2017). Determinants of foreign direct investment in developing countries: A panel data study. *International Journal of Emerging Markets*, *12*(4), 658–682. DOI: 10.1108/IJoEM-10-2014-0169

Lee, S. J., Kang, S. J., & Lee, S. (2024). Economic, social and institutional determinants of FDI inflows: A comparative analysis of developed and developing economies. *Transnational Corporations Review*, *16*(3), 200074. DOI: 10.1016/j.tncr.2024.200074

Lensink, R., & Morrissey, O. (2001). Foreign direct investment: Flows, volatility and growth in developing countries (No. 01/06). CREDIT Research Paper.

Liu, Q., Zhang, G., Yu, J., Kong, G., Cao, T., Ji, G., & Han, L. (2024). Machine learning-aided hydrothermal carbonization of biomass for coal-like hydrochar production: Parameters optimization and experimental verification. *Bioresource Technology*, *393*, 130073. DOI: 10.1016/j.biortech.2023.130073

Lundberg, S. M., & Lee, S. I. (2017). A unified approach to interpreting model predictions. *Advances in Neural Information Processing Systems*, 30.

Mahmood, N., Shakil, M. H., Akinlaso, I. M., & Tasnia, M. (2019). Foreign direct investment and institutional stability: Who drives whom? *Journal of Economics, Finance and Administrative Science*, *24*(47), 145–156. DOI: 10.1108/JEFAS-05-2018-0048

Mapendo, J. J., Senadjki, A., & Choong, Y. O. (2025). Stock market development and foreign direct investment: The moderating role of government effectiveness. *International Journal of Emerging Markets*. Advance online publication. DOI: 10.1108/IJOEM-04-2024-0597

Martinez-Vazquez, J., Zhang, L., & Goodspeed, T. (2011). Public policies and FDI location: Differences between developing and developed countries. FinanzArchiv / Public Finance Analysis, 67(2), 171–191. DOI: 10.1628/001522111X588736

Mavruk, T. (2022). Analysis of herding behavior in individual investor portfolios using machine learning algorithms. *Research in International Business and Finance*, *62*, 101740. DOI: 10.1016/j.ribaf.2022.101740

Mienye, I. D., Sun, Y., & Wang, Z. (2019). Prediction performance of improved decision tree-based algorithms: A review. *Procedia Manufacturing*, *35*, 698–703. DOI: 10.1016/j.promfg.2019.06.011

Mirkovikj, B. K., Gkasis, P., & Golitsis, P. (2024). Regulatory quality and foreign direct investment: A case analysis of North Macedonia. *Theoretical Economics Letters*, *14*(5), 1883–1913. DOI: 10.4236/tel.2024.145095

Mongi, C., & Saidi, K. (2024). The impact of corruption, government effectiveness, FDI, and GFC on economic growth: New evidence from global panel of 48 middle-income countries. *Journal of the Knowledge Economy*, *15*(3), 10696–10721. DOI: 10.1007/s13132-023-01509-0

Mottaleb, K., & Kalirajan, K. (2010). Determinants of foreign direct investment in developing countries: A comparative analysis. *Margin*, *4*(4), 369–404. DOI: 10.1177/097380101000400401

Nagelkerke, N. J. (1991). A note on a general definition of the coefficient of determination. *Biometrika*, *78*(3), 691–692. DOI: 10.1093/biomet/78.3.691

Oberhauser, M. (2024). The Chinese belt and road initiative: Development project with strings attached? *International Journal of Development Issues*, *23*(2), 212–244. DOI: 10.1108/IJDI-03-2023-0073

Ohashi, H. (2018). The Belt and Road Initiative (BRI) in the context of China's opening-up policy. *Journal of Contemporary East Asia Studies*, *7*(2), 85–103. DOI: 10.1080/24761028.2018.1564615

Okara, A. (2023). Does foreign direct investment promote political stability? Evidence from developing economies. *Economic Modelling*, *123*, 106249. DOI: 10.1016/j.econmod.2023.106249

Ono, S., & Sekiyama, T. (2024). The impact of official development assistance on foreign direct investment: The case of Japanese firms in India. *Frontiers in Political Science*, *6*, 1351285. DOI: 10.3389/fpos.2024.1351285

Paul, J., & Feliciano-Cestero, M. M. (2021). Five decades of research on foreign direct investment by MNEs: An overview and research agenda. *Journal of Business Research*, *124*, 800–812. DOI: 10.1016/j.jbusres.2020.04.017

Peres, M., Ameer, W., & Xu, H. (2018). The impact of institutional quality on foreign direct investment inflows: Evidence for developed and developing countries. *Ekonomska Istrazivanja*, *31*(1), 626–644. DOI: 10.1080/1331677X.2018.1438906

Petrov, A. V., Baynova, M. S., & Jiaerheng, J. (2022). Features of Russian and Chinese direct investments in Kazakhstan. *Spatial Economics*, *8*(1), 148–167. DOI: 10.14530/se.2022.1.148-167

Poulsen, L., & Hufbauer, G. (2011). Foreign direct investment in times of crisis. *Transnational Corporations*, *20*(1), 19–38. DOI: 10.18356/138883a0-en

Ranjan, V., & Agrawal, G. (2011). FDI inflow determinants in BRIC countries: A panel data analysis. *International Business Research*, *4*(4), 255. DOI: 10.5539/ibr.v4n4p255

Revilla, M. L. D. (2016). Cross-country econometric study on the impact of fiscal incentives on FDI. Econstor - PIDS Discussion Paper Series, 2016–17. Retrieved from http://hdl.handle.net/10419/173538

Sabir, S., Rafique, A., & Abbas, K. (2019). Institutions and FDI: Evidence from developed and developing countries. *Financial Innovation*, *5*(1), 1–20. DOI: 10.1186/s40854-019-0123-7

Saha, S., Sadekin, M. N., & Saha, S. K. (2022). Effects of institutional quality on foreign direct investment inflow in lower-middle income countries. *Heliyon*, *8*(10), e10828. DOI: 10.1016/j.heliyon.2022.e10828

Sahoo, P. (2006). Foreign direct investment in South Asia: Policy, trends, impact and determinants. ADB Institute Discussion Paper No. 56.

Saidi, Y., Ochi, A., & Maktouf, S. (2023). FDI inflows, economic growth, and governance quality trilogy in developing countries: A panel VAR analysis. *Bulletin of Economic Research*, *75*(2), 426–449. DOI: 10.1111/boer.12364

Saini, N., & Singhania, M. (2018). Determinants of FDI in developed and developing countries: A quantitative analysis using GMM. *Journal of Economic Studies (Glasgow, Scotland)*, *45*(2), 348–382. DOI: 10.1108/JES-07-2016-0138

Sarno, L., & Taylor, M. P. (1998). Exchange controls, international capital flows and saving-investment correlations in the UK: An empirical investigation. *Weltwirtschaftliches Archiv*, *134*(1), 69–98. DOI: 10.1007/BF02707579

Schneider, F., & Frey, B. S. (1985). Economic and political determinants of foreign direct investment. *World Development*, *13*(2), 161–175. DOI: 10.1016/0305-750X(85)90002-6

Shapley, L. S. (1953). Stochastic games. *Proceedings of the National Academy of Sciences of the United States of America*, *39*(10), 1095–1100. DOI: 10.1073/pnas.39.10.1095

Sinha, C., Saha, S., & Vasilev, A. (2024). Institutional quality and US FDI outflows: Do political regimes matter? *Economic Systems*, *48*(3), 101241. DOI: 10.1016/j.ecosys.2024.101241

Strumbelj, E., & Kononenko, I. (2010). An efficient explanation of individual classifications using game theory. *Journal of Machine Learning Research*, *11*, 1–18.

Thierry Mayer & Soledad Zignago. (2011). Notes on CEPII's distances measures: The GeoDist database. Working Papers 2011-25, CEPII research center.

Vasilyeva, R., & Mariev, O. (2021). Determinants of foreign direct investment in developed and developing countries: Impact of political stability. *Economy of Regions, 17*(4), 1390–1404. DOI: 10.17059/ekon.reg.2021-4-24

Wiessner, Y. T., Giuliani, E., Wijen, F., & Doh, J. (2024). Towards a more comprehensive assessment of FDI's societal impact. *Journal of International Business Studies, 55*(1), 50–70. DOI: 10.1057/s41267-023-00636-9

Yusuf, F. A., Alfaridzi, M., & Herdi, T. (2022). Penerapan algoritma decision tree untuk klasifikasi KIPI vaksin Covid-19. *Jurnal Ilmiah FIFO, 14*(2), 155. DOI: 10.22441/fifo.2022.v14i2.005

Zardoub, A., & Sboui, F. (2023). Impact of foreign direct investment, remittances and official development assistance on economic growth: Panel data approach. *PSU Research Review, 7*(2), 73–89. DOI: 10.1108/PRR-04-2020-0012

KEY TERMS AND DEFINITIONS

Crisis-Responsive Determinants: Factors influencing FDI that exhibit altered importance during economic crises, indicating adjustments in investor decision-making.

Emerging Countries: Countries experiencing fast industrial progress, expanding financial markets and higher-risk yet high-return investment opportunities compared to developed economies.

Feature Importance Ranking: The ranking of factors in modeling FDI, using machine learning models and SHAP analysis to prioritize policy actions.

Foreign Direct Investment (FDI): Cross-border financial long-term investments made by foreign investors seeking to establish a lasting stake or operational control in companies to leverage market access, resources, or cost efficiencies.

Geopolitical Risk: Political turbulence, territorial disputes, or diplomatic tensions that can reduce investor confidence and FDI flows, measured using indices related to governance or security conditions.

SHAP (SHapley Additive exPlanations) Values: A metric derived from game theory that quantifies the extent to which each feature influences FDI inflows, allowing for the ranking and identification of their contributions.

Tree-Based Machine Learning: Predictive algorithms (e.g., decision trees, random forests, XGBoost) which employ hierarchical splitting rules to examine interactions between predictors and outcomes, ensuring interpretability and effectively handling non-linear relationships.

APPENDIX

Table A1. Data definition and summary statistics

Variable	Definition	Source	Obs	Mean	Std. Dev.	Min	Max
WPANUI	World PANdemic Uncertainty Index.	FRED database	437	6,911	17,813	0,000	68,915
Distance capitals	Distance between capitals (km).	(Thierry Mayer & Soledad Zignago, 2011)	440	9084,217	3195,244	4180,438	16353,900
GEOPR	The GEOPolitical Risk index per country.	(Caldara et al.,2022)	460	0,151	0,322	0,000	3,690
GEPUI	The Global Economic Policy Uncertainty Index	(Davis,2016)	460	1936,606	913,502	777,460	3930,286
CAPOPEN	The capital openness index.	Chinn and Ito (2008), updated	460	-0,119	1,240	-1,931	2,299
CPI	The Consumer Price Index % of change.		427	4,778	0,406	3,809	7,916
SR	The Stock market Return.		262	2,793	1,388	-2,600	10,018
EXPORT	EXPORTs of goods and services (% of GDP)		450	3,479	0,528	2,337	4,748
IMPORT	IMPORTs of goods and services (% of GDP)		450	3,463	0,504	2,421	4,554
REERV	The Real Effective Exchange Rate Volatility (standard deviation)		271	0,403	1,183	-3,779	5,375
GDPGROWTH	Annual percentage growth rate of GDP.		451	3,786	4,282	-28,759	18,287

continued on following page

Table A1. Continued

Variable	Definition	Source	Obs	Mean	Std. Dev.	Min	Max
INTERST	The real interest rate.		354	4,233	9,288	-20,497	44,635
ShipConnec	Liner Shipping Connectivity Index score.		352	43,124	27,266	5,624	171,178
NATRESSRENT	Total natural resources rents.	World Bank database	407	7,002	8,510	0,205	55,024
BROA	Banks' Return On Assets.		398	1,291	1,609	-23,887	6,091
MARKETCAP	Stock MARKET CAPitalization.		340	3,812	0,808	1,216	5,845
UNEMP	UNEMPloyment rate.		458	7,535	4,963	0,249	28,838
STDEBT	The Short-Term DEBT (% of exports of goods, services and primary income)		336	2,996	0,611	1,478	5,006
DIGI	The DIGItilization composite index measure with the Principal Component Analysis method while considering these variables: Mobile cellular subscriptions (per 100 people), Fixed telephone subscriptions, Mobile cellular subscriptions, Fixed broadband subscriptions (per 100 people), and Individuals using the Internet (% of population). Kaiser Meyer Olkin measure of sampling adequacy equals 0,6007 for the digitalization composite index		419	0,303	1,341	-2,514	3,558

continued on following page

Table A1. Continued

Variable	Definition	Source	Obs	Mean	Std. Dev.	Min	Max
PROVNNLOAN	PROVisions to NoNperforming LOANs.		364	4,425	0,614	1,946	6,404
INSTQ	Is it an institutional quality composite index obtained by using the principal component analysis method. To have the composite index reflecting the institutional quality we considered a set of six variables, namely control of corruption, political stability and absence of violence, rule of law, voice and accountability, regulatory quality, government effectiveness. Kaiser Meyer Olkin measure of sampling adequacy was launched and gave us a value of 0.8780.		437	-0,115	1,9271	-6,416	5,048
TOR	The stock market TurnOver Ratio. It stands for the value of domestic shares traded divided by their market capitalization.		333	3.422	1.139	-1.308	6.174

Table A2. List of countries

Countries
Argentina; Brazil; Chile; China; Colombia; Egypt; Hungary; India; Indonesia; Malaysia; Mexico; Peru; Philippines; Poland; Russian Federation; Saudi Arabia; South Africa; Thailand; Tunisia; Turkey; Ukraine; Venezuela; Viet Nam.

Chapter 10
Recasting International Trade Law in the Age of Geopolitical Shifts and Geo-Economic Pressures

Sheikh Inam Ul Mansoor
https://orcid.org/0000-0001-8636-4769
Symbiosis Law School, Symbiosis International University, Pune, India

Syed Shahid Rashid
https://orcid.org/0009-0008-8450-0091
Symbiosis Law School, Symbiosis International University, Pune, India

ABSTRACT

This research focuses on the dynamics of international trade laws within the rapidly changing geopolitical and geo-economic environment for trade. It analyses the emergence of new powers, China, and the place of the U.S., given protectionism, focusing on the impact on the multilateral trading system. The chapter analyses the issues which relate to the WTO, the dispute settlement, relationship between national security and free trade, and the role of regional trade agreements. Moreover, it continues where others start: the intricacies of law in the use of trade as an instrument of foreign policy, export controls, tariffs, and sanctions. The chapter outlines recommendations for the enhancement of the organization's structure, modern issues' incorporation into the WTO, and rebuilding of multilateralism. Finally, it seeks to establish the course of law for obtaining a sustainable, equitable, and integration of international trade amidst the modern issues.

DOI: 10.4018/979-8-3373-7907-4.ch010

INTRODUCTION

International trade law as a field of law regulates trade in goods and services, transfer of technology and intellectual property. It covers rules, trade and partnership deals and frameworks that aim at balancing the trading relations between countries (Cohen, 2018). Traditionally, this body of law has developed to support globalization, foster business relations and adopt clear regulations on disagreements (Benalleg, 2023). Nevertheless, the world of the 21st century has been characterized by challenges to the global trading system due to geopolitical tensions, economic patriotism and decline of multilateralism (Luo, 2024). All these advances require a fundamental re-evaluation of the proclaimed and stipulated goals as well as of the normative and institutional framework of international trade law in the context of a more diverse and complex international political economy (Benalleg, 2023). It is with reference to such a context that the following interrelated factors can be used to explain the contemporary context of international trade law. Prominent among these are the geopolitical shifts that have changed the location of power in world trade management (Góes & Bekkers, 2022). With the help of China and some other emerging countries, the USA and other countries of the Western world have faced competition in the international market structure (Ul Mansoor, 2023). The BRI as well as infrastructure and technology investments have upended global supply chains; legal issues related to transparency and reciprocity as well as compliance with existing trade laws have emerged regarding these investments (Ni, 2024). At the same time, now, there are tendencies toward more protectionism, for instance, the United States withdrew from multilateral trade agreements, and applied unilateral tariffs which have pressure the very fundamental bases of the international trade law (Zahoor, et al., 2023).

Development of the regional trade agreements (RTAs) has added more problems to the multilateral trading system (Kaushal, 2021). Despite the contribution of RTAs in liberalization and deeper integration among the participating societies, they are conducted beyond the WTO's domains, thus developing segmented legal structures and making it difficult to coordinate the principles of trades (Chandran, 2017). Furthermore, the elevation of trade as a weapon of geopolitics, sanctions, export controls, trade wars has in turn injected new layers into the legal debate around trade (Mansoor et al., 2025). These anvil points raise concern on the capacity of flows prevailing traditional trade norms to address interaction between trade interests and political processes (Barbieri, 2024). In this regard, WTO, which has taken central stage of the international trade system since its establishment in 1995 has been in crisis. The judicial system of the organization that was once regarded as serving as an excellent basis for settling international disputes has recently come to a halt because the United States failed to confirm the members of the Appellate

Body (Simões, 2019). This has weakened the WTO's Dispute Settlement Body in managing trade rivalry and ensuring compliance with the WTO procedures and regulations and diminished multipurpose confidence (Lehne, 2019). Also, WTO has not been forthcoming with emerging trends like digital trade, climate change and data protection leading to its guidelines and regulation framework becoming more and more useless in the face of technological and climate change realities (Horváthy, 2020) The interaction of geopolitics and geo-economics raises monumental challenges for the legal regime of international trade. Measured in the broadest sense, economic sanctions, as tools of foreign policy, are problematic in relation to the principles of non-discrimination and market access that underpin trade liberalisation (Hurrell, 2024). In the same regard, the use of tariffs and export controls in strategic products such as semiconductors and artificial intelligence has been in doubt concerning WTO compliance (Huzaifa & Legacy, 2024). The use of national security as the reason for implementing policies that are protectionist makes the distinction between legitimate security concerns and rational self-serving by countries' interests less clear (Rasch & Shrimali, 2024).

The objective of this chapter is to identify the reform measures in international trade law that would be required to respond to the contemporary world that entails a geopolitics-inspired topography together with an economic globalization-driven structure. The first question asks whether the currently applicable laws can cope with new phenomena connected with changing power relations, protectionism, and the use of trade as a weapon. Besides reviewing current reigning trade rules and institutions, the research seeks to explain possible changes to make the international trading system stronger and more transparent.

Pivotal to this, is analysis on how international trade law is still being shaped and if the world trade law system is capable of handling the modern forces (Cottier, 2015). The chapter examines how the political shifts contributes to the creation and use of the trade regulations. It also looks at legal aspects of geo-economics: sanctions & export controls, as well as the RTAs which fragment trading systems. Further, it looks for measures hoping to bring a revival within the WTO's Dispute Settlement Body (DSB) (Guan, 2024). This research focuses on developing and the least developed countries in the new trade order to look at trade law in relation to environmental law, human rights and geo-political dynamics.

GEOPOLITICAL SHIFTS IN INTERNATIONAL TRADE

The field of international trade law has always been shaped by the political processes and cyclises of the world affecting the forms of global trade and regulating legal and organizational relations in the sphere of trade (Aliaj & Mekaj, 2019). The post-Cold War period indeed has noted new changes in the international structure that has redrawn the power relations and changed the legal framework of the Global trade. Such developments have appeared through the rise of new players within the international system, decline of old rim dealers, the emergence of the Regional Trade Agreements, each of which poses various changes and prospects in the nature and regulation of international trade law (Roberts, 2008). The new comers, especially China, have become one of the most transformative forces in global trade governance. The unprecedented economic rise China saw especially in the twentieth century placed it at the fore-front of export oriented economies that had for long been dominated by western economies (Ul Mansoor, 2023). It is not only an economic dominance, but it comes with an aggressive legal and institutional agenda to refashion legal and institutional structures of trade to suit it. One of the ways through which China sought to restructure the new world order is through BRI which is a development model through infrastructure investment and trade and financial integration across Asia Africa and beyond (Khan et al., 2018). The legal nature of such initiatives is very significant because such measures work beyond WTO and disturb the classical multilateral systems and principles of international trade law as such as transparency, non-discrimination, and reciprocity (Khatoon & Sakeena, 2022).

China's interaction with regional trade partners also evident in its participation in trade relations frameworks also supports this supposed strategic approach to trade governance (Sampson, 2019). Its membership in various pacts like the Regional Comprehensive Economic Partnership (RCEP), the latest being a clear plan to centralize economic power within the Asia-Pacific realm as well as its companies (Liu, Xu, & Lim, 2023). These agreements, while integrating the economies and promoting trade create legal issues in that they put in place parallel systems that are often in conflict with multilateral trade norms (Ren, 2023). For instance, focus on provisions like rules of origin, preference, and enforcement mechanisms under such deals pose a danger of Balkanizing the trading arena and makes a synchronization of trade laws more challenging (James, 2005). This however comes with the emergent economies which also included India, Brazil and South Africa that also seek to enjoy their authority in the trade system of the world. These nations have been leading a process of change within the WTO to correct injustices of the past and increase the representation of developing countries (Bıçakcıoğlu-Peynirci, 2023). However, their struggle for special treatment and the right to policy space is ill at odds with the qualitative neoliberal trade environment that integrates the principles of market access and liberalization favored by the developed countries, resulting in technical legalization that challenges the ability of GATS to address the structural difference of economic interests in the international trade legal order (Garcia, 2007).

On one hand there are countries of new emerging powers, on the other hand, there is the waning dominance of the United States, change which has brought unpredictability to the international trading system (Chin, 2010). For a long time the architect and guarantor of the post-war economic order America has lately been turning into protectionism vision that is working against the principles of multilateralism and liberalization the country once defended (Dadkhah, 2009). Having seen instances of such measures as the imposition of tariffs under the Trade Expansion Act of 1962 Section 232 and invocation of national Security to justify measures that are restrictive in nature undermines the rule based nature of the WTO (Hanada, 2020). The America's pull out from the international trade partnership like the TPP also depicts the country's planned retreat from its traditional hegemonic domination of the international trade (Narine, 2018). This retreat has not only left strategic room for others, particularly China, to increase their influence while simultaneously casting doubts on the effectiveness of multilateralism as an organizing principle of trade governance (Janusch & Mucha, 2017). On a legal level, this shift poses important consequences because it reduce the enforceability of the multilateral trade regime and increases the number of preferential agreements that are not signed within the WTO framework (Bouët & Laborde, 2018). It is therefore clear that protectionism in the United States of America has deeper geo-economics structuring factors including perceived decline in industrial capacity, and the need to safeguard vital supply chains (Fajgelbaum et al., 2020). These pressures have been enacted by the return of manufacturing to their countries and the limitation of foreign investment in strategic industries as well as the export restrictions of high-tech products (Zahoor, Wu, Khan, et al., 2023). Measures, which, under the cloak of economic security, are contrary to the non-discrimination and market access norms of contemporary trade treaties, throw up issues that challenge the robustness of international trade law (Diebold, 2011).

The relative decline of the US hegemony is also best illustrated by its behaviour at the WTO by which America has vetoed appointments to the Appellate Body grinding reforms at the WTO's dispute-settlement mechanism (Ashraf, 2023). This situation does not only endanger the WTO but also cause member states to look for other ways to solve the dispute such as bilateral and regionalism (Bäumler, 2020). The outcomes are fragmentation and hitches in the consistent application and interpretation of trade norms, signalling the importance of more legal and institutional change to renegotiate the WTO's centrality in international trade (Duong, 2024). In the context of these geopolitical changes, the analysis of the role of regional trade agreements (RTAs) for the configurations of world trade has become crucial (Kaushal, 2021). A surge in the number of RTAs is evidence of shifts in economic realism by individuals who find incongruities with the multilateral system and the core freedom to take more complex economic relations or trade relations within focused geo-strategic agendas (Kaushal, 2021). By doing so they develop new legal systems apart from WTO rules, which are opposed in such areas as IPR, labour, and environment contrary to legitimacy questions on multilateral frameworks (Martínez-Zarzoso et al., 2021). In RTAs, there is much emphasis on rules of origin which distort the supply chain since the exporter has to meet at least one of the several and perhaps conflicting standards to avail the preference (Kim, 2012). This legal fragmentation subtracts from the stability and the certainty of the international trade regime, which attempts to bring together regionalism and multilateralism.

The phenomenon of so-called mega-regional FTAs including the CPTPP and the AfCFTA is a perfect example of the increased role that RTAs play in shaping trader relations (Aggarwal, 2016). These arrangements cover a vast area of the subject such as investment and services, digital trade, and even environmental standards aspects of the modern international trade (Zuev, 2022). Disputes involve RTAs' availability because fundamental tycoons are not involved and use of non-centralized approaches to enforcing them. Such geopolitical measures are as old as CPTPP, where China is excluded which in turn increases the complexity of the trade law and geopolitical factors (Li & Wang, 2024). As a common trend, the AfCFTA, which was aimed at promoting economic integration in Africa has legal and institutional constraints when establishing, implementing and monitoring the various trade systems of member states' and ensuring their compliance with the set objectives (Samunderu, 2024). Thus, there is no inherent contradiction between regionalization and globalization, and the relationship between these two processes should be adjusted by legal means and turned into a clearly complementary one (Chen & De Lombaerde, 2019). Mere attempts to synchronize RTA provisions with WTO rules including by other measures like transparency measures and compatibility checks are imperative to avoid the danger of legal bifurcation (Shadikhodjaev, 2011). Further, anything that contributes to the DCs being as part of a RTA that is consistent with the WTO jurisprudence will improve the legitimacy and thus the predictability of such agreements.

GEO-ECONOMIC PRESSURES AND THEIR LEGAL IMPLICATIONS

This chapter will go on to demonstrate the co-production of actors in the international trade law with geo-economic forces that are produced by political and economic tools for the services of political economic interests. These pressures are thus not simply economic entities although they are embedded in or originated from the legal systems governing international business (Breslin & Nesadurai, 2023). The use of trade measures as instruments of foreign policy, the management of tariff rates, export controls, and the growing rivalry in technological spheres for the multilateral trading system (Charnovitz, 1996). In order for the international trade system of law to emerge and to work, legal scholarship has to engage with these problems in order to preserve the stability and fairness of the genuinely international trade and to assuage or articulate the genuinely international politics and economics at the same time (Chow et al., 2021). Trade is connected to foreign policy in geographical economics, as is retaliation as an instrument of economic coercion. Sanctions present legal concerns on GATT/WTO's non-cury of discrimination and the MFN principle (Martin & Vergote, 2008). Preferential measures, frequently applied extra regionally and rarely with the UN's endorsement, destabilize the multilateralism as they sup national interests on international decision-making (Falvey & Foster-McGregor, 2022). They also illustrate the subject of trade institutions to other branches of international law, including laws of state responsibility and human rights, as they imply extraterritorial impact on the third states and non-state actors for the sanctioning state.

Countermeasures are considered as a part of the applicable law to the extent of developing legal uncertainty in the relations of international trade (Jackson & Paddeu, 2024). Sanctions in relation to what is believed to be trade infringement as allowed under the WTO, Dispute Settlement system whilst allowing for countermeasures may in most circumstances avoid legal redress in favour of self-help measures (Egger et al., 2024). Measures of this nature are also against the doctrine of legal certainty, and give a wrong signal to the multilateralism. For example, protective tariffs set during contentious trade matters, including the ongoing trade relations between China and the United States, distort supply chain and engender notable legal risk for every contractual party and administration (Ma & Ning, 2024). To read the use of these measures into the WTO is the real conundrum for International trade law, given the WTO principles of proportionality, necessity and good faith (Andenas & Zleptnig, 2007). Tariffs, export restraints and Technological rivalry is another side of geo economic pressures that have great legal relevance. The use of tariffs for the purpose of shielding industries or for correcting currency differentials creates concerns about compliance with WTO regulation especially the non-derogable provision that bars discrimination in tariffs and the undertaking that certain tariff levels have been agreed (Doan & Zhang, 2024). Tariffs, a classic measure of trade policy, have come as a tool of economic nationalism more recently as part of shifts in global economic governance system (Jakubik et al., 2022). The use of U-turns; invocation of Article XXI of the GATT under the trade name of security to put tariffs on steel and aluminium for example, as well as the dispute that has surrounded the interpretation and understanding of the said particular article have been key issues of concern (Mansoor & Inam, 2024). This exception provides states broad discretion, which compromises stability in the multilateral trading system, particularly export control to dual-use technologies and strategic products (Kanetake, 2021). Controlling exports of some strategic technologies including those used in semiconductors and artificial intelligence is now an area of conflict between states where power is seen in possessing superior technology while denying it to a rival (Nesselrodt, 2023). These controls have legal consequences in its relationship with WTO rules on quantitative restrictions on controls, relationships with intellectual property rights, and compatibility with trade agreements with other countries. The difficulty is to approach these measures in a way that is transparent and reasonable viewed under the scope of the state legal obligation (Marceau, 2016).

Technological competition also bring out the integration of trade law with geo-economics since states compete in new frontiers like digital trade, green techs and artificial intelligence. The key role of these sectors has prompted the use of trade measures designed to stimulate domestic innovation, protect IPR, and establish data ownership (ThankGod, 2023). Still, such measures raise legal issues concerning the conflict of market access and non-discrimination to which much attention needs to be paid. For instance, domestic data localisation policy measures that serve the declared purpose of national security and data protection, may be deemed as qualifications to free flow of services violate Paragraph 3 of the GATS (Abugre, Nellis, & Ofosu-Dorte, 2024). Likewise subsidization of green technologies as progressive towards environmental goals may also contravene the WTO Anti-Subsidy regulation on subsidies and countervailing mechanisms requiring a tension between globalization and sustainability (Wang et al., 2021). Geo-economic pressures also impact the rest of the multilateral trading system facing which has increasingly experienced enormous pressure over time. As the WTO at the heart of this system, it seems to be suffering a crisis of both its authority and efficiency, endogenous and exogenous factors (Breslin & Nesadurai, 2023). Protectionism, the emergence of regions 'trade arrangements, and stifling of the WTO's Dispute Settlement Mechanism have highlighted the WTO complex as unable to address the modern trade issues. Beneath this problem, the absence of consensus among member states over more fundamental concerns like agricultural subsidies, digital trade and the standards still present problems affecting the idea of multilateralism in a world which is divided geopolitically (Park, 2020).

The legal barriers to the multilateral trading system are exacerbated by the progressive reliance on bilateral practices that circumvent or violate WTO norms. This is evident in the recent shift to unilateral tariffs, export controls as well as sanctions which is also a half-baked compliance with the multilateral order where states only act where their best interest is not compromised (Abbas & Duchesne, 2023). Continuing along this trajectory may have begun to balkanise the WTO system, erode multilateral confidence and push for changes in the Rules-Baselining, Verification, Sanctions, and Construction of Fairness within the WTO (Stephen & Parízek, 2018). The biggest problem of the WTO is currently the paralysis of the Dispute Settlement System, in particular the Appellate Body, due to the lack of appointments from the United States. It has not only damaged the position of the

WTO but also caused a number of member states to lack a competent platform for solving conflicts in the sphere of trade (Stephen & Parízek, 2018). Disappearing appellate system has forced the DSU to resort to the application of other forms of the dispute resolution particularly the arbitration under Article 25 of DSU and has shifted emphasis on the bilateral and regionalism. However, they are all temporary measures that cannot provide legal certainty and coming from multiple sources in the same way as a multilateral system does (Gao, 2021). This suggests that addressing this crisis especially requires rebranding of multilateralism and preparedness to achieve for compromises of the new realities of the geopolitical and geo-economic worlds (Mansoor, 2025).

RTAs can offer examples of new trade rules or trade practices by which multilateral can be inspired. In contrast, the growth of RTAS threatens to produce a legal mosaic of disparate and conflicting norms that erode the cohesiveness of the international trading system (Kaushal, 2021). The problem for international trade law lies in the fact that current RTAs appear to have the potential to compete with 'proper' multilateral norms, but rather, the relevant provisions of international trade agreements should be made more compatible and coherent (Shaffer, 2021). Solving issues of regionalism must be approached through openness, interoperability and harmonisation. Transparency, informational effect, and non-discrimination rules are crucial for the proper functioning of the multilateral trading system to be legitimate (Wang, 2023). These principles cannot be bolstered by top-down legal or institutional transformations alone but must be grounded in the shared commitment to the values that form the foundation of the current WTO-centred liberal trade regime – equality, non-discrimination, and cooperation (Matsushita et al., 2003). Geo-economic pressures are dynamic, and thus require a sophisticated legal structure that will balance all stake holders' needs while at the same time preserving the multilateral trading system (Lipkan et al., 2023).

CHALLENGES TO THE WTO AND MULTILATERALISM

Global trade, regulated and supervised by the WTO as the most important organization, has become increasingly challenged, which undermines the principles of multilateralism that became the foundation of this organization (Ababakr, 2024). Such challenges distort the structural pulling forces, geopolitical realignments, and flaws in its architecture to respond to modern dynamics in trade relations (Sampson, 2018). While the multilateral trading system confronts even keener and speedier changes in the international political economy, the sustainability and effectiveness of the system are increasingly doubted. At the heart of this debate are questions of the specificity of the DSM, the employment of the national security exception, and such general questions as the diversification and fairness in representation within the WTO (Mansoor & Inam, 2024). Such problems show that it becomes crucial to overhaul the WTO to remain effective; its Appellate Body is critical for addressing the dispute, however, is currently dormant (Garner-Knapp et al., 2022). This has not only paralysed the working of the dispute settlement system but also jeopardy the rule-oriented spirit of WTO. The inactivation of the Appellate Body system erodes legal predictability and effectiveness that are critical to the achievement of compliance with multilateral trade commitments (Sacerdoti et al., 2021). Without it, members have opted to deal with matters unilaterally, or bilaterally in some cases to seek solutions for their disputes, which continues to destabilize the multilateral system.

There are basic strategic disagreements in this respect on the nature and place of the Appellate Body in the equal, value added WTO system. Its critics say that the body has transgressed its role by being judicial and departing with the WTO agreements in a manner that thrust responsibilities that are not agreed by the members of the WTO (Ansong, 2019). This has inspired demands for the organization to be more cautious when interpreting its decisions, with reforms recommending more specific demarcation of the organization's jurisdiction. Meanwhile, the Appellate Body which likewise benefits from the support of the United States affirms that there is need for a strong and independent mechanism of dispute settlement for the preservation of the multilateral trading system (Yang, 2021). In order to harmonise these conflicting observations, the WTO system requires such changes in the Appellate body that will balance the sovereignty of this judicial arm and the concerns of the member states on the same (Garner-Knapp et al., 2022). Only the reforms may guarantee fair decisions and involvement of the member-states in the decision making process. Here the measures invoked through Article XXI of GATT are issues of potential abuse and broad discretion (Malikova, 2021). The existence of national security measures for tariffs and restrictions raised a question of sovereignty versus international trade system, which contrary to the WTO rule, is based on non-discrimination and legal predictability (Wang, 2019).

Since the existence of the provision makes the interpretation of Article XXI subject to legal controversy, it makes the application of the provision even more worrisome as the WTO has only exercised reluctance in handling disputes that incorporate national security arguments. This has resulted to the absence of regulation whereby some states will use the provision for small economic or strategic gains (Alexandroff & Sharma, 2005). To counter this problem, a compromise appears essential: stabilising states' security interests without over-regulating free trade, perhaps relying on guidelines that emerged during the member negotiation (Malikova, 2021). These guidelines give a new form of understanding the role of trade measures in question of sovereignty and commitments, it is also revealing a continued controversy of define 'trade' and who governs the policy (Cottier, 2021).

While it has a worldwide membership, the WTO has been accused, more often than not of failing to protect the interest of developing and least developed countries. The decision-making instrument that involves consultation of the members has often ignored the small economy, who have little influence in the system (Mansoor & Chopra, 2022). This structural issue has given a perception of unfairness of the multilateral trading system, making it to be less legitimate and less effective.

The nature of this asymmetry is compounded by an element of capability to engage the WTO trade negotiation process and domestic implementation of the WTO rules. The technical capabilities, financial endowment, or institutional framework of developing countries and LDCs are frequently insufficient to enable them to actively participate in trade negotiations or to fulfill the demanding conditions of the WTO accords (Mansoor, 2021). Not only do they find it difficult to be integrated into the international trading system but also they are restricted to use trade as an instrument of economic growth. In order to overcome such difficulties, deeper strengthening of the capacity of the WTO and further development of technical assistance measures and targeted assistance for developing countries are needed (Mansoor, 2021). Another aspect of the openness is related to the 'what' of the WTO which has hitherto been dominated by the conventional categorisation: market access and trade liberalisation. As valid as these concerns are, the contemporary trade regime foregrounds newly emerging challenges including, digital trade, environmental standards, and labor standards (Howse & Langille, 2023). These problems are almost always linked to other broader development goals, requiring a systemic and pluralist approach to trade regulation. Mainstreaming these concerns into the WTO work programme means not only the transformational changes in work programme content but also in the process by which they are set up and implemented and in inclusiveness of civil society, academia, and business (Bacchus, 2022).

The issues that the WTO is experiencing are an expression of the more profound crisis of the multilateral system in the context of the post-2015 shift in the structures of the global economy to nationalism and bipolarity (Hopewell, 2020). Regional trade has been evident together with bilateralism due to dwindling faith in multilateralism as could complement WTO, but may also lead to different legal frameworks in the international trade (Freund & Ornelas, 2010). As WTO challenges worsen and competition in the U.S.-China trade intensifies, Hicks calls for better coordination between multilateral and regional trade measures to safeguard non-discrimination and transparency (Hoekman, Tu, & Wolfe, 2023). This standoff is indicative of not only specific policy differences but also a trend decline of the depositor of multilateralism, where states now resort to unilateralism or regionalism. They argue that in order to redefine the WTO and breathe life into the institution, there is a need to return to talking and selling the idea to the members as it was in

1994, and recognize the quid pro quo of the system governed by rules at the multilateral level (Mansoor, 2023).

Therefore, reforming the WTO to coherently respond to these diversified challenges is a tremendous challenge but an imperative too. Core concepts of non-discrimination as well as transparency and certainty in trading useful today as they were when the organization was established (Smeets et al., 2023). It can only be achieved by restructuring the WTO system, values, and policies in terms of dispute resolution, national security and its members' engagement.

PROPOSED REFORMS TO INTERNATIONAL TRADE LAW

Given the continuous changes in the legal framework governing international trade as well as the emerging challenges on the international trade scene in the 21st century, there is need to undertake a critical review of the subject matter. The principles on which the MTN and the WTO were built are still sound at their core but they are running into increasing difficulty in the light of contemporary politics and economics (Suwanprasert, 2020). For the subject of international trade law to remain meaningful, it needs to develop changes which will include the WTO regime reforms to enhance the multifaceted international organization, adapt to new challenges like digital trade or environmental protection, and, finally, bring together the interests of various states, more often than not, opposite (Cima & Esty, 2024). The WTO can be reformed only if such global multilateral goals are complemented by respective needs of the individual countries. As demonstrated the RTP has its advantages, however the consensus nature of the body hinders accomplishments and change (Abuseridze, 2023). While it can often lead to stability, the consensus decision-making model slows down decision making as far as major geopolitical issues are concerned (Ul Mansoor, 2023). Changing voting or creating more open Coalitions can de-marginalise non-consensus topics enhancing WTO (Xiao, Peng, & Yu, 2024).

One of the WTO's core elements, the Dispute Settlement Mechanism, is in need of reform, given the suspension of the Appellate Body; candidate solutions deal with interpretive roles and members' participation (Madhumitha, 2020). The above changes intended to ensure the balance between judicial independence and the excesses presumed by the member states. As the WTO debate has realised so well, a functional dispute settlement mechanism is needed not only to settle trade disputes but also to provide continuity to the system through the strengthening of GATT/WTO principles (Jackson, Hudec, & Davis, 2000). New phenomena like digital trade and sustainability are features of the contemporary legal order that offer both possibilities and complex for the regulation of international trade. E-commerce and data flows have become new unparalleled trends of the global trade which have developed due to the growth of the digital economy (Herman & Oliver, 2023). However, the trade rules that are currently in place are rather inadequate given that new generation trade rules were developed to govern the conventional trade of goods and services. Others are data localization policies, cross border transfers of data, cybersecurity, and protection of intellectual property in the new paradigm(Zhao, 2023). Countries desiring efficient cooperation define digital trade through formulation of a coherent and comprehensible legal system encouraging openness, non-discrimination and level playing field enforcement for economic prosperity.

Environmental issues such as those brought out by climate change also require inclusion into international trade law. Policies on trade are useful in increasing adoption and implementation of environmental friendly technologies, decreasing on carbon emission, and discouraging environmentally negative trade (Tamiotti, 2010). However, activities in the trading context as such frequently raise controversies and this is evidenced by trade and environment conflicts with regard to carbon border adjustment measures and subsidies for green energy as well as restriction on green averse importation (Felbermayr et al., 2024). Addressing these concerns poses a relatively finely-sliced task of harmonizing trade frameworks with climate obligations accepted under other multilateral arrangements like the Paris Accord. This could mean the integration of environmental measures into the trade agreements; the acknowledgement of environmental amenities as allowable under the GATT and the WTO; and the establishment of sustainable development as one of the principal goals of the liberal trade system (Segger, 2021).

Preserving geopolitical imperatives as a counterpoint to cooperation within multilateral structures constitutes perhaps the most essential and at the same time most complex task of international trade legal regulation (Muhammad, 2023). Non-discrimination and market openness principles are under pressure from nationalism trends, protectionism and strategic competition. The science of multilateral cooperation calls for political will and commitment and trust restoration among members of any international organization (Singh & Woolcock, 2022). These efforts encourage fairness in the trade negotiation procedure to make WTO legitimate. It is seen that plurilateral deals relate to the geopolitics while working for the cause of liberalizing the multilateral trade (Green, 2023). These agreements focus on information technology products and services, the environment, services, and intellectual property right, supporting innovation within WTO, but may helmet the WTO trade or exclude members that are not part of the agreement (Deane et al., 2024). In order to increase the role of plurilateral processes in the WTO, the issue of transparency and openness becomes critical. The hinderances for developing and least developed countries include for instance infrastructure, and market access (Zahoor et al., 2023). Thus, development of WTO's inclusiveness through such measures as capacity building, technical cooperation and special and differential treatment should be accompanied by structural changes that would allow for decision-making by small economies (Draper et al., 2018).

RTAs are useful supplements to the multilateral system insofar as they fill gaps in WTO governance; however, they are detrimental to the coherence of global trade commitments insofar as there is governance fragmentation due to a profusion of RTAs (Brandi & Morin, 2023). Attempting to enhance the roles of the WTO in supervision of RTAs and their conformity with multilateral systems is likely to reduce these risks and increase the compatibility of regional and global trade systems (Shadikhodjaev, 2011). Technology and innovation enhance the pressure and demand for flexibility in international trade law. For trade the new technologies like artificial intelligence, blockchain, and biotechnology have brought significant changes and new legal and regulatory challenges (Rabajante, 2024). There is therefore need to be vigilante in implementing and updating trade rules to be in tandem with technology standards in which there are provisions for review of trade agreements as well (Burri et al., 2024). It should do so in a clear, consultative, and pro-innovation manner, that recognised remarkable advances in technology for what they are — a force for productive and sustainable respective development.

Last but not least, whether the states will pursue the proposed reforms of international trade law depends on the development of the truly common value of multilateralism and cooperation based on it. This means that changes on the institutional and legal level are necessary as well as changes within the culture of the member states accepting the mutual respect and cooperation (Cottier, 2015). Achieving consensus for matters of controversy which include the subsidies for agriculture, property rights, and markets, requires member states to be ready to let go of vested interests and put the general interest first. The WTO, and other international bodies that deal with trade relations must therefore act as forums where States can discuss and make negotiations to overcome these challenges.

CONCLUSION

The reform of international trade law is a pertinent exercise since the world is ever transforming at the regional, international and national level due to changed geopolitics, trade dynamics, and new challenges. As the unipolar system shifts from the American hegemony, new economic players have emerged and China has emerged to challenge the status quo of global trade. Various aspects of this change have profound implications for the legal structures of the multilateral trading system, and it becomes imperative that international trade law adapts to these changes. The WTO has been the key institution governing the international trade because it provided a framework for the relationship in the global market. But there are numerous challenges that the organization has to overcome in this new geopolitics world. Nevertheless, the WTO's most formidable asset, the Dispute Settlement Mechanism, is at present in severe turmoil and its Appellate Body cannot function since December 2019. This has created paralysis in the institution leading to poor or lack of enforcement of trade rules thus ridiculing the credibility of the institution. These reforms must be designed to correct such a dysfunction and ensure that the process of settling the dispute is revived and opened for all Members. This could mean changing the mechanism of handling disputes with a view of fast-tracking the processes and handling challenges that have held the system emanating procedural complications. Improvement of the WTO capability would therefore help extend a social fabric that adequately provides for the evolution of new trade challenges and sustenance of the rule based system. In addition to these institutional matters, there is a question of the post-1990s so-called regional trade agreements (RTAs). These agreements involve more involvement and more particular provisions than the WTO arrangement; however, they may have the WTO's proliferation problem in world exchange. Thus, although RTAs can be helpful in supporting multilateral work, their growing number can pose a threat to the new Pos and fairness of the GTS. But change to the international trade law must take account of the need for RTAs not to undermine the WTO accord or multilateralism. This can be done through better coordination of regional and global trade machinery and the harmonization of this with wider international goals and policies. Through spurring of coherence and inclusion in the global trade system, these reforms will increase guaranty that RTAs are not going to result in fragmentation of trade rules.

This chapter argues that emerging powers led by China have revolutionised the global economy. This new power wish to engage in the direction of the organization and trade governance, they deny the principles and rules long applied in international trade law. Such change means that international trade law must search for ways of balancing these emerging nations' needs and aspirations with the extant legal framework. One aspect of this is there is evidence that there is rising trend in economic nationalism, whereby states are using trade instruments for geopolitical and security reasons. The measures of trade sanctions, export controls, tariffs, and other protectionisms measures have increased over time which are prejudicial to non-discriminatory plus open-market ethos that the WTO aims to champion. These measures are sometimes used on the pretext of national security although their application should be more thoroughly controlled to meet the obligations under the GATT. Thus while the use of the national security exceptions are important in some instance they should not be deployed in a way that at end distorts the trading system. There is no doubt that legal systems have to address the reasonable threats which the sovereign states pose, while keeping in mind the principles of an open and equitable commerce.

New and inherently more contemporary themes like digital trade or environmental sustainability are also becoming core to the discursive formation of the future of the international trade law. Digital trade and technological advancement has therefore introduced new trade characteristics which traditional trade systems are not well designed to address. The present structure of international trade law, developed currently for tangible items and services, is not suited for digital trade. In this area, legal reform should focus on fulfilling clear, non-discriminatory and transparent rules on transfer and protection of data, intellectual property and digital commerce in order to meet the necessary legal frameworks of digital trade for the future technological advancements without prejudice to anyone. Also, environmental issues are gradually becoming the subject of discourses on trade liberalization. Trade policy has his prerogative in engaging sustainable development and the contingent legal regime of trade ought to evolve into another world to approve environmental problems. With rising upheaval of global climate and environmental standards, trade law can act as a drive towards adoption of green technologies and sustainable conducts. Trade related environmental measures can facilitate the promotion of environmental opportunities in trade while at the same time ensuring that the promotion of trades does not compromise the capacity of countries to pursue their environmental objectives. On the positive side, attempts such as the process of involving environmental standards into trade relations and creation of ways, which would allow combating with CO2 emissions based on trade relations, are significant steps towards linking trade law with more general processes of global sustainability.

The idea of using trade as an instrument of foreign policy has been extended noticeably, the economic lever is actively applied to put pressure on certain state or to defend national interests. Sanction, tariffs, export control and certain measure of ban are commonly used for geopolitical motives. These practices have generated considerable legal issues on the conformity with international trade relation. National security exceptions in ILA reveal relative discretion, however, their misuse comprise diminishing the fact of trade reputable structure. Any reform must aim at improving such measures for them to meet the international law and WTO Regex framework in the application of measures that are transparent, accountable and proportional.

REFERENCES

Ababakr, A. (2024). Global trade governance and WTO: Beyond the model of the club. *Asian Social Science, 18*(2), 32–32. DOI: 10.5539/ass.v18n2p32

Abbas, M., & Duchesne, E. (2023). Beyond the failure of the WTO: Resilience of trade multilateralism. In Guilbaud, A., Petiteville, F., & Ramel, F. (Eds.), *Crisis of multilateralism? Challenges and resilience* (pp. 211–227). Palgrave Macmillan. DOI: 10.1007/978-3-031-39671-7_10

Abugre, J. A., Nellis, J., & Ofosu-Dorte, D. (2024). Impact of political and legal environments on international trade. In Ocran, M. K., & Abor, J. Y. (Eds.), *The Palgrave handbook of international trade and development in Africa* (pp. 47–67). Palgrave Macmillan. DOI: 10.1007/978-3-031-65715-3_3

Abuseridze, G. (2023). The multifaceted landscape of WTO law: A comprehensive examination of its principles, rules and institutional structure. *Innovative Economics and Management, 10*(2), 18–25. DOI: 10.46361/2449-2604.10.2.2023.18-25

Aggarwal, V. K. (2016). Mega-FTAs and the trade-security nexus: The Trans-Pacific Partnership (TPP) and Regional Comprehensive Economic Partnership (RCEP). *East-West Center*. https://www.jstor.org/stable/resrep06450

Alexandroff, A. S., & Sharma, R. (2005). The national security provision—GATT Article XXI. In Macrory, P. F. J., Appleton, A. E., & Plummer, M. G. (Eds.), *The World Trade Organization: Legal, economic and political analysis* (pp. 701–716). Springer. DOI: 10.1007/0-387-22688-5_35

Aliaj, K., & Mekaj, G. (2019). Legal aspects of international trade. *ILIRIA International Review, 8*(2). Advance online publication. DOI: 10.21113/iir.v8i2.444

Andenas, M., & Zleptnig, S. (2007). Proportionality and balancing in WTO law: A comparative perspective. *Cambridge Review of International Affairs, 20*(1), 71–92. DOI: 10.1080/09557570701232233

Ansong, A. (2019). The WTO Appellate Body: Are there any viable solutions? *Global Trade and Customs Journal, 14*(3), 169–178. DOI: 10.54648/GTCJ2019016

Ashraf, N. (2023). Revisiting international relations legacy on hegemony: The decline of American hegemony from comparative perspectives. *Review of Economics and Political Science, 8*(6), 410–426. DOI: 10.1108/REPS-05-2019-0061

Bacchus, J. (2022, June 17). WTO steps back from the abyss of irrelevance . . . but crucial issues remain unresolved. *Cato Institute*. https://www.cato.org/blog/wto-steps-back-abyss-irrelevance-crucial-issues-remain-unresolved

Barbieri, K. (2024). Geopolitics and international trade. In Cope, Z. (Ed.), *The Palgrave handbook of contemporary geopolitics* (pp. 49–1). Palgrave Macmillan. DOI: 10.1007/978-3-031-25399-7_49-1

Bäumler, J. (2020). The WTO's crisis: Between a rock and a hard place. In Bungenberg, M., Krajewski, M., Tams, C. J., Terhechte, J. P., & Ziegler, A. R. (Eds.), *European Yearbook of International Economic Law 2020* (Vol. 11). Springer. DOI: 10.1007/8165_2020_60

Benalleg, H. (2023). *International laws of trade and investment: A comprehensive study of legal frameworks, challenges, and implications* (02). DOI: 10.5281/zenodo.8083049

Bıçakcıoğlu-Peynirci, N. (2023). Internationalization of emerging market multinational enterprises: A systematic literature review and future directions. *Journal of Business Research, 164*, 114002. Advance online publication. DOI: 10.1016/j.jbusres.2023.114002

Bouët, A., & Laborde, D. (2018). US trade wars in the twenty-first century with emerging countries: Make America and its partners lose again. *World Economy, 41*(9), 2276–2319. DOI: 10.1111/twec.12719

Brandi, C., & Morin, J.-F. (2023). *Trade and the environment: Drivers and effects of environmental provisions in trade agreements*. Cambridge University Press. DOI: 10.1017/9781009461825

Breslin, S., & Nesadurai, H. E. S. (2023). Economic statecraft, geoeconomics and regional political economies. *The Pacific Review, 36*(5), 927–948. DOI: 10.1080/09512748.2023.2200030

Burri, M., Vásquez Callo-Müller, M., & Kugler, K. (2024). The evolution of digital trade law: Insights from TAPED. *World Trade Review, 23*(2), 190–207. DOI: 10.1017/S1474745623000472

Chandran, S. (2017). Why do countries enter into regional trade agreements? Insights from the literature. SSRN *Electronic Journal*. DOI: 10.2139/ssrn.3024684

Charnovitz, S. (1996). Trade measures and the design of international regimes. *Journal of Environment & Development, 5*(2), 168–196. DOI: 10.1177/107049659600500204

Chen, L., & De Lombaerde, P. (2019). ASEAN between globalization and regionalization. *Asia Pacific Business Review*, *25*(1), 1–22. DOI: 10.1080/13602381.2019.1652982

Chin, G. (2010). The emerging countries and China in the G20: Reshaping global economic governance. *Studia Diplomatica, 63*(2), 105–123. https://www.jstor.org/stable/44838598

Chow, D. C. K., Schoenbaum, T. J., & Dorris, G. C. (2021). *International trade law: Problems, cases, and materials* (Ohio State Legal Studies Research Paper No. 654). Aspen Publishers. DOI: 10.2139/ssrn.3924952

Cima, E., & Esty, D. C. (2024). Making international trade work for sustainable development: Toward a new WTO framework for subsidies. *Journal of International Economic Law*, *27*(1), 1–17. DOI: 10.1093/jiel/jgae008

Cohen, H. G. (2018). What is international trade law for? *American Journal of International Law*, 113(4), forthcoming. IILJ Working Paper 2018/6 (MegaReg Series). University of Georgia School of Law Legal Studies Research Paper No. 2018-44. Dean Rusk International Center Research Paper No. 2018-08. https://ssrn.com/abstract=3298389

Cottier, T. (2015). The common law of international trade and the future of the World Trade Organization. *Journal of International Economic Law*, *18*(1), 3–20. DOI: 10.1093/jiel/jgv005

Cottier, T. (2021). Recalibrating the WTO dispute settlement system: Towards new standards of appellate review. *Journal of International Economic Law*, *24*(3), 515–533. DOI: 10.1093/jiel/jgab024

Dadkhah, K. (2009). The post-war economic order. In *The evolution of macroeconomic theory and policy* (pp. [insert page numbers]). Springer. DOI: 10.1007/978-3-540-77008-4_2

Deane, F., Woolmer, E., Cao, S., & Tranter, K. (2024). Trade in the digital age: Agreements to mitigate fragmentation. *Asian Journal of International Law*, *14*(1), 154–179. DOI: 10.1017/S204425132300036X

Diebold, N. F. (2011). Standards of non-discrimination in international economic law. *The International and Comparative Law Quarterly*, *60*(4), 831–865. DOI: 10.1017/S0020589311000418

Doan, H. T. T., & Zhang, H. (2024). Technical barriers to trade, product quality and trade margins: Firm-level evidence. *Review of World Economics*, *160*(3), 785–811. DOI: 10.1007/s10290-023-00514-4

Draper, P., Freytag, A., Dörffel, C., & Schuhmann, S. (2018). Trade, inclusive development, and the global order. *Global Summitry*, *4*(1), 30–49. DOI: 10.1093/global/guz001

Duong, T. T. T. (2024). International law: From fragmentation to integration? An analysis of the relationship between international trade law and international labor law in multilateral and regional trade law frameworks. *Asia Europe Journal*, *22*(2), 293–311. DOI: 10.1007/s10308-024-00701-4

Egger, P., Syropoulos, C., & Yotov, Y. V. (2024). Analyzing the effects of economic sanctions: Recent theory, data, and quantification. *Review of International Economics*, *32*(1), 1–11. DOI: 10.1111/roie.12724

Fajgelbaum, P. D., Goldberg, P. K., Kennedy, P. J., & Khandelwal, A. K. (2020). The return to protectionism. *The Quarterly Journal of Economics*, *135*(1), 1–55. DOI: 10.1093/qje/qjz036

Falvey, R., & Foster-McGregor, N. (2022). The breadth of preferential trade agreements and the margins of exports. *Review of World Economics*, *158*(1), 181–251. DOI: 10.1007/s10290-021-00430-5

Felbermayr, G., Peterson, S., & Wanner, J. (2024). Trade and the environment, trade policies and environmental policies—How do they interact? *Journal of Economic Surveys*, 1–37. DOI: 10.1111/joes.12628

Freund, C., & Ornelas, E. (2010). Regional trade agreements. *Annual Review of Economics*, *2*(1), 139–166. DOI: 10.1146/annurev.economics.102308.124455

Gao, H. (2021). Finding a rule-based solution to the Appellate Body crisis: Looking beyond the multiparty interim appeal arbitration arrangement. *Journal of International Economic Law*, *24*(3), 534–550. DOI: 10.1093/jiel/jgab031

Garcia, F. J. (2007). Developing a normative critique of international trade law: Special & differential treatment. *TranState Working Papers* (No. 66). Universität Bremen, Collaborative Research Center 597 - Transformations of the State. https://hdl.handle.net/10419/2497

Garner-Knapp, L., Western, S. D., & Lovat, H. (2022). The US, the WTO, and the Appellate Body: From Great Expectations to Hard Times. In J. Bäumler et al. (Eds.), *European Yearbook of International Economic Law 2021* (Vol. 12). Springer. DOI: 10.1007/8165_2021_76

Góes, C., & Bekkers, E. (2022). The impact of geopolitical conflicts on trade, growth, and innovation. *arXiv*.

Green, P. F. (2023). Ameliorating global challenges: Globalization, geopolitics, basic & applied research, and research security. *MRS Bulletin*, *48*(10), 964–967. DOI: 10.1557/s43577-023-00600-w

Guan, H. (2024). On the reform of WTO dispute settlement mechanism and suggestions. *Advances in Economics. Management and Political Sciences*, *71*(1), 185–191. DOI: 10.54254/2754-1169/71/20241487

Hanada, E. (2020). Trump vs. China? Tariffs under Section 232 of the Trade Expansion Act of 1962 revisited. *Vienna Journal of East Asian Studies*, *12*(1), 207–251. DOI: 10.2478/vjeas-2020-0008

Herman, P. R., & Oliver, S. (2023). Trade, policy, and economic development in the digital economy. *Journal of Development Economics*, *164*, 103135. DOI: 10.1016/j.jdeveco.2023.103135

Hoekman, B., Tu, X., & Wolfe, R. (2023). China and WTO reform. In Gao, H., Raess, D., & Zeng, K. (Eds.), *China and the WTO: A twenty-year assessment* (pp. 275–298). Cambridge University Press. DOI: 10.1017/9781009291804.017

Hopewell, K. (2020). Trump & trade: The crisis in the multilateral trading system. *New Political Economy*, *26*(1), 1–12. DOI: 10.1080/13563467.2020.1841135

Horváthy, B. (2020). International trade law and emerging technologies: A conceptual framework. *Bratislava Law Review*, *4*(2), 9–20. DOI: 10.46282/blr.2020.4.2.201

Howse, R., & Langille, J. (2023). Continuity and change in the World Trade Organization: Pluralism past, present, and future. *The American Journal of International Law*, *117*(1), 1–47. DOI: 10.1017/ajil.2022.82

Hurrell, A. (2024). Geopolitics and global economic governance. *Oxford Review of Economic Policy*, *40*(2), 220–233. DOI: 10.1093/oxrep/grae013

Huzaifa, A., & Legacy, S. (2024). Trade wars and tariffs: Examining the intersection of international relations and economic security. *ResearchGate*. https://doi.org/DOI: 10.13140/RG.2.2.22058.73928

Jackson, J. H., Hudec, R. E., & Davis, D. (2000). The role and effectiveness of the WTO dispute settlement mechanism [with comments and discussion]. *Brookings Trade Forum*, *2000*(1), 179–236. https://www.jstor.org/stable/25063150. DOI: 10.1353/btf.2000.0007

Jackson, M., & Paddeu, F. I. (2024). The countermeasures of others: When can states collaborate in the taking of countermeasures? *The American Journal of International Law*, *118*(2), 231–274. DOI: 10.1017/ajil.2024.8

Jakubik, A., Keck, A., & Piermartini, R. (2022). Trade policy implications of a changing world: Tariffs and market power. *Applied Economics Letters*, *31*(9), 783–787. DOI: 10.1080/13504851.2022.2150140

James, W. E. (2005). Rules of origin and rules of preference and the World Trade Organization: The challenge to global trade liberalization. In P. F. J. Macrory, A. E. Appleton, & M. G. Plummer (Eds.), *The World Trade Organization: Legal, economic and political analysis* (pp. [insert specific pages]). Springer. DOI: 10.1007/0-387-22688-5_48

Janusch, H., & Mucha, W. (2017). America first: Power and geopolitics in US trade policy under President Trump. *Sicherheit und Frieden (S+F) / Security and Peace, 35*(3), 110–114. https://www.jstor.org/stable/26428648

Kanetake, M. (2021). Dual-use export control: Security and human rights challenges to multilateralism. In Bungenberg, M., Krajewski, M., Tams, C. J., Terhechte, J. P., & Ziegler, A. R. (Eds.), *European Yearbook of International Economic Law 2020* (Vol. 11). Springer. DOI: 10.1007/8165_2021_67

Kaushal, L. A. (2021). Impact of regional trade agreements on export efficiency – A case study of India. *Cogent Economics & Finance*, *10*(1), 2008090. Advance online publication. DOI: 10.1080/23322039.2021.2008090

Khan, M., Sandano, I., Pratt, C., & Farid, T. (2018). China's Belt and Road Initiative: A global model for an evolving approach to sustainable regional development. *Sustainability (Basel)*, *10*(11), 4234. DOI: 10.3390/su10114234

Khatoon, A., & Sakeena, . (2022). China's Belt and Road Initiative: An analysis of its role in global peace, development, and implications. *Journal of Humanities Social and Management Sciences*, *3*(2), 40–61. DOI: 10.47264/idea.jhsms/3.2.3

Kim, J. (2012). The evolution of preferential rules of origin in ASEAN's RTAs: A guide to multilateral harmonization. *Journal of World Trade*, *46*(6), 1343–1364. DOI: 10.54648/TRAD2012042

Lehne, J. (2019). Crisis at the WTO: Is the blocking of appointments to the WTO Appellate Body by the United States legally justified? *SSRN*. DOI: 10.24921/2019.94115941

Li, S., & Wang, Y. (2024). China's perspective on applying for the CPTPP: Enhancing economic interdependence as a hedging approach in great power rivalry. *China International Strategy Review*, *6*(1), 78–99. DOI: 10.1007/s42533-024-00154-9

Lipkan, V., Kuznichenko, O., & Ivanov, A. (2023). Geoeconomics as a tool of modern geostrategy. *Baltic Journal of Economic Studies*, *9*(1), 113–123. DOI: 10.30525/2256-0742/2023-9-1-113-123

Liu, H., Xu, C., & Lim, G. (2023). The China effect on regional economic integration: A longitudinal study of Central, South, and Southeast Asia. *Journal of the Asia Pacific Economy*, *29*(4), 2110–2132. DOI: 10.1080/13547860.2023.2258018

Luo, Y. (2024). Paradigm shift and theoretical implications for the era of global disorder. *Journal of International Business Studies*, *55*(1), 127–135. DOI: 10.1057/s41267-023-00659-2

Ma, H., & Ning, J. (2024). The return of protectionism: Prospects for Sino-US trade relations in the wake of the trade war. *China Economic Quarterly International*, *4*(3), 182–211. DOI: 10.1016/j.ceqi.2024.09.003

Madhumitha, B. (2020). WTO—Analysis of issues with the dispute settlement mechanism. *Beijing Law Review*, *11*(4), 879–888. DOI: 10.4236/blr.2020.114052

Malikova, R. (2021). National security exception under the GATT Article XXI as the most problematic issue of today's trading system. *SSRN*. DOI: 10.2139/ssrn.3759338

Mansoor, I. U. (2021). Globalization and role of WTO in bridging the inequalities between member countries. *SSRN*. DOI: 10.2139/ssrn.5019105

Mansoor, S. I. (2025). Renewable energy and international law: Managing risk in relation to economic volatility and geopolitical instability. In Özsungur, F., Chaychi Semsari, M., & Küçük Bayraktar, H. (Eds.), *Geopolitical landscapes of renewable energy and urban growth* (pp. 97–124). IGI Global Scientific Publishing. DOI: 10.4018/979-8-3693-8814-3.ch004

Mansoor, S. I., Shah, M. A., Khan, H., Ghazali, A., Jan, S., & Utagi, S. H. (2025). Modern democracies and economic sanctions: A legal perspective on security and sovereignty. In Alaverdov, E., & Abuseridze, G. (Eds.), *Globalization, global security, and new international realities for modern democracies* (pp. 173–198). IGI Global Scientific Publishing. DOI: 10.4018/979-8-3373-1355-9.ch008

Mansoor, S. I. U. (2021). TRIPS Agreement's obligations and their repercussion on developing countries during emergency situations. *Ilkogretim Online*, *20*(1), 6021–6031.

Mansoor, S. I. U. (2023). China's geopolitical strategy: Crafting a new world order. *China Quarterly of International Strategic Studies*, *9*(1), 337–359. DOI: 10.1142/S2377740023500161

Mansoor, S. I. U., & Chopra, M. (2022). WTO and developing nations: Disparities in the WTO dispute settlement mechanism. *International Journal of Early Childhood Special Education*, *10*, 4441–4449.

Mansoor, U., & Inam, S. (2024). National security or trade openness? The balancing act in contemporary trade relations. *IUP Law Review, 14*(3).

Marceau, G. (2016). The World Trade Organization and export restrictions. In Matsushita, M., & Schoenbaum, T. (Eds.), *Emerging issues in sustainable development: Economics, law, and institutions in Asia Pacific* (pp. 113–136). Springer. DOI: 10.1007/978-4-431-56426-3_6

Martin, A., & Vergote, W. (2008). On the role of retaliation in trade agreements. *Journal of International Economics*, *76*(1), 61–77. DOI: 10.1016/j.jinteco.2008.03.009

Martínez-Zarzoso, I., & Chelala, S. (2021). Trade agreements and international technology transfer. *Review of World Economics*, *157*(3), 631–665. DOI: 10.1007/s10290-021-00420-7

Matsushita, M., Schoenbaum, T., Mavroidis, P., & Hahn, M. (2003). *The World Trade Organization: Law, practice, and policy*. DOI: 10.1093/law/9780199571857.001.0001

Muhammad, A. (2023). The geopolitical implications of shifting alliances in a multipolar world. *Zenodo*. https://doi.org/DOI: 10.5281/zenodo.8382207

Narine, S. (2018). US domestic politics and America's withdrawal from the Trans-Pacific Partnership: Implications for Southeast Asia. *Contemporary Southeast Asia*, *40*(1), 50–76. DOI: 10.1355/cs40-1c

Nesselrodt, R. (2023). Controlling for X: Export controls and emerging technology competition. *Journal of Science Policy & Governance*, *22*(3). Advance online publication. DOI: 10.38126/JSPG220306

Ni, J. (2024). A decade of the Belt and Road Initiative and its global impact. *China Economic Journal*, *17*(2), 137–139. DOI: 10.1080/17538963.2024.2345532

Park, S. C. (2020). Protectionism as challenges for the global trade governance. In Rewizorski, M., Jędrzejowska, K., & Wróbel, A. (Eds.), *The future of global economic governance* (pp. 99–113). Springer. DOI: 10.1007/978-3-030-35336-0_7

Rabajante, M. D. F. (2024). Artificial Intelligence and international trade law. In A. Poorhashemi (Ed.), *Artificial intelligence and the future of international law* (pp. 35–50). SpringerBriefs in Law. Springer. DOI: 10.1007/978-3-031-73334-5_3

Rasch, F. A., & Shrimali, M. (2024). Protectionism by governments, the retrenchment of globalization and national security. In A. K. Nagar, D. S. Jat, D. Mishra, & A. Joshi (Eds.), *Intelligent sustainable systems. WorldS4 2023* (Vol. 812, pp. 523-536). Lecture Notes in Networks and Systems. Springer. DOI: 10.1007/978-981-99-8031-4_42

Ren, Z. (2023). Analysis of trade competitiveness and complementarity between China and RCEP members. *Advances in Economics. Management and Political Sciences, 18*(1), 150–160. DOI: 10.54254/2754-1169/18/20230067

Roberts, A. (2008). International relations after the Cold War. *International Affairs (Royal Institute of International Affairs 1944-), 84*(2), 335–350. https://www.jstor.org/stable/25144768

Sacerdoti, G., Semercioglu, N., Famà, R., Assenza, E., Wade, D., & Lapa, V. (2021). *The WTO Dispute Settlement System in 2020: Facing the Appellate Body Paralysis*. Bocconi Legal Studies Research Paper No. 37944327. DOI: 10.2139/ssrn.3794327

Sampson, G. P. (2018). Challenges facing the World Trade Organization: An overview. *The Australian Economic Review, 51*(4), 453–473. DOI: 10.1111/1467-8462.12301

Sampson, M. (2019). The evolution of China's regional trade agreements: Power dynamics and the future of the Asia-Pacific. *The Pacific Review, 34*(2), 259–289. DOI: 10.1080/09512748.2019.1660397

Samunderu, E. (2024). Liberalisation of trade regime under AfCFTA: A perspective analysis on Africa's single market. In *The Economic Effects of Air Transport Market Liberalisation. Advances in African Economic, Social and Political Development* (pp. 123–145). Springer. DOI: 10.1007/978-3-031-61864-2_7

Segger, M.-C. (2021). Integrating social and environmental considerations into trade and investment agreements, for sustainable development. In *Sustainable Development in International Trade and Investment Law* (Chapter 22). DOI: 10.1093/oso/9780198831341.003.0022

Shadikhodjaev, S. (2011). Checking RTA compatibility with global trade rules: WTO litigation practice and implications from the transparency mechanism for RTAs. *Journal of World Trade, 45*(3), 529–551. DOI: 10.54648/TRAD2011018

Shaffer, G. (2021). The challenges of international trade law. In *Emerging powers and the world trading system: The past and future of international economic law* (pp. 58–78). Cambridge University Press. DOI: 10.1017/9781108861342.004

Simões, F. D. (2019). The Appellate Body of the WTO: An international court by another name. In Bungenberg, M., Krajewski, M., Tams, C. J., Terhechte, J. P., & Ziegler, A. R. (Eds.), *European Yearbook of International Economic Law 2019* (Vol. 10, pp. 8165–8179). Springer. DOI: 10.1007/8165_2019_33

Singh, J. P., & Woolcock, M. (2022). The future of multilateralism and global development: Opportunities for constitutive and functional reform. *Global Perspectives, 3*(1), 57594. DOI: 10.1525/gp.2022.57594

Smeets, M., Berger, A., Akman, S., Aran, B., Braga, C., Kher, R., Lippoldt, D., Mildner, S., Nair, A., & Schmucker, C. (2023). Reforming the WTO through inclusive and development-friendly plurilaterals. *Journal of World Trade*, *57*, 875–888. DOI: 10.54648/TRAD2023036

Stephen, M. D., & Parízek, M. (2018). New powers and the distribution of preferences in global trade governance: From deadlock and drift to fragmentation. *New Political Economy*, *24*(6), 735–758. DOI: 10.1080/13563467.2018.1509065

Suwanprasert, W. (2020). The role of the most favored nation principle of the GATT/WTO in the new trade model. *Review of International Economics*, *28*(3), 760–798. Advance online publication. DOI: 10.1111/roie.12470

Tamiotti, L. (2010). Trade and the environment: Fundamental issues in international law, WTO law and legal theory by Erich Vranes. *World Trade Review*, *9*(1), 285–288. DOI: 10.1017/S147474560999022X

ThankGod. (2023). *Artificial intelligence and international trade law: Navigating legal challenges in the age of automation*. SSRN. DOI: 10.2139/ssrn.4706943

Ul Mansoor, S. I. (2023). China's geopolitical strategy: Crafting a new world order. *China Quarterly of International Strategic Studies*, *9*(1–4), 337–359. DOI: 10.1142/S2377740023500161

Ul Mansoor, S. I. (2023). China's geopolitical strategy: Crafting a new world order. *China Quarterly of International Strategic Studies*, *9*(01–04), 337–359.

Wang, C. (2019). Invocation of national security exceptions under GATT Article XXI: Jurisdiction to review and standard of review. *Chinese Journal of International Law*, *18*(4), 695–712. DOI: 10.1093/chinesejil/jmz029

Wang, J. (2023). China and international trade law: Rising from within the system or always an outlier? *International Journal of Environmental Research and Public Health*, *18*(22), 11991. DOI: 10.3390/ijerph182211991

Xiao, B., Peng, Y., & Yu, W. (2024). The WTO institutional structure and dispute settlement practice. In *The practice of WTO dispute settlement: Modern China and international economic law*. Springer. DOI: 10.1007/978-981-97-0185-8_1

Yang, Y. (2021). Crisis and reform direction of WTO Appellate Body. *Advances in Social Science, Education and Humanities Research*. Advance online publication. DOI: 10.2991/assehr.k.210916.015

Zahoor, N., Wu, J., Khan, H., & Khan, Z. (2023). De-globalization, international trade protectionism, and the reconfigurations of global value chains. *MIR. Management International Review*, *63*(5), 823–859. DOI: 10.1007/s11575-023-00522-4

Zhao, L. (2023). The reconstruction and innovation of international economic and trade rules. In *Modern China and international rules. Modern China and international economic law*. Springer. DOI: 10.1007/978-981-19-7576-9_3

Zuev, V. (2022). Regional trade agreements: A hope or a threat to the global trade? In Karhu, A., & Haaja, E. (Eds.), *Global trade and trade governance during deglobalization* (pp. 55–72). International Political Economy Series. Palgrave Macmillan. DOI: 10.1007/978-3-031-13757-0_4

Compilation of References

Aaltola, M., Käpylä, J., Mikkola, H., & Behr, T. (2014). *Towards the Geopolitics of Flows: Implications for Finland, FIIA Report No. 40*. The Finnish Institute of International Affairs. Available at www.fiia.fi/en/publication/towards-the-geopolitics-of-flows

Ab Aziz, N. H., & Alshdaifat, S. M. (2025). ESG Reporting: Impacts, Benefits and Challenges. In Alshurafat, H., Hamdan, A., & Sands, J. (Eds.), *Sustainable Horizons for Business, Education, and Technology* (pp. 69–76). Springer Nature.

Ababakr, A. (2024). Global trade governance and WTO: Beyond the model of the club. *Asian Social Science*, *18*(2), 32–32. DOI: 10.5539/ass.v18n2p32

Abbas, M., & Duchesne, E. (2023). Beyond the failure of the WTO: Resilience of trade multilateralism. In Guilbaud, A., Petiteville, F., & Ramel, F. (Eds.), *Crisis of multilateralism? Challenges and resilience* (pp. 211–227). Palgrave Macmillan. DOI: 10.1007/978-3-031-39671-7_10

Abdallah, S., & Nizamuddin, N. (2023). Blockchain-based solution for pharma supply chain industry. *Computers & Industrial Engineering*, *177*, 108997. Advance online publication. DOI: 10.1016/j.cie.2023.108997

Abdellatif, H., & Graham, S. (2019). Green Supply Chain Management Practices in Developing Countries - A Case Study from Jordan. *International Journal of Simulation: Systems, Science & Technology*, 10.1-10.6.

Abdelsalam, M. A. M. (2023). Oil price fluctuations and economic growth: The case of MENA countries. Review of Economics and Political Science. DOI: 10.1108/REPS-12-2019-0162

Abdul-Salam, Y. (2022). Examining the effect of the UK oil and gas windfall tax on the economics of new fields in the UKCS province. *SSRN*. DOI: 10.2139/ssrn.4220963

Abid, M. (2016). Does economic, financial and institutional developments matter for environmental quality? A comparative analysis of EU and MEA countries. *Journal of Environmental Management*, 183–194.

Abugre, J. A., Nellis, J., & Ofosu-Dorte, D. (2024). Impact of political and legal environments on international trade. In Ocran, M. K., & Abor, J. Y. (Eds.), *The Palgrave handbook of international trade and development in Africa* (pp. 47–67). Palgrave Macmillan. DOI: 10.1007/978-3-031-65715-3_3

Abuseridze, G. (2023). The multifaceted landscape of WTO law: A comprehensive examination of its principles, rules and institutional structure. *Innovative Economics and Management, 10*(2), 18–25. DOI: 10.46361/2449-2604.10.2.2023.18-25

Adjei-Bamfo, P., Maloreh-Nyamekye, T., & Ahenkan, A. (2019). The role of e-government in sustainable public procurement in developing countries: A systematic literature review. *Resources, Conservation and Recycling*, 189–203.

Adrian, T. (2022). Interest rate increases and volatile markets signal rising financial stability risks. International Monetary Fund. https://www.imf.org/en/Blogs/Articles/2022/10/11/interest-rate-increases-volatile-markets-signal-rising-financial-stability-risks

AFDB. (2022). *How Rwanda is using Artificial Intelligence to improve healthcare*. Retrieved from African Development Bank: https://www.afdb.org/en/success-stories/how-rwanda-using-artificial-intelligence-improve-healthcare-55309

AfDB. (2025). *East Africa Economic Outlook 2024*. Retrieved from afdb.org: https://www.afdb.org/sites/default/files/documents/publications/reo_east_africa_english_2024.pdf

Africa, E. (2025). *Kenyan Startup Leta Raises $5 Million to Boost AI-Powered Logistics Platform in Africa*. Retrieved from Empower Africa: https://empowerafrica.com/kenyan-startup-leta-raises-5-million-to-boost-ai-powered-logistics-platform-in-africa/

Aggarwal, V. K. (2016). Mega-FTAs and the trade-security nexus: The Trans-Pacific Partnership (TPP) and Regional Comprehensive Economic Partnership (RCEP). *East-West Center*. https://www.jstor.org/stable/resrep06450

Ahearn, R. J. (2009, March). *The global economic downturn and protectionism*. Congressional Research Service, Library of Congress.

Ahmad, A., Ikram, A., Rehan, M. F., & Ahmad, A. (2022). Going green: Impact of green supply chain management practices on sustainability performance. *Frontiers in Psychology*, 1-12.

Aizenman, J., Lindahl, R., Stenvall, D., & Uddin, G. S. (2024). Geopolitical shocks and commodity market dynamics: New evidence from the Russia-Ukraine conflict. *European Journal of Political Economy, 85*, 102574. DOI: 10.1016/j.ejpoleco.2024.102574

Ajayi, S. I. (2006). *FDI and economic development in Africa*. ADB/AERC International.

Ajide, F. M., Osinubi, T. T., Oladipupo, S. A., & Soyode, E. O. (2025). Economic complexity in Africa: The role of Chinese FDI and trade. *Journal of Chinese Economic and Foreign Trade Studies, 18*(1), 86–108. DOI: 10.1108/JCEFTS-07-2024-0063

Akizhanov, K. B. (2023). Argentina: Entrenching Income Inequality. In *Finance Capitalism and Income Inequality in the Contemporary Global Economy: A Comparative Study of the USA, South Korea, Argentina and Sweden* (pp. 125–152). Springer International Publishing. DOI: 10.1007/978-3-031-21768-5_6

Al Mustofa, M. U., & Risyad, M. H. (2025). Geopolitical risk and foreign direct investment: The role of liberalization, institutions and financial markets. *Studies in Economics and Finance, 42*(4), 730–758. DOI: 10.1108/SEF-09-2024-0621

Alessandrini, D. (2010). *Developing countries and the multilateral trade regime: The failure and promise of the WTO's development mission*. Bloomsbury Publishing.

Alexandroff, A. S., & Sharma, R. (2005). The national security provision—GATT Article XXI. In Macrory, P. F. J., Appleton, A. E., & Plummer, M. G. (Eds.), *The World Trade Organization: Legal, economic and political analysis* (pp. 701–716). Springer. DOI: 10.1007/0-387-22688-5_35

Alfaro, L., & Chor, D. (2023). Global supply chains: The looming "great reallocation". https://www.nber.org/papers/w31661

Alfaro, L. (2017). Gains from foreign direct investment: Macro and micro approaches. *The World Bank Economic Review, 30*(Supplement_1), S2–S15.

Al-Farsi, S., Rathore, M. M., & Bakiras, S. (2021). Security of blockchain-based supply chain management systems: Challenges and opportunities. *Applied Sciences (Basel, Switzerland), 11*(12), 5585. Advance online publication. DOI: 10.3390/app11125585

Aliaj, K., & Mekaj, G. (2019). Legal aspects of international trade. *ILIRIA International Review, 8*(2). Advance online publication. DOI: 10.21113/iir.v8i2.444

Ali, Z. H., Ali, H. A., & Badawy, M. M. (2015). Internet of Things (IoT): Definitions, Challenges, and Recent Research Directions. *International Journal of Computer Applications*, 37–46.

Aljohani, A. (2023). Predictive analytics and machine learning for real-time supply chain risk mitigation and agility. *Sustainability (Basel)*, *15*(20), 15088. Advance online publication. DOI: 10.3390/su152015088

Allee, T. (2012). The role of the United States: A multilevel explanation for decreased support over time. Academic Press.

Allison, R. (2023). Russia's Case for War against Ukraine: Legal Claims, Political Rhetoric, and Instrumentality in a Fracturing International Order. *Problems of Post-Communism*, *71*(3), 271–282. DOI: 10.1080/10758216.2023.2254915

Almazán-Gómez, M. Á., Llano, C., Pérez, J., & Rauhut, D. (2023). Socioeconomic impacts of Russian invasion of Ukraine: A multiregional assessment for Europe. *Journal of Regional Science*, *64*(2), 333–354. DOI: 10.1111/jors.12676

Al-Saidi, M. (2023). Caught off guard and beaten: The Ukraine war and food security in the Middle East. *Frontiers in Nutrition*, *10*, 983346. Advance online publication. DOI: 10.3389/fnut.2023.983346 PMID: 36895270

Althaf, S., & Babbitt, C. W. (n.d.). Disruption risks to material supply chains in the electronics sector. Resources. https://www.elsevier.com/open-access/userlicense/1.0/

Alvstam, C., Ivarsson, I., & Petersen, B. (2020). Are Multinationals and Governments from Emerging Economies Configuring Global Value Chains in New Ways? *International Journal of Emerging Markets*, *15*(1), 111–130. DOI: 10.1108/IJOEM-02-2017-0055

AMC. (2025, 04 20). *Unilever Kenya to Source US $50 million worth of Raw Materials locally by 2025*. Retrieved from African Marketing Confederation: https://africanmarketingconfederation.org/unilever-kenya-to-source-us50m-worth-of-raw-materials-locally-by-2025/#:~:text=According%20to%20Unilever%2C%20the%20company,%2468%2Dmillion%20in%20supplier%20diversity

Amul, G. G., Ang, M., Kraybill, D., Ong, S. E., & Yoong, J. (2022). Responses to COVID-19 in Southeast Asia: Diverse paths and ongoing challenges. *Asian Economic Policy Review*, *17*(1), 90–110. DOI: 10.1111/aepr.12362

An, T.-H. T., Chen, S.-H., & Yeh, K.-C. (2023). Does financial development enhance the growth effect of FDI? A multidimensional analysis in emerging and developing Asia. *International Journal of Emerging Markets*. Advance online publication.

Andenas, M., & Zleptnig, S. (2007). Proportionality and balancing in WTO law: A comparative perspective. *Cambridge Review of International Affairs*, *20*(1), 71–92. DOI: 10.1080/09557570701232233

Anderer, C., Dür, A., & Lechner, L. (2020). Trade policy in a "GVC World": Multinational corporations and trade liberalization. *Business and Politics*, *22*(4), 639–666. DOI: 10.1017/bap.2020.4

Ansong, A. (2019). The WTO Appellate Body: Are there any viable solutions? *Global Trade and Customs Journal*, *14*(3), 169–178. DOI: 10.54648/GTCJ2019016

Antwi-Boateng, O., & Al Jaberi, N. H. S. (2022). The post-oil strategy of the UAE: An examination of diversification strategies and challenges. *Politics & Policy*, *50*(2), 380–407. Advance online publication. DOI: 10.1111/polp.12457

Anyanwu, J. C. (2012). Why does foreign direct investment go where it goes? New evidence from African countries. *Annals of Economics and Finance*, *13*(2), 425–462.

APICS. (2017). Supply Chain Operations Reference Model. Chicago, Illinois, USA.

ASEAN. (2020). *RCEP Agreement* (full text). Available at https://asean.org/wp-content/uploads/2024/10/Regional-Comprehensive-Economic-Partnership-RCEP-Agreement-Full-Text.pdf&sa=D&source=docs&ust=1739948329527261&usg=AOvVaw1UEpjIv-z9prOG8nRVTmrH

Ashraf, N. (2023). Revisiting international relations legacy on hegemony: The decline of American hegemony from comparative perspectives. *Review of Economics and Political Science*, *8*(6), 410–426. DOI: 10.1108/REPS-05-2019-0061

Ashurov, S., Abdullah Othman, A. H., & Rosman, R. (2020). The determinants of foreign direct investment in Central Asian region: A case study of Tajikistan, Kazakhstan, Kyrgyzstan, Turkmenistan and Uzbekistan (A quantitative analysis using GMM). *Russian Journal of Economics*, *6*(2), 162–176. DOI: 10.32609/j.ruje.6.48556

ASPK. (2025). *Safaricom Takes A Leap On Its Sustainability Goals in becoming a 'green' organization*. Retrieved from Association of Sustainability Practitioners in Kenya: https://aspkenya.org/general/safaricom-takes-a-leap-on-its-sustainability-goals-in-becoming-a-green-organization/

Astrov, V., Ghodsi, M., Grieveson, R., Holzner, M., Kochnev, A., Landesmann, M., Pindyuk, O., Stehrer, R., Tverdostup, M., & Bykova, A. (2022). Russia's invasion of Ukraine: Assessment of the humanitarian, economic, and financial impact in the short and medium term. *International Economics and Economic Policy*, *19*(2), 331–381. DOI: 10.1007/s10368-022-00546-5 PMID: 40478010

Ateed, E. H. (2023). The impact of Russia-Ukraine war on the global energy crisis. In *Advances in public policy and administration (APPA) book series* (pp. 119–138). DOI: 10.4018/979-8-3693-0440-2.ch007

Atkinson, A. B., & Stiglitz, J. E. (2015). *Lectures on public economics: Updated edition*. Princeton University Press.

Auerbach, A. J., Kotlikoff, L. J., & Koehler, D. (2016). U.S. inequality and fiscal progressivity: An intragenerational accounting (NBER Working Paper No. 22032). National Bureau of Economic Research. https://ssrn.com/abstract=2747187

Aunesluoma, J. (2022). Global Trade Policy Regimes and Previous Crises. In *Global Trade and Trade Governance During De-Globalization: Transforming Trade Policy for Not-So-United World* (pp. 19–30). Springer International Publishing. DOI: 10.1007/978-3-031-13757-0_2

Avi-Yonah, R. S. (2003). National regulation of multinational enterprises: An essay on comity, extraterritoriality, and harmonization. *Colum. J. Transnat'l L.*, *42*, 5.

Aydın, F. (2025). BRICS: The archetype of 21st century international cooperation alternative or challenge? In Yazdani, E. (Ed.), *Implications, prospects, and challenges in China's Global South strategy* (pp. 207–232). IGI Global. DOI: 10.4018/979-8-3373-0938-5.ch008

Ayinde, T. O., Fatai, B. O., & Adeyemi, F. A. (2024). Macroeconomic determinants of foreign direct investment in emerging economies in turbulent times–A case of COVID'19 pandemic. *Transnational Corporations Review*, *16*(4), 200079. DOI: 10.1016/j.tncr.2024.200079

Ayob, A. H., & Senik, Z. C. (2015). The role of competitive strategies on export market selection by SMEs in an emerging economy. *International Journal of Business and Globalisation*, *14*(2), 208–225. DOI: 10.1504/IJBG.2015.067436

Babić, M., Dixon, A. D., & Liu, I. T. (2022). Geoeconomics in a changing global order. In *The political economy of geoeconomics: Europe in a changing world* (pp. 1–27). Springer International Publishing. DOI: 10.1007/978-3-031-01968-5_1

Bacchus, J. (2022, June 17). WTO steps back from the abyss of irrelevance . . . but crucial issues remain unresolved. *Cato Institute*. https://www.cato.org/blog/wto-steps-back-abyss-irrelevance-crucial-issues-remain-unresolved

Bagchi, B., Paul, B., & Ghosh, R. (2024). Dynamic effects of crude oil price shocks on stock markets and exchange rates: Evidence from major oil importing countries amid Russia-Ukraine conflict. *Global Business and Economics Review*, *30*(2), 234–257. DOI: 10.1504/GBER.2024.136424

Baggs, J., & Brander, J. A. (2006). Trade liberalization, profitability, and financial leverage. *Journal of International Business Studies*, *37*(2), 196–211. DOI: 10.1057/palgrave.jibs.8400183

Bagheri, M., & Jahromi, M. J. G. (2016). Globalization and extraterritorial application of economic regulation: Crisis in international law and balancing interests. *European Journal of Law and Economics*, *41*(2), 393–429. DOI: 10.1007/s10657-012-9351-2

Baier, S. L., & Bergstrand, J. H. (2007). Do free trade agreements actually increase members' international trade? *Journal of International Economics*, *71*(1), 72–95. DOI: 10.1016/j.jinteco.2006.02.005

Balasubramanyam, V. N., Salisu, M. A., & Sapsford, D. (1996). Foreign direct investment, trade policy and economic growth. In *Trade and Development: Essays in Honour of Jagdish Bhagwati* (pp. 3–21). Palgrave Macmillan UK. DOI: 10.1007/978-1-349-25040-0_1

Balmaceda, M., Högselius, P., Johnson, C., Pleines, H., Rogers, D., & Tynkkynen, V. (2024). Rethinking energy materialities in the shadow of Russia's war on Ukraine. *Energy Research & Social Science*, *117*, 103678. DOI: 10.1016/j.erss.2024.103678

Balma, L., Heidland, T., Jävervall, S., Mahlkow, H., Mukasa, A. N., & Woldemichael, A. (2024). Long-run impacts of the conflict in Ukraine on grain imports and prices in Africa. *African Development Review*, *36*(S1). Advance online publication. DOI: 10.1111/1467-8268.12745

Balteanu, I., & Viani, F. (2023). The energy dependency of the EU and Spain. Banco de España. *Economic Bulletin*, *2023*(Q3). https://ssrn.com/abstract=4488293

Banco de Portugal. (2023). Financial stability report 2023. https://www.bportugal.pt/sites/default/files/documents/2024-02/ref_11_2023_pt.pdf

Bandekar, B. N., & Sankaranarayanan, K. G. (2017). Trends and determinants of FDI in BRICS countries: A panel data analysis. *ZENITH International Journal of Business Economics & Management Research*, *7*(11), 53–65.

Barbieri, K. (2024). Geopolitics and international trade. In Cope, Z. (Ed.), *The Palgrave handbook of contemporary geopolitics* (pp. 49–1). Palgrave Macmillan. DOI: 10.1007/978-3-031-25399-7_49-1

Barney, J. B. (1991). Firm Resources and Sustained Competitive Advantage. *Journal of Management*, 99–120.

Barro, R. J. (1981). Output effects of government purchases. *Journal of Political Economy*, *89*(6), 1086–1121. DOI: 10.1086/261024

Barton, J. H. (2006). *The Evolution of the Trade Regime: Politics, Law, and Economics of the GATT and the WTO*. Princeton University Press.

Bashar, A. M., Taher, M. A., Islam, M. K., & Ahmed, H. (2024). The Impact of Advanced Robotics and Automation on Supply Chain Efficiency in Industrial Manufacturing: A Compartive Analysis between the US and Bangladesh. *Global Mainstream Journal of Business, Economics, Development & Project Management*, 2834-2739.

Batchelder, L. L., & Kamin, D. (2019). Policy options for taxing the rich. In M. Kearney & A. Ganz (Eds.), Maintaining the strength of American capitalism (pp. 183–210). The Aspen Institute. https://ssrn.com/abstract=3634117

Bäumler, J. (2020). The WTO's crisis: Between a rock and a hard place. In Bungenberg, M., Krajewski, M., Tams, C. J., Terhechte, J. P., & Ziegler, A. R. (Eds.), *European Yearbook of International Economic Law 2020* (Vol. 11). Springer. DOI: 10.1007/8165_2020_60

Becchetti, L., Bruni, L., & Zamagni, S. (2020). The utilitarian view of welfare economics. In *The microeconomics of wellbeing and sustainability* (pp. 227–269). Springer. DOI: 10.1016/B978-0-12-816027-5.00008-2

Bednarski, L., Roscoe, S., Blome, C., & Schleper, M. C. (2024). Geopolitical disruptions in global supply chains: A state-of-the-art literature review. *Production Planning and Control*, 1–27. DOI: 10.1080/09537287.2023.2286283

Bei, G., & Celata, F. (2023). Challenges and effects of short-term rentals regulation: A counterfactual assessment of European cities. *Annals of Tourism Research, 101*, 103605. Advance online publication. DOI: 10.1016/j.annals.2023.103605

Belhadi, A., Kamble, S., Subramanian, N., Singh, R. K., & Venkatesh, M. (2024). Digital capabilities to manage agri-food supply chain uncertainties and build supply chain resilience during compounding geopolitical disruptions. *International Journal of Operations & Production Management*, *44*(11), 1914–1950. DOI: 10.1108/IJOPM-11-2022-0737

Ben Hassen, T., & El Bilali, H. (2022). Impacts of the Russia-Ukraine war on global food security: Towards more sustainable and resilient food systems? *Foods*, *11*(15), 2301. Advance online publication. DOI: 10.3390/foods11152301 PMID: 35954068

Benalleg, H. (2023). *International laws of trade and investment: A comprehensive study of legal frameworks, challenges, and implications* (02). DOI: 10.5281/zenodo.8083049

Bénassy-Quéré, A., Coupet, M., & Mayer, T. (2007). Institutional determinants of foreign direct investment. *World Economy*, *30*(5), 764–782. DOI: 10.1111/j.1467-9701.2007.01022.x

Bentham, J. (1789). *An introduction to the principles of morals and legislation*. Oxford University Press. DOI: 10.1093/oseo/instance.00077240

Bergstra, J., & Bengio, Y. (2012). Random search for hyper-parameter optimization. *Journal of Machine Learning Research*, *13*(1), 281–305.

Beverelli, C., Gourevich, I., Heiland, I., Keck, A., Larch, M., & Yotov, Y. (2023). *Trade and welfare effects of the WTO Trade Facilitation Agreement* (No. ERSD-2023-04). WTO Staff Working Paper.

Bhatnagr, P., Rajesh, A., & Misra, R. (2024a). The impact of Fintech innovations on digital currency adoption: a blockchain-based study in India. *International Journal of Accounting and Information Management*. DOI: 10.1108/IJAIM-11-2023-0275

Bhatnagr, P. (2024). Consumer insights on cultural appropriation in fashion: A Douyin analysis. *Asia Pacific Journal of Marketing and Logistics*. Advance online publication. DOI: 10.1108/APJML-07-2024-0893

Bhatnagr, P., & Rajesh, A. (2024). Artificial intelligence features and expectation confirmation theory in digital banking apps: Gen Y and Z perspective. *Management Decision*. Advance online publication. DOI: 10.1108/MD-07-2023-1145

Bhatnagr, P., Rajesh, A., & Misra, R. (2024). Neobank adoption: Integrating the information systems effectiveness framework with the innovation resistance model. *Management Decision*, *62*(10), 3315–3352. Advance online publication. DOI: 10.1108/MD-06-2023-0977

Bhatnagr, P., Rajesh, A., & Misra, R. (2024b). Continuous intention usage of artificial intelligence enabled digital banks: A review of expectation confirmation model. *Journal of Enterprise Information Management*, *37*(6), 1763–1787. DOI: 10.1108/JEIM-11-2023-0617

Bhatnagr, P., Rajesh, A., & Misra, R. (2024c). A study on driving factors for enhancing financial performance and customer-centricity through digital banking. *International Journal of Quality and Service Sciences*, *16*(2), 218–250. DOI: 10.1108/IJQSS-09-2023-0141

Bhattacharjee, A., Gaur, D., & Gupta, K. (2023). Russia–Ukraine war and the impact on Indian economy. *Journal of Economic Studies (Glasgow, Scotland)*, *51*(4), 841–858. DOI: 10.1108/JES-03-2023-0136

Bıçakcıoğlu-Peynirci, N. (2023). Internationalization of emerging market multinational enterprises: A systematic literature review and future directions. *Journal of Business Research*, *164*, 114002. Advance online publication. DOI: 10.1016/j.jbusres.2023.114002

Bieron, B., & Ahmed, U. (2012). Regulating e-commerce through international policy: Understanding the international trade law issues of e-commerce. *Journal of World Trade*, *46*(3).

Bilali, H. E., & Hassen, T. B. (2024). Disrupted harvests: How Ukraine – Russia war influences global food systems – a systematic review. *Policy Studies*, *45*(3–4), 310–335. DOI: 10.1080/01442872.2024.2329587

Binswanger, M. (2004). Stock returns and real activity in the G-7 countries: Did the relationship change during the 1980s? *The Quarterly Review of Economics and Finance*, *44*(2), 237–252. DOI: 10.1016/j.qref.2003.07.001

Blackwill, R. D., & Harris, J. M. (2016). *War by other means: Geoeconomics and statecraft*. Harvard University Press.

Blanchard, O. (2017). *Macroeconomics* (7th ed.). Pearson.

Blomstrom, M., & Kokko, A. (2001). Foreign direct investment and spillovers of technology. *International Journal of Technology Management*, *22*(5-6), 435–454. DOI: 10.1504/IJTM.2001.002972

Boddewyn, J. J., & Goodnow, J. D. (2020) A Short history of the Academy of International Business. https://www.aib.world/about/history/

Borensztein, E., De Gregorio, J., & Lee, J. W. (1998). How does foreign direct investment affect economic growth? *Journal of International Economics*, *45*(1), 115–135. DOI: 10.1016/S0022-1996(97)00033-0

Borghi, R. A. Z. (2024). Challenges of the global economy in the face of escalating armed conflicts in the post-pandemic era. Jornal do Economista. https://www.corecon-rj.org.br/anexos/5CAA993B73E3D62F8845C563ECB1D711.pdf

Bouët, A., & Laborde, D. (2018). US trade wars in the twenty-first century with emerging countries: Make America and its partners lose again. *World Economy*, *41*(9), 2276–2319. DOI: 10.1111/twec.12719

Boungou, W., & Yatié, A. (2024). Uncertainty, stock and commodity prices during the Ukraine-Russia war. *Policy Studies*, *45*(3-4), 1–17. DOI: 10.1080/01442872.2024.2302440

Bowden, P. (2009). In defense of utilitarianism. *Annual Conference: Australian Association for Professional and Applied Ethics*. DOI: 10.2139/ssrn.1534305

Boyko, N., Nes, K., & Schaefer, K. A. (2023). International trade and Ukraine's pursuit of self-determination. *World Economy*, *47*(4), 1460–1477. DOI: 10.1111/twec.13493

Brandao-Marques, L., Casiraghi, M., Gelos, R. G., Harrison, O., & Kamber, G. (2023). Is high debt constraining monetary policy? Evidence from inflation expectations (IMF Working Paper No. 2023/143). https://ssrn.com/abstract=4501248 or https://doi.org/DOI: 10.5089/9798400249822.001

Brandi, C., & Morin, J.-F. (2023). *Trade and the environment: Drivers and effects of environmental provisions in trade agreements*. Cambridge University Press. DOI: 10.1017/9781009461825

Breiman, L. (1996). Bagging predictors. *Machine Learning*, *24*(2), 123–140. DOI: 10.1023/A:1018054314350

Breiman, L. (2001). Random forests. *Machine Learning*, *45*(1), 5–32. DOI: 10.1023/A:1010933404324

Breslin, S., & Nesadurai, H. E. S. (2023). Economic statecraft, geoeconomics and regional political economies. *The Pacific Review*, *36*(5), 927–948. DOI: 10.1080/09512748.2023.2200030

Brosig, M., & Verma, R. (2024). The war in Ukraine, the Global South and the evolving global order. *Global Policy*, *15*(4), 740–745. Advance online publication. DOI: 10.1111/1758-5899.13366

Browder, R. E., Dwyer, S. M., & Koch, H. (2024). Upgrading adaptation: How digital transformation promotes organizational resilience. *Strategic Entrepreneurship Journal*, *18*(1), 128–164. DOI: 10.1002/sej.1483

Bryman, A., & Bell, E. (2011). *Business research methods* (3rd ed.). Oxford University Press.

Buckley, P. J., & Casson, M. (1976). *The future of the multinational enterprises*. Macmillan. DOI: 10.1007/978-1-349-02899-3

Buckley, P. J., Clegg, J., Cross, A. R., Liu, X., Voss, H., & Zheng, P. (2007). The determinants of Chinese outward foreign direct investment. *Journal of International Business Studies*, *8*(4), 499–518. DOI: 10.1057/palgrave.jibs.8400277

Budiono, S., & Purba, J. T. (2023). Factors of foreign direct investment flows to Indonesia in the era of COVID-19 pandemic. *Heliyon, 9*(4), e15429. DOI: 10.1016/j.heliyon.2023.e15429

Bunjaku, F. (2024). Decoding the stock market and GDP relationship over the long term: Implications for index fund investments. *International Journal of Management and Applied Research, 12*(1), 1–13. DOI: 10.5281/zenodo.10654133

Burri, M., Vásquez Callo-Müller, M., & Kugler, K. (2024). The evolution of digital trade law: Insights from TAPED. *World Trade Review, 23*(2), 190–207. DOI: 10.1017/S1474745623000472

Čábelková, I., Smutka, L., Rotterova, S., Zhytna, O., Kluger, V., & Mareš, D. (2022). The sustainability of international trade: The impact of ongoing military conflicts, infrastructure, common language, and economic wellbeing in Post-Soviet region. *Sustainability (Basel), 14*(17), 10840. DOI: 10.3390/su141710840

Caldara, D., & Iacoviello, M. (2022). Measuring Geopolitical Risk. *The American Economic Review, 112*(4), 1194–1225. DOI: 10.1257/aer.20191823

Calvo, G. A., Leiderman, L., & Reinhart, C. M. (1993). Capital inflows and real exchange rate appreciation in Latin America: The role of external factors. *Staff Papers - International Monetary Fund. International Monetary Fund, 40*(1), 108–151. DOI: 10.2307/3867379

Calvo, S. G., & Reinhart, C. (1996). Capital flows to Latin America: is there evidence of contagion effects? Available at *SSRN* 636120.

Calzolari, G. (2004). Incentive regulation of multinational enterprises. *International Economic Review, 45*(1), 257–282. DOI: 10.1111/j.1468-2354.2004.00125.x

Cargill. (2025). *Impact Report 2024.* Retrieved from Cargill: https://www.cargill.com/sustainability/doc/1432270798723/2024-impact-report.pdf

Carrere, C. (2006). Revisiting the effects of regional trade agreements on trade flows with proper specification of the gravity model. *European Economic Review, 50*(2), 223–247. DOI: 10.1016/j.euroecorev.2004.06.001

Cashin, P., Mohaddes, K., Raissi, M., & Raissi, M. (2014). The differential effects of oil demand and supply shocks on the global economy. *Energy Economics, 44*, 113–134. DOI: 10.1016/j.eneco.2014.03.014

Caso, N., Hilhorst, D., Mena, R., & Papyrakis, E. (2023). Does disaster contribute to armed conflict? A quantitative analysis of disaster–conflict co-occurrence between 1990 and 2017. *International Journal of Development Issues*, *23*(1), 1–23. DOI: 10.1108/IJDI-01-2023-0015

Cavusgil, S. T., & Knight, G. (2009). *Born global firms: A new international enterprise*. Business Expert Press. DOI: 10.4128/9781606490136

CCICED. (2021). *Green Recovery with Resilience and High Quality Development*. Springer.

Celasun, O., Gelos, G., & Prati, A. (2004). Obstacles to disinflation: What is the role of fiscal policy? *IMF Staff Papers*, *51*(3), 1–24. https://www.imf.org/external/pubs/ft/wp/2004/wp04111.pdf

Chaisse, J. (2016). Untangling the triangle: issues for state-controlled entities in trade, investment, and competition law. In *International Economic Law and Governance: Essays in Honour of Mitsuo Matsushita* (pp. 233-258). Oxford University Press.

Chai, T., & Draxler, R. R. (2014). Root mean square error (RMSE) or mean absolute error (MAE). *Geoscientific Model Development Discussions*, *7*(1), 1525–1534.

Chandran, S. (2017). Why do countries enter into regional trade agreements? Insights from the literature. SSRN *Electronic Journal*. DOI: 10.2139/ssrn.3024684

Charnovitz, S. (1996). Trade measures and the design of international regimes. *Journal of Environment & Development*, *5*(2), 168–196. DOI: 10.1177/107049659600500204

Chatterjee, N. (2024). Impact of economic crises on economic development of developing nations in a globalised world. In *Emerald Publishing Limited eBooks* (pp. 299–313). DOI: 10.1108/978-1-83753-586-620241020

Chen, L., & De Lombaerde, P. (2019). ASEAN between globalization and regionalization. *Asia Pacific Business Review*, *25*(1), 1–22. DOI: 10.1080/13602381.2019.1652982

Chen, P., & Semmler, W. (2024). Wage – price dynamics and financial market in a disequilibrium macro model: A Keynes – Kaldor – Minsky modeling of recession and inflation using VECM. *Journal of Economic Behavior & Organization*, *220*, 433–452. DOI: 10.1016/j.jebo.2024.01.012

Chen, T., & Guestrin, C. (2016, August). XGBoost: A scalable tree boosting system. In *Proceedings of the 22nd ACM SIGKDD International Conference on Knowledge Discovery and Data Mining* (pp. 785-794).

Chen, W., & Zhao, X. (2023). Understanding global rice trade flows: Network evolution and implications. *Foods, 12*(17), 3298. Advance online publication. DOI: 10.3390/foods12173298 PMID: 37685236

Chen, X., Yuan, L., & Song, C. (2023). Investigating merchandise trade structure in the RCEP region from the perspective of regional integration. *Journal of Geographical Sciences, 33*(6), 1185–1204. DOI: 10.1007/s11442-023-2125-7

Chiappini, R., Coupaud, M., & Viaud, F. (2022). Does attracting FDI affect population health? New evidence from a multi-dimensional measure of health. *Social Science & Medicine, 301*, 114878. DOI: 10.1016/j.socscimed.2022.114878

Chin, G. (2010). The emerging countries and China in the G20: Reshaping global economic governance. *Studia Diplomatica, 63*(2), 105–123. https://www.jstor.org/stable/44838598

Chin, T. A., Tat, H. H., & Sulaiman, Z. (2015). Green Supply Chain Management, Environmental Collaboration and Sustainability Performance. *Science Direct*, 695-699.

Chinn, M. D., & Ito, H. (2008). A new measure of financial openness. *Journal of Comparative Policy Analysis, 10*(3), 309–322. DOI: 10.1080/13876980802231123

Chordia, A., & Gurbani, K. (2021). How is economic growth correlated to index growth? *Journal of Student Research, 10*(3), 1–12. DOI: 10.47611/jsrhs.v10i3.1775

Chow, D. C. K., Schoenbaum, T. J., & Dorris, G. C. (2021). *International trade law: Problems, cases, and materials* (Ohio State Legal Studies Research Paper No. 654). Aspen Publishers. DOI: 10.2139/ssrn.3924952

Chung, C., Park, I., & Park, S. (2022). Estimating the Impact of Cumulative Rules of Origin on Trade Costs: An Application to Mega-regional Free Trade Agreements in the Asia-Pacific Region. *Asian Economic Papers, 21*(1), 92–109. DOI: 10.1162/asep_a_00846

Chung, H. (2023). When utilitarianism dominates justice as fairness: An economic defence of utilitarianism from the original position. *Economics and Philosophy, 39*(2), 308–333. DOI: 10.1017/S0266267122000098

Cima, E., & Esty, D. C. (2024). Making international trade work for sustainable development: Toward a new WTO framework for subsidies. *Journal of International Economic Law, 27*(1), 1–17. DOI: 10.1093/jiel/jgae008

Claessen, E. (2021). The making of a narrative: The use of geopolitical othering in Russian strategic narratives during the Ukraine crisis. *Media, War & Conflict, 16*(1), 82–99. DOI: 10.1177/17506352211029529

Cohen, H. G. (2018). What is international trade law for? *American Journal of International Law*, 113(4), forthcoming. IILJ Working Paper 2018/6 (MegaReg Series). University of Georgia School of Law Legal Studies Research Paper No. 2018-44. Dean Rusk International Center Research Paper No. 2018-08. https://ssrn.com/abstract=3298389

Contractor, F. J., Dangol, R., Nuruzzaman, N., & Raghunath, S. (2020). How do country regulations and business environment impact foreign direct investment (FDI) inflows? *International Business Review*, *29*(2), 101640. DOI: 10.1016/j.ibusrev.2019.101640

Cooper, J. (2024). The machine tool industry of Russia at a time of war and sanctions. *Post-Communist Economies*, *36*(5), 1–35. DOI: 10.1080/14631377.2024.2325787

Cottier, T. (2015). The common law of international trade and the future of the World Trade Organization. *Journal of International Economic Law*, *18*(1), 3–20. DOI: 10.1093/jiel/jgv005

Cottier, T. (2021). Recalibrating the WTO dispute settlement system: Towards new standards of appellate review. *Journal of International Economic Law*, *24*(3), 515–533. DOI: 10.1093/jiel/jgab024

Csurgai, G. (2018). The increasing importance of geoeconomics in power rivalries in the twenty-first century. *Geopolitics*, *23*(1), 38–46. DOI: 10.1080/14650045.2017.1359547

Cui, J., Maghyereh, A., & Liao, D. (2024). Risk connectedness between international oil and stock markets during the COVID-19 pandemic and the Russia-Ukraine conflict: Fresh evidence from the higher-order moments. *International Review of Economics & Finance*, *103470*, 103470. Advance online publication. DOI: 10.1016/j.iref.2024.103470

Cui, T., Jia, S., & Lavastida, T. (2023). From stream to pool: Pricing under the law of diminishing marginal utility. arXiv. https://arxiv.org/abs/2305.03689

Cui, V., Vertinsky, I., Wang, Y., & Zhou, D. (2023). Decoupling in international business: The 'new'vulnerability of globalization and MNEs' response strategies. *Journal of International Business Studies*, *54*(8), 1562–1576. DOI: 10.1057/s41267-023-00602-5 PMID: 36846272

Curran, L. (2017). EU trade policy after the GFC: The geoeconomics of shifting EU trade policy priorities. In *Advances in Geoeconomics* (pp. 132–140). Routledge. DOI: 10.4324/9781315312132-11

Curran, L. (2022). Future challenges to trade policy in support of international business. In *Global trade and trade governance during de-globalization: Transforming trade policy for not-so-united world* (pp. 161–179). Springer International Publishing. DOI: 10.1007/978-3-031-13757-0_10

Dadkhah, K. (2009). The post-war economic order. In *The evolution of macroeconomic theory and policy* (pp. [insert page numbers]). Springer. DOI: 10.1007/978-3-540-77008-4_2

Daily, B. (2023, 10 31). Carbacid joins list of companies ditching KPLC for solar power. Nairobi, Nairobi, Kenya.

Darie, F. C., Miron, A. D., & Ciurea, I. C. (2024). Geoeconomic Dynamics in a New Economic Global Order from West to East. In *Proceedings of the International Conference on Business Excellence* (Vol. 18, No. 1, pp. 469-481). Sciendo. DOI: 10.2478/picbe-2024-0041

Das, D. K. (2006). The Doha Round of multilateral negotiations and the embellishing role of the developing economies. *The International Trade Journal*, *20*(3), 307–354. DOI: 10.1080/08853900600784070

David, M., & LD, N. (2024). Russia's war on Ukraine: Unbottled emotions and the conditioning of the EU's Russia policy. *Revue D'intégration Européenne. Journal of European Integration*, *46*(5), 661–684. DOI: 10.1080/07036337.2024.2363613

Davis, S. J. (2016). *An index of global economic policy uncertainty (No. w22740).* National Bureau of Economic Research. DOI: 10.3386/w22740

Davis, S. J., Peters, G. P., & Caldeira, K. (2011). The supply chain of CO2 emissions. *Proceedings of the National Academy of Sciences*, 18554-18559.

De Carvalho, G., Anand, J., & Naidu, S. (2025). BRICS expansion: Adaptive response or proactive restructuring of global governance? *The South African Journal of International Affairs*, 1–24. DOI: 10.1080/10220461.2025.2525312

De Castro, P. G., Fernandes, E. A., & Campos, A. C. (2013). The determinants of foreign direct investment in Brazil and Mexico: An empirical analysis. *Procedia Economics and Finance*, *5*, 231–240. DOI: 10.1016/S2212-5671(13)00029-4

De Freitas, M. V. (2025). *BRICS: A new framework for New South inclusiveness.* Policy Center for the New South. https://www.policycenter.ma/publications/brics-new-framework-new-south-inclusiveness

de Moura, A. C., Quaresma, S. F., & Salum, M. I. (2021). Application of Fuzzy Logic to Analyze the Performance of Sustainability Logistics in Industrial Departments. *International Journal for Innovation Education and Research*, 306–327.

De Ville, B. (2013). Decision trees. *Wiley Interdisciplinary Reviews: Computational Statistics*, *5*(6), 448–455. DOI: 10.1002/wics.1278

Deane, F., Woolmer, E., Cao, S., & Tranter, K. (2024). Trade in the digital age: Agreements to mitigate fragmentation. *Asian Journal of International Law*, *14*(1), 154–179. DOI: 10.1017/S204425132300036X

DECO. (2023). The impact of rising cost of living on household budgets. DECO Proteste. https://deco.pt/protecao-financeira/o-impacto-do-aumento-do-custo-de-vida-nos-orcamentos-familiares/

Del Rosal, I. (2023). Trade effects of liner shipping across world regions. *Maritime Business Review*, *9*(1), 2–16. DOI: 10.1108/MABR-06-2023-0040

Delanty, G. (2023). Introduction to the special issue on the Russo-Ukrainian War: A new European war? Considerations on the Russo-Ukrainian War. *European Journal of Social Theory*, *26*(4), 431–449. DOI: 10.1177/13684310231174098

Delios, A., Perchthold, G., & Capri, A. (2021). Cohesion, COVID-19 and contemporary challenges to globalization. *Journal of World Business*, *56*(3), 1–8. DOI: 10.1016/j.jwb.2021.101197

Delmonte Kenya Ltd. (2022). *2022 Sustainability Report.* Retrieved from https://freshdelmonte.com/wp-content/uploads/2023/10/FDM_2022_SustainabilityReportFINAL.pdf

Dent, C. M. (2010). Freer trade, more regulation? Commercial regulatory provisions in Asia-Pacific free trade agreements. *Competition & Change*, *14*(1), 48–79. DOI: 10.1179/102452910X12587274068114

Desai, R. M., & Vreeland, J. R. (2011). Global governance in a multipolar world: The case for regional monetary funds. *International Studies Review*, *13*(1), 109–121. DOI: 10.1111/j.1468-2486.2010.01002.x

De, U. K., & Mallik, G. (2024). Crude oil price, manufacturing index, and consumer price index: Is there any temporal link in India? *IIMB Management Review*, *36*(2), 137–145. Advance online publication. DOI: 10.1016/j.iimb.2024.03.007

Devadoss, S., & Ridley, W. (2024). Impacts of the Russian invasion of Ukraine on the global wheat market. *World Development*, *173*, 106396. DOI: 10.1016/j.worlddev.2023.106396

Diageo. (2024, 09 05). *Diageo partners with tech innovators to help build resilience in Sub-Saharan African agriculture*. Retrieved from Diageo: https://www.diageo.com/en/news-and-media/press-releases/2024/diageo-partners-with-tech-innovators-to-help-build-resilience-in-sub-saharan-african-agriculture#:~:text=5th%20September%202024%3A%20Diageo,Diageo%20Sustainable%20Solutions%20(DSS)

Dias, M., Dias, J., & Hirata, J. (2014). Foreign Direct Investment in Brazil: The effects of productivity and aggregate consumption. *Journal of Stock and Forex Trading*, *3*(127), 59–73. DOI: 10.4172/2168-9458.1000127

Dib, G., Huang, F., & Poulou, A. (2020). *RCEP: Common rule of origin could boost regional trade by around USD90BN annually*. Allianz Research.

Diebold, N. F. (2011). Standards of non-discrimination in international economic law. *The International and Comparative Law Quarterly*, *60*(4), 831–865. DOI: 10.1017/S0020589311000418

Digdowiseiso, K., & Sugiyanto, E. (2020). The effects of multinational companies on deforestation: The building block or stumbling block. *Journal of Environmental Management and Tourism*, *11*(1 (41)), 5. DOI: 10.14505//jemt.v11.1(41).01

DiMaggio, P., & Powell, W. (1983). The iron cage revisited: Institutional isomorphism and collective rationality in organizational fields. *American Sociological Review*, 147–160.

Dimitrova, A., Rogmans, T., & Triki, D. (2020). Country-specific determinants of FDI inflows to the MENA region: A systematic review and future research directions. *Multinational Business Review*, *28*(1), 1–38. DOI: 10.1108/MBR-01-2019-0003

Dindorf, R., & Wos, P. (2024). Challenges of Robotic Technology in Sustainable Construction Practice. *Sustainability*, 1–26.

Ding, S., Ward, H., & Tukker, A. (2023). How Internet of Things can influence the sustainability peformance of logistics industries - A Chinese case study. *Cleaner Logistics and Supply Chain*, 1-14.

Dinkar, N., & Rahul, C. N. (2014). A selective review of foreign direct investment theories. Asia-Pacific Research and Training Network on Trade, 2-26.

Doan, H. T. T., & Zhang, H. (2024). Technical barriers to trade, product quality and trade margins: Firm-level evidence. *Review of World Economics, 160*(3), 785–811. DOI: 10.1007/s10290-023-00514-4

Dollar, D. (2007). Poverty, inequality, and social disparities during China's economic reform (Policy Research Working Paper No. 4253). World Bank. https://documents1.worldbank.org/curated/en/182041468241155669/pdf/wps4253.pdf

Domanski, D., Drehmann, M., & Juselius, M. (2016). Wealth inequality and monetary policy. BIS Quarterly Review. https://www.bis.org/publ/qtrpdf/r_qt1603f.htm

Domanski, D., Scatigna, M., & Zabai, A. (2016). Wealth inequality and monetary policy. BIS Quarterly Review, March 2016. https://ssrn.com/abstract=2744862

Dong, Y., & Whalley, J. (2010). Carbon, trade policy and carbon free trade areas. *World Economy, 33*(9), 1073–1094. DOI: 10.1111/j.1467-9701.2010.01272.x

Drabek, Z. (2024). *Is the WTO terminally ill? Threats to the international trading system*. Asia and the Global Economy. DOI: 10.1016/j.aglobe.2024.100078

Draghi, M. (2014, August 22). Unemployment in the euro area. European Central Bank. https://www.ecb.europa.eu/press/key/date/2014/html/sp140822.en.html

Draper, P., Freytag, A., Dörffel, C., & Schuhmann, S. (2018). Trade, inclusive development, and the global order. *Global Summitry, 4*(1), 30–49. DOI: 10.1093/global/guz001

Drieghe, L. (2020). The first Lomé Convention between the EEC and ACP group revisited: Bringing geopolitics back in. *Journal of European Integration, 42*(6), 783–798. DOI: 10.1080/07036337.2019.1682566

Drucker, P. F. (1974). Multinationals and developing countries: Myths and realities. *Foreign Affairs, 53*(1), 121. DOI: 10.2307/20039495

Dua, P., & Garg, R. (2015). Macroeconomic determinants of foreign direct investment: Evidence from India. *Journal of Developing Areas, 49*(1), 133–155. DOI: 10.1353/jda.2015.0025

Du, J., & Shepotylo, O. (2024). Brexit and the services trade—A longitudinal analysis. *Journal of Service Research*. DOI: 10.1177/10946705241271384

Duncan, D., & Sabirianova Peter, K. (2008). Tax progressivity and income inequality (Andrew Young School of Policy Studies Research Paper Series No. 08-26). SSRN. DOI: 10.2139/ssrn.1260860

Dunning, J. H. (1991). The eclectic paradigm of international production. *The nature of the transnational firm, 121*, 173-190.

Dunning, J. H., & Lundan, S. M. (2011). The changing political economy of foreign investment: Finding a balance between hard and soft forms of regulation. *The evolving international investment regime: Expectations, realities, options*, 125-52.

Dunning, J. H. (1977). Trade location of economic activity and the MNE: A search of an eclectic approach. In Ohlin, B., Hesselborn, P. O., & Wijkman, P. J. (Eds.), *The international allocation of economic activity*. DOI: 10.1007/978-1-349-03196-2_38

Dunning, J. H. (1993). International direct investment patterns. In *The global race for foreign direct investment: Prospects for the future* (pp. 107–132). Springer Berlin Heidelberg. DOI: 10.1007/978-3-642-78309-8_5

Dunning, J. H., & Lundan, S. M. (2008). *Multinational enterprises and the global economy*. Edward Elgar Publishing.

Duong, T. T. T. (2024). International law: From fragmentation to integration? An analysis of the relationship between international trade law and international labor law in multilateral and regional trade law frameworks. *Asia Europe Journal, 22*(2), 293–311. DOI: 10.1007/s10308-024-00701-4

Durán, J. E. (1999). *Los determinantes de la IED en los países de América Latina y el Caribe: Su impacto sobre el comercio y la integración regional*. ECLAC, Mimeo.

Dutta, P., Choi, T.-M., Somani, S., & Butala, R. (2020). Blockchain technology in supply chain operations: Applications, challenges and research opportunities. *Transportation Research Part E, Logistics and Transportation Review*.

Dworschak, C. (2023). Bias mitigation in empirical peace and conflict studies: A short primer on posttreatment variables. *Journal of Peace Research*. Advance online publication. DOI: 10.1177/00223433221145531

EABL. (2025). *EABL Sustainability Report 2024*. Retrieved from East African Breweries Ltd: https://www.eabl.com/sites/default/files/2024-10/EABL-2024-Sustainability-Report.pdf

EABL. (2025). *East African Breweries Ltd*. Retrieved from Our Business: https://www.eabl.com/our-business

Easterlin, R. A. (2005). Diminishing marginal utility of income? Caveat emptor. *Social Indicators Research, 70*(3), 243–255. https://www.jstor.org/stable/27522165. DOI: 10.1007/s11205-004-8393-4

Economou, F., Hassapis, C., Philippas, N., & Tsionas, M. (2017). Foreign direct investment determinants in OECD and developing countries. *Review of Development Economics, 21*(3), 527–542. DOI: 10.1111/rode.12269

Edler, J., Blind, K., Kroll, H., & Schubert, T. (2023). Technology sovereignty as an emerging frame for innovation policy. Defining rationales, ends and means. *Research Policy, 52*(6), 104765. Advance online publication. DOI: 10.1016/j.respol.2023.104765

Egger, P., Syropoulos, C., & Yotov, Y. V. (2024). Analyzing the effects of economic sanctions: Recent theory, data, and quantification. *Review of International Economics, 32*(1), 1–11. DOI: 10.1111/roie.12724

Elsayed, A. H., & Helmi, M. H. (2021). Volatility transmission and spillover dynamics across financial markets: The role of geopolitical risk. *Annals of Operations Research, 305*(1-2), 1–22. Advance online publication. DOI: 10.1007/s10479-021-04081-5

Emako, E., Seid, N., & Mesfin, M. (2022). The effect of foreign direct investment on economic growth in developing countries. *Transnational Corporations Review, 14*(4), 382–401. DOI: 10.1080/19186444.2022.2146967

Epoh, R. L., Langton, I., & Mafini, C. (2024). A model for green supply chain management in the South African manufacturing sector. *Cogent Business & Management.*

Erb, C. B., & Harvey, C. R. (2013). The golden dilemma. *Financial Analysts Journal, 69*(4), 10–42. https://ssrn.com/abstract=2078535. DOI: 10.2469/faj.v69.n4.1

Erdal, F., & Tatoglu, E. (2002). Locational determinants of foreign direct investment in an emerging market economy: Evidence from Turkey. *Multinational Business Review, 10*(1).

Erixon, F., Guinea, O., Lamprecht, P., du Roy, O., Sisto, E., & Zilli, R. (2024). *Trading up: An EU trade policy for better market access and resilient sourcing* (No. 08/2024). ECIPE Policy Brief.

Esclanda-Lo, C. G., Masangkay, G. A., Ong, C. A. S., & Reyes, R. S. (2024). *Exploring the evolving determinants of foreign direct investment and the investing country preferences in developing Asian economies using machine learning* (Vol. 62). Bank for International Settlements.

Estrada, M. A. R. & Koutronas, E. (2022). The impact of the Russian aggression against Ukraine on the Russia-EU trade. Journal of Policy Modeling. tDOI: 10.1016/j.jpolmod.2022.06.004

Estrades, C., Maliszewska, M., Osorio-Rodarte, I., & Pereira, M. S. (2023). Estimating the economic impacts of the regional comprehensive economic partnership. *Asia and the Global Economy*, *3*(2), 100060. DOI: 10.1016/j.aglobe.2023.100060

European Parliament. (2025). Small and medium-sized enterprises. Factsheets on the European Union. https://www.europarl.europa.eu/erpl-app-public/factsheets/pdf/pt/FTU_2.4.2.pdf

Eurostat. (2021). Income and living conditions - Income distribution and poverty. https://ec.europa.eu/eurostat/web/income-and-living-conditions

Eurostat. (2022). European Union annual inflation was 10.6% in October 2022. https://ec.europa.eu/eurostat/documents/2995521/15265521/2-17112022-AP-EN.pdf/b6953137-786e-ed9c-5ee2-6812c0f8f07f

Fajgelbaum, P. D., Goldberg, P. K., Kennedy, P. J., & Khandelwal, A. K. (2020). The return to protectionism. *The Quarterly Journal of Economics*, *135*(1), 1–55. DOI: 10.1093/qje/qjz036

Falvey, R., & Foster-McGregor, N. (2022). The breadth of preferential trade agreements and the margins of exports. *Review of World Economics*, *158*(1), 181–251. DOI: 10.1007/s10290-021-00430-5

Fasanya, I. O., Oyewole, O. J., Adekoya, O. B., & Badaru, F. O. (2021). Oil price and stock market behaviour in GCC countries: Do asymmetries and structural breaks matter? *Energy Strategy Reviews*, *36*, 100682. DOI: 10.1016/j.esr.2021.100682

Fath, B., Fiedler, A., Sinkovics, N., Sinkovics, R. R., & Sullivan-Taylor, B. (2021). International relationships and resilience of New Zealand SME exporters during COVID-19. *Critical Perspectives on International Business*, *17*(2), 359–379. DOI: 10.1108/cpoib-05-2020-0061

Felbermayr, G., Peterson, S., & Wanner, J. (2024). Trade and the environment, trade policies and environmental policies—How do they interact? *Journal of Economic Surveys*, 1–37. DOI: 10.1111/joes.12628

Feldstein, M. (2008). The effects of taxes on economic behavior (NBER Working Paper No. 13745). National Bureau of Economic Research. https://www.nber.org/system/files/working_papers/w13745/w13745.pdf

Ferragamo, M. (2025). *What is the BRICS group and why is it expanding?* Council on Foreign Relations. https://www.cfr.org/backgrounder/what-brics-group-and-why-it-expanding

Ferragamo, M. (2024). From dollar dependency to BRICS autonomy: Legal and economic impacts on global trade governance. *Acta Universitatis Danubius Oeconomica, 20*(6), 21–38. https://www.researchgate.net/publication/387275679_From_Dollar_Dependency_to_BRICS_Autonomy_Legal_and_Economic_Impacts_on_Global_Trade_Governance

Ferrández-Serrano, V., & Angosto-Fernández, P. L. (2022). A Russian carol: Impact and dependence on global equity markets during the Ukraine invasion. *Journal of Economic Studies (Glasgow, Scotland), 50*(7), 1399–1412. DOI: 10.1108/JES-06-2022-0364

Fichtner, F., & Joebges, H. (2024). *Does the stock market predict GDP? Revisiting the empirical evidence for G7 countries. IMK Studies, 90*, 1–38. Düsseldorf: Macroeconomic Policy Institute (IMK). https://www.econstor.eu/bitstream/10419/283065/1/p-imk-study-90-2024.pdf

Firdos, R., Subhan, M., Mansuri, B. B., & Alharthi, M. (2024). Unraveling the impact of COVID-19 pandemic on foreign direct investment and its determinants: Empirical insights from SAARC countries. *Journal of Economic Studies (Glasgow, Scotland), 51*(6), 1247–1265. DOI: 10.1108/JES-08-2023-0420

Fjäder, C. O. (2018). Interdependence as dependence: Economic security in the age of global interconnectedness. In *Geo-economics and power politics in the 21st Century* (pp. 28–42). Routledge. DOI: 10.4324/9781351172288-3

Flach, L., & Gräf, F. (2020). The impact of trade agreements on world export prices. *Review of International Economics, 28*(1), 168–208. DOI: 10.1111/roie.12446

Fleurbaey, M., & Maniquet, F. (2008). Utilitarianism versus fairness in welfare economics. In Fleurbaey, M., Salles, M., & Weymark, J. A. (Eds.), *Justice, political liberalism, and utilitarianism: Themes from Harsanyi and Rawls* (pp. 263–280). Cambridge University Press. DOI: 10.1017/CBO9780511619595.012

Fleurbaey, M., & Zuber, S. (2021). Fair utilitarianism. *American Economic Journal. Microeconomics, 13*(2), 370–401. DOI: 10.1257/mic.20170234

Fliagin, D., & Abdulganiyu, M. (2025). Impact of intra-BRICS trade on the share of United States dollar in international reserve composition. *BRICS Journal of Economics, 6*(2), 5–20. DOI: 10.3897/brics-econ.6.e143810

Fliess, B., & Busquets, C. (2006). The role of trade barriers in SME internationalisation. OECD Papers, 6(13).

Forgey, Q., & Kine, P. (2022). Blinken calls China 'most serious long-term' threat to world order. https://www.politico.com/news/2022/05/26/blinken-biden-china-policy-speech-00035385

Forsgren, M. (2024). *Theories of the Multinational Firm. A Multidimensional Creature in the Global Economy* (4th ed.). Edward Elgar Publishing.

Forsgren, M., & Yamin, M. (2023). The source of MNE superiority from within or from outside?–A response to "the importance of being transnational". *Critical Perspectives on International Business*, *19*(4), 523–525. DOI: 10.1108/cpoib-03-2023-0019

Frederick, S., Bair, J., & Gereffi, G. (2015). Regional trade agreements and export competitiveness: The uncertain path of Nicaragua's apparel exports under CAFTA. *Cambridge Journal of Regions, Economy and Society*, *8*(3), 403–420. DOI: 10.1093/cjres/rsv015

Freeman, E. (1984). *Strategic Management: A Stakeholder Approach*. Pitman.

Freidin, E. (2024). *BRICS Pay as a challenge to SWIFT network*. Lowy Institute. https://www.lowyinstitute.org/the-interpreter/brics-pay-challenge-swift-network

Freund, C. L., & Weinhold, D. (2004). The effect of the Internet on international trade. *Journal of International Economics*, *62*(1), 171–189. DOI: 10.1016/S0022-1996(03)00059-X

Freund, C., & Ornelas, E. (2010). Regional trade agreements. *Annual Review of Economics*, *2*(1), 139–166. DOI: 10.1146/annurev.economics.102308.124455

Friedman, M. (1957). *A theory of the consumption function*. Princeton University Press. DOI: 10.1515/9780691188485

Friedman, M. (1968). The role of monetary policy. *The American Economic Review*, *58*(1), 1–17. https://www.jstor.org/stable/1831652

Galbraith, J. K., & Kum, H. (2002). Inequality and economic growth: Data comparisons and econometric tests (University of Texas Inequality Project Working Paper No. 21). https://ssrn.com/abstract=315699 or DOI: 10.2139/ssrn.315699

Gao, H. (2021). Finding a rule-based solution to the Appellate Body crisis: Looking beyond the multiparty interim appeal arbitration arrangement. *Journal of International Economic Law*, *24*(3), 534–550. DOI: 10.1093/jiel/jgab031

Gao, J., Zhao, Y., & Jia, R. (2025). RCEP regional value chain construction and global value chain position enhancement: A measurement analysis based on regional value chains. *Economia e Politica Industriale*, *52*(1), 27–58. DOI: 10.1007/s40812-024-00320-5

Garcia, F. J. (2007). Developing a normative critique of international trade law: Special & differential treatment. *TranState Working Papers* (No. 66). Universität Bremen, Collaborative Research Center 597 - Transformations of the State. https://hdl.handle.net/10419/2497

Garner-Knapp, L., Western, S. D., & Lovat, H. (2022). The US, the WTO, and the Appellate Body: From Great Expectations to Hard Times. In J. Bäumler et al. (Eds.), *European Yearbook of International Economic Law 2021* (Vol. 12). Springer. DOI: 10.1007/8165_2021_76

Gawande, K., Hoekman, B., & Cui, Y. (2011). Determinants of trade policy responses to the 2008 financial crisis. *World Bank Policy Research Working Paper*, (5862).

Gera, R., Chadha, P., Nag, M. B., Sharma, S., Arora, H., Parvez, A., & Sergeevna, L. Y. (2021). A systematic review of green supply chain management practices in firms. *Journal of Cleaner Production*, 535–542.

Gereffi, G., Lim, H. C., & Lee, J. (2021). Trade policies, firm strategies, and adaptive reconfigurations of global value chains. *Journal of International Business Policy*, *4*(4), 506–522. DOI: 10.1057/s42214-021-00102-z

Ghauri, P., Strange, R., & Cooke, F. L. (2021). Research on international business: The new realities. *International Business Review*, *30*(2), 101794. DOI: 10.1016/j.ibusrev.2021.101794

Giuffrida, M., Jiang, H., & Mangiaracina, R. (2021). Investigating the relationships between uncertainty types and risk management strategies in cross-border e-commerce logistics. *International Journal of Logistics Management*, *32*(4), 1406–1433. DOI: 10.1108/IJLM-04-2020-0158

Góes, C., & Bekkers, E. (2022). The impact of geopolitical conflicts on trade, growth, and innovation. *arXiv*.

Goldberg, P. K., & Reed, T. (2023, June). Growing threats to global trade. *Finance & Development*.

Goldstein, I., & Razin, A. (2006). An information-based trade off between foreign direct investment and foreign portfolio investment. *Journal of International Economics*, *70*(1), 271–295. DOI: 10.1016/j.jinteco.2005.12.002

Gondim, I. J. C., Morandier, N., Dias, I. R. R., Couto, C. A. P., & Charotta, T. C. A.GONDIM. (2017). Analysis of domestic factors affecting outward foreign direct investment in Brazil. *Latin American Business Review*, *18*(1), 1–18. DOI: 10.1080/10978526.2016.1251821

Goodspeed, T. J., Martinez-Vazquez, J., & Zhang, L. (2011). *The role of public services and taxes in attracting 'foreign' direct investment (No. 433)*. Hunter College Department of Economics.

Govindan, K., Azevedo, S. G., Carvalho, H., & Cruz-Machado, V. (2015). Lean, green and resilient practices influence on supply chain performance: Interpretive structural modeling approach. *International Journal of Environmental Science and Technology*, 15–34.

Greene, J. D., & Baron, J. (2000). Intuitions about declining marginal utility. *Journal of Behavioral Decision Making*, *14*(3), 243–255. DOI: 10.1002/bdm.375

Green, K. W., Zelbst, P. J., Meacham, J., & Bhadauria, V. S. (2012). Green supply chain management practices: Impact on performance. *Supply Chain Management*, 290–305.

Green, P. F. (2023). Ameliorating global challenges: Globalization, geopolitics, basic & applied research, and research security. *MRS Bulletin*, *48*(10), 964–967. DOI: 10.1557/s43577-023-00600-w

Greenwald, D., Leombroni, M., Lustig, H. N., & Van Nieuwerburgh, S. (2022). Financial and total wealth inequality with declining interest rates. Stanford University Graduate School of Business Research Paper, Columbia Business School Research Paper. DOI: 10.2139/ssrn.3789220

Grosse, R. (Ed.). (2005). *International business and government relations in the 21st century*. Cambridge University Press.

Grosse, R., Gamso, J., & Nelson, R. C. (2021). China's rise, world order, and the implications for international business. *Management International Review*, *61*(1), 1–26. Advance online publication. DOI: 10.1007/s11575-020-00433-8 PMID: 33679004

Grossfeld, E. (2024). Russia's declining satellite reconnaissance capabilities and its implications for security and international stability. *International Journal of Intelligence and CounterIntelligence*, *38*(1), 1–30. DOI: 10.1080/08850607.2024.2330848

Guan, H. (2024). On the reform of WTO dispute settlement mechanism and suggestions. *Advances in Economics. Management and Political Sciences*, *71*(1), 185–191. DOI: 10.54254/2754-1169/71/20241487

Gulyas, O., & Kiss, G. (2023). Impact of cyber-attacks on the financial institutions. *Procedia Computer Science*, *219*, 84–90. Advance online publication. DOI: 10.1016/j.procs.2023.01.267

Gunneriusson, H., & Ratsiborynska, V. (2024). Geopolitics in the Contested Areas. In *Geopolitics in the Contested Areas* (pp. 1–15). DOI: 10.1007/978-3-031-25399-7_59-1

Guo, Y., Zheng, H., Zeng, Y., Fan, W., Albahooth, B., & Bhuiyan, R. A. (2023). Natural resources extraction of RCEP trade bloc: Examining geopolitical risk and economic situation. *Resources Policy*, *86*, 104227. DOI: 10.1016/j.resourpol.2023.104227

Gupta, P. (2025). BRICS vs G7: The data behind the new global economic power shift. *Medium*. https://medium.com/@guptaprashant0999/brics-vs-g7-the-data-behind-the-new-global-economic-power-shift-b2ef15f7c12b

Gupta, S., Yadav, S. S., & Jain, P. K. (2024). Does institutional quality matter for foreign direct investment flows? Empirical evidence from BRICS economies. *International Journal of Emerging Markets*, *19*(12), 4431–4458. DOI: 10.1108/IJOEM-11-2021-1713

Habib, A. M., & Kayani, U. N. (2024). Price reaction of global economic indicators: Evidence from the COVID-19 pandemic and the Russia–Ukraine conflict. *SN Business & Economics*, *4*(1), 19. Advance online publication. DOI: 10.1007/s43546-023-00619-w

Håkansson, C. (2023). The Ukraine war and the emergence of the European commission as a geopolitical actor. *Journal of European Integration*, *46*(1), 25–45. DOI: 10.1080/07036337.2023.2239998

Hamdani, M., & Belfencha, I. (2024). Strategic implications of the US-China semiconductor rivalry. *Discover Global Society*, *2*(1), 67. Advance online publication. DOI: 10.1007/s44282-024-00081-5

Hanada, E. (2020). Trump vs. China? Tariffs under Section 232 of the Trade Expansion Act of 1962 revisited. *Vienna Journal of East Asian Studies*, *12*(1), 207–251. DOI: 10.2478/vjeas-2020-0008

Hannan, S. A. (2018). *Revisiting the determinants of capital flows to emerging markets—A survey of the evolving literature*. International Monetary Fund.

Hanousek, J., Kočenda, E., & Vozárová, P. (2020). Impact of multinational enterprises on competition, productivity and trade spillovers across European firms. *KIER Discussion Paper*, 1028, 1-44.

Harvey, C. R., & Rabetti, D. (2024). International business and decentralized finance. *Journal of International Business Studies*, *55*(7), 840–863. Advance online publication. DOI: 10.1057/s41267-024-00705-7

Hasibuan, S., Yunita, I., & Zulkarnaen, I. (2025). Evaluating supply chain sustainability and agility using fuzzy logic approach: a case in Indonesian agroindustry. *BIO Web of Conferences*. EDP Sciences.

Hassan, Q., Viktor, P., Al-Musawi, T. J., Ali, B. M., Algburi, S., Alzoubi, H. M., & Jaszczur, M. (2024). The renewable energy role in the global energy Transformations. *Renewable Energy Focus*, *48*, 100545. DOI: 10.1016/j.ref.2024.100545

Hausman, D., McPherson, M., & Satz, D. (2017). *Economic analysis, moral philosophy, and public policy*. Cambridge University Press.

Head, J. (2021). *The future of the global economic organizations: an evaluation of criticisms leveled at the IMF, the multilateral development banks, and the WTO* (Vol. 5). BRILL.

Hejazi, M. T., Batati, B. A., & Bahurmuz, A. (2023). The Influence of Green Supply Chain Management Practices on Corporate Sustainability Performance. *Sustainability*.

Hellani, H., Sliman, L., Samhat, A. E., & Exposito, E. (2021). On blockchain integration with supply chain: Overview on data transparency. *Logistics (Basel)*, *5*(3), 46. Advance online publication. DOI: 10.3390/logistics5030046

Helleiner, E. (2024). Economic globalization's polycrisis. *International Studies Quarterly*, *68*(2), sqae024. DOI: 10.1093/isq/sqae024

Helmy, N. (2025). BRICS' game-changing blockchain payment system: The future of global transactions. *Modern Diplomacy*. https://moderndiplomacy.eu/2025/03/27/brics-game-changing-blockchain-payment-system-the-future-of-global-transactions/

Helpman, E., Melitz, M., & Rubinstein, Y. (2008). Estimating trade flows: Trading partners and trading volumes. *The Quarterly Journal of Economics*, *123*(2), 441–487. DOI: 10.1162/qjec.2008.123.2.441

Henderson, J. (2024). The impact of the Russia-Ukraine war on global gas markets. *Current Sustainable/Renewable. Energy Reports*, *11*(1), 1–9. DOI: 10.1007/s40518-024-00232-x

Herman, P. R., & Oliver, S. (2023). Trade, policy, and economic development in the digital economy. *Journal of Development Economics*, *164*, 103135. DOI: 10.1016/j.jdeveco.2023.103135

Herold, D. M. & Marzantowicz, Ł (2023). Supply chain responses to global disruptions and its ripple effects: an institutional complexity perspective. Operations management research. DOI: 10.1007/s12063-023-00404-w

Herszenhorn, D. M. (2021). Biden's team wants EU allies to get real on 'strategic autonomy'. https://www.politico.eu/article/joe-biden-us-eu-strategic-autonomy-brussels-g20/

Hitt, M. A., Holmes, R. M.Jr, & Arregle, J. L. (2021). The (COVID-19) pandemic and the new world (dis) order. *Journal of World Business*, *56*(4), 101210. Advance online publication. DOI: 10.1016/j.jwb.2021.101210

Hoekman, B., Tu, X., & Wolfe, R. (2023). China and WTO reform. In Gao, H., Raess, D., & Zeng, K. (Eds.), *China and the WTO: A twenty-year assessment* (pp. 275–298). Cambridge University Press. DOI: 10.1017/9781009291804.017

Hofmann, C., Osnago, A., & Ruta, M. (2019). The content of preferential trade agreements. *World Trade Review*, *18*(3), 365–398. DOI: 10.1017/S1474745618000071

Hopewell, K. (2020). Trump & trade: The crisis in the multilateral trading system. *New Political Economy*, *26*(1), 1–12. DOI: 10.1080/13563467.2020.1841135

Horner, R. (2016). A New Economic Geography of Trade and Development? Governing South–South Trade, Value Chains and Production Networks. *Territory, Politics, Governance*, *4*(4), 400–420. DOI: 10.1080/21622671.2015.1073614

Horobet, A., Popovici, O. C., & Bela cu, L. (2021). Shaping competitiveness for driving FDI in CEE countries. *Romanian Journal of European Affairs*, *21*(2).

Horváthy, B. (2020). International trade law and emerging technologies: A conceptual framework. *Bratislava Law Review*, *4*(2), 9–20. DOI: 10.46282/blr.2020.4.2.201

Hossain, A. T., & Masum, A. A. (2022). Russian invasion of Ukraine, geopolitical risk, and global financial markets. SSRN *Electronic Journal*. DOI: 10.2139/ssrn.4056137

Hossain, A. T., Masum, A., & Saadi, S. (2024). The impact of geopolitical risks on foreign exchange markets: Evidence from the Russia–Ukraine war. *Finance Research Letters*, *59*, 104750. DOI: 10.1016/j.frl.2023.104750

Howse, R., & Langille, J. (2023). Continuity and change in the World Trade Organization: Pluralism past, present, and future. *The American Journal of International Law*, *117*(1), 1–47. DOI: 10.1017/ajil.2022.82

Huang, Y. (2022). China's changing economic relations with the world: Introduction. *China Economic Journal*, *15*(3), 231–234. DOI: 10.1080/17538963.2022.2118458

Hurrell, A. (2024). Geopolitics and global economic governance. *Oxford Review of Economic Policy, 40*(2), 220–233. DOI: 10.1093/oxrep/grae013

Huzaifa, A., & Legacy, S. (2024). Trade wars and tariffs: Examining the intersection of international relations and economic security. *ResearchGate*. https://doi.org/DOI: 10.13140/RG.2.2.22058.73928

Hymer, S. H. (1960). *The international operations of national firms, a study of direct foreign investment*. Doctoral dissertation, Massachusetts Institute of Technology.

Hymer, S. H. (1976). The international operations of national firms: A study of direct foreign investment. Cambridge, MA: The MIT Press. (Original publication 1960)

Hymer, S. H. (1968). The large multinational corporation: An analysis of some motives for the international integration of business. *Revista de Economia (Curitiba), 19*(6), 949–973.

IIF. (2023). The Institute of International Finance, https://www.iif.com/publications/capital-flows

Ikegbu, E. A., & Diana-Abasi, F. I. (2017). Utilitarianism as a veritable vehicle for the promotion of a just society. *LWATI: A Journal of Contemporary Research, 14*(2), 121–137.

IMF. (2024). Emerging Markets Show Resilience Despite Global Monetary Tightening, https://www.imf.org/en/Blogs/Articles/2024/07/12/emerging-markets-show-resilience-despite-global-monetary-tightening

IMF. (2024). https://data.imf.org/?sk=9D6028D4-F14A-464C-A2F2-59B2CD424B85

Imran-Ur-Rahman, I., Shafi, M., Fauzi, M. A., & Fetuu, E. (2024). Examining trade flow dynamics in the face of deglobalization and decoupling: A comparative analysis of developing and developed nations. *Kybernetes*. Advance online publication. DOI: 10.1108/K-02-2024-0503

Instituto Nacional de Estatística. (2023). Rendimento e condições de vida: 2023 – versão retificada em 13/12/2023. Instituto Nacional de Estatística. https://www.ine.pt/ngt_server/attachfileu.jsp?look_parentBoui=638979246&att_display=n&att_download=y

International Monetary Fund. (2018). Addressing global imbalances requires cooperation. https://www.imf.org/en/Blogs/Articles/2018/07/24/blog-addressing-global-imbalances-requires-cooperation

International Monetary Fund. (2022). *Global financial stability report.* https://www.imf.org/

International Monetary Fund. (2023). *Global financial stability report: Market resilience amid tightening global conditions.* https://www.imf.org/en/Publications/GFSR

International Monetary Fund. (2024). *Geopolitics, global trade, and the U.S. dollar: Insights from Gita Gopinath.* https://www.imf.org/en/News/Articles/2024/05/07/sp-geopolitics-impact-global-trade-and-dollar-gita-gopinath

Jackson, J. H., Hudec, R. E., & Davis, D. (2000). The role and effectiveness of the WTO dispute settlement mechanism [with comments and discussion]. *Brookings Trade Forum, 2000*(1), 179–236. https://www.jstor.org/stable/25063150. DOI: 10.1353/btf.2000.0007

Jackson, M., & Paddeu, F. I. (2024). The countermeasures of others: When can states collaborate in the taking of countermeasures? *The American Journal of International Law, 118*(2), 231–274. DOI: 10.1017/ajil.2024.8

Jagtap, S., Trollman, H., Trollman, F., Garcia-Garcia, G., Parra-López, C., Duong, L., Martindale, W., Munekata, P., Lorenzo, J., Hdaifeh, A., Hassoun, A., Salonitis, K., & Afy-Shararah, M. (2022). The Russia-Ukraine Conflict: Its implications for the global food supply chains. *Foods, 11*(14), 2098. DOI: 10.3390/foods11142098 PMID: 35885340

Jakubik, A., Keck, A., & Piermartini, R. (2022). Trade policy implications of a changing world: Tariffs and market power. *Applied Economics Letters, 31*(9), 783–787. DOI: 10.1080/13504851.2022.2150140

Jakupec, V. (2024). Dynamics of the Ukraine War. DOI: 10.1007/978-3-031-52444-8

James, W. E. (2005). Rules of origin and rules of preference and the World Trade Organization: The challenge to global trade liberalization. In P. F. J. Macrory, A. E. Appleton, & M. G. Plummer (Eds.), *The World Trade Organization: Legal, economic and political analysis* (pp. [insert specific pages]). Springer. DOI: 10.1007/0-387-22688-5_48

Janusch, H., & Mucha, W. (2017). America first: Power and geopolitics in US trade policy under President Trump. *Sicherheit und Frieden (S+F) / Security and Peace, 35*(3), 110–114. https://www.jstor.org/stable/26428648

Jasinskaja-Lahti, I., Szebeni, Z., Birman, D., Mitikka, E., & Renvik, T. A. (2024). Diasporas during conflict: A mixed-method analysis of attitudes of the Russian-speaking community in Finland towards the Russia-Ukraine war. *Journal of Community & Applied Social Psychology*, *34*(4), e2824. Advance online publication. DOI: 10.1002/casp.2824

Javaid, M., Haleem, A., Khan, I. H., & Suman, R. (2023). *Understanding the potential applications of Artificial Intelligence in Agriculture Sector*. Advanced Agrochem., DOI: 10.1016/j.aac.2022.10.001

Jia, L. (2020). The role of big data analytics in enabling green supply chain management: A literature review. *Journal of Data, Information and Management*, 75–83.

Jiang, H., & Yu, M. (2021). Understanding RCEP and CPTPP: From the perspective China's dual circulation economic strategy. *China Economic Journal*, *14*(2), 144–161. DOI: 10.1080/17538963.2021.1933055

Jiang, W., & Chen, Y. (2024). Impact of Russia-Ukraine conflict on the time-frequency and quantile connectedness between energy, metal and agricultural markets. *Resources Policy*, *88*, 104376. DOI: 10.1016/j.resourpol.2023.104376

Jiménez, A., & Herrero, Á. (2019). Selecting features that drive internationalization of Spanish firms. *Cybernetics and Systems*, *50*(1), 25–39. DOI: 10.1080/01969722.2018.1558012

Kammer, A. (2022, April 22). The war in Ukraine is a serious setback to Europe's economic recovery. International Monetary Fund. https://www.imf.org/en/Blogs/Articles/2022/04/21/blog042222-eurreo-war-in-ukraine-is-serious-setback-to-europe-economic-recovery

Kashwan, P., & Lee, H. (2024). Beyond stakeholder consultations: Red-green coalition democratizes Maine's offshore wind energy policymaking. *Energy Research & Social Science*, *116*, 103692. DOI: 10.1016/j.erss.2024.103692

Katenova, M. (2018). Foreign direct investment and gross domestic product in Kazakhstan. International Journal of Economics. *Business and Management Studies*, *5*(1), 40–45. DOI: 10.20448/802.51.40.45

Kaushal, L. A. (2021). Impact of institutional and regulatory quality on FDI inflow: Case of a developing Indian economy. *Cogent Economics & Finance*, *9*(1), 1985201. DOI: 10.1080/23322039.2021.1985201

Kaushal, L. A. (2022). Impact of regional trade agreements on export efficiency–A case study of India. *Cogent Economics & Finance*, *10*(1), 2008090. DOI: 10.1080/23322039.2021.2008090

Keohane, R. O. (1984). *After hegemony: Cooperation and discord in the world political economy*. Princeton University Press. DOI: 10.2307/j.ctt7sq9s

Keohane, R., & Nye, J. S. (1998). Power and Interdependence in the Information Age. *Foreign Affairs, 20*(5), 81–94. DOI: 10.2307/20049052

Khamisu, M. S., & Paluri, R. A. (2024). *Emerging trends of environmental social and governance (ESG) disclosure research.* Cleaner Production Letters.

Khamphengvong, V., Xia, E., & Srithilat, K. (2018). Inflow determinants of foreign direct investment. *Human Systems Management, 37*(1), 57–66. DOI: 10.3233/HSM-17229

Khan, S. A., & Qianli, D. (2017). Impact of Green Supply Chain Management Practices on Firms' Performance: An Empiral Study from the Perspective of Pakistan. *Environmental Science Pollution*, 16829-16844.

Khan, M., Sandano, I., Pratt, C., & Farid, T. (2018). China's Belt and Road Initiative: A global model for an evolving approach to sustainable regional development. *Sustainability (Basel), 10*(11), 4234. DOI: 10.3390/su10114234

Khan, N., Mejri, S., & Hammoudeh, S. (2024). How do global commodities react to increasing geopolitical risks? New insights into the Russia-Ukraine and Palestine-Israel conflicts. *Energy Economics, 107812*. Advance online publication. DOI: 10.1016/j.eneco.2024.107812

Khan, Y., Su'ud, M. B., Alam, M. M., Ahmad, F. S., Ahmad, A. Y., & Khan, N. (2022). Application of Internet of Things (IoT) in Sustainable Supply Chain Management. *Sustainability*, 1–14.

Khatoon, A., & Sakeena, . (2022). China's Belt and Road Initiative: An analysis of its role in global peace, development, and implications. *Journal of Humanities Social and Management Sciences, 3*(2), 40–61. DOI: 10.47264/idea.jhsms/3.2.3

Kimball, M. S., Ohtake, F., Reck, D., Tsutsui, Y., & Zhang, F. (2015). Diminishing marginal utility revisited. *SSRN*. DOI: 10.2139/ssrn.2592935

Kim, J. (2012). The evolution of preferential rules of origin in ASEAN's RTAs: A guide to multilateral harmonization. *Journal of World Trade, 46*(6), 1343–1364. DOI: 10.54648/TRAD2012042

Kindleberger, C. P. (2013). *The world in depression, 1929–1939*. University of California Press. https://www.ucpress.edu/books/the-world-in-depression-1929-1939/paper

Kireyev, A., & Osakwe, C. (2017). Making Trade Multilateralism Work for All: The Role of WTO Accessions. *Trade Multilateralism in the Twenty-First Century: Building the Upper Floors of the Trading System Through WTO Accessions*, 1.

Kizilova, K., & Norris, P. (2023). "Rally around the flag" effects in the Russian–Ukrainian war. *European Political Science*. Advance online publication. DOI: 10.1057/s41304-023-00450-9

Kizys, R., & Pierdzioch, C. (2009). Changes in the international comovement of stock returns and economic activity: Evidence from the G7 countries. *Journal of International Financial Markets, Institutions and Money*, *19*(2), 289–305. DOI: 10.1016/j.intfin.2008.01.002

Kong, Q., Yamada, M., Yang, C., & Nie, H. (2025). Competition or complementarity? Assessing the interaction effects of RCEP and CPTPP on agricultural and non-agricultural trade flows. *International Economics and Economic Policy*, *22*(1), 7. DOI: 10.1007/s10368-024-00628-6

Kormych, B., & Malyarenko, T. (2022). From gray zone to conventional warfare: The Russia-Ukraine conflict in the Black Sea. *Small Wars & Insurgencies*, *34*(7), 1235–1270. DOI: 10.1080/09592318.2022.2122278

Korsah, E., Amanamah, R. B., & Gyimah, P. (2025). Drivers of foreign direct investment: New evidence from West African regions. *Journal of Business and Socio-economic Development*, *5*(1), 3–19. DOI: 10.1108/JBSED-12-2021-0173

Köseoğlu, S. D., Mercangöz, B. A., Khan, K., & Sarwar, S. (2023). The impact of the Russian-Ukraine war on the stock market: A causal analysis. *Applied Economics*, 1–11. DOI: 10.1080/00036846.2023.2188168

Kovvuri, V. R. R., Fu, H., Fan, X., & Seisenberger, M. (2023). Fund performance evaluation with explainable artificial intelligence. *Finance Research Letters*, *58*, 104419. DOI: 10.1016/j.frl.2023.104419

Kozielec, A., Piecuch, J., Daniek, K., & Luty, L. (2024). Challenges to food security in the Middle East and North Africa in the context of the Russia–Ukraine conflict. *Agriculture*, *14*(1), 155. DOI: 10.3390/agriculture14010155

Koziuk, V. (2023). The geopolitical "puzzle" of the central bank's switch to gold. *Economics-Innovative and Economics Research Journal*, *11*(2), 225–243. DOI: 10.2478/eoik-2023-0018

Kozyrev, V. (2024). The war in Ukraine and its impact on the US perspective of Europe. In *Global power shift* (pp. 17–43). DOI: 10.1007/978-3-031-48117-8_2

Krishna, E. S. A., Tom, A., & Joseph, D. (2025). Evaluating the impact of BRICS+ trade policies: A comparative analysis before and after the Russia-Ukraine conflict. In Mbandlwa, Z., Netswera, F. G., & Smirnov, S. A. (Eds.), *Analyzing the impact of BRICS+ nations' trade policies on global economies* (pp. 123–144). IGI Global. DOI: 10.4018/979-8-3693-7969-1.ch005

Kuhla, K., Willner, S. N., Otto, C., & Levermann, A. (2023). Resilience of international trade to typhoon-related supply disruptions. *Journal of Economic Dynamics & Control, 151*, 104663. DOI: 10.1016/j.jedc.2023.104663

Kumari, R., & Sharma, A. K. (2017). Determinants of foreign direct investment in developing countries: A panel data study. *International Journal of Emerging Markets, 12*(4), 658–682. DOI: 10.1108/IJoEM-10-2014-0169

Kumar, N., & Singhal, N. (2022). Role of outward foreign direct investment in economic growth of India: Evidence from non-linear ARDL approach. *Jindal Journal of Business Research, 11*(2), 187–204. DOI: 10.1177/22786821221127670

Kumar, S. (2022). Regional organizations and States in international Relations: A study of India's approach towards regional organizations. *Millennial Asia, 15*(2), 259–277. DOI: 10.1177/09763996221105148

Kumar, V., Pallathadka, H., Sharma, S. K., Thakar, C. M., Singh, M., & Pallathadka, L. K. (2022). *Role of machine learning in green supply chain management and operations management. Materials Today: Proceedings*. Elsevier.

Kushwaha, S., Kafle, S. C., & Khanal, B. (2023). Impact of GDP and inflation on stock market in India: A case study of BSE index. *BMC Journal of Scientific Research, 6*(1), 136–148. DOI: 10.3126/bmcjsr.v6i1.60961

Kuźnar, A. (2024). Shaping the economic resilience in East Asia through international trade. In *Regional Cooperation and Resilience in East Asia* (pp. 52–73). Routledge. DOI: 10.4324/9781003458357-4

Laboure, M., Müller, M. H.-P., Heinz, G., Singh, S., & Köhling, S. (2021). Cryptocurrencies and CBDC: The route ahead. *Global Policy, 12*(5), 98–110. DOI: 10.1111/1758-5899.13017

Lagarde, M. C. (2014). *A new multilateralism for the 21st century*. International Monetary Fund.

Lambert, L. A., Tayah, J., Lee-Schmid, C., Abdalla, M., Abdallah, I., Ali, A. H., Esmail, S., & Ahmed, W. (2022). The EU's natural gas Cold War and diversification challenges. *Energy Strategy Reviews, 43*, 100934. DOI: 10.1016/j.esr.2022.100934

Lampe, M., & Sharp, P. (2024). Cliometric approaches to international trade. In *Springer eBooks* (pp. 859–897). DOI: 10.1007/978-3-031-35583-7_8

Larch, M., & Yotov, Y. V. (2024). Estimating the effects of trade agreements: Lessons from 60 years of methods and data. *World Economy*, *47*(5), 1771–1799. Advance online publication. DOI: 10.1111/twec.13569

Lawton, T. C., Lindeque, J. P., & McGuire, S. M. (2009). Multilateralism and the multinational enterprise. *Business and Politics*, *11*(2), 1–26. DOI: 10.2202/1469-3569.1274

Lebepe, P. & Mathaba, T. N. D. (2025). Enhancing energy resilience in manufacturing enterprises: A systematic mapping of challenges to strategies. *Journal of Economy and Technology*. DOI: 10.1016/j.ject.2025.01.002

Lee, H. S. (2014). Outward Foreign Direct Investment, Interindustry Networks, and US Trade Politics. *Guoji Maoyi Wenti*, *28*(2), 140–168.

Lee, S. J., Kang, S. J., & Lee, S. (2024). Economic, social and institutional determinants of FDI inflows: A comparative analysis of developed and developing economies. *Transnational Corporations Review*, *16*(3), 200074. DOI: 10.1016/j.tncr.2024.200074

Lehne, J. (2019). Crisis at the WTO: Is the blocking of appointments to the WTO Appellate Body by the United States legally justified? *SSRN*. DOI: 10.24921/2019.94115941

Lekić, M., & Osakwe, C. (2017). WTO rules, accession protocols and mega-regionals: Complementarity and governance in the rules-based global economy. *Trade Multilateralism in the Twenty-First Century: Building the Upper Floors of the Trading System Through WTO Accessions*.

Lensink, R., & Morrissey, O. (2001). Foreign direct investment: Flows, volatility and growth in developing countries (No. 01/06). CREDIT Research Paper.

Lenza, M., & Slacalek, J. (2018). How does monetary policy affect income and wealth inequality? Evidence from quantitative easing in the Euro area (ECB Working Paper No. 2190). DOI: 10.2139/ssrn.3275976

Lesne, J. (2016). On the necessity of requiring international free trade agreements to provide stronger protection of human health and the environment. *Environnement, Risques & Santé : ERS*, *15*(3), 238–247.

Leta. (2025). *Your deliveries,* Retrieved from Leta: https://leta.ai/

Li, C., & Whalley, J. (2021). Effects of the comprehensive and progressive agreement for trans-pacific partnership. *World Economy*, *44*(5), 1312–1337. DOI: 10.1111/twec.13026

Li, F. (2024). Challenges and Opportunities for Sustainable Supply Chain Management. *Frontiers in Business, Economics and Management*, 160–163.

Lin, C.-C., & Peng, S.-S. (2019). The role of diminishing marginal utility in the ordinal and cardinal utility theories. ERN: Other Macroeconomics: Employment. Academic Press.

Lin, K. K., Arya, N., Malik, S., & Diaz, M. (2024). Continuous variable analyses. In *Elsevier eBooks* (pp. 141–145). DOI: 10.1016/B978-0-323-85663-8.00078-7

Lind, M. (2019). The return of geo-economics. *National Interest*, (164), 12–18.

Linnenluecke, M. K. (2017). Resilience in business and management research: A review of influential publications and a research agenda. *International Journal of Management Reviews*, *19*(1), 4–30. DOI: 10.1111/ijmr.12076

Linnenluecke, M. K. (2022). Environmental, social and governance (ESG) performance in the context of multinational business research. *Multinational Business Review*, *30*(1), 1–16. Advance online publication. DOI: 10.1108/MBR-11-2021-0148

Li, P. P. (2020). Organizational resilience for a new normal: Balancing the paradox of global interdependence. *Management and Organization Review*, *16*(3), 503–509. DOI: 10.1017/mor.2020.30

Lipkan, V., Kuznichenko, O., & Ivanov, A. (2023). Geoeconomics as a tool of modern geostrategy. *Baltic Journal of Economic Studies*, *9*(1), 113–123. DOI: 10.30525/2256-0742/2023-9-1-113-123

Li, Q., & Moon, H. C. (2018). The trade and income effects of RCEP: Implications for China and Korea. *Journal of Korea Trade*, *22*(3), 306–318. DOI: 10.1108/JKT-03-2018-0020

Li, S., & Wang, Y. (2024). China's perspective on applying for the CPTPP: Enhancing economic interdependence as a hedging approach in great power rivalry. *China International Strategy Review*, *6*(1), 78–99. DOI: 10.1007/s42533-024-00154-9

Liu, H., Xu, C., & Lim, G. (2023). The China effect on regional economic integration: A longitudinal study of Central, South, and Southeast Asia. *Journal of the Asia Pacific Economy*, *29*(4), 2110–2132. DOI: 10.1080/13547860.2023.2258018

Liu, Q., Zhang, G., Yu, J., Kong, G., Cao, T., Ji, G., & Han, L. (2024). Machine learning-aided hydrothermal carbonization of biomass for coal-like hydrochar production: Parameters optimization and experimental verification. *Bioresource Technology*, *393*, 130073. DOI: 10.1016/j.biortech.2023.130073

Liu, Y., Zhang, Y., Jiang, R., Cheng, J., & Dai, J. (2024). Limiting heterogeneity in cross-border data flow: Impact on domestic value chains stability and the role of innovation. *PLoS One*, *19*(8), e0308716. DOI: 10.1371/journal.pone.0308716 PMID: 39159215

Li, X., & Hsee, C. K. (2021). The psychology of marginal utility. *The Journal of Consumer Research*, *48*(1), 169–188. DOI: 10.1093/jcr/ucaa064

Locoman, E., & Lau, R. R. (2024). Narratives of conflict: Russian media's evolving treatment of Ukraine (2013–2022). *Media, War & Conflict*. Advance online publication. DOI: 10.1177/17506352241257053

Lohani, K. K. (2020). Trade Flow of India with BRICS Countries: A Gravity Model Approach. *Global Business Review*, *25*(1), 22–39. DOI: 10.1177/0972150920927684

Lori Systems Ltd. (2025). *Transport Empowerment*. Retrieved from Lori Systems Ltd: https://www.lorisystems.com/impact.html#transport

Lu, S. (2019). Regional Comprehensive Economic Partnership (RCEP): Impact on the integration of textile and apparel supply chain in the Asia-Pacific region. *Fashion Supply Chain Management in Asia: Concepts, Models, and Cases*, 21-41.

Luiz, J. M., & Barnard, H. (2022). Home country (in) stability and the locational portfolio construction of emerging market multinational enterprises. *Journal of Business Research*, *151*, 17–32. Advance online publication. DOI: 10.1016/j.jbusres.2022.06.042

Lundberg, S. M., & Lee, S. I. (2017). A unified approach to interpreting model predictions. *Advances in Neural Information Processing Systems*, 30.

Luo, Y. (2024). Paradigm shift and theoretical implications for the era of global disorder. *Journal of International Business Studies*, *55*(2), 127–135. Advance online publication. DOI: 10.1057/s41267-023-00659-2

Luthra, K. S., Vinod, K., Sanjay, A., & Haleem, A. (2016). Barriers to implement green supply chain management in automobile industry using interpretive structural modeling technique: An Indian perspective. *Journal of Industrial Engineering and Management*, 231–257.

Luttwak, E. N. (1990). From geopolitics to geoeconomics: Logic of conflict, grammar of commerce. *National Interest*, (20), 17–23. https://www.jstor.org/stable/42894676

Madhumitha, B. (2020). WTO—Analysis of issues with the dispute settlement mechanism. *Beijing Law Review*, *11*(4), 879–888. DOI: 10.4236/blr.2020.114052

Maftouh, A., El Fatni, O., Fayiah, M., Liew, R. K., Lam, S. S., Bahaj, T., & Butt, M. H. (2022). The application of water–energy nexus in the Middle East and North Africa (MENA) region: A structured review. *Applied Water Science*, *12*(5), 83. DOI: 10.1007/s13201-022-01613-7

Ma, H., & Ning, J. (2024). The return of protectionism: Prospects for Sino-US trade relations in the wake of the trade war. *China Economic Quarterly International*, *4*(3), 182–211. DOI: 10.1016/j.ceqi.2024.09.003

Mahmood, F., & Jongwanich, J. (2018). Export-enhancing effects of free trade agreements in South Asia: Evidence from Pakistan. *Journal of South Asian Development*, *13*(1), 24–53. DOI: 10.1177/0973174118764925

Mahmood, N., Shakil, M. H., Akinlaso, I. M., & Tasnia, M. (2019). Foreign direct investment and institutional stability: Who drives whom? *Journal of Economics, Finance and Administrative Science*, *24*(47), 145–156. DOI: 10.1108/JEFAS-05-2018-0048

Malhotra, G., Yadav, M. P., Tandon, P., & Sinha, N. (2023). An investigation on dynamic connectedness of commodity market with financial market during the Russia–Ukraine invasion. *Benchmarking*, *31*(2), 439–465. DOI: 10.1108/BIJ-11-2022-0727

Malikova, R. (2021). National security exception under the GATT Article XXI as the most problematic issue of today's trading system. *SSRN*. DOI: 10.2139/ssrn.3759338

Malle, S. (2017). Russia and China in the 21st century. Moving towards cooperative behaviour. *Journal of Eurasian Studies*, *8*(2), 136–150. DOI: 10.1016/j.euras.2017.02.003

Malyarenko, T., & Kormych, B. (2023). Russian policy towards the economy of occupied Ukrainian territories: Crawling de-modernization. *Eurasian Geography and Economics*, *64*(2), 220–237. DOI: 10.1080/15387216.2023.2167097

Mansoor, U., & Inam, S. (2024). National security or trade openness? The balancing act in contemporary trade relations. *IUP Law Review, 14*(3).

Mansoor, I. U. (2021). Globalization and role of WTO in bridging the inequalities between member countries. *SSRN*. DOI: 10.2139/ssrn.5019105

Mansoor, S. I. (2025). Renewable energy and international law: Managing risk in relation to economic volatility and geopolitical instability. In Özsungur, F., Chaychi Semsari, M., & Küçük Bayraktar, H. (Eds.), *Geopolitical landscapes of renewable energy and urban growth* (pp. 97–124). IGI Global Scientific Publishing. DOI: 10.4018/979-8-3693-8814-3.ch004

Mansoor, S. I. U. (2021). TRIPS Agreement's obligations and their repercussion on developing countries during emergency situations. *Ilkogretim Online*, *20*(1), 6021–6031.

Mansoor, S. I. U. (2023). China's geopolitical strategy: Crafting a new world order. *China Quarterly of International Strategic Studies*, *9*(1), 337–359. DOI: 10.1142/S2377740023500161

Mansoor, S. I. U., & Chopra, M. (2022). WTO and developing nations: Disparities in the WTO dispute settlement mechanism. *International Journal of Early Childhood Special Education*, *10*, 4441–4449.

Mansoor, S. I., Shah, M. A., Khan, H., Ghazali, A., Jan, S., & Utagi, S. H. (2025). Modern democracies and economic sanctions: A legal perspective on security and sovereignty. In Alaverdov, E., & Abuseridze, G. (Eds.), *Globalization, global security, and new international realities for modern democracies* (pp. 173–198). IGI Global Scientific Publishing. DOI: 10.4018/979-8-3373-1355-9.ch008

Mapendo, J. J., Senadjki, A., & Choong, Y. O. (2025). Stock market development and foreign direct investment: The moderating role of government effectiveness. *International Journal of Emerging Markets*. Advance online publication. DOI: 10.1108/IJOEM-04-2024-0597

Marceau, G. (2016). The World Trade Organization and export restrictions. In Matsushita, M., & Schoenbaum, T. (Eds.), *Emerging issues in sustainable development: Economics, law, and institutions in Asia Pacific* (pp. 113–136). Springer. DOI: 10.1007/978-4-431-56426-3_6

Mardones, C. (2022). Economic effects of isolating Russia from international trade due to its 'special military operation' in Ukraine. *European Planning Studies*, *31*(4), 663–678. DOI: 10.1080/09654313.2022.2079074

Mariotti, S. (2022). A warning from the Russian–Ukrainian war: Avoiding a future that rhymes with the past. *Economia e Politica Industriale*, *49*(4), 761–782. Advance online publication. DOI: 10.1007/s40812-022-00219-z

Maris. (2021). *Meta Electric Partners with Sendy to Provide Cleaner, Cheaper Deliveries*. Retrieved from Marisafrica: https://marisafrica.com/meta-electric-sendy-partnership/

Marketforce. (2025). *Facilitating growth across the African retail ecosystem in a digital age*. Retrieved from Marketforce360: https://marketforce360.com/company.html

Marshall, A. (1890). *Principles of economics*. Macmillan.

Martin, A., & Vergote, W. (2008). On the role of retaliation in trade agreements. *Journal of International Economics*, *76*(1), 61–77. DOI: 10.1016/j.jinteco.2008.03.009

Martinez-Vazquez, J., Zhang, L., & Goodspeed, T. (2011). Public policies and FDI location: Differences between developing and developed countries. FinanzArchiv / Public Finance Analysis, 67(2), 171–191. DOI: 10.1628/001522111X588736

Martínez-Zarzoso, I., & Chelala, S. (2021). Trade agreements and international technology transfer. *Review of World Economics*, *157*(3), 631–665. DOI: 10.1007/s10290-021-00420-7

Ma, S., Shen, Y., & Fang, C. (2023). Can data flow provisions facilitate trade in goods and services?—Analysis based on the TAPED database. *The Journal of International Trade & Economic Development*, *33*(3), 343–368. DOI: 10.1080/09638199.2023.2179860

Maśniak, J., & Jędruchniewicz, A. (2024). Foreign Trade as a Channel of Pandemic Transmission to the Agricultural Sector in Poland. *Sustainability (Basel)*, *16*(16), 7072. DOI: 10.3390/su16167072

Mathews, S., & Healy, M. (2008). 'From garage to global': The internet and international market growth, an SME perspective. *International Journal of Internet Marketing and Advertising*, *4*(2-3), 179–196. DOI: 10.1504/IJIMA.2008.017021

Matsushita, M., Schoenbaum, T., Mavroidis, P., & Hahn, M. (2003). *The World Trade Organization: Law, practice, and policy*. DOI: 10.1093/law/9780199571857.001.0001

Maurya, P. K., Bansal, R., & Mishra, A. K. (2023). Russia–Ukraine conflict and its impact on global inflation: An event study-based approach. *Journal of Economic Studies (Glasgow, Scotland)*, *50*(8), 1824–1846. DOI: 10.1108/JES-01-2023-0003

Mavruk, T. (2022). Analysis of herding behavior in individual investor portfolios using machine learning algorithms. *Research in International Business and Finance*, *62*, 101740. DOI: 10.1016/j.ribaf.2022.101740

McDonald, F., Josef Tüselmann, H., Voronkova, S., & Golesorkhi, S. (2011). The strategic development of subsidiaries in regional trade blocs. *Multinational Business Review, 19*(3), 256–271. DOI: 10.1108/15253831111172685

McDowell, D. (2023). *Bucking the buck: U.S. financial sanctions and the international backlash against the dollar.* Oxford University Press. DOI: 10.1093/oso/9780197679876.001.0001

Mchopa, A. D., Kazungu, I. E., & Changalima, I. A. (2024). Green Supply Chain Management Among Small and Medium Manufacturing Firms in East Africa: A Review of Practices and Antecedents for Sustainability. *Sustainable Education and Development - Clean Energy* (pp. 243-257). Springer Nature.

Meixell, M. J., & Gargeya, V. B. (2005). Global supply chain design: A literature review and critique. *Transportation Research*, 531–550.

Menzl, V. (2021). Alternative views on the link between risk aversion and diminishing marginal utility of wealth. *European Financial and Accounting Journal, 16*(2), 51–72. DOI: 10.18267/j.efaj.255

Meyer, K. E., & Li, C. (2022). The MNE and its subsidiaries at times of global disruptions: An international relations perspective. *Global Strategy Journal, 12*(3), 555–577. Advance online publication. DOI: 10.1002/gsj.1436

Meyer, K. E., Mudambi, R., & Narula, R. (2011). Multinational enterprises and local contexts: The opportunities and challenges of multiple embeddedness. *Journal of Management Studies, 48*(2), 235–252. DOI: 10.1111/j.1467-6486.2010.00968.x

MHCL. (2025). mkulazi.co.tz. Retrieved from About Mkulazi: https://www.mkulazi.co.tz/about

Mienye, I. D., Sun, Y., & Wang, Z. (2019). Prediction performance of improved decision tree-based algorithms: A review. *Procedia Manufacturing, 35*, 698–703. DOI: 10.1016/j.promfg.2019.06.011

Mill, J. S. (1863). Utilitarianism. Longmans, Green, Reader, and Dyer.

Milner, H. (2009). Power, Interdependence, and Nonstate Actors in World Politics: Research Frontiers. In Milner, H. V., & Moravcsik, A. (Eds.), *Power, Interdependence, and Nonstate Actors in World Politics* (pp. 3–28). Princeton University Press. DOI: 10.2307/j.ctt7t8fk.6

Mirkovikj, B. K., Gkasis, P., & Golitsis, P. (2024). Regulatory quality and foreign direct investment: A case analysis of North Macedonia. *Theoretical Economics Letters, 14*(5), 1883–1913. DOI: 10.4236/tel.2024.145095

Miró, J. (2023). Responding to the global disorder: The EU's quest for open strategic autonomy. *Global Society*, *37*(3), 315–335. Advance online publication. DOI: 10.1080/13600826.2022.2110042

Miroudot, S., & Rigo, D. (2022). Multinational production and investment provisions in preferential trade agreements. *Journal of Economic Geography*, *22*(6), 1275–1308. DOI: 10.1093/jeg/lbab031

Mishkin, F. S. (2011). Monetary policy strategy: Lessons from the crisis (NBER Working Paper No. 16755). National Bureau of Economic Research.

MIT. (2020). *Massachusetts Institute of Technology*. Retrieved from Improving global health equity by helping clinics do more with less: https://news.mit.edu/2020/macro-eyes-vaccine-chain-health-equity-0626

Mody, A., & Sandri, D. (2011). The Eurozone crisis: How banks and sovereigns came to be joined at the hip (IMF Working Paper No. 11/269). https://www.imf.org/external/pubs/ft/wp/2011/wp11269.pdf

Mohamad, A. (2024). Herding behaviour surrounding the Russo–Ukraine war and COVID-19 pandemic: Evidence from energy, metal, livestock and grain commodities. *Review of Behavioral Finance*, *16*(5), 925–957. Advance online publication. DOI: 10.1108/RBF-12-2023-0339

Mohammed, A. (2023). The Utilization of Robotics in Supply Chain Management and its Various Applicatons. *International Journal of Information Technology, Modeling and Computing*, 1-9.

Mohazzem Hossain, S., Biswas, S., & Raihan Uddin, M. (2024). Sustainable energy transition in Bangladesh: Challenges and pathways for the future. *Engineering Reports*, *6*(1), e12752. DOI: 10.1002/eng2.12752

Mohd Sofian, D. R., & Mohd Redzuan, D. M. (2023). The impact of US monetary policy tools on exchange rates of major European currencies: Tools or games? *SSRN*. DOI: 10.2139/ssrn.4497922

Mongi, C., & Saidi, K. (2024). The impact of corruption, government effectiveness, FDI, and GFC on economic growth: New evidence from global panel of 48 middle-income countries. *Journal of the Knowledge Economy*, *15*(3), 10696–10721. DOI: 10.1007/s13132-023-01509-0

Moore, R. M. (1972). The Role of International Firms in Latin American Automotive Industry. *Journal of International Business Studies*, *3*(1), 51–67. DOI: 10.1057/palgrave.jibs.8490741

Moral-Muñoz, J. A., Herrera-Viedma, E., Santisteban-Espejo, A., & Cobo, M. J. (2020). Software tools for conducting bibliometric analysis in science: An up-to-date review. *El Profesional de la Información, 29*(1), e290103. DOI: 10.3145/epi.2020.ene.03

Moschieri, C., Ravasi, D., & Huy, Q. (2024). Why do some multinational firms respond better than others to the hostility of host governments? Proximal embedding and the side effects of local partnerships. *Journal of Management Studies, 61*(2), 627–685. Advance online publication. DOI: 10.1111/joms.12809

Moshiri, S., & Kheirandish, E. (2023). Global impacts of oil price shocks: The trade effect. *Journal of Economic Studies (Glasgow, Scotland), 51*(1), 126–144. DOI: 10.1108/JES-08-2022-0455

Mottaleb, K., & Kalirajan, K. (2010). Determinants of foreign direct investment in developing countries: A comparative analysis. *Margin, 4*(4), 369–404. DOI: 10.1177/097380101000400401

Moutik, B., Summerscales, J., Jones, J. G., & Pemberton, R. (2023). Life Cycle Assessment Research Trends and Implications: A Bibliometric Analysis. *Sustainability*.

Mrindoko, A. E., & Mollel, A. B. (2024). Impacts of Non-Tariff Barriers to International Trade on the Growth of Small Business in Tanzania. *International Journal of Management, Accounting & Economics, 11*(6).

Muchlinski, P. (2021). *Multinational enterprises and the law*. Oxford University Press. DOI: 10.1093/law/9780198824138.001.0001

Mueller, M. L., & Farhat, K. (2022). Regulation of platform market access by the United States and China: Neo-mercantilism in digital services. Policy & Internet. https://ssrn.com/abstract=3896517 DOI: 10.1002/poi3.305

Muhammad, A. (2023). The geopolitical implications of shifting alliances in a multipolar world. *Zenodo*. https://doi.org/DOI: 10.5281/zenodo.8382207

Mukwano Industries Ltd. (2025). *Mukwano Industries Uganda Ltd*. Retrieved from https://mukwano.com/about-us/: https://mukwano.com/about-us/

Murphy, J. P., & McLarney, C. (2018). Regionalism and the Multilateral Trading System: The Role of Regional Trade Agreements. In *Geopolitics and strategic management in the global economy* (pp. 1-18). IGI Global Scientific Publishing.

Mwanaumo, E. T., Mwanza, B. M., & Siaminwe, L. (2023). Green Supply Chain Management Practices and Effects on Organizational Performance in the Zambian Beverage Manufacturing Industry . *Logistics and Operation Management*, 15-30.

Nagelkerke, N. J. (1991). A note on a general definition of the coefficient of determination. *Biometrika, 78*(3), 691–692. DOI: 10.1093/biomet/78.3.691

Namagembe, S., Ryan, S., & Ramaswami, S. (2019). Green supply chain practice adoption and firm performance: Manufacturing SMEs in Uganda. *Management of Environmental Quality*, 5–35.

Nam, H., & Ryu, D. (2024). Does trade openness promote economic growth in developing countries? *Journal of International Financial Markets, Institutions and Money*, *93*, 101985. DOI: 10.1016/j.intfin.2024.101985

Napshin, S., & Brouthers, L. E. (2015). Intermediary products: FDI strategies, imports, exports, and trade balances in developed economies. *Thunderbird International Business Review*, *57*(4), 311–322. DOI: 10.1002/tie.21673

Narens, L., & Skyrms, B. (2020). *The pursuit of happiness: Philosophical and psychological foundations of utility*. Oxford University Press. DOI: 10.1093/oso/9780198856450.001.0001

Narine, S. (2018). US domestic politics and America's withdrawal from the Trans-Pacific Partnership: Implications for Southeast Asia. *Contemporary Southeast Asia*, *40*(1), 50–76. DOI: 10.1355/cs40-1c

Nasiche, F., & Ngugi, G. K. (2014). Determinants of Adoption of Green Procurement in the Public Sector: A Case Study of Kenya Pipeline Company. *International Journal of Social Sciences and Entrepreneurship*, 351-372.

Nasir, M. A., Nugroho, A. D., & Lakner, Z. (2022). Impact of the Russian–Ukrainian conflict on global food crops. *Foods*, *11*(19), 2979. Advance online publication. DOI: 10.3390/foods11192979 PMID: 36230055

Nelson, E. (2007). Milton Friedman on inflation. Economic Synopses, 1, Federal Reserve Bank of St. Louis. https://files.stlouisfed.org/files/htdocs/publications/es/07/ES0701.pdf

Nelson, R. M. (2010). *G-20 and International Economic Cooperation: Background and Implications for Congress*. DIANE Publishing.

Nesselrodt, R. (2023). Controlling for X: Export controls and emerging technology competition. *Journal of Science Policy & Governance*, *22*(3). Advance online publication. DOI: 10.38126/JSPG220306

Nguyen, H. H., Van Nguyen, P., & Ngo, V. M. (2024). Energy security and the shift to renewable resources: The case of Russia-Ukraine war. *The Extractive Industries and Society*, *17*, 101442. DOI: 10.1016/j.exis.2024.101442

Nguyen, T. T., Timilsina, R. R., Sonobe, T., & Rahut, D. B. (2023). Interstate war and food security: Implications from Russia's invasion of Ukraine. *Frontiers in Sustainable Food Systems*, *7*, 1080696. Advance online publication. DOI: 10.3389/fsufs.2023.1080696

Nielsen, B. B., Wechtler, H., & Zheng, L. G. (2023). Disasters and international business: Insights and recommendations from a systematic review. *Journal of World Business*, *58*(4), 101458. DOI: 10.1016/j.jwb.2023.101458

Ni, J. (2024). A decade of the Belt and Road Initiative and its global impact. *China Economic Journal*, *17*(2), 137–139. DOI: 10.1080/17538963.2024.2345532

Nizhnikau, R., & Moshes, A. (2024). The war in Ukraine, the EU's geopolitical awakening and implications for the "contested neighbourhood.". *Policy Studies*, *45*(3-4), 1–18. DOI: 10.1080/01442872.2024.2306972

Noosuwan, C., Autsadee, Y., Saengsupavanich, C., & Açık, A. (2024). Measuring economic convergence: Evidence from container throughputs of ASEAN-5 countries. *World Review of Intermodal Transportation Research*, *12*(1), 44–63. DOI: 10.1504/WRITR.2024.140467

Oberhauser, M. (2024). The Chinese belt and road initiative: Development project with strings attached? *International Journal of Development Issues*, *23*(2), 212–244. DOI: 10.1108/IJDI-03-2023-0073

Ohashi, H. (2018). The Belt and Road Initiative (BRI) in the context of China's opening-up policy. *Journal of Contemporary East Asia Studies*, *7*(2), 85–103. DOI: 10.1080/24761028.2018.1564615

Oh, C. H., Shin, J., & Oetzel, J. (2021). How does experience change firms' foreign investment decisions to non-market events? *Journal of International Management*, *27*(1), 100802. DOI: 10.1016/j.intman.2020.100802

Ojo, L. D., Adeniyi, O., Ogundimu, O. E., & Alaba, O. O. (2022). Rethinking Green Supply Chain Management Practices Impact on Company Performance: A Close-Up Insight. *Sustainability*, 2–19.

Okabe, M. (2015). Impact of free trade agreements on trade in East Asia. *ERIA Discussion Paper Series, 1*, 48.

Okara, A. (2023). Does foreign direct investment promote political stability? Evidence from developing economies. *Economic Modelling*, *123*, 106249. DOI: 10.1016/j.econmod.2023.106249

Okoye, K., & Hosseini, S. (2024). Choosing Between Parametric and Non-parametric Tests in Statistical Data Analysis. In *springer* (pp. 87–98). DOI: 10.1007/978-981-97-3385-9_4

Olayungbo, D. O., Zhuparova, A., Al-Faryan, M. S., & Ojo, M. S. (2024). Global oil price and stock markets in oil exporting and European countries: Evidence during the Covid-19 and the Russia-Ukraine war. *Research in Globalization*, *8*, 100199. DOI: 10.1016/j.resglo.2024.100199

Ono, S., & Sekiyama, T. (2024). The impact of official development assistance on foreign direct investment: The case of Japanese firms in India. *Frontiers in Political Science*, *6*, 1351285. DOI: 10.3389/fpos.2024.1351285

Organisation for Economic Co-operation and Development. (2023). Economic policy reforms 2023: Going for growth. OECD Publishing. https://www.oecd.org/content/dam/oecd/en/publications/reports/2023/10/economic-policy-reforms-2023_6ffe1e12/9953de23-en.pdf

Organisation for Economic Co-operation and Development. (2023). Revenue statistics 2023. https://www.oecd.org/en/publications/revenue-statistics-2023_9d0453d5-en.html

Organisation for Economic Co-operation and Development. (2024). Tax and benefit policy descriptions for Portugal 2024. OECD Publishing. https://www.oecd.org/content/dam/oecd/en/topics/policy-sub-issues/incomes-support-redistribution-and-work-incentives/TaxBEN-Portugal-latest.pdf

Organization for Economic Co-operation and Development. (2021). *Financial markets and economic cycles.* https://www.oecd.org/

Orhangazi, Ö., & Yeldan, A. E. (2021). The re-making of the Turkish crisis. *Development and Change*, *52*(3), 460–503. Advance online publication. DOI: 10.1111/dech.12644

Oxford Analytica (2024). China trade deal has pros and cons for Ecuador. *Emerald Expert Briefings*, (oxan-db).

Oyebamiji, S. I., Ashe, M. O., & Kiyala, K. J. C. (2024). Russia-Ukraine War: Impacts on energy market and food security in Africa. In *˜The œanthropocene: Politik - economics - society - science* (pp. 419–441). DOI: 10.1007/978-3-031-48375-2_19

Oyewo, A. S., Sterl, S., Khalili, S., & Breyer, C. (2023). Highly renewable energy systems in Africa: Rationale, research and recommendations. *Joule*, 1437–1470.

Ozili, P. K. (2024). Global economic consequences of Russian invasion of Ukraine. In *Advances in human services and public health (AHSPH) book series* (pp. 195–223). DOI: 10.4018/978-1-6684-9467-7.ch010

Ozili, P. K., & Arun, T. (2020). Spillover of COVID-19: Impact on the global economy (March 27, 2020). *SSRN*. DOI: 10.2139/ssrn.3562570

Özocakli, D., Başar, B. D., Ekşi, İ. H., & Ginn, W. (2024). Effect of Grain Corridor Agreement on grain prices. *International Economic Journal*, *38*(3), 1–18. DOI: 10.1080/10168737.2024.2372764

Pagano, M. (2015). Lessons from the European financial crisis. In Faia, E., Hackethal, A., Haliassos, M., & Langenbucher, K. (Eds.), *Financial regulation: A transatlantic perspective* (pp. 23–48). Cambridge University Press. DOI: 10.1017/CBO9781316026649.004

Paiola, M., & Gebauer, H. (2020). Internet of things technologies, digital servitization and business model innovation in BtoB manufacturing firms. *Industrial Marketing Management*, 245–264.

Palmunen, L.-M., Pelto, E., & Karhu, A. (forthcoming). Blockchain technology and the consequences for trust in international business relations. *European Journal of International Management*.

Panagariya, A. (2013). Challenges to the multilateral trading system and possible responses. *Economics*, *7*(1), 20130010. DOI: 10.5018/economics-ejournal.ja.2013-10

Pandey, D. K., & Kumar, R. (2022). Russia-Ukraine War and the global tourism sector: A 13-day tale. *Current Issues in Tourism*, *26*(5), 692–700. DOI: 10.1080/13683500.2022.2081789

Papadopoulos, G. D., Magafas, L., Demertzis, K., & Antoniou, I. (2023). Analyzing global geopolitical stability in terms of world trade network analysis. Information. mdpi.comDOI: 10.3390/info14080442

Park, C. Y., Petri, P. A., & Plummer, M. G. (2021). The economics of conflict and cooperation in the Asia-pacific: RCEP, CPTPP and the US-China trade war. *East Asian Economic Review*, *25*(3), 233–272. DOI: 10.11644/KIEP.EAER.2021.25.3.397

Park, S. C. (2020). Protectionism as challenges for the global trade governance. In Rewizorski, M., Jędrzejowska, K., & Wróbel, A. (Eds.), *The future of global economic governance* (pp. 99–113). Springer. DOI: 10.1007/978-3-030-35336-0_7

Parmar, Y. (2023). An empirical impact of GDP and inflation on Indian stock market inclusive with Sensex. *International Journal of Creative Research Thoughts, 11*(2), 688–694. https://www.ijcrt.org/papers/IJCRT2302082.pdf

Paul, J., & Feliciano-Cestero, M. M. (2021). Five decades of research on foreign direct investment by MNEs: An overview and research agenda. *Journal of Business Research, 124*, 800–812. DOI: 10.1016/j.jbusres.2020.04.017

Pellegrino, R., Gaudenzi, B., & Zsidisin, G. A. (2024). Mitigating foreign exchange risk exposure with supply chain flexibility: A real option analysis. *Journal of Business Logistics, 45*(1), e12338. DOI: 10.1111/jbl.12338

Pereira, P., Bašić, F., Bogunovic, I., & Barcelo, D. (2022). Russian-Ukrainian war impacts the total environment. *The Science of the Total Environment, 837*, 155865. DOI: 10.1016/j.scitotenv.2022.155865 PMID: 35569661

Peres, M., Ameer, W., & Xu, H. (2018). The impact of institutional quality on foreign direct investment inflows: Evidence for developed and developing countries. *Ekonomska Istrazivanja, 31*(1), 626–644. DOI: 10.1080/1331677X.2018.1438906

Petrov, A. V., Baynova, M. S., & Jiaerheng, J. (2022). Features of Russian and Chinese direct investments in Kazakhstan. *Spatial Economics, 8*(1), 148–167. DOI: 10.14530/se.2022.1.148-167

Piketty, T. (2014). Capital in the twenty-first century. In L. W. R. (Ed.), The economics of inequality (pp. 23–45). Harvard University Press. https://www.jstor.org/stable/j.ctt6wpqbc

Piketty, T. (2020). *Capital and ideology*. Harvard University Press.

Piketty, T., Saez, E., & Zucman, G. (2018). Distributional national accounts: Methods and estimates for the United States. *The Quarterly Journal of Economics, 133*(2), 553–609. DOI: 10.1093/qje/qjx043

Pistilli, M. (2025). How would a new BRICS currency affect the U.S. dollar? *Investing News Network*. https://investingnews.com/brics-currency/

Podgórska, K., Jekaterynczuk, A., Yarosh, O., Kuzmuk, O., & Liubchuk, V. (2023). Support for Ukrainian refugees after Russia's invasion of Ukraine: Aid structure and resilience factors. Case studies of Lublin and Lutsk. *European Societies*, 1–25. DOI: 10.1080/14616696.2023.2206892

Pomfret, R. (2021). 'Regionalism'and the global trade system. *World Economy, 44*(9), 2496–2514. DOI: 10.1111/twec.13155

Poulsen, L., & Hufbauer, G. (2011). Foreign direct investment in times of crisis. *Transnational Corporations, 20*(1), 19–38. DOI: 10.18356/138883a0-en

PR Newswire. (2020). Retrieved from Macro-eyes receives $2.2M grant from the Bill & Melinda Gates Foundation to bring AI to low income countries: https://www.prnewswire.com/news-releases/macro-eyes-receives-2-2m-grant-from-the-bill--melinda-gates-foundation-to-bring-ai-to-low-income-countries-300999849.html

Prachowny, M. F. J. (1993). Okun's law: Theoretical foundations and revised estimates. *The Review of Economics and Statistics, 75*(2), 331–336. DOI: 10.2307/2109440

Prause, G., Olaniyi, E. O., & Gerstlberger, W. (2023). Ammonia production as alternative energy for the Baltic Sea region. *Energies, 16*(4), 1831. DOI: 10.3390/en16041831

Puhr, H., & Müllner, J. (2022). Foreign to all but fluent in many: The effect of multinationality on shock resilience. *Journal of World Business, 57*(6), 101370. DOI: 10.1016/j.jwb.2022.101370

Pushp, P., Sharma, A., & Ahmed, F. (2024). Flexibility in the WTO: Navigating the dynamics of multilateralism using Grounded theory. *Global Journal of Flexible Systems Management*. DOI: 10.1007/s40171-024-00413-z

Quaglia, L., & Verdun, A. (2023). Weaponisation of finance: The role of European central banks and financial sanctions against Russia. *West European Politics, 46*(5), 872–895. DOI: 10.1080/01402382.2022.2155906

Qu, C., & Kim, E. (2024). Reviewing the roles of AI-integrated technologies in sustainable supply chain management: Research propositions and a framework for future directions. *Sustainability*, •••, 6186.

Quiambao, J. E. A. (2022). Thinking ethically: The utilitarianism approach in moral decision making. *International Journal of Multidisciplinary Research and Growth Evaluation, 3*(3), 602–604. DOI: 10.54660/anfo.2022.3.3.30

Rabajante, M. D. F. (2024). Artificial Intelligence and international trade law. In A. Poorhashemi (Ed.), *Artificial intelligence and the future of international law* (pp. 35–50). SpringerBriefs in Law. Springer. DOI: 10.1007/978-3-031-73334-5_3

Rabbi, M. F., Ben Hassen, T., El Bilali, H., Raheem, D., & Raposo, A. (2023). Food security challenges in Europe in the context of the prolonged Russian–Ukrainian conflict. *Sustainability (Basel), 15*(6), 4745. DOI: 10.3390/su15064745

Rahman, M. A., Saha, P., Ratul, S. H., & Graham, G. (2024). Big data analytics capability and supply chain sustainability: Analyzing moderating role of green supply chain management practices. *Benchmarking*.

Rajput, N., & Sufiya, . (2022). Impact of COVID-19 on financial integration: Study on BRICS. *Investment Management and Financial Innovations*, *19*(2), 119–129. DOI: 10.21511/imfi.19(2).2022.10

Raju, J. K., Manjunath, B. R., & Pradeep, K. S. (2018). Impact of inflation and GDP on CNX Nifty. *Adarsh Journal of Management Research*, *11*(1). Advance online publication. DOI: 10.21095/ajmr/2018/v11/i1/139602

Ranjan, V., & Agrawal, G. (2011). FDI inflow determinants in BRIC countries: A panel data analysis. *International Business Research*, *4*(4), 255. DOI: 10.5539/ibr.v4n4p255

Rasch, F. A., & Shrimali, M. (2024). Protectionism by governments, the retrenchment of globalization and national security. In A. K. Nagar, D. S. Jat, D. Mishra, & A. Joshi (Eds.), *Intelligent sustainable systems. WorldS4 2023* (Vol. 812, pp. 523-536). Lecture Notes in Networks and Systems. Springer. DOI: 10.1007/978-981-99-8031-4_42

Raut, R. D., Mangla, S. K., Narwane, V. S., Dora, M., & Liu, M. (2021). Big Data Analytics as a mediator in Lean, Agile, Resilient, and Green (LARG) practices effects on sustainable supply chains. *Transportation Research Part E, Logistics and Transportation Review*.

Rawls, J. (1971). *A theory of justice*. Harvard University Press. DOI: 10.4159/9780674042605

Reinhart, C. M., & Rogoff, K. S. (2010). Growth in a time of debt. *The American Economic Review*, *100*(2), 573–578. DOI: 10.1257/aer.100.2.573

Ren, Z. (2023). Analysis of trade competitiveness and complementarity between China and RCEP members. *Advances in Economics. Management and Political Sciences*, *18*(1), 150–160. DOI: 10.54254/2754-1169/18/20230067

Reserve Bank of India. (2023). *Annual report 2022–2023.* https://www.rbi.org.in/

Revilla, M. L. D. (2016). Cross-country econometric study on the impact of fiscal incentives on FDI. Econstor - PIDS Discussion Paper Series, 2016–17. Retrieved from http://hdl.handle.net/10419/173538

Richter, W. F. (2024). Residual profit splitting: A theory-based approach to tax multinationals. *International Tax and Public Finance*, 1–21.

Ritala, P. (2024). Grand challenges and platform ecosystems: Scaling solutions for wicked ecological and societal problems. Journal of Product Innovation Management. DOI: 10.1111/jpim.12682

Roberts, A. (2008). International relations after the Cold War. *International Affairs (Royal Institute of International Affairs 1944-), 84*(2), 335–350. https://www.jstor.org/stable/25144768

Root, F. R. (2019). Independence and Adaptation: Response Strategies of US-Based Multinational Corporations to a Restrictive Public Policy World. In *Controlling Multinational Enterprises* (pp. 101-110). Routledge.

Røseth, T. (2017). Russia's energy relations with China: Passing the strategic threshold? *Eurasian Geography and Economics, 58*(1), 23–55. DOI: 10.1080/15387216.2017.1304229

Rout, B. S., & Das, N. M. (2024). BRICS stock markets performances during COVID-19: Comparison with other economic crises. *Vikalpa, 49*(3), 230–243. Advance online publication. DOI: 10.1177/02560909241264430

Saaida, M. (2024). BRICS Plus: De-dollarization and global power shifts in new economic landscape. *BRICS Journal of Economics, 5*(1), 13–33. DOI: 10.3897/brics-econ.5.e117828

Sabir, S., Rafique, A., & Abbas, K. (2019). Institutions and FDI: Evidence from developed and developing countries. *Financial Innovation, 5*(1), 1–20. DOI: 10.1186/s40854-019-0123-7

Sabljic, S., Rakovic, T. S., & Vasic, V. (2023). The new challenges of the Western Balkan banking industry during ongoing global crisis. *Journal of Balkan & Near Eastern Studies, 25*(4), 671–682. DOI: 10.1080/19448953.2023.2167166

Sacerdoti, G., Semercioglu, N., Famà, R., Assenza, E., Wade, D., & Lapa, V. (2021). *The WTO Dispute Settlement System in 2020: Facing the Appellate Body Paralysis.* Bocconi Legal Studies Research Paper No. 37944327. DOI: 10.2139/ssrn.3794327

Saeed, S., Altamimi, S. A., Alkayyal, N. A., Alshehri, E., & Alabbad, D. A. (2023). Digital transformation and cybersecurity challenges for businesses resilience: Issues and recommendations. Sensors, 23(15), 6666. DOI: 10.3390/s23156666

Safaricom. (2025). *2024 Sustainable Business Report.* Retrieved from safaricom.co.ke: https://www.safaricom.co.ke/images/Downloads/Safaricom-Sustainable-Report-2024-compressed.pdf

Saha, S., Sadekin, M. N., & Saha, S. K. (2022). Effects of institutional quality on foreign direct investment inflow in lower-middle income countries. *Heliyon*, *8*(10), e10828. DOI: 10.1016/j.heliyon.2022.e10828

Sahoo, P. (2006). Foreign direct investment in South Asia: Policy, trends, impact and determinants. ADB Institute Discussion Paper No. 56.

Saidi, Y., Ochi, A., & Maktouf, S. (2023). FDI inflows, economic growth, and governance quality trilogy in developing countries: A panel VAR analysis. *Bulletin of Economic Research*, *75*(2), 426–449. DOI: 10.1111/boer.12364

Saini, N., & Singhania, M. (2018). Determinants of FDI in developed and developing countries: A quantitative analysis using GMM. *Journal of Economic Studies (Glasgow, Scotland)*, *45*(2), 348–382. DOI: 10.1108/JES-07-2016-0138

Salamatov, V., Tangaeva, A. V., & Kolomin, V. O. (2022). RCEP in the System of Mega-Regional Trade Agreements. *Mirovaia Ekonomika i Mezhdunarodnye Otnosheniia*, *66*(2), 23–32. DOI: 10.20542/0131-2227-2022-66-2-23-32

Sampson, G. P. (2018). Challenges facing the World Trade Organization: An overview. *The Australian Economic Review*, *51*(4), 453–473. DOI: 10.1111/1467-8462.12301

Sampson, M. (2019). The evolution of China's regional trade agreements: Power dynamics and the future of the Asia-Pacific. *The Pacific Review*, *34*(2), 259–289. DOI: 10.1080/09512748.2019.1660397

Samunderu, E. (2024). Liberalisation of trade regime under AfCFTA: A perspective analysis on Africa's single market. In *The Economic Effects of Air Transport Market Liberalisation. Advances in African Economic, Social and Political Development* (pp. 123–145). Springer. DOI: 10.1007/978-3-031-61864-2_7

Santomero, A. M., & Seater, J. J. (1978). The inflation-unemployment trade-off: A critique of the literature. *Journal of Economic Literature*, *16*(2), 499–544. https://www.jstor.org/stable/2722879

Santos, J. R., & Sousa, M. J. (2022). Public administration and new information: Increasing utility. In A. Ullah, S. Anwar, Á. Rocha, & S. Gill (Eds.), Proceedings of International Conference on Information Technology and Applications (Lecture Notes in Networks and Systems, Vol. 350). Springer. DOI: 10.1007/978-981-16-7618-5_33

Santos, J. R., de Bem Machado, A., Sousa, M. J., & Fonseca, R. B. (2024). War in Ukraine and inflation in the Eurozone: Combining monetary and fiscal policies with a new "savings policy" as a more utilitarian solution to combat the inflationary surge. In New Research on Leadership Styles and Performance (pp. 273–292). DOI: 10.52305/ZKQP3465

Santos, J. R. (2020). *Economia indispensável*. Lisbon International Press.

Sarkar, M., & Cavusgil, S. T. (1996). Trends in international business thought and literature: A review of international market entry mode research: Integration and synthesis. *The International Executive*, *38*(6), 825–847. DOI: 10.1002/tie.5060380608

Sarno, L., & Taylor, M. P. (1998). Exchange controls, international capital flows and saving-investment correlations in the UK: An empirical investigation. *Weltwirtschaftliches Archiv*, *134*(1), 69–98. DOI: 10.1007/BF02707579

Saxena, P. (2022). An empirical study on implications and impact of GDP on the Indian stock market. *NeuroQuantology : An Interdisciplinary Journal of Neuroscience and Quantum Physics*, *20*(22), 938–950. DOI: 10.48047/nq.2022.20.22.NQ10070

Scherrer, C. (2004). Global governance: From fordist trilateralism to Neoliberal constitutionalism. In *New rules for global markets: Public and private governance in the world economy* (pp. 109–129). Palgrave Macmillan UK. DOI: 10.1057/9780230524361_6

Schmitz, L. & Seidl, T. (2023). As open as possible, as autonomous as necessary: Understanding the rise of open strategic autonomy in EU trade policy. JCMS: journal of common market studies. DOI: 10.1111/jcms.13428

Schneider, F., & Frey, B. S. (1985). Economic and political determinants of foreign direct investment. *World Development*, *13*(2), 161–175. DOI: 10.1016/0305-750X(85)90002-6

Schotter, A. (2021). Resilient or not: boundary-spanning in innovation focused MNEs during global crises. *Critical Perspectives on International Business*, *17*(2), 342-358.

Segger, M.-C. (2021). Integrating social and environmental considerations into trade and investment agreements, for sustainable development. In *Sustainable Development in International Trade and Investment Law* (Chapter 22). DOI: 10.1093/oso/9780198831341.003.0022

Semenenko, O., Sliusarenko, M., Onofriichuk, A., Onofriichuk, V., & Remez, A. (2023). Impact of the Russian–Ukrainian war on the national economy of Russia. *Journal of Interdisciplinary Economics*, *36*(1), 41–57. DOI: 10.1177/02601079231207489

Sen, A. (1997). Welfare economics, utilitarianism, and equity. In *On economic inequality* (pp. 1–19). Clarendon Press. DOI: 10.1093/0198281935.003.0001

Settembre-Blundo, D., González-Sánchez, R., Medina-Salgado, S., & García-Muiña, F. E. (2021). Flexibility and resilience in corporate decision making: a new sustainability-based risk management system in uncertain times. Global Journal of Flexible Systems Management, 22(Suppl 2), 107-132. DOI: 10.1007/s40171-021-00277-7

Seyoum, B. (2024). International Trade Policy for growth and Prosperity. In *Palgrave studies in democracy, innovation, and entrepreneurship for growth* (pp. 275–314). DOI: 10.1007/978-3-031-44776-1_7

Shadikhodjaev, S. (2011). Checking RTA compatibility with global trade rules: WTO litigation practice and implications from the transparency mechanism for RTAs. *Journal of World Trade*, *45*(3), 529–551. DOI: 10.54648/TRAD2011018

Shaffer, G. (2021). The challenges of international trade law. In *Emerging powers and the world trading system: The past and future of international economic law* (pp. 58–78). Cambridge University Press. DOI: 10.1017/9781108861342.004

Shapley, L. S. (1953). Stochastic games. *Proceedings of the National Academy of Sciences of the United States of America*, *39*(10), 1095–1100. DOI: 10.1073/pnas.39.10.1095

Sharma, P., & Shrivastava, A. K. (2021). Economic activities and oil price shocks in Indian outlook: Direction of causality and testing cointegration. *Global Business Review*, *097215092199049*. Advance online publication. DOI: 10.1177/0972150921990491

Sherraden, M. (1991). *Assets and the poor: New American welfare policy*. M.E. Sharpe.

Shih, W. C. (2020). Global supply chains in a post-pandemic world. *Harvard Business Review*, *98*(5), 82–89.

Short, J. L. (2021). The politics of regulatory enforcement and compliance: Theorizing and operationalizing political influences. Regulation & Governance. DOI: 10.1111/rego.12291

Silva, J. S., & Tenreyro, S. (2006). The log of gravity. *The Review of Economics and Statistics*, *88*(4), 641–658. DOI: 10.1162/rest.88.4.641

Simchi-Levi, D., & Haren, P. (2022). How the war in Ukraine is further disrupting global supply chains. https://hbr.org/2022/03/how-the-war-in-ukraine-is-further-disrupting-global-supply-chains

Simões, F. D. (2019). The Appellate Body of the WTO: An international court by another name. In Bungenberg, M., Krajewski, M., Tams, C. J., Terhechte, J. P., & Ziegler, A. R. (Eds.), *European Yearbook of International Economic Law 2019* (Vol. 10, pp. 8165–8179). Springer. DOI: 10.1007/8165_2019_33

Singh, C., Thakkar, R., & Jatinder, W. (2022). Blockchain in Supply Chain Management. *European Journal of Engineering and Technology Research*, 60-69.

Singh, J. P., & Woolcock, M. (2022). The future of multilateralism and global development: Opportunities for constitutive and functional reform. *Global Perspectives, 3*(1), 57594. DOI: 10.1525/gp.2022.57594

Singh, S. K., & Roy, S. (2020). Lecture Notes in Electrical Engineering. In Mandal, V. N. (Ed.), *Lecture Notes in Electriacl Engineering* (pp. 301–313). Springer.

Sinha, C., Saha, S., & Vasilev, A. (2024). Institutional quality and US FDI outflows: Do political regimes matter? *Economic Systems, 48*(3), 101241. DOI: 10.1016/j.ecosys.2024.101241

Sin, K. Y., Osman, A., Salahuddin, S. N., Abdullah, S., Lim, Y. J., & Sim, C. L. (2016). Relative advantage and competitive pressure towards implementation of e-commerce: Overview of small and medium enterprises (SMEs). *Procedia Economics and Finance, 35*, 434–443. DOI: 10.1016/S2212-5671(16)00054-X

Smeets, M., Berger, A., Akman, S., Aran, B., Braga, C., Kher, R., Lippoldt, D., Mildner, S., Nair, A., & Schmucker, C. (2023). Reforming the WTO through inclusive and development-friendly plurilaterals. *Journal of World Trade, 57*, 875–888. DOI: 10.54648/TRAD2023036

Sölvell, Ö., & Zander, I. (1995). Organization of the dynamic multinational enterprise: The home-based and the heterarchical MNE. *International Studies of Management & Organization, 25*(1-2), 17–38. DOI: 10.1080/00208825.1995.11656650

Song, L., & Agarwal, V. (2023). The Future of Multilateralism in the Post-pandemic World. *China & World Economy, 31*(1), 62–87. DOI: 10.1111/cwe.12459

Sönmez, A., Uysal, D., & Amirzai, F. R. (2025). Importance of BRICS countries in the world economy. In Gedikli, A., Erdogan, S., & Çalışkan Terzioğlu, H. (Eds.), *Changing the global political economy: BRICS countries and alternative relations strategies* (pp. 1–48). IGI Global. DOI: 10.4018/979-8-3693-7393-4.ch001

Stark, K. J. (2004). Fiscal federalism and tax progressivity: Should the federal income tax encourage state and local redistribution? *SSRN*. https://ssrn.com/abstract=546584

Statsenko, L., Jayasinghe, R. S., & Soosay, C. (2023). Supply network resilience capabilities: A social–ecological perspective. *Supply Chain Management*, *29*(1), 1–26. DOI: 10.1108/SCM-11-2022-0438

Stephen, M. D., & Parízek, M. (2018). New powers and the distribution of preferences in global trade governance: From deadlock and drift to fragmentation. *New Political Economy*, *24*(6), 735–758. DOI: 10.1080/13563467.2018.1509065

Stiglitz, J. E. (2012). The price of inequality: How today's divided society endangers our future. W. W. Norton & Company. https://business.columbia.edu/sites/default/files-efs/imce-uploads/Joseph_Stiglitz/Price%20of%20Inequality%20for%20Sustainable%20Humanity.pdf

Stiglitz, J. E. (2022). The causes of—and responses to—today's inflation. Roosevelt Institute. https://rooseveltinstitute.org/publications/the-causes-of-and-responses-to-todays-inflation/

Stiglitz, J. E. (2020). *People, power, and profits: Progressive capitalism for an age of discontent.* W. W. Norton & Company.

Strumbelj, E., & Kononenko, I. (2010). An efficient explanation of individual classifications using game theory. *Journal of Machine Learning Research*, *11*, 1–18.

Sujatmiko, Krisnanto, B., Sasmita, H., & Wahab, A. (2024). Global Supply Chain Management: Trends, Challenges, and Strategies. *Vifada Management and Digital Business*, 20-38.

Sunstein, C. R. (2020). Behavioral welfare economics. *Journal of Benefit-Cost Analysis*, *11*(1), 1–25. DOI: 10.1017/bca.2020.14

Suresh Kumar, K., Nassa, V. K., Uike, D., Kalra, A., Sahu, A. K., Athavale, V. A., & Saravanan, V. (2022). [Retracted] A Comparative Analysis of Blockchain in Enhancing the Drug Traceability in Edible Foods Using Multiple Regression Analysis. Journal of Food Quality, 2022(1), 1689913. DOI: 10.1155/2024/9837204

Suwanprasert, W. (2020). The role of the most favored nation principle of the GATT/WTO in the new trade model. *Review of International Economics*, *28*(3), 760–798. Advance online publication. DOI: 10.1111/roie.12470

Tadesse, G., Yitayih, S., Gashaw, F., Fentahun, S., Amare, A., Kibralew, G., & Zeleke, T. A. (2024). Magnitude and factors associated with post-traumatic stress disorder among war-affected internally displaced people in northwest Ethiopia, 2022. *SAGE Open Medicine*, *12*, 20503121241259629. Advance online publication. DOI: 10.1177/20503121241259629 PMID: 39086554

Taj, S., Imran, A. S., Kastrati, Z., Daudpota, S. M., Memon, R. A., & Ahmed, J. (2023). IoT-based supply chain management: A systematic literature review. *Ineternet of Things*.

Takáts, E., & Papp, T. K. (2008). Tax rate cuts and tax compliance: The Laffer curve revisited (IMF Working Paper No. 08/7). *SSRN*. https://ssrn.com/abstract=1087186 DOI: 10.5089/9781451868692.001

Tamiotti, L. (2010). Trade and the environment: Fundamental issues in international law, WTO law and legal theory by Erich Vranes. *World Trade Review*, *9*(1), 285–288. DOI: 10.1017/S147474560999022X

Tan, L., & Zhang, Y. (2015). Optimal resource allocation with principle of equality and diminishing marginal utility in wireless networks. *Wireless Personal Communications*, *84*(1), 671–693. DOI: 10.1007/s11277-015-2655-0

TBL. (2025). *Welcome to Tanzania Breweries Ltd PLC, Tanzania's Oldest and #1 Brewer*. Retrieved from Tanzania Breweries Ltd: https://www.tanzaniabreweries.co.tz/

Thakkar, C. (2024). Russia-Ukraine War, India, and US grand strategy: Punishing or leveraging neutrality? *Policy Studies*, *45*(3-4), 1–19. DOI: 10.1080/01442872.2024.2302437

Thangavel, P., & Chandra, B. (2024). Impact of sanctions on Russia on global economy. *International Journal of Business Forecasting and Marketing Intelligence*, *9*(1), 1–8. DOI: 10.1504/IJBFMI.2024.135717

ThankGod. (2023). *Artificial intelligence and international trade law: Navigating legal challenges in the age of automation*. SSRN. DOI: 10.2139/ssrn.4706943

Thierry Mayer & Soledad Zignago. (2011). Notes on CEPII's distances measures: The GeoDist database. Working Papers 2011-25, CEPII research center.

Tideman, N., & Plassmann, F. (2019). Utilitarianism as a criterion for state action. In Congleton, R. D., Grofman, B., & Voigt, S. (Eds.), *The Oxford Handbook of Public Choice* (Vol. 1, pp. 365–384). Oxford University Press.

Tinbergen, J. (1962). Shaping the world economy; suggestions for an international economic policy. Academic Press.

Tiwari, M., Ferrill, J., & Allan, D. M. (2024). Trade-based money laundering: A systematic literature review. *Journal of Accounting Literature*. Advance online publication. DOI: 10.1108/JAL-11-2022-0111

Todorova, T. (2021). Diminishing marginal utility and the teaching of economics: A note. [JRES]. *Journal of Research in Educational Sciences*, *12*(14), 25–31. DOI: 10.14505/jres.v12.14.02

Tong, E. (2024). Repercussions of the Russia–Ukraine war. *International Review of Economics & Finance*, *89*, 366–390. DOI: 10.1016/j.iref.2023.07.064

Tooze, A., & Odendahl, C. (2022). Economic consequences of the war: How the Ukraine crisis is reshaping Europe's economic agenda. Centre for European Reform. https://www.cer.eu/publications/archive/policy-brief/2022/economic-consequences-war

Tosun, O. K., Eshraghi, A., & Vigne, S. A. (2024). Firms entangled in geopolitical conflicts: Evidence from the russia – Ukraine war. *Journal of International Money and Finance*, *103137*, 103137. Advance online publication. DOI: 10.1016/j.jimonfin.2024.103137

Trabandt, M., & Uhlig, H. (2011). The Laffer curve revisited. *Journal of Monetary Economics*, *58*(4), 305–327. Advance online publication. DOI: 10.1016/j.jmoneco.2011.07.003

Travaly, Y., & Muvunyi, K. (2020). *The future is intelligent: Harnessing the potential of artificial intelligence in Africa*. Retrieved from Brookings: https://www.brookings.edu/articles/the-future-is-intelligent-harnessing-the-potential-of-artificial-intelligence-in-africa/

Treiblmaier, H. (2018). The impact of the blockchain on the supply chain: A theory-based research framework and a call for action. *Supply Chain Management*, 545–559.

Tsai, T. Y., & Urmetzer, F. (2024). A decisional framework for manufacturing relocation: Consolidating and expanding the reshoring debate. International Journal of Management Reviews, 26(2), 254-284. DOI: 10.1111/ijmr.12352

Tukiran, M., Candra, T., & Hendri, K. (2023). The ethics of utilitarianism in a circular economy. *Jurnal Filsafat*, *33*(2), 270–289. DOI: 10.22146/jf.74664

Tundys, B., & Wisniewski, T. (2023). Triple Bottom Line Aspects and Sustainable Supply Chain Resilience: A structural equation modelling approach. *Frontiers in Environmental Science*.

Tuzova, Y., & Qayum, F. (2016). Global oil glut and sanctions: The impact on Putin's Russia. *Energy Policy*, *90*, 140–151. DOI: 10.1016/j.enpol.2015.12.008

Ul Mansoor, S. I. (2023). China's geopolitical strategy: Crafting a new world order. *China Quarterly of International Strategic Studies*, *9*(01–04), 337–359.

Unilever. (2025). *Unilever Sustainable Sourcing Programme for Agricultural Raw Materials*. Retrieved from unilever.com: https://www.unilever.com/files/archive-unilever-sustainable-sourcing-programme-for-agricultural-raw-materials-scheme-rules.pdf

United Nations. (2024). Asia–Pacific Trade Facilitation Report 2024 - Promoting sustainability and resilience in global value chains. ESCAP - The Economic and Social Commission for Asia and the Pacific; available online at https://repository.unescap.org/server/api/core/bitstreams/cb7a1b8a-77c2-4f60-a656-1fd49a983e49/content

Usher, D. (2016). A utilitarian measure of economic growth. Queen's University Economics Department. *Working Paper, 1356*, 1–14.

Vaidya, S., Ambad, P., & Bhosle, S. (2018). Industry 4.0 - A Glimpse. *2nd International Conference on Materials Manufacturing and Design Engineering* (pp. 233-238). Amsterdam: Elsevier B.V.

Vargas-Hernández, J. G., & Vargas-González, O. C. (2024). Global supply, production and value chains. In *Emerald Publishing Limited eBooks* (pp. 277–297). DOI: 10.1108/978-1-83753-586-620241019

Varian, H. R. (2014). *Intermediate microeconomics with calculus: A modern approach*. W. W. Norton & Company.

Vasani, S. V. (2020). Analysis of impact of gross domestic product (GDP) on stock market movement in India. *Global Journal of Management and Business Research: B Economics and Commerce, 20*(8), 35–43. https://globaljournals.org

Vasilyeva, R., & Mariev, O. (2021). Determinants of foreign direct investment in developed and developing countries: Impact of political stability. *Economy of Regions*, *17*(4), 1390–1404. DOI: 10.17059/ekon.reg.2021-4-24

Verma, R., & Düben, B. A. (2024). The Russia–Ukraine war and inter-state dynamics in the Indo-Pacific. *International Politics*, *61*(5), 903–922. Advance online publication. DOI: 10.1057/s41311-023-00551-8

Viebeg Medical. (2025). *Artificial Intelligence*. Retrieved from Viebeg Medical: https://www.viebeg.com/philosophy/ai/

Vlados, C., & Chatzinikolaou, D. (2024). The emergence of the new globalization: The approach of the evolutionary structural triptych. *Journal of Global Responsibility*. Advance online publication. DOI: 10.1108/JGR-04-2023-0063

Volkov, A. D., Roslyakova, N. A., Vasilieva, A. V., Averyanov, A. O., Tishkov, S. V., & Nalivaychenko, E. V. (2024). Preferential Regime of the Russian Arctic: Tendencies and First Results from Realization of the World's Largest Special Economic Zone. *Journal of Risk and Financial Management, 17*(1), 28. DOI: 10.3390/jrfm17010028

Von Below, D., & Vezina, P. F. (2016). The trade consequences of pricey oil. *IMF Economic Review, 64*(2), 303–318. DOI: 10.1057/imfer.2016.3

Walker, H., Di Sisto, L., & McBain, D. (2008). Drivers and Barriers to Environmental Supply Chain Management Practices: Lessons from the public and private sectors. *Journal of Purchasing and Supply Management*, 69–85.

Wang, Y., Lucey, B. M., Vigne, S. A., & Yarovaya, L. (2022). The effects of central bank digital currencies news on financial markets. Technological Forecasting and Social Change, 180, 121715. DOI: 10.1016/j.techfore.2022.121715

Wang, C. (2019). Invocation of national security exceptions under GATT Article XXI: Jurisdiction to review and standard of review. *Chinese Journal of International Law, 18*(4), 695–712. DOI: 10.1093/chinesejil/jmz029

Wang, J. (2023). China and international trade law: Rising from within the system or always an outlier? *International Journal of Environmental Research and Public Health, 18*(22), 11991. DOI: 10.3390/ijerph182211991

Weber, R. H., & Grosz, M. (2009). Governments' Interventions into the Real Economy under WTO Law Revisited: New Tendencies of Governmental Support of the Automobile Industry. *Journal of World Trade, 43*(5).

WEF. (2023). This is why 'polycrisis' is a useful way of looking at the world right now. https://www.weforum.org/stories/2023/03/polycrisis-adam-tooze-historian-explains/

White, G. O.III, Rajwani, T., & Lawton, T. C. (2021). Open for business in a closed world? Managing MNE nonmarket strategy in times of populism and geopolitical uncertainty. *Multinational Business Review, 29*(4), 441–450. DOI: 10.1108/MBR-06-2021-0077

Wiessner, Y. T., Giuliani, E., Wijen, F., & Doh, J. (2024). Towards a more comprehensive assessment of FDI's societal impact. *Journal of International Business Studies, 55*(1), 50–70. DOI: 10.1057/s41267-023-00636-9

Wilhelm, M. (2024). Mandatory due diligence legislation: a paradigm shift for the governance of sustainability in global value chains? Journal of International Business Policy. DOI: 10.1057/s42214-024-00193-4

Willemyns, I. (2020). Agreement forthcoming? A comparison of EU, US, and Chinese RTAs in times of plurilateral e-commerce negotiations. *Journal of International Economic Law*, *23*(1), 221–244. DOI: 10.1093/jiel/jgz048

Wilson, A., Connor, P., & Hardy, J. (2024). Fighting the past to win the future: Regulatory roulette, institutional inertia and the challenge of enabling military energy security. *Energy Research & Social Science*, *114*, 103584. DOI: 10.1016/j.erss.2024.103584

Wiśniewski, T. P. (2023). Investigating Divergent Energy Policy Fundamentals: Warfare Assessment of past dependence on Russian energy raw materials in Europe. *Energies*, *16*(4), 2019. DOI: 10.3390/en16042019

WITS. (2022). WITS. https://wits.worldbank.org/countrystats.aspx?lang=en

Witt, M. A. (2019). De-globalization: Theories, predictions, and implications for international business research. *Journal of International Business Studies*, *50*(7), 1053–1077. DOI: 10.1057/s41267-019-00219-7

Witt, M. A., Lewin, A. Y., Li, P. P., & Gaur, A. (2023). Decoupling in international business: Evidence, drivers, impact, and implications for IB research. *Journal of World Business*, *58*(1), 101399. DOI: 10.1016/j.jwb.2022.101399

Witt, M. A., Li, P. P., Välikangas, L., & Lewin, A. Y. (2021). De-globalization and decoupling: Game changing consequences? *Management and Organization Review*, *17*(1), 6–15. DOI: 10.1017/mor.2021.9

World Bank. (2023). *Market capitalization of listed domestic companies.* https://www.worldbank.org/

World Economic Forum. (2025). *Lori Systems*. Retrieved from weforum.org: https://www.weforum.org/organizations/lori-systems-corp/

Wright, R. W., & Dana, L. P. (2003). Changing paradigms of international entrepreneurship strategy. *Journal of International Entrepreneurship*, *1*(1), 135–152. DOI: 10.1023/A:1023384808859

WTO. (2025). Evolution of trade under the WTO: handy statistics. WTO webpages. Available: https://www.wto.org/english/res_e/statis_e/trade_evolution_e/evolution_trade_wto_e.htm

Wu, T., & Zuo, M. (2023). Green supply chain transformation and emission reduction based on machine learning. *Science Progress*, 1–15.

Xia, X., & Li, A. (2024). Global natural gas market and changing trends of natural gas trade. In *Current Chinese economic report series* (pp. 139–152). DOI: 10.1007/978-981-99-7289-0_9

Xiao, B., Peng, Y., & Yu, W. (2024). The WTO institutional structure and dispute settlement practice. In *The practice of WTO dispute settlement: Modern China and international economic law*. Springer. DOI: 10.1007/978-981-97-0185-8_1

Yang, T., Dong, Q., Du, M., & Du, Q. (2023). Geopolitical risks, oil price shocks and inflation: Evidence from a TVP–SV–VAR approach. *Energy Economics, 127*, Part B. DOI: 10.1016/j.eneco.2023.1070.99

Yang, Y. (2021). Crisis and reform direction of WTO Appellate Body. *Advances in Social Science, Education and Humanities Research*. Advance online publication. DOI: 10.2991/assehr.k.210916.015

Young, A. R. (2013). The rise (and fall?) of the EU's performance in the multilateral trading system. In *The Performance of the EU in International Institutions* (pp. 117–131). Routledge.

Yu, Z., Razzaq, A., Rehman, A., Shah, A., Jameel, K., & Mor, R. S. (2021). Disruption in global supply chain and socio-economic shocks: a lesson from COVID-19 for sustainable production and consumption. Operations Management Research, 1-16. DOI: 10.1007/s12063-021-00179-y

Yusuf, F. A., Alfaridzi, M., & Herdi, T. (2022). Penerapan algoritma decision tree untuk klasifikasi KIPI vaksin Covid-19. *Jurnal Ilmiah FIFO, 14*(2), 155. DOI: 10.22441/fifo.2022.v14i2.005

Zahoor, N., Wu, J., Khan, H., & Khan, Z. (2023). De-globalization, international trade protectionism, and the reconfigurations of global value chains. *MIR. Management International Review, 63*(5), 823–859. DOI: 10.1007/s11575-023-00522-4

Zardoub, A., & Sboui, F. (2023). Impact of foreign direct investment, remittances and official development assistance on economic growth: Panel data approach. *PSU Research Review, 7*(2), 73–89. DOI: 10.1108/PRR-04-2020-0012

Zavershinskaia, P. (2024). State's Legitimisation of Violence through Strategic Narration: How the Kremlin Justified the Russian Invasion of Ukraine. *The International Spectator, 59*(2), 1–19. DOI: 10.1080/03932729.2024.2327492

Zejjari, I., & Benhayoun, I. (2024). The use of artificial intelligence to advance sustainable supply chain: Retrospective and future avenues explored through bibliometric analysis. *Discover Sustainability*.

Zenchenko, S., Strielkowski, W., Smutka, L., Vacek, T., Radyukova, Y., & Sutyagin, V. (2022). Monetization of the Economies as a Priority of the New Monetary Policy in the Face of Economic Sanctions. Journal of Risk and Financial Management, 15(3), 140. DOI: 10.3390/jrfm15030140

Zhang, L., Fu, S., Tian, J., & Peng, J. (2022). A review of energy industry chain and energy supply chain. *Energies, MDPI*, 1-32.

Zhang, D., Wang, C., & Wang, Y. (2024). Unveiling the critical nexus: Volatility of crude oil future prices and trade partner's cash holding behavior in the face of the Russia–Ukraine conflict. *Energy Economics*, *132*, 107413. DOI: 10.1016/j.eneco.2024.107413

Zhao, C. (2024). Russia and the war in Ukraine: The Chinese perspective on Europe's role. In *Global power shift* (pp. 45–60). DOI: 10.1007/978-3-031-48117-8_3

Zhao, S., & Hu, J. (2023). Gao zhiliang shishi "Quyu Quanmian Jingji Huoban Guanxi Xieding" (RCEP) (High-quality implementation of the "Regional Comprehensive Economic Partnership" (RCEP). *Qiushi*. Available at: https://www.qstheory.cn/dukan/hqwg/2023-07/11/c_1129742844.htm

Zhao, L. (2023). The reconstruction and innovation of international economic and trade rules. In *Modern China and international rules. Modern China and international economic law*. Springer. DOI: 10.1007/978-981-19-7576-9_3

Zhu, Q., Sarkis, J., & Lai, K.-h. (2013). Institutional-based antecedents and performance outcomes of internal and external green supply chain management practices. *Journal of Purchasing and Supply Management*, 106–117.

Zuev, V. (2022). Regional trade agreements: A hope or a threat to the global trade? In Karhu, A., & Haaja, E. (Eds.), *Global trade and trade governance during deglobalization* (pp. 55–72). International Political Economy Series. Palgrave Macmillan. DOI: 10.1007/978-3-031-13757-0_4

About the Contributors

Bryan Christiansen is an Adjunct Business Professor at Southern New Hampshire University and the Chief Executive Officer of the management consultancy, Soluvex, LLC in New Mexico, USA. He is currently Editor-in-Chief of the IGI Global Book Series, "Advances in Digital Crime, Forensics, and Cyber Terrorism" as well as "Advances in Psychology, Mental Health, and Behavioral Studies". Christiansen is fluent in Chinese, Japanese, and Spanish, and is currently learning Russian. He has presented at several universities in other countries including Oxford University in the United Kingdom. He earned an MBA from Capella University and a BS in Marketing from the University of the State of New York. Christiansen's extensive travels around the world since 1973 have enabled him to produce 50 Reference books on a variety of subjects ranging from cultural studies to organizational sociology. Over 70 percent of these publications have become Scopus- and/or Web of Science-indexed.

John Branch currently teaches a variety of marketing and international business courses at the undergraduate, MBA, and executive levels at the Stephen M Ross School of Business at the University of Michigan (USA), and serves as Co-Director of the Yaffe Digital Media Initiative. Previously, he was the Academic Director of the School's weekend and evening MBA programs as well as the Director of Educational Outreach at the University's William Davidson Institute. John also holds an appointment at the University's Center for Russian, East European, & Eurasian Studies, and maintains a Research Fellowship at the William Davidson Institute. John holds a Bachelor of Engineering Science in electronics from the University of Western Ontario (Canada), a Master of Business Administration from the University of New Brunswick (Canada), a Master of Arts in education from Washington University in Saint Louis (USA), a Doctor of Philosophy in marketing from the University of Cambridge (England), a Doctor of Education from the University of

Michigan (USA), and a Doctor of Professional Studies from Middlesex University (England).

* * *

Carla Gomes Costa is Director of the Faculty of Social Sciences and Technology at the European University (Portugal). She has a PhD in Management and Development of Human Resources from ISCTE-IUL. She has a Master's degree in Social and Organizational Psychology and a degree in Sociology and Psychology. She has postgraduate degrees in: Human Resources Management; Training Management and Planning; Psychological Coaching and specializations in Psychotherapy and as a Senior Occupational Health and Safety Technician. Her areas of research interest include leadership; performance management; emotional management and the promotion of occupational health; and corporate coaching. She has published articles in the Journal of Organizational Behavior, the Journal of Creative Behavior and the International Journal of Environmental Research and Public Health.

Anna Karhu, PhD., is a Research Manager at the Pan-European Institute (PEI) in Turku School of Economics, University of Turku. Her research focuses on the intersection of business and policy by examining how these two spheres of society interact through the business environment. She has studied these dynamics through an institutional change perspective in the context of the pharmaceutical industry, international retailing and trade policy systems.

Rehema Kiarie is a Lecturer at the Riara School of Business (Kenya) and also the faculty in charge of industrial attachment at the School of Business. She holds a Master's degree in Business Administration and is currently pursuing her PhD at the University of Nairobi. Rehema is an accomplished researcher and writer and some her notable writings include; Ethics in Mobile Banking: A Case Study of Kenya's Mobile Money Platforms and Impact of Mobile Payment Applications and Transfers on Business and Technology and Social Media in Customer Service Management in Africa; A Strategic and Operational Perspective (co-author).

Andreia Machado, PhD in Engineering and Knowledge Management; Master in Scientific and Technological Education. Ad Hoc evaluator of National and International Journals. He has been working in the educational area for over 25 years. He has experience in the area: Education, Distance Education, management, hybrid teaching, digital technologies, active methodology, knowledge media, entrepreneurship, sustainability, innovation habitat and knowledge management.

Sheikh Inam Ul Mansoor (BA.LLB Hon's, LLM, CPCT WIPO, Ph.D. International Trade Law) is a highly accomplished academician presently working as an Assistant Professor Law at the Symbiosis Law School Hyderabad Campus, Symbiosis International (Deemed University), Pune, India. With a strong background in law and a passion for academia, Dr. Sheikh has made significant contributions to the field through his extensive research and publications. Pursued his BA. LLB (Hon's) from University of Kashmir, LLM from JNU Jaipur and Ph.D. International Trade Law from LPU Punjab. Prior to his academic career, Dr. Sheikh served as an Advocate and Solicitor at the Jammu and Kashmir High Court and other subordinate courts in Jammu and Kashmir. This experience as a legal practitioner has provided him with valuable insights into the practical application of law and enhanced his understanding of legal dynamics.

Baso R. is a lecturer in the Accounting Study Program at the Faculty of Economics and Business, Universitas Wira Bhakti. He earned his Bachelor's degree in Accounting (S.E., Ak) from Universitas Hasanuddin (Unhas) in August 2000 and is currently pursuing a Doctoral degree at Universitas Islam Negeri (UIN) Makassar. His academic expertise lies in the integration of Accounting and Religious Studies, a unique interdisciplinary approach that he applies in teaching accounting courses within the Faculty of Economics and Business. He previously served as Head of the Institute for Quality Assurance and Internal Audit (LPMI) from 2015 to 2017 and as Head of the Accounting Study Program at Universitas Wira Bhakti from 2017 to 2024. Baso R holds several prestigious certifications, including Certified Sustainability Reporting Specialist (CSRS), Certified Sustainability Reporting Assurer (CSRA), and Certified Sustainability Professional (CSP). In addition, he has authored numerous publications in the fields of financial accounting, Islamic accounting, auditing, and tax accounting, contributing significantly to the academic community.

Syed Shahid Rashid is an Assistant Professor at Symbiosis Law School, Hyderabad, Symbiosis International (Deemed) University, Pune. He holds a Ph.D., LL.M., LL.B., and B.Com. His teaching and research interests span across Family Law, Jurisprudence, Constitutional Law, and Interpretation of Statutes. His specialized areas of scholarship include inheritance law, property rights of women, constitutional interpretation in India, and the need for Ijtihad in Islamic jurisprudence. He is actively engaged in advancing research and academic discourse in these domains.

Rismawati is a distinguished academic and consultant with a robust focus on sustainability reporting. She currently holds the position of lecturer and Head of the Quality Assurance Institute at Universitas Muhammadiyah Palopo, where she has been pivotal in ensuring the quality of university processes and outputs since February 2020. Additionally, she serves as an Assurer for Sustainability Reporting at the National Center for Sustainability Reporting in Jakarta, specializing in the evaluation of sustainability reports for mining companies across Indonesia. Her academic qualifications are extensive, comprising a Bachelor's degree in Economics and Accounting, a Master's degree in Accounting Science, and a Doctorate in Accounting from Universitas Brawijaya, Malang. Rismawati is also a certified specialist in sustainability reporting, risk management, and tax planning, holding several prestigious certifications including Certified Sustainability Reporting Specialist (CSRS), Certified Risk Management Practitioner (CRMP), Certified Management Accountant (CMA) and Certified Enterprise Risk Analysis (CERA). In her professional capacity, she has provided consultancy services in financial management and tax compliance for companies such as PT. Reski Barito Timur and PT. Helay Raya. Furthermore, she has authored multiple publications on Social Accounting, Sustainability Accounting, Management Accounting and CSR, contributing significantly to the academic community. Her interests in reading, writing, and travel reflect her commitment to lifelong learning and professional growth in her field.

João Rodrigues dos Santos is an Associate Professor at the Universidade Europeia (Portugal) and a Visiting Professor at the Instituto Superior de Educação e Ciências (ISEC Lisbon). At the Universidade Europeia, he is the Scientific and Vertical Coordinator of the Management and Economics area. He has a PhD in Economics and Business (Universidad Europea de Madrid), a Master's degree in International Security and Civil Protection Management and a Degree in Geography and Territorial Planning (Universidade Nova de Lisboa). As an Integrated Researcher, he is a member of the Center for Transdisciplinary Development Studies at the Universidade de Trás-os-Montes e Alto Douro. He is the author of two books in two of his areas of interest (Economics and Territorial Management) and frequently publishes chapters and articles of an academic, technical and scientific nature. João Rodrigues dos Santos currently collaborates with CNN Portugal, analyzing and commenting on national and international economic news.

Sumarni S. is an Associate Professor in Management Science at Universitas Wira Bhakti, South Sulawesi, Indonesia. Her research interests include financial management, financial literacy, and Micro, Small, and Medium Enterprise (MSME) finance. Since 2024, she has been serving as the Dean of the Faculty of Economics and Business. Her academic qualifications include a Bachelor's degree in Economics (SE) and a Master of Science (M.Si) in Management from Universitas

Hasanuddin, as well as a Doctorate in Management Science from Universitas Brawijaya, Malang. Sumarni S has published several articles in nationally accredited journals on topics such as financial management, MSME financial governance, village financial accountability, and culturally based financial literacy. She also holds professional certifications, including Certified Lecturer and BKD Assessor. To date, she remains actively engaged in teaching and academic writing, including authorship of academic books.

António Sacavém, PhD in Management. Collaboratively engaged in research focused on leader-follower dynamics, and digital transformation in organizations. Contributions to the academic community include publications in international journals and academic books. As a complement to academic responsibilities worked closely with global organizations as a strategic consultant and advisor (e.g., Delta) and developed and delivered core-skills training (e.g., Toyota, NATO, Fujitsu, PwC). Work has been featured in Portuguese media (e.g., CNN, NOW).

Pasquale Sarnacchiaro is an Associate Professor of Statistics at the Department of Economics, Management, Institutions of Università Federico II in Naples. He is a member of the PhD program in Management at the same university. Since 2022, he has served as the National Co-Coordinator of the Italian Society of Statistics group "Statistics for Evaluation and Service Quality." He has been a visiting professor at the Academy of Economic Studies in Bucharest and the University of Granada. His research interests include factor analysis, structural equation models, and hierarchical composite indicators for performance measurement. Pasquale has participated as a statistical coordinator in numerous national and international projects and has presented and organized many conferences at both national and international levels. He is the author of numerous publications in peer-reviewed journals and has served as Guest Editor for special issues on statistical methods for decision-making.

Rossana Simeoli is a PhD student in Management at the University of Naples Federico II, Department of Economics, Management, Institutions. She earned her Master's degree from the University of Naples "L'Orientale," where she developed a thesis examining the economic impacts of the Regional Comprehensive Economic Partnership (RCEP). Her current research focuses on the New Space Economy as an emerging managerial and business phenomenon. Specifically, she investigates how innovations and transformations developed within the space sector can influence firms operating both inside and outside the space industry. Her broader academic interests include innovation dynamics and the evolving role of Asian economies—particularly China—in shaping global technological and industrial transformations.

Surjit Singha is an academician with a broad spectrum of interests, including UN Sustainable Development Goals, Organizational Climate, Workforce Diversity, Organizational Culture, HRM, Marketing, Finance, IB, Global Business, Business, AI, K12 & Higher Education, Gender and Cultural Studies. Currently a faculty member at Kristu Jayanti College, Dr. Surjit also serves as an Editor, reviewer, and author for prominent global publications and journals, including being on the Editorial review board of Information Resources Management Journal and contributor to various publications. With over 16 years of experience in Administration, Teaching, and Research, Dr. Surjit is dedicated to imparting knowledge and guiding students in their research pursuits. As a research mentor, Dr. Surjit has nurtured young minds and fostered academic growth. Dr. Surjit has an impressive track record of over 150+ publications (SCOPUS Indexed 100+), including articles, book chapters, and textbooks, holds two US Copyrights, one patent granted, and has successfully completed and published two fully funded minor research projects from Kristu Jayanti (Deemed to be University).

Maria José Sousa (Ph.D. in Management) is a University Professor and a research fellow at ISCTE/IUL. Her research interests currently are public policies, information science, and innovation. She is a best seller author in Research Methods, ICT and People Management fields and has co-authored over 80 articles and book chapters and published in several scientific journals (e.g. Journal of Business Research, Journal of Medical Systems, Information Systems Frontiers, European Planning Studies, Systems Research and Behavioral Science, Computational and Mathematical Organization Theory, Future Generation Computer Systems, and others), she has also organized and peer-reviewed international conferences, and is the guest-editor of several Special Issues from Springer and Elsevier.

Marco Tregua is an Associate Professor in Management at University of Naples Federico II; he teaches International Management and Business Ethics. His main areas of interest are service logic, service ecosystems, and innovation. He participated to national and international conferences and he published papers on value creation, service research, and ethics on international journals, including Journal of Business Ethics, Journal of Service Theory and Practice, International Journal of Public Sector Management, and European Journal of Marketing. He is associate editor in international journals and he edited books on innovation in cities management and management of cultural heritage.

Index

I

M

N

P

R

S

T

W

www.ingramcontent.com/pod-product-compliance
Lightning Source LLC
LaVergne TN
LVHW081543300926
849161LV00006B/1503